The Political Economy of State-Society Relations in Hungary and Poland

From Communism to the European Union

In *The Political Economy of State-Society Relations in Hungary and Poland*, Anna Seleny contends that the profound transformations that preceded the downfall of communism originated in Poland and Hungary but played out in strikingly different ways – Hungary led through economic reform, Poland through open political struggle.

Seleny's analysis of these transformational variants yields important insights into systemic change, marketization, and democratization. She shows how these changes were possible in authoritarian regimes as, over time, state and society became mutually vulnerable, neither fully able to dictate the terms of engagement. For Poland this meant principled confrontation; for Hungary, innovative accommodation.

The book argues that different conceptual frameworks and strategies of persuasion account for these divergences in nearly identical institutional settings. Seleny traces the different political-institutional residues that, in both Hungary and Poland, now function as constraining or enabling legacies. In particular, she demonstrates that state-socialist legacies account for salient differences between these two new capitalist democracies, and they now condition their prospects in the European Union.

Anna Seleny is Visiting Associate Professor at the Fletcher School, Tufts University. Previously she was Assistant Professor at Princeton University; in Princeton she also spent a year at the Institute for Advanced Studies. She has published in *World Politics, International Studies Quarterly, Comparative Politics, Law and Policy, East European Politics and Societies*, and in edited volumes. Seleny has held fellowships from the American Council of Learned Societies, the German Marshall Fund, the MacArthur Foundation, the International Research and Exchange Commission, and Fulbright-Hayes.

The Political Economy of State-Society Relations in Hungary and Poland

From Communism to the European Union

ANNA SELENY
Tufts University

CAMBRIDGE
UNIVERSITY PRESS

CAMBRIDGE UNIVERSITY PRESS
Cambridge, New York, Melbourne, Madrid, Cape Town, Singapore, São Paulo

Cambridge University Press
40 West 20th Street, New York, NY 10011-4211, USA

www.cambridge.org
Information on this title: www.cambridge.org/9780521835640

© Anna Seleny 2006

First published 2006

Printed in the United States of America

A catalog record for this publication is available from the British Library.

Library of Congress Cataloging in Publication Data

Seleny, Anna.
The political economy of state-society relations in Hungary and Poland :
from communism to the European Union / Anna Seleny.
    p.   cm.
Includes bibliographical references and index.
ISBN 0-521-83564-x (hardback)
1. Social change – Hungary.   2. Social change – Poland.   3. Post-communism –
Hungary.   4. Post-communism – Poland.   5. Hungary – Economic policy – 1968–1989.
6. Hungary – Economic policy – 1945–1968.   7. Poland – Politics and government –
1980–1989.   8. Poland – Politics and government – 1945–1980.   I. Title.
HN420.5.A8S45   2006
306.2'09438'09045–dc22   2005010536

ISBN-13   978-0-521-83564-0 hardback
ISBN-10   0-521-83564-x hardback

To my parents and Marika, who saw the beginning
To Moni, who never got to see
and to Alex, who is free of its legacy

Contents

List of Tables

List of Abbreviations

Hungary

FIDESZ	Alliance of Young Democrats (now FIDESZ – Hungarian Civic Party)
GYOSZ	National Association of (private, large) Factory Owners
HSP	Hungarian Socialist Party (post-1989)
HSWP	Hungarian Socialist Workers Party (pre-1989)
IPOSZ	National Association of Manufacturers
KIOSZ	National Association of Small Manufacturers
KISOSZ	National Association of Small Retailers
MGTSZ	State Agricultural Cooperatives
NEM	New Economic Mechanism
OKISZ	National Association of Small Industrial Cooperatives
SZDSZ	Alliance of Free Democrats
SZOT	National Council of Trade Unions
TOT	National Association of Agricultural Cooperatives
VOSZ	National Association of Entrepreneurs

Poland

CRZZ	Central Council of Trade Unions
KKP	Solidarity National Coordinating Commission
KOR	Committee for the Defense of the Workers
KOR-KSS	Committee for Social Self-Defense
KOS	Committees for Social Resistance
KPN	Confederation of Independent Poland
MKZ	Regional Solidarity Inter-Factory Strike Committee
NSZZ	Independent Self-Governing Trade Union (Solidarity)
PUWP	Polish United Workers Party (pre-1989)
ROPCiO	Movement for the Defense of Human and Civil Rights

SLD	Alliance of the Democratic Left (Social Democratic Party, whose original membership drew mostly on the PUWP)
TKN	Flying University
WRON	Military Council of National Salvation

Acknowledgments

In researching and writing this book, I have incurred more than the usual debts of gratitude across three countries and four disciplines, over the course of nearly a decade.

Among the earliest and most enduring of these debts are those owed to exemplary friends and mentors János Kornai and István Gábor, from whom I learned so much about the political economy of state-socialist systems; and Suzanne Berger and Donald Blackmer, whose guidance and support were indispensable at the earliest stages of my academic career. My deepest debt of all is to Consuelo Cruz, who challenged and inspired me both directly and by example, and without whose help and encouragement this book would never have been completed.

At Princeton University and at professional gatherings, many colleagues helped to clarify my thinking about the significance of my research findings for the field of comparative politics. Several offered helpful comments on earlier drafts of this manuscript or on articles on which I drew for the final version. I am especially grateful to Sheri Berman, Nancy Bermeo, Stephen Cohen, Elizabeth Kiss, Atul Kohli, Minxin Pei, and John Waterbury. I am also thankful to Princeton's Center of International Studies for financial support in the transcription of taped interviews and to the university's Committee on Research in the Humanities and Social Sciences for research support. Jan Kubik and Jakub Grygiel helped me to disentangle Polish politics and to think more deeply about a number of the theoretical issues that arise in the comparisons of Poland and Hungary, the two countries that form the empirical backbone of the book. During a year spent at the Institute for Advanced Studies in Princeton, I benefited from discussions with Clifford Geertz and Albert Hirschman, both of whom also offered comments on work that would ultimately inform the concluding chapter of this book.

Other scholars on this side of the Atlantic shaped my work through their own research, challenging discussions at conferences, or by commenting on parts of the manuscript. Some – David Bartlett, Michael Bernhard, Tomasz

Inglot, Jeffrey Kopstein, Ákos Róna-Tas, Alfred Stepan, Iván Szelényi, and Ding Xeuliang – graciously did all three. Still others helped me through thought-provoking exchanges and comments on related work: Andrew Arato, Zoltán Bárány, Valerie Bunce, Dan Chirot, Grzegorz Ekiert, Peter Hall, Susan Gál, Andrew C. János, Michael Kennedy, Gail Kligman, Andrei Markovitz, Kazimierz Poznański, Gideon Rose, Andreas Ryll, James Scott, Ben Slay, Vladimir Tismaneanu, Katherine Verdery, Andrew Walder, and Jason Wittenberg.

In Eastern Europe, I benefited from the assistance of more people than I can name here, but even an abbreviated list includes many remarkable scholars, entrepreneurs and government officials. In Hungary, I must thank the late Rudolf Andorka, Kati Balog, László Egyed, Judit Fekete, Péter Futó the entrepreneur, as well as the eponymous Péter Futó, researcher and journalist; Pétér Gerő, István Hetényi, Tamás Hofer, Mihály Laki, Teréz Laky, György Lengyel, Kati Lorschy, Mária Kovács, György Kővári, Iván Pető, Endre Sík, Zsuzsa Szántó, Péter Szirácki, Tamás Szabó, Anna Székács, and János Timár. Many others at the Institute of International Economics of the Hungarian Academy of Sciences gave me essential intellectual advice, among them Tamás Bauer, Mária Lackó, and Aladár Sipos. Scholars and policymakers at a variety of other research institutes and universities helped me to clarify confusing data and to sharpen interpretations, in particular László Antal, István Bretter, László Bruszt, Ildikó Ékes, Gábor Halmai, Tibor Kuczi, János Palotás, András Sajó, Tamás Sárközy, Péter Tölgyessy, István Tóth, and Agnes Vajda.

In Poland, too, many researchers and scholars gave generously of their time. Among them I must thank, first and foremost, Agnieszka Julita Rybczynska, for untiring research assistance, careful interpretation of statistical data, and sharp analytical critiques. Mira Marody shared her own research in progress and helped elucidate many of the subtleties of Polish political life. Beata Chaikowska helped with translation and logistics. I am grateful for in-depth discussions with Marek Bednarski, Tomasz Bichta, Tomasz Charanzkiński, Zbigniew Hołda, Ryszard Kokoszczynski, Jacek Kochaonowicz, Lena Kolarska-Bobinska, Ireneusz Krzeminski, the late Jacek Kurón, Janusz Levandowski, Jan Rutkowski, Andrzej Rychard, Jacek Tarkowski, and Jacek Wasilewski, Miroslav Zeliński, and Marek Zmigrodzk. The late Czeslaw Miłosz influenced the book through his own classic works and also through illuminating discussions on the links between post-socialist Polish politics and Polish history.

I owe debts of gratitude elsewhere in Eastern Europe as well. Jozef Kotrba and Martin Palous; Zora Butórova and Martin Butora; and Daniel Daianu each helped me to sort out the relevance of my research findings for the Czech Republic, Slovakia, and Romania, respectively.

I also want to thank Jason Parker and the American Council of Learned Societies, the German Marshall Fund, the MacArthur Foundation, IREX, and the Fulbright Commission for their support of my research in Eastern Europe. At the Fletcher School at Tufts, I am particularly grateful to Tamás Kovács, who read the manuscript for errors and deftly corrected many while offering extremely useful comments. Ioli Christopholu ably assisted me in gathering material on Eastern Europe and the European Union. At Princeton, Andrew Barnes and Robert Cronin skillfully assembled data for the tables.

Finally, there are my editors. At Cambridge University Press, Senior Acquisitions Editor Lewis Bateman's keen intellect, patience, and kindness made the manuscript possible, and better. Manuscript editor Ronald Cohen's marvelous precision, sharp eye for detail, and fine sensibility for language and structure improved the manuscript tremendously. No author could be more fortunate.

The Political Economy of State-Society Relations in Hungary and Poland

From Communism to the European Union

Introduction

Points of Permeable Contact

Not everything went according to plan in the state-socialist world. This much is well-known. The reasons, however, remain poorly understood. Invoking modernization's prophecy, some analysts contend that state socialism collapsed because economic development must eventually lead to political democracy.[1] Others draw on liberal conceptions of human nature to argue that capitalism was bound to triumph, because people are too self-interested to sustain the practice of communist ideals; because dissidents, acting as the conscience of society, brought an unjust system to its knees; or because the demise of an unreformable system was inherent in its Leninist logic.[2] From a Cold War

---

[1] Beginning in the 1960s, as the rule of terror eased in the East, scholarly consensus in the West moved away from totalitarian accounts of immutability and, via modernization/convergence theories, toward pluralist accounts of gradual change. Modernization and pluralist theories recognized the possibility of gradual change, but they grafted the internal logic of capitalist democracies onto socialist systems. Modernization theorists posited that with economic progress, the Schmittian politics of friend and foe would be subsumed under an Eastonian allocative imperative (see fn 49, Chapter 1). Moreover, such theories typically viewed the state-socialist economy as underdeveloped capitalism, and party-states as underdeveloped versions of democratic political structures. See Ellen Comisso, "Where Have We Been and Where Are We Going? Analyzing Post-Socialist Politics in the 1990s," in William Crotty, ed., *Political Science: Looking to the Future* (Evanston: Northwestern University Press, 1991), 96. One among many popular contemporary versions of this interpretation is Francis Fukuyama's "The Modernizing Imperative: The USSR as an Ordinary Country," *The National Interest* (Spring 1993). Another strain of modernization theory holds that the pressures of globalization brought state-socialist systems down. Charles Maier, *Dissolution: The Crisis of Communism and the End of East Germany* (Princeton: Princeton University Press, 1997), 91.

[2] Interest-group theorists studied bargaining relations within the socialist state, and tended to describe socialist politics as corporatist, or alternatively, as an "institutional" variant of pluralism. Prominent works under this rubric include Jerry F. Hough, *The Soviet Prefects: The Local Party Organs in Industrial Decision-Making* (Cambridge: Harvard University Press, 1969); Jerry F. Hough, *The Soviet Union and Social Science Theory* (Cambridge: Harvard University Press, 1977); and H. Gordon Skilling and Franklyn Griffiths, eds., *Interest Groups in Soviet Politics* (Princeton: Princeton University Press, 1971). On the role of civil society, see Blair Ruble, "The

perspective, some proclaim that the West's superior strength of arms and will prevailed. Even the great-man theory has made a comeback: either Gorbachev did it or, or as other commentators assert, Ronald Reagan vanquished the "evil empire."[3]

Revisionist accounts also surfaced. State socialism, say some, had nothing to do with true socialism, let alone communism. Others posit that state socialism was not an economic failure until the 1980s, when it became the victim of a world-market downturn.[4] Some assert that in retrospect 1989 will mark socialism's rebirth in a truer form.[5] The claims about economic performance

Soviet Union's Quiet Revolution," in George Breslauer, ed., *Can Gorbachev's Reforms Succeed?* (Berkeley: University of California Press, 1990); Moshe Lewin, *The Gorbachev Phenomenon* (Berkeley: University of California Press, 1988); S. Frederick Starr, "Soviet Union: A Civil Society," *Foreign Policy* 70 (Spring 1988): 26–41; and Vladimir Tismaneanu, *Reinventing Politics: Eastern Europe from Stalin to Havel* (New York: Free Press, 1992). Among political commentators, one stand-out is John P. Maynard, "What's Sad About the Soviet Collapse," *Conservative Review* (April 1992). On the role of injustice in the fall of communism, see Richard Pipes, *Communism: The Vanished Specter* (New York: Oxford University Press, 1994), especially the chapter "A Warning to the West"; and Theodore Von Laue, *Why Lenin, Why Stalin: The Rise and Fall of the Soviet System*, 3rd Edition (New York: Harper Collins, 1993). The best-known proponent of the "inherent logic" thesis is Martin Malia, presented in his "Leninist Endgame," in Stephen Graubard, ed., *Exit from Communism* (New Brunswick, NJ: Transaction Publishers, 1993).

[3] A claim Reagan never made on his own behalf. In part because both theories of totalitarianism and later theories of modernization left unspecified the precise mechanisms of collapse and transformation, they opened up space, by default, for the subsequent view of Gorbachev as the primary agent of change. See, for instance, Archie Brown, *The Gorbachev Factor* (Oxford: Oxford University Press, 1997) and Robert Kaiser, *Why Gorbachev Happened: His Triumph and His Failure* (New York: Simon and Schuster, 1991). Jacques Lévesque offers a multi-causal explanation for the fall of communism, but nevertheless presents Gorbachev as the prime mover. See Jacques Lévesque, *The Enigma of 1989: The USSR and the Liberation of Eastern Europe* (Berkeley: University of California Press, 1997). Numerous other analyses give primacy either to Gorbachev's reforms and/or to his political leadership. See, for instance, Larry Elliot and Dan Atkinson, *The Age of Insecurity* (New York: Verso, 1998), 220–221. Still others emphasize Gorbachev's role in the breakup of the Soviet Union without making larger claims about his role in the collapse of communism *per se*. For an illustration, see Michael Mandelbaum, "Coup de Grace: The End of the Soviet Union," *Foreign Affairs* (Autumn/Winter 1991/1992). Some contemporary commentators fit both the "triumph against evil" and the "Reagan did it" categories. See George Urban, "After the Fall," *The Heritage Lecture Series*, September 24, 1992, and also Edwin Meese III, *With Reagan: The Inside Story* (Washington D.C.: Regnery Gateway, 1992). Some sophisticated analysts emphasize both Gorbachev and Reagan's roles not so much in the demise of communism as in the timing of the Cold War's end. See, for instance, Daniel Deudney and G. John Ikenberry, "Who Won the Cold War?" *Foreign Policy* 87 (Summer 1992): 123–138.

[4] Charles Maier, "Why Did Communism Collapse in 1989?" Central and Eastern Europe Working Paper Series #7 (Cambridge: Minda de Gunzburg Center for European Studies, Harvard University, 1991), and quoted in Michael Doyle, "Liberalism and the End of the Cold War," in Richard Ned Lebow and Thomas Risse-Kappen, eds, *International Relations Theory and the End of the Cold War* (New York: Columbia University Press, 1995).

[5] See Pranab K. Bardhan and John E. Romer, eds. *Market Socialism: The Current Debate* (New York: Oxford University Press, 1993); Frank Roosevelt and David Belkin, eds., *Why Market Socialism? Voices from Dissent* (Armonk, NY: M.E. Sharpe, 1994); and David Schweickart, *Against Capitalism* (Cambridge: Cambridge University Press, 1993, as well as David Schweickart,

are both fanciful and demonstrably wrong;[6] on the latter, the foggy future must have the last word.[7] Meanwhile, revisionism, like determinism, has little to tell us about the actual processes through which human agency brought down existing state socialism.[8]

Sophisticated scholarly accounts of the fall of state-socialist regimes continue to range widely, from the structural-systemic to the highly political. In structural-systemic accounts, collapse generally results from the accumulated weight of economic failures, and then construction of the new begins amidst the ruins of the old. Political accounts, in contrast, offer a variety of stories based on keen contestation, typically culminating in zero-sum outcomes. The most familiar variant features a protracted battle in which the state – still full of resolve but acutely short of material resources – finally loses to society, which, long repressed, has nonetheless somehow grown politically resourceful.

The fall of state socialism is not the principal concern of this book, although a clear perspective on the events of 1989 does emerge. Nor, like so much recent work on the region, does it ask how East European cases fit existing theories.[9] Instead, the book shows how the internal transformations of communist ideals and state socialist institutions challenge established theory. The analytical focus

"Socialism After Communism: The New Market Socialism," review of work by Christopher Pierson, *American Political Science Review* 91, no. 1 (March 1997): 221–222. See also Alex Callinicos, *The Revenge of History: Marxism and the East European Revolutions* (Oxford: Polity Press/Basil Blackwell, 1991).

[6] See, for instance, W. Easterly, and Stanley Fischer, "The Soviet Economic Decline: Historical and Republican Data" (NBER Working Paper #4735, 1994, which concluded that "Soviet economic performance conditional on investment and human capital accumulation was the worst in the world over the period 1960–1989." See also Adam Bergson, "USSR Before the Fall: How Poor and Why?" *Economic Perspectives* (Fall 1991); and Daniel Gros and Alfred Steinherr, *Winds of Change: Economic Transition in Central and Eastern Europe* (New York: Longman, 1995), especially Chapter 3.

[7] It is fair to say, however, that many treatises on "market socialism" appear to be ignorant of the dismal results of the Yugoslav, Hungarian, and Polish experiments with some of the proposals that contemporary authors now present as if they had never been tried.

[8] Revisionism partially echoes older, class-based theories in its assumption that a more rational and/or more egalitarian socialism would produce a similarly rational and just political structure. Such theories turned totalitarianism on its head: socialist power structures and politics were natural outgrowths of a prevailing logic of production and allocation, rather than the other way around. But these theories became entrapped in circularity, since the state itself had imposed the new economic order and set the parameters of class relations through its administrative policies. As a result, they simply could not explain departures from the classical bureaucratic socialist model, or the failure of class-based support for that model. Thus, like the older totalitarian view of state-socialist societies as frozen in terror, neither interest group nor class theories lent themselves to analysis of the *process* of reform and transformation. For a review of class-based theories as applied to socialist systems, see Iván Szelényi, "The Intelligentsia in the Class Structure of State-Socialist Societies," in Michael Burawoy and Theda Skocpol, eds., *Marxist Inquiries: Studies of Labor, Class, and States*, Supplement to the *American Journal of Sociology*, Vol. 88, S287-S327 (Chicago: Chicago University Press, 1982).

[9] Charles King, "Post-Post Communism: Transition, Comparison and the End of Eastern Europe," *World Politics* 53, no. 1 (October 2000): 143–72, 144.

therefore is on the decades *prior* to the drama of 1989, and on the difference that earlier transformations now make in post-communist societies.

The cases under consideration are Poland and Hungary, the two countries that, via radically different routes, led Eastern Europe out of communism. The book also establishes a broad comparative context for its core cases through references to the Soviet Union/Russia, and other East European countries. These countries are all of interest to theorists and students of systemic change, largely because they highlight questions of general import. One such question, at the center of this book, is as fundamental as it is enduring: why and how, even in hermetically closed systems, do power relations become open to negotiation and contestation?

Juxtaposed, Poland and Hungary also raise intriguing questions for students of comparative politics. Why do distinctive patterns of negotiation and contestation emerge where the formal rules of the game are virtually identical? This question is especially germane because whereas Hungary was the undisputed leader of economic reform in the communist world, Poland led dramatically and decisively in the field of open political struggles. Moreover, whereas Hungarians – especially after 1956 but even before – revolted by reform, the Poles had to revolt before the country's equally talented economists and technocrats could achieve significant institutional reform.

From a comparative perspective, the book also explores the role of legacies. Specifically, what do different histories of state-society relations mean for the countries' post-communist political and economic development? Hungary and Poland, again, offer contrasting outcomes. Hungary's marketization and privatization programs were comparatively depoliticized and proceeded rapidly, while Poland's privatization and restructuring programs have been much slower and more contentious. Moreover, Poland's democracy has been plagued by high governmental instability, low administrative continuity, and continued state-labor confrontation. In 2005, a decade and a half after the Roundtable Agreements, the main parties of both the Polish Left and the Right of the political spectrum are in shambles, leaving a vacuum that invites the emergence of extremist parties. Meanwhile, Hungarian democracy has exhibited nearly opposite traits, with increasingly strong and stable parties, which in many respects are very similar to their West European analogues.

Finally, the book seeks to clarify micro/macro connections at different levels of social and political action. It asks, for instance: how is individual rationality tied to collective action? How are the boundaries of principal-agent dynamics set? And what is the impact of the state's "moral-ideological"[10] function on its economic programmatic competence and policymaking capacity?

The strategic behavior of Polish and Hungarian workers and entrepreneurs suggests that when building and negotiating the micro-foundations of incipient markets, rational agents repeatedly confirm the validity of both methodological

---

[10] Michael Mann, *The Sources of Social Power, Volume II: The Rise of Classes and Nation-States, 1760–1914* (New York: Cambridge University Press, 1993), 44.

individualism *and* Weberian economics. Similarly, the workings of informal and hybrid institutions suggest that, given the porousness of internal systemic boundaries, command-chain dilemmas like the principal-agent problem can only be properly understood in the broader context of state-society relations. We will see, among other things, the inadequacy of the widely accepted notion that the problems facing principals *vis-à-vis* agents are either conflicts of interest or problems arising from imperfect information, say, regarding agents' motives.[11] For important as they are, these two categories of challenges facing principals in an organization hardly exhaust the possibilities.

The cases of state-socialist Poland and Hungary present two seemingly contradictory dynamics and outcomes of principal-agent relations. On the one hand, in both countries (as in all state-socialist systems), there is ample evidence of collusion – tacit and explicit – between state-firm managers and workers against an "unjust" and "irrational" state. On the other hand, the ultimate "principal" – the top echelons of the party-state – often has perfectly good information about the motives and strategies of both managers and workers. Yet in Poland, the higher-ups insisted on maintaining an ideologically grounded institutional structure, whereas in Hungary they responded by altering the structure as far as possible without directly confronting their Soviet overlords.

Finally, the key role played by reformist technocrats in Hungary's transformation, and the relative weakness of their Polish counterparts, calls for a closer look at two additional and important factors. One is the generation and depletion of power by subordinate officialdom; the other is the political-discursive capacity of the state. On both these points, it is worth anticipating a theme from Chapter 5: by the early 1980s, key officials of the Hungarian communist state were ready *and* able to make an astonishing claim. They would argue that *large state enterprises – not private firms*, as Leninist ideology held – had turned into "vehicles of particular interest [that] obstructed the assertion of general economic interests."[12]

Thus, not only did extensive monitoring imposed from above fail to constrain agents, but in Hungary, principals actually led the subversion of the system's structure, whereas in Poland they faced revolt. If we are to understand the causes, mechanisms, and patterns of change in the relationship between structural context and agents' politics, we must carefully examine the ideologies, dependencies, and conflicts that, in the dynamics of history, shape state-society relations.[13] It is to this task that I now turn.

---

[11] Morris Fiorina and Kenneth Schepsle, "Formal Theories of Leadership: Agents, Agenda-Setters, and Entrepreneurs," in Bryan D. Jones, ed., *Leadership and Politics: New Perspectives in Political Science* (Lawrence, KS: University Press of Kansas, 1989).

[12] László Bruszt, "The Politics of Private Business and Public Enterprises," EUI Colloquium Papers, Doc. IUE 261/87 Col. 45 (Florence: European University Institute, June 1988), 41.

[13] For an excellent treatment of the agency-structure problem in state-socialist and post-socialist settings see Mark Beissinger, *Nationalist Mobilization and the Collapse of the Soviet State* (New York: Cambridge University Press, 2002).

The Argument in Preview

In addressing the puzzles at its core, the book develops a tripartite argument. First, the potential for self-transformation was present in most, if not all, state-socialist countries from the start: underneath the strict formality of their total-itarian design, state-socialist institutions in both countries began early on to develop what I call *points of permeable contact* with society. These were points at which neither citizens nor states could fully dictate the terms of engagement, and the highly asymmetrical power relations between state and society could even attain a rough informal equality.

Both in Poland and Hungary, for example, the terms of engagement were contested as follows: citizens *qua* economic agents informally reshaped the formal rules upheld by an extremely powerful party-state, gradually riddling the economic sphere with structural dualities, while party-state leaders, indu-bitably dominant yet constrained by ideological dictates, searched for addi-tional degrees of freedom in the official sphere of economic policymaking. Yet despite this fundamental similarity in state-society engagement, the countries not only underwent remarkably distinctive transformations, but in Hungary, the transformative process was ultimately characterized by a positive-sum solu-tion in state-society relations, whereas in Poland the opposite occurred.[14]

This leads to the second part of the argument. At crucial moments, the ruling elites' practical competence can hinge on political-discursive adaptations of the dominant ideology. In Eastern Europe, party-state leaders' capacity to loosen ideological constraints on economic policymaking shaped their ability to launch and sustain meaningful economic reforms. Put more directly, because commu-nist ideology straitjacketed reformist political elites, the crafting and execution of liberalizing economic reforms prior to 1989 required an official discourse that presented such reforms not as dangerous breaks with the system's guiding ideology, but rather as consistent with state-socialist pragmatism. At various key junctures between 1949 and 1989, Hungarian elites succeeded in this del-icate task much better than their Polish counterparts. In fact, close historical inspection of the institutional bases of reform indicates that the reform capabil-ities of the Hungarian state outstripped those of the Polish state because pro-reform Hungarian leaders, public functionaries, and professional economists effectively crafted political-discursive strategies that stretched the boundaries of the ideologically permissible.

Ideological adaptation, both among elites and societal groups, can set in motion subtle, sometimes unintended, and perhaps intractable processes of economic and political restructuring. In our two cases, reform programs, even when inadequate or belated, interacted from above with citizens' *de facto* alter-ations of state-socialist practices from below. This interactive process of official

---

[14] This is in no way to deprecate the remarkable political consensus achieved by the Polish Roundtable Agreements between the opposition and the party-state. It refers, however, to the much older trend of deep socio-political cleavage evident both before and after the Roundtable (see Chapters 3 and 4).

reform and informal practice determined the extent to which each party-state could deliver some measure of what we might call "just rationality." Rationality, as understood at the time by the countries' citizenries, may be defined as the tangible convergence between the economic system's *potential* for improved efficiency and its *actual* performance. Justice, in turn, refers to citizens' perception of the party-state's demonstrable *willingness* to design and implement the requisite policy initiatives.

More specifically, the high reform capabilities of the Hungarian state translated into waves of economic reform, which in turn led to a robust, increasingly diversified and better integrated *second economy*[15] whose networks of production and exchange eventually suffused the entire economic system with an increasingly marked degree of "rationality," and beginning in the early 1980s, a rough economic "justice" between private and public enterprise. In Poland, by contrast, attempts to loosen ideological constraints generally failed, and sometimes backfired, further restricting the state's reform capabilities. This meant a poorly integrated second economy. Moreover, the failure of Polish elites to mediate state-society conflicts through *either* official economic reforms *or* via informal means and hybrid economic institutions fed the image of the party-state as "unjustly" bent on executing "irrational" economic policies. The party-state's unjust irrationality, in fact, served as the organizing theme for societal arguments against the state and as a focal point for the formation of Solidarity itself.

The third and final part of the argument flows from the previous two. State-society relations, as described earlier, shaped labor's veto instruments over economic policy in different ways, and engendered two hallmark hybrids: an increasingly institutionalized second economy in Hungary, and Solidarity in Poland. To phrase it yet another way, the rough, informal equality previously mentioned found different institutional expressions in each country. In Hungary, labor's veto was exercised on the shop-floor through complex bargaining processes between state-management and *individual* workers. In Poland, labor exercised its veto power collectively. Moreover, whereas in Hungary the state's economic reforms "de-politicized" workers' material demands, in Poland these demands were closely entwined with an increasingly generalized normative outrage provoked by the state's "irrational" policies.

---

[15] Defined as the sum total of all non-state private economic activity: licensed and informal; legal, illegal, and on the borderline of illegality. The state sector, by contrast, or "first" economy, encompassed state-owned firms, state-controlled cooperatives, government agencies, and registered non-profit institutions. Definitions of the second economy vary significantly with the analyst's focus, assumptions, and ideological perspective. This simplified working-definition draws on those used by István Gábor and Péter Galasi, "Second Economy, State and Labour Market" in Galasi and Sziráczki, eds., *Labour Market and Second Economy in Hungary*, and by János Kornai both in "The Hungarian Reform Process: Visions, Hopes and Reality," *Journal of Economic Literature* XXIV, no. 4 (December 1986) and in his book *The Socialist System: The Political Economy of Communism* (Princeton: Princeton University Press, 1992).

The upshot of all this is that the two countries developed distinctive *selection patterns of core conflicts* and *specific modes of core-conflict resolution*, which in turn led to sharp variations in the substance and stability of power settlements. By *selection of core conflicts*, I mean the articulation and prioritization of stakes contested by state and societal actors. By *mode of core-conflict resolution*, I mean the institutional mechanisms deployed by agents in the settlement of clashing political and economic agendas. In Hungary, for instance, the early 1960s brought an official policy of reconciliation between state and society that enabled professional economists, reformist technocrats, and Party ideologues to communicate more freely and constructively than elsewhere in the bloc. Conversely, Poland was rocked in the late 1960s and early 1970s by student strikes, serious labor unrest, and the Party's violent responses. Power settlements differed as well. In 1980, Poland produced the politically radical but inherently unstable Gdańsk Accords, whereas Hungary produced a property-rights reform in 1982 that served as the launching platform for subsequent, even more radical reforms.

If the Hungarians "reformed Communism to death," as Lonnie R. Johnson has quipped,[16] the Poles protested it into agony. Or so it would seem from the vantage point of system collapse. But when viewed from the perspective of systemic transformation, a more dynamic picture emerges – one in which negotiation and contestation, stemming from various points of permeable contact between state and society, generate legacies of their own. Indeed, once we take such legacies into account, it becomes clear why it is that institutional frameworks are often much more than mere functional arrangements designed to consolidate the "political advantages" of powerful actors.[17] Moreover, once we incorporate the legacy factor, the different institutional residues of state socialism(s) become discernable, not only under the transforming *ancien régime*, but also as they came into play during the dual transition to democracy and market. In the transition to democracy, legacy effects appeared paradoxical. The contentious Poles negotiated their way out of party rule; the pragmatic Hungarians opted for a competitive route. But this paradox, we will see, dissolves once we probe more deeply into the political calculations of protagonists and the institutional conditions in which they operated. The implications for democratic consolidation are more obvious and straightforward, and throughout most of the 1990s could be seen in Poland's relatively contentious and unstable democracy, and in Hungary's more quiescent politics.

Economic legacies, too, had a straightforward effect on privatization, marketization, and even on the relative strength of key economic sectors,

---

[16] Lonnie R. Johnson, *Central Europe: Enemies, Neighbors, Friends* (New York: Oxford University Press, 2002), 278.

[17] Allison Stanger, "Leninist Legacies and Legacies of State Socialism in Post-Communist Central Europe's Constitutional Development," and Paul Pierson, "Epilogue: From Area Studies to Contextualized Comparisons," 361, both in Grzegorz Ekiert and Stephen Hanson, eds., *Capitalism and Democracy in Central and Eastern Europe: Assessing the Legacy of Communist Rule* (New York: Cambridge University Press, 2003).

most notably agriculture. Hungary's precocious institutionalization of property rights under state socialism allowed for a swifter post-socialist privatization program that was also largely depoliticized early on. Similarly, the country's waves of reform under state socialism increasingly gave the indigenous private sector a "corporate" character, which, in contradistinction to Poland's "unincorporated" variant,[18] paved the way for a relatively smooth transition to a market economy. Finally, the liberal agricultural policies of the Hungarian party-state left domestic agriculture far better positioned to meet the competitive challenges of a global economy.

These post-socialist processes and structural conditions, shaped to a significant degree by the socialist past, would in turn later shape both countries' accession paths to the European Union (EU), as well as their adjustment as new members. In this regard, it matters that Poland's privatization and marketization programs were relatively slow and problematic. But it is Polish agriculture that is most instructive, though it has so rarely been the subject of serious analysis.[19] At least 70 percent of this sector remained in private hands under state socialism, yet food shortages (or very high prices) persisted throughout much of that country's state-socialist experience, in part because private Polish farmers were not allowed to attain economies of scale, and were offered modest opportunities for modernization only in the late 1980s. Today, Polish agriculture remains a potentially serious stumbling block to the country's successful integration into Europe.[20]

Organization and Sources

This book is based on a wide variety of sources from Eastern and Western Europe and the United States. Between 1989 and 1996, I conducted rounds of extensive interviews with ministerial level and other high officials, second-economy entrepreneurs, economists, and sociologists involved in policy formulation, or active as dissidents and later, in new democratic parliaments. In many cases, I was able to conduct follow-on correspondence after 1996, as well as several new interviews between 1998 and 2003. My analysis also relies heavily on a broad array of unpublished government documents and other primary

---

[18] Simon Johnson and Gary W. Loveman, *Starting Over in Eastern Europe: Entrepreneurship and Economic Renewal* (Cambridge: Harvard Business School Press, 1995).

[19] At least by Western scholars. Notable exceptions are Andrzej Korbonski's *Politics of Socialist Agriculture in Poland: 1945–60* (NY: Columbia University Press 1965); Zvi Lerman, Csaba Csáki, Gershon Feder, *Agriculture in Transition: Land Policies and Evolving Farm Structures in Post-Soviet Countries* (NY: Lexington Books 2004); Ivan Szelényi, *Privatizing the Land: Rural Political Economy in Post-Communist Societies* (NY: Routledge, 1998); and Joseph Brada and Karl-Eugen Wadekin, eds. *Socialist Agriculture in Transition: Organizational Response to Failing Performace* (NY: Westview, 1987).

[20] In 2000, for example, Poland ran a $600 million trade deficit in agricultural products (compared, for instance, with Romania's $311 million deficit). "Poverty in Eastern Europe: The Land That Time Forgot," *The Economist*, September 23, 2000, 27–30.

sources to which I gained access in Eastern Europe, as well as on the more broadly available U.S. data sources. The book is also informed throughout by hundreds of empirical and theoretical studies by economists, sociologists, political scientists, and anthropologists in Eastern and Western Europe and the United States.[21]

The book is ordered both thematically and chronologically. Chapter 1 sketches the historical development of the relevant *points of permeable contact* between state and society. To this end, it highlights some key political and discursive initiatives of state actors in each country. Think of this as the view from above. It also highlights some of the adaptive strategies of societal actors: the view from below. These macro- and micro-perspectives are interlaced with outlines of the hybrid institutions and transformative processes that set Poland and Hungary apart from other state socialist countries, but also from one another.

The discussion in Chapter 1 sets the stage for a more detailed discussion of the book's theoretical implications (Conclusion), and serves as a background for Chapters 2 and 3, which paint a picture of political-economic relations between state and society in Poland and Hungary as the Stalinist and classical-bureaucratic periods draw to a close. Here the focus is on economic reforms and reform attempts, with special attention to their impact on the second economy, as well as on informal property relations inside state firms and cooperatives, in both industry and the agricultural sector.

Chapter 2 covers the period between 1948 and 1968 in Hungary, with comparative references to several other East European countries as well as more extended comparisons to Poland. This chapter traces Hungary's rich early history of economic reform, but also shifts attention away from the issue of the economic success or failure of reforms to their *political* implications, and argues that reforms, even when truncated or ineffective, invariably led to an informal redistribution of control over economic activities. Specifically, the chapter examines the mechanisms whereby reforms aimed at improving the efficiency of state firms created new principal-agent problems in the attempt to solve old ones, and implicitly increased the power of workers and peasants *vis-à-vis* managers.

In this chapter, we see that in their second-economy activities, peasants and workers occupied dual positions in socialism: not, as has so often been suggested, because of an inexorable split between the public and private realms, but because actors' strategies blurred the boundaries between the two, creating both a hybrid mode of production and a hybrid realm of social relations profoundly influenced by the former.

Chapter 2 also shows how reform-minded politicians started to craft a specialized language based on the accumulated weight of experiments in agriculture. Because these were seen by ideologues as less important and less threatening than potential changes in industry, party-state pragmatists were

---

[21] For further details on methodology of interviews with entrepreneurs, see fn 8, Chapter 6.

able to use reforms in agriculture as a basis from which to begin a long, slow process of reconciliation with society after the devastation of the 1956 revolution.

Chapter 3 traces the history of economic reform and reform attempts in Poland from the early 1950s to the late 1970s. Like the preceding companion chapter on Hungary, this chapter seeks to explain not only the economic results, but also the broader political impact of reforms, reform attempts, and the Polish leadership's *promises* of reform. Both Chapters 2 and 3 pay close attention to the agricultural sector, but because private agriculture played such an important economic – and political – role in Poland, Chapter 3 devotes considerable attention to explaining the party-state's attitude toward and treatment of Poland's large private agricultural sector. We see that despite some short-lived periods of modest liberalization, Polish leaders shied away from all serious reform of either the state sector or the small remaining formal private sector outside agriculture. Private farmers, meanwhile, were either harassed (because the majority refused to join state-controlled cooperatives) or abandoned to their own devices, without sufficient reliable access to inputs or technical assistance.

Because the Polish party-state failed to collectivize most of the agricultural sector, Poland's orthodox party leaders in this period tried to subdue the sector as best they could without provoking open conflict. We see in this chapter that the party-state's first failure in this regard – the Poznań riots of 1956 – though far less dramatic than Hungary's 1956, was equally important to the construction of state-society relations and political discourse in Poland. By the time Gierek took over as First Secretary, workers were highly politicized, and in particular were angered by what they saw as the government's irrationality and failure to make good on its promises to include them in decision-making. Despite massive stimulus of the economy through Western credits – and despite high hopes among the leadership for the potential of socialist development in this period – by the end of the 1970s the government had lost what managerial credibility it had with much of the Polish citizenry.

Chapter 4 treats the rise of Solidarity as Poland's most important hybrid institution, linking its evolution to the party-state's failure to reach a workable economic accommodation with society. The chapter covers the period from 1980 to 1990, and focuses in addition to Solidarity, on the particular characteristics of the Polish non-agricultural second economy that began to expand in the mid-1980s, and especially on its political-ideological genesis. From interviews and scholarly accounts alike, we see how the party-state's treatment of the second economy over the preceding thirty years resulted in an incipient private sector that differed from its Hungarian counterpart both in its institutional forms and in the degree of security and legitimacy it enjoyed. The expansion in this period of the legal, non-agricultural private sector in Poland provides a window onto the Polish party-state's last-ditch efforts to coopt a thoroughly polarized society that regarded it with deepening suspicion and hostility. The government selectively permitted the expansion of the second economy into a more institutionalized private sector, but neither extended clear and binding contractual guarantees like those of the Hungarian reform that made private enterprise a citizen's *right,* nor educated the public, as the Hungarian government tried to do. The result was growing public hostility to the increasingly visible wealth of the most dynamic segment of private firms: foreign-owned companies.

Chapter 5 follows the development of a formal private sector in Hungary from the inception of the reform in 1979 to its enactment in 1982. Here we see clearly how old concessions became the basis for new reforms, like buried blueprints for change later rediscovered and adapted to new circumstances. The chapter traces the links between reform precedents from the 1950s and 1960s and the legalization of the second economy. The 1982 reform changed the basis of entrepreneurship and private business ownership in Hungary from *privilege* – small numbers of licenses granted at the discretion of local authorities – to that of a *right* based on government decree and on a broad regulatory mechanism. By transforming a "privilege" into a "right," this reform led to the dramatic growth of the second economy into a new, significantly expanded formal private sector. We see, too, that although the 1982 statutes created at least half-a-dozen new company and partnership forms for private business, it also legalized several pre-existing second-economy practices already familiar from Chapter 2, and called them "new."

The chapter surveys some of the numerous radical institutional reforms that followed in the remainder of the 1980s. In particular, it shows why, after 1982, the government faced intense pressure from entrepreneurs to codify – in a uniform law passed by Parliament, not contingent on state administrative directives – the mix of *de facto* and *de jure* rights granted to them in 1982. Pressure from below combined with the frustration of officials (who faced a now unintelligible and largely unworkable regulatory framework that no longer fit Hungary's rapidly evolving economic reality), and culminated in the 1988 Corporations Act (sometimes also called the Enterprise Law in English translations).[22] This comprehensive new law unified the complex of regulations introduced in 1982 and thereafter, equalized virtually all public and private sector prerogatives, and presented an explicit framework for the outright privatization of state firms.

Perhaps most interesting for political scientists are the insights this chapter affords into the policymaking process in a communist state through detailed interviews with key functionaries involved in the 1982 reform. The chapter uses these interviews, along with numerous unpublished internal government documents, to demonstrate in some detail that while systemic exigencies argued for radical reform, only intense political-discursive adaptation of communist ideology by reformers within the party-state made it possible. Finally, the chapter demonstrates how the effect of this political-discursive adaptation – a seemingly

---

[22] "A gazdasági társaágokról szóló 1988. évi VI. törvény" ("Act VI of the 1988 law on business associations"), which defined the statutorily sanctioned institutional forms of economic enterprise – e.g., limited liability company, stock company limited by shares.

simple task that in fact required great entrepreneurial tenacity and complex ideological maneuvers – stabilized expectations throughout the party-state in general and among hard-liners in particular.

Here, there is no counterpart chapter for Poland, because there was no analogous Polish reform; this fact is an important part of the story itself. The chapters wholly devoted to Poland do, however, draw on interviews with Polish economists who had a close view of that country's quite different forms of economic liberalization under martial law during the 1980s, and discuss the private cooperatives that were established after the repression of Solidarity.

Chapter 6 presents in-depth case-studies of modern entrepreneurs who emerged as highly successful manufacturers from Hungary's early 1980s reform of property rights. These case-studies are a small cross-section of a much larger set of interviews with Hungarian private manufacturers that I conducted from late 1988 to 1996. The chapter places the studies in broader socio-political context using two large-*n* surveys undertaken by sociologists and economists of the Hungarian Academy of Sciences. Through the accounts of the entrepreneurs themselves, we see firsthand how and why individuals decided to leave the security of the state sector and/or the cover of the informal economy; what incentives, difficulties, risks, and rewards were involved; how they dealt with an often still-hostile bureaucracy and an infrastructure unsuited to their needs; and finally, how individually and collectively they pleaded, bribed, pressured, sued, and ultimately organized to change regulations that blocked some of their efforts to promote the development of increasingly sophisticated private enterprises that would be at home in the global economy.

Chapter 7 seeks a deeper yet more precise understanding of the relationship between economic and political pressures. It demonstrates how the Hungarian party-state's formal recognition of private enterprise triggered a complex transformation of interest-representation institutions, which in turn led to a radical political change two years before the fall of the Hungarian Socialist Workers Party (HSWP). In 1987, entrepreneurs formed their own independent interest representation organization to extract concessions for the private sector from the authorities. A year later, entrepreneurs formed a political party. More importantly, the chapter also shows that while the institutional shock to the Hungarian system of command and interest transmission was much greater than in Poland, the Hungarian transformative process nevertheless retained its pragmatic, even cooperative, character.

The Conclusion examines the problems and prospects of Hungary and Poland as they integrate into a wider Europe. This final chapter also summarizes the book's main arguments, and presents in more detailed fashion their implications for existing theories of transition and political-economic change more generally

I

History and Theory in Practice

By now it is obvious that even though the blueprint of classical state socialism aimed for uniformity across countries and within societies, a *variety* of national hybrids actually developed in the state-socialist world.[1] The most casual observers intuit, for instance, that Romania was not Poland, and specialists are keenly aware of the myriad ways in which the developmental paths of Czechoslovakia and Hungary diverged from one another, or from those of the Soviet Union, Bulgaria, and the German Democratic Republic.[2] Some have

[1] See, among others, Grzegorz Ekiert, "Patterns of Post-Communist Transitions," in Karen Dawisha and Bruce Parrot, eds., *Conflict, Cleavage and Change in Central Asia and the Caucasus* (Cambridge: Cambridge University Press, 1997), and Valerie Bunce, "Postsocialisms," in Sorin Antohi and Vladimir Tismaneanu, eds., *Between Past and Future: The Revolutions of 1989 and Their Aftermath* (Budapest: CEU Press, 2000).

[2] On Czechoslovakia, see, for instance, Sharon L. Wolchick, *Czechoslovakia in Transition: Politics, Economics and Society* (New York: Pinter, 1991); on Hungary, see Gábor Révész, *Perestroika in Eastern Europe: Hungary's Economic Transformation, 1945–1988* (Boulder: Westview, 1990); Bennett Kövrig, *Communism in Hungary: From Kun to Kádár* (Stanford: Hoover Institution Press 1979); János Kornai, "The Hungarian Reform Process: Visions, Hopes and Reality," *Journal of Economic Literature* 24 (4) December 1986, 1687–1737; Paul Hare, Hugo Radice, and Nigel Swain, eds., *Hungary: A Decade of Economic Reform* (London: George Allen and Unwin, 1981); Rudolf Tőkés, *Hungary's negotiated revolution: Economic reform, social change and political succession* (New York: Cambridge University Press, 1996); Nigel Swain, *Hungary: The Rise and Fall of Feasible Socialism* (New York: Verso, 1992); on the GDR, see Jeffrey Kopstein, *The Politics of Economic Decline, 1945–1989* (Chapel Hill: University of North Carolina Press, 1997); and A. James McAdam, *Germany divided: From the wall to reunification* (Princeton: Princeton University Press, 1993); on Poland, Kazimierz Poznański, *Poland's Protracted Transition: Institutional Change and Economic Growth, 1970–1994* (New York: Cambridge University Press, 1996); Bartołmiej Kaminski, *The Collapse of State Socialism: The Case of Poland* (Princeton: Princeton University Press, 1991); Ben Slay, *The Polish Economy: Crisis, Reform, and Transformation* (Princeton: Princeton University Press, 1994); on Bulgaria, see Iliana Zloch-Christy, ed., *Bulgaria in a Time of Change: Economic and Political Dimensions* (Brookfield, VT: Avebury, 1996); John D. Bell, ed., *Bulgaria in transition: politics, economics, society, and culture after communism* (Boulder, CO: Westview Press, 1998); *Bulgaria: the dual challenge of transition and accession* (Washington, D.C.: World Bank, 2001).

also explored the similarities and differences amongst the Chinese, Hungarian, and Yugoslav "reform" variants,[3] while a smaller group has focused on the East Asian or Latin American experiences with the state-socialist blueprint.[4]

Even analysts sensitive to such differences, however, have generally grouped Hungary and Poland together as very similar pre-1989 "reformers." This cat-egorization, to be sure, makes a certain amount of sense. After all, Hungary, Poland, and Yugoslavia appeared *avant garde* beside the Soviet Union and other more "conservative" countries. (Outside the region, only China could be con-sidered a serious economic reformer.)[5] But closer inspection of the prolonged internal transformations of Hungary and Poland suggests that in many ways it is precisely these two countries that represented *opposing* variants of state socialism. One came to resemble a laboratory for controlled economic experi-mentation, the other held out the ironic image of a workers' state buffeted by overt labor-state conflict. One became the undisputed leader of economic reform in the communist world; the other led dramatically and decisively in the field of open political struggles. One was characterized by accommodation and stability; the other by upheaval and hardship.

These differences between the Polish and Hungarian political economies are as intriguing as the differences that obtain among West European nations and attract the attention of scholars working on that region. But as in the case of Western Europe, understanding them fully requires deep knowledge of the various countries' political-economic trajectories. Indeed, one way to explain the origins and persistence of the different cleavages and settlements is to go back in history in search of a single, determinative juncture. Yu-Shan Wu, for one, argues that "traumatic imprinting events" – the suppression of the 1956 revolution in Hungary; the civil war and War Communism in the Soviet

---

[3] On China and Hungary, see Victor Nee and David Stark eds., *Remaking the Economic Insti-tutions of Socialism: China and Eastern Europe* (Stanford: Stanford University Press, 1989); Andrew Walder, ed., *The Waning of the Communist State: Economic Origins of Political Decline in China and Hungary* (Berkeley: University of California Press, 1995); Yu-Shan Wu, *Comparative Economic Transformations: Mainland China, Hungary, the Soviet Union, and Taiwan* (Stanford: Stanford University Press, 1994); on Yugoslavia, see Debrorah Milenkovitch, *Plan and market in Yugoslav economic thought* (New Haven: Yale University Press, 1971); Ellen Comisso, *Workers' control under plan and market implications of Yugoslav self-management* (New Haven: Yale University Press, 1979); Susan Woodward, *Socialist Unemployment: The Political Economy of Yugoslavia, 1945–1990* (Princeton: Princeton University Press, 1995).

[4] On Vietnam, see Benedict J. Tria Kerkvliet and Doug. J. Porter, *Vietnam's Rural Transforma-tion* (New York: Westview Press, 1995); on Vietnam and North Korea, see Doug J. Porter in Maria Łos, ed., *The Second Economy in Marxist States*. London: Macmillan, 1990. On Cuba, see, among others, Susan Eckstein, *Back from the Future: Cuba Under Castro* (Princeton: Prince-ton University Press, 1994); on Nicaragua (a partially consolidated state-socialist system between 1979–1990), see Forrest D. Colburn, *Managing the commanding heights: Nicaragua's state enter-prises* (Berkeley: University of California Press, 1990).

[5] In brief, a reform in a state-socialist system is significant, or even "radical" and potentially transformative, only if it alters *at least one* of the system's defining attributes: ideology, property rights, or bureaucratic coordination. János Kornai, *The Socialist System: The Political Economy of Communism* (Princeton: Princeton University Press, 1992), 36–50, 71, 361, 388.

Union; the havoc wreaked by the Cultural Revolution in mainland China – leave ruling elites "desperate" for legitimacy and, by extension, lead them to adopt radical policy measures aimed at providing the population with its "most basic needs." Hence the agricultural orientation of early reforms in both Hungary and China.[6]

In a similar vein, Grzegorz Ekiert makes the case that diverse post-crisis policies account for divergences in countries' state-society relations. In post-1956 Hungary, he posits, repressive demobilization was followed by re-equilibration policies that ushered in the formation of "a paternalistic regime characterized by a pragmatic approach to economic policies and a relative flexibility in political and ideological matters." In 1980s Poland, by way of contrast, the post-martial law regime failed "to rebuild the party-state's authority and institutions, to destroy political opposition, to prevent large-scale collective protest, to arrest economic crisis, and to introduce effective political and economic reforms."[7]

Both Wu's and Ekiert's claims, grounded in careful empirical research and refined analysis, insightfully synthesize complex political and economic developments spanning long periods in multiple countries. Yet by focusing on 1956, Wu underestimates the significance of a prior turning point in Hungary – namely, the "New Course" reforms of 1953 – whereas Ekiert, by focusing on the 1980s, underestimates the significance of 1956 in Poland, and the betrayal by subsequent regimes, of the social pact workers understood to have emerged from the settlement of that crisis. Indeed, transformative paths in Hungary and Poland were shaped by *multiple* junctures: 1953, 1956, and 1963, as well as the early 1980s in Hungary; 1956, 1968, the early 1970s, and 1980–1981 in Poland. The analytical narrative that follows renders these junctures more easily discernable by showing in stylized form key actors' adaptations to the system's structural rigidities.

State Actors: Official Realism and Legacies

Under the *ancien régime*, Hungarian politicians developed an approach to policy legitimation that we might call *official pragmatism*. This approach traced its distinct rhetorical framework back to 1953, when the Imre Nagy leadership selectively deployed a Marxist-Leninist analytical discourse to argue two points: first, leaders should not forget that raising the population's standard of living was the ultimate goal of state socialism; and second, a "balanced" program of economic development was the best means to attain that goal.

This formulation had several advantages. To begin with, it borrowed its tactical applications from Marxist-Leninist "realism." Advocates of the New Course

---

[6] Yu-Shan Wu, *Comparative Economic Transformations: Mainland China, Hungary, the Soviet Union, and Taiwan* (Stanford: Stanford University Press, 1994), 12–13, 199.

[7] Grzegorz Ekiert, *The State Against Society: Political Crises and Their Aftermath in East Central Europe* (Princeton: Princeton University Press, 1996), 24–25.

(1953–1955), for example, were able to defend the program's "deviationist" policies as both pragmatic and legitimate. After all, had not Marx and Lenin themselves stressed the point that every country faces its own peculiar developmental stages and challenges? In addition, a "realistic" assessment of Hungary's particularities implied that the agricultural sector was of paramount importance to the progress of the general economy and that peasants were indispensable political allies of the party-state. Finally, if the fathers of Marxist-Leninist realism had faced the facts of life squarely without abandoning the ultimate goal of socialism, then so too could "objective" Hungarian experts. Hence the early "professionalization" of Hungarian economics under Nagy's regime – a process that afforded economists the credibility to claim that the practice of undogmatic (non-normative, positivist) science was the only way to understand and transform the unique "realities" of the Hungarian economy.

The enemies of the New Course resisted its policies and 1956 temporarily put an end to the experiment. But the New Course also left crucial discursive and structural-institutional legacies. Because the New Course legitimated itself by articulating its own brand of Marxist-Leninist realism, the party's official line shielded the economics profession behind the armature of an "objective-scientific" identity and, equally important, mandated a "pragmatic politics" for state officials. One key consequence of armored economists and flexible ideologues was their joint ability to foster a particular type of informal networking – that is to say, the forging of close links between intellectuals and scholars, on the one hand, and party-state functionaries, on the other. These networks proved so resilient, in fact, that later, under the Kádár regime, they thrived despite the nearly overwhelming vertical bureaucratization and distrustful compartmentalization that characterized all state-socialist regimes. As Chapter 6 shows, they became increasingly predominant in the formulation and implementation of "realistic" economic policy.

Beyond the high valorization of pragmatic realism, the New Course policies yielded undeniable material success both in agriculture and small private (non-agricultural) enterprise, thus altering the structure of production and, by extension, further enhancing the prestige and influence of reformers. These legacies left the country well-positioned to take advantage of the enhanced degrees of policy freedom that flowed from Soviet elites' political learning during the 1956 crisis. Perhaps the most pertinent lesson was summed up by Nikita Khrushchev at the time: "Ideological work alone will be of no avail if we do not ensure that living standards rise. It is no accident that Hungary and Poland are the countries in which unrest has occurred."[8]

Khrushchev's statement underscored the historical irony that while the New Course was defunct by 1956, the highest level of the Soviet power structure

[8] Mark Kramer, "New Evidence on Soviet Decision-Making and the 1956 Polish and Hungarian Crises," in *Cold War International History Project Bulletin 8/9* (Washington DC: Woodrow Wilson International Center For Scholars, Winter 1996/97), 376.

now embraced its primary goal. The statement also pointed to the possible expansion of opportunity structures. During moments of expansion, in the words of Valerie Bunce,

there is a growing elasticity in the environment, wherein existing political alignments are disturbed, political access widens, the policy agenda is reordered, and the costs of mobilization decline alongside the benefits of standing passive on the sidelines.[9]

The aftermath of 1956 in both Hungary and Poland indicates that this was indeed a critical moment for the future of these countries. The quest for higher living standards soon became the signal feature of Hungary's hybrid model. But what of Poland? As is well-known, Gomułka proposed a pragmatic approach to collectivization, but he did this in the late 1940s, when Stalinism was still in force. Hence the truncation of his "deviationist path" to socialism. It was only with the advent of the post-Stalinist thaw and the end of the 1956 crisis that the Gomułka regime reached a *modus vivendi* with the Soviet Union: Poland would remain a steady ally, and in return it would be accorded greater leeway in domestic policy.

In the context of this mutual understanding, Gomułka recognized the legitimacy of workers' councils, as well as their active participation in economic management. In short, he used Poland's newly enhanced degrees of freedom to acknowledge openly Polish workers' vocal and effective rights in the determination of "economic rationality." But as it became clear that this radical concession to workers put at risk the party-state's leading role, the Gomułka regime proceeded to eviscerate *de facto* workers' rights. The consequences of this about-face were as profound as they were lasting. Most significantly, the regime lost credibility with the citizenry and, by extension, the ability to project a persuasive vision of state-socialist pragmatism. If anything, Gomułka's regime crucified itself to the rigid principle that political loyalty did *not* require economic incentives. In so doing, the regime made economic rationality a permanent object of contestation between state and society.

In Hungary, meanwhile, Kádár subdued all post-1956 revolutionary remnants, smashing workers' councils in the process. As Henryk Szlajfer wrote in *Krytyka*, the Kádár leadership spent the next six years "brutally dismantling" the "revolt syndrome."[10] But once that awful task had been accomplished, this same repressive regime faced a critical choice – namely, which exit path to take "out of the freeze," to borrow yet another apt phrase from Szlajfer. The legacies of the New Course proved crucial at this juncture, ultimately enabling Kádár to bring about what Szlajfer called an "innovative restoration" from above in the early 1960s.

---

[9] Valerie Bunce, *Subversive Institutions: The Design and Destruction of Socialism and the State* (New York: Cambridge University Press, 1999), 18.

[10] Henryk Szlajfer, "Under the Military Dictatorship: Between the 'Freeze Frame' and 'Restoration,'" in Michael Bernhard and Henryk Szlajfer, eds., *From the Polish Underground: Selections from Krytyka* (University Park, PA: The Pennsylvania State University Press, 1995), 13.

In the context of innovative restoration, Hungarian experiments in economic reform generated their *own* legacies – legacies that in turn stimulated, often inadvertently, the diversification of the second economy, and promoted, not so inadvertently, its integration with the state sector. Thus, the critical juncture of 1963 became the founding moment of Hungary's famous Alliance Policy and the reform program to which it gave rise in 1968, known as the New Economic Mechanism (NEM; see Chapter 2). But by the late 1970s, state reformers faced a new critical choice: with economic crisis intensifying and international debt growing, could the thriving second economy be harnessed to help stabilize consumption, or would it destabilize the polity? Just as the *New Course* legacies had made possible Kádár's innovative restoration, now it was the legacies of the *Alliance Policy* and the NEM that allowed for a third round of innovations – namely, the radical property rights reform of 1982 and the numerous other economic policy and legal changes of the 1980s that dramatically altered the political economic landscape of Hungarian state socialism (Chapter 6).

If the quest for official pragmatism can be traced back to the early 1950s in Hungary, in Poland it is only in the early 1970s, after the party-state had accumulated a dismal record of economic mismanagement and broken political commitments, that we finally detect a serious political-discursive attempt to increase the party-state's flexibility. Under Edward Gierek, the party-state elaborated a vision at once moralistic and instrumental. On the one hand, material values were denigrated. On the other hand, they were now seen as incentives to be used selectively to reward the work of "good" citizens.

The contradictory elements of this "pragmatic approach" were seemingly dissolved by the political-discursive move to downplay the principle of class struggle while emphasizing the importance of the nation's "moral-political unity" (Chapter 4). But as the party-state itself failed to make a significant contribution to the people's welfare, old popular grievances associated with Gomułka's evisceration of the workers' councils fueled state-society disagreements about how best to attain economic rationality. Moreover, as these disagreements went unresolved, and as the party-state proved incapable of "rationalizing" the economic system, political identities hardened. Ultimately, official moral instrumentalism itself became the weapon that societal forces wielded against the party-state's legitimacy. Specifically, opposition groups transposed moral instrumentalism, and used its inverted version to create a plausible image of the Polish party-state as a throughly destructive force that threatened both the moral and the material fabric of the polity. The explosive events that rocked Poland in the 1980s stemmed partly from this political-discursive dynamic, just as Hungary's calm stemmed partly from the political-discursive underpinnings of reform waves (Chapters 5 and 6).

Long before 1989, then, it was already evident that prominent actors had developed and privileged distinctive *selection patterns* of core conflicts and particular *modes* of core-conflict resolution. In Hungary, core conflicts were articulated in purely economic terms, although, as is clear from the previous discussion, this economicism was itself a political artifact: a product of complex shifts in power relations, interest configurations, and ideological parameters. In Poland, meanwhile, core conflicts were articulated in both economic *and* increasingly in normative terms. The close link between the material and the normative, in fact, became the hallmark of Solidarity, the most salient institutional hybrid produced in Poland under state socialism.

Like Hungary's economic hybrids, Solidarity was a political construct. Different hybrids, however, engendered different patterns of conflict resolution. The compound nature of societal grievances during Poland's communist period, for example, helps explain the cyclical confrontations and fragile compromise settlements that plagued state-society relations. The nearly unalloyed economicism of the Hungarian system, in contrast, allowed for cycles of reformism and more sustainable accommodation between state and society.

These historical junctures created still new roles, opportunities, and constraints for actors whose social and political identities had already been reshaped in the previous decades. Gdańsk, for example, led Polish workers and intellectuals to build societal networks – that is, to transform solidaristic but heretofore relatively discrete associations into a united front that stood in confrontation with the party-state. In Hungary, on the other hand, the 1982 reform turned private entrepreneurs into *de facto* associates of the internally transforming party state. The inevitable frictions notwithstanding, entrepreneurs and state officials carried out together the task of reinventing the administrative and legal machinery undergirding the mixed economy (Chapter 7).

Societal Actors: Structural Dualism and Just Rationality

The early hallmark of communist systems was as distinct as it was severe. Under the party's unquestionable authority, the state lay monopolistic claims to the organization of work, the ordering values, the standing of groups in the public arena, and the rules of entry and exit across the various spheres of the political-economic domain. Yet in Poland and Hungary, citizenries that initially intended merely to carve out refuges in a system that had "hardened" and "thickened" and "could not be otherwise,"[11] gradually began to repossess small pieces of the party-state's turf. In so doing, they ultimately changed the "balance of interests" and even the way in which political struggles were organized.[12]

Both the initial repossession efforts of Polish and Hungarian citizens and the impotence that hegemonic party-states showed in the face of these implicit, informal challenges emerged in the context of systemic rigidities common to all state-socialist systems. Ranging from perpetual shortages of goods and services to artificially petrified labor markets under full employment, these rigidities compelled peasants, workers, and even state-firm managers and bureaucrats

---

[11] Peter Berger and Thomas Luckmann, *The Social Construction of Reality*, quoted in Mark Granovetter and Richard Swedberg, *The Sociology of Economic Life* (Boulder, CO: Westview Press, 1992), 17.

[12] Pierre Bourdieu, quoted in Granovetter and Swedberg, *The Sociology of Economic Life*, 16.

to seek – initially in hidden and limited ways – some sort of just rationality. In the case of peasants and workers, for example, these efforts often took the form of reflexive labor hoarding – that is, workers and peasants conserved their own labor time and labor power for use in the second economy. Workers and peasants, to be sure, typically entered the second economy just to try and make ends meet. But once established in their informal niches, both groups used them to reclaim from the state what they deemed to be rightfully theirs: the *de facto* property rights inherent in private labor that the state had arrogated and essentially externalized by pronouncing them inalienably public.[13]

Although particularistic in character, these repossession acts had a broad impact, if only because as the second economy grew, the entire economic system became permeated with positional dualities. By the 1960s, for example, Hungarian workers, peasants, and professionals were at once state employees and private producers[14] – formally embedded in the socialist structure yet able to transfer state resources and individual competencies to their second-economy niches.[15] This pervasive duality gradually altered power relations in the state sector between employees and management in favor of employees, starting a bottom-up chain reaction whereby subordinates in the hierarchy of the planned economy routinely compromised the interests of superiors. Thus the terms of engagement, initially set from above, were amended by the practice of labor hoarding by firms, which in turn fomented the growth of the second economy.

Communist party-states, especially in their early years of rule, considered the second economy a serious threat to the integrity of the socialized economy and an affront to socialist principles. Party leaders might tolerate second-economy activity temporarily and on a limited scale in order to ease social pressure in

[13] External dis-economies of scale are generally understood as the beneficial or negative effects that the production activities of firms bring to bear on one another. Here I generalize the concept to include the beneficial or harmful effects that a group of state monopolies – socialist firms – may have on a factor of production: in this case, labor. In state-socialist systems, several externality generating activities lower the production or utility of the externally affected parties. These included maintenance of administrative labor markets until 1968 in Hungary, and until the mid-1980s in Poland, as well as wage controls in both. But state-socialism's fundamental externality generating activity is the curtailment of workers' choice between self-employment and employment by the state: that is, the effective abolition of private enterprise. On externalities more generally, see Harold Demsetz, *Ownership, Control and the Firm: The Organization of Economic Activity*, Vol. 1 (London: Basil Blackwell, 1988), especially chapters 2 and 7.

[14] István Kemény, "The Unregistered Economy in Hungary," *Soviet Studies* 34, no. 3 (July 1982): 349–366. Most of these positions were part-time – hence the "duality," as contrasted with Polish peasant farmers, who had at least nominal private property rights to their farms and the right to work them full-time.

[15] Far fewer studies focus on the informal sector in Poland, but it does appear that workers' opportunities for this kind of transfer were more restricted there in this period, although the basic dynamic was the same. See Anders Åslund, "The Functioning of Private Enterprise in Poland," *Soviet Studies* 36 (1984):427–44, and Anders Åslund, *Private Enterprise in Eastern Europe: The Non-Agricultural Private Sector in Poland and the GDR, 1945–1983* (New York: St. Martin's Press,1985).

times of extreme scarcity. But the second economy's extirpation remained their ultimate goal. In the meantime, participants in the large *informal* – unlicensed and illegal – sector of the second economy ran the risk of steep fines and long prison terms. In order to avoid these punitive costs, individuals resorted to *repossession strategies*.

Individuals' repossession strategies hinged on complicity, trust, and mutual masking. Complicity was the only measure of assurance shared by mutually unknown parties, one of whom might be acting in bad faith. Trust, on the other hand, was qualitatively different from complicity, since it was cultivated through repeated dealings between familiar parties: every time a client was satisfied with the goods and services provided by his or her purveyor, the former grew less inclined to denounce the latter; and conversely, the purveyor was able to add one more name to his roster of trustworthy clients. Dense informal networks grew out of the multiplicity of similar transactions taking place throughout the system, particularly in Hungary, with the result that circulating second-economy purveyors and clients could routinely access stored information on potential transaction partners (Chapter 6).

Finally, there was one additional precaution that transacting parties could take: "mutual masking." The idea behind mutual masking was to commit two individuals to share in the illusion that neither one was engaging in criminal activity. The extensiveness of mutual masking was perhaps most striking in Poland during the economic crisis of the 1980s, a period when supply and demand met neither in the tangle of bottlenecks and shortages that was the planned economy nor in the kind of self-regulating market that Alfred Marshall once envisioned. Rather, supply and demand met in a multiplicity of "chat" circles: people "innocently" talking in euphemisms. In the chatters' realm, payments were not really payments; they were a way of "returning favors." And pilfering was not really pilfering, but a form of repossession: a way of "making something belong to one."[16]

Repossession acts by citizens caught in the rigidities of the planned economy were in the first instance the acts of *individuals*. In fact, the practice of particularistic repossession confirmed a fundamental tenet of micro-economic theory: individuals are sovereign actors unconcerned with the wishes of others. And yet the coordination of repossession acts *via* informal second-economy activity was an extremely complex process precisely because no sovereign decision-maker could *by himself* avoid or even minimize the harshly punitive costs the party-state attached to informal activity.

Indeed, had the individual decision-maker of neoclassical theory remained true to his sovereign impulse, he would almost certainly have foundered in the nether world of the informal sector. The millions of citizens who participated in the informal sector in Poland and Hungary alike were able to transact repeatedly precisely because they were aware, as Weberian social economics argues, that

---

[16] Janine R. Wedel, ed., *The Unplanned Society: Poland During and After Communism* (New York: Columbia University Press, 1992), 79.

they were tied to other decision-makers by "ongoing networks of personal relationships."[17] The framework of this book, then, is built on the premise that informal networks were more than random events, and that in Hungary in particular, they actually became "regular and general processes": in short, informal *organizations.*[18]

The book's framework, more importantly, incorporates the notion that under certain conditions, decision-makers must be concerned with what Timur Kuran calls "reputational utility." Complicity, trust, and mutual masking all required actors' recognition that in "certain fields of action" – in our case, the perilous informal economy – "people have an abiding interest in one another's preferences."[19] Ironically, however, the net result of this "abiding interest" contradicts Kuran's larger claim, which is that East European societies lived under veils of ignorance until tipping points and cascades rent those previously impregnable veils.[20] True, given the strict control of the press, citizens' information about high politics was far more limited than in the Western democracies. But at the broader societal level, almost the opposite was true. People lived in what we might call worlds of feathered foxes: roosts in which prey and predator could be, and often were, one and the same. For this reason, societies were characterized by highly anticipatory behavior, with actors constantly focusing on the future implications of both the long-range plans *and* the quotidian actions of everyone else in the system.

Consider, for a moment, the palpable anxieties that permeated the consumption/demand side of the equation. Will there be sufficient meat next month; how much should I pay the surgeon or the dentist under the table; will I be able to find decent shoes for the children; will we have oranges for the holidays; will I be able to obtain a washing machine next year, a car within three years, or building materials to repair my house? These perennial question marks required

---

[17] Granovetter and Swedberg, *The Sociology of Economic Life,* 9.

[18] Lajos Héthy and Csaba Makó, *Patterns of Workers' Behavior and the Business Enterprise* (Budapest: Institute of Sociology, Hungarian Academy of Sciences, 1989), 88.

[19] Timur Kuran, *Private Truths, Public Lies: The Social Consequences of Preference Falsification* (Cambridge: Harvard University Press, 1995), 42.

[20] *Via* a very different line of reasoning and analytical perspective, Kuran's conclusions converge with those of older formalist models. By focusing on formal economic and political structures, these models came to view socialist citizens as apolitical, notwithstanding the fact that "intimacy with political issues" was part of quotidian socialist life. Denied rights of free speech and assembly, how could they be "political" at all? Besides, socialist citizenries themselves seemed, on the surface, to know only that a powerful party-state affected every aspect of their lives: choice of residence, work, consumption, and, to varying degrees in different times and places, even their forms of self-expression. And yet it was precisely this pervasive control over the lives of individuals that made politics "palpable," and produced "politicized citizens." Hence the puzzle of apparent political inactivity among politicized citizens, a puzzle one East European scholar solved by offering the seemingly oxymoronic suggestion that people were political in the private realm. See Elemér Hankiss, *East European Alternatives: Are There Any?* (Oxford: Oxford University Press, 1990); and Elemér Hankiss, *Diagnózisok* (Diagnoses) (Budapest: Magvető Kiadó, 1982). See also Slavenka Drakulic, *How We Survived Communism and Even Laughed* (Hutchinson: London, 1992), 17.

citizens not only to try to establish with some degree of accuracy the goals of opaque state planners, but above all to craft effective approaches for operating the system and manipulating its rules. Successfully jumping queues, for example, called for more than independently acquired resources for bribery; outright bribery was not even always possible, let alone advisable. It called simultaneously for the cultivation of reliable contacts and for the evasion of vigilantes. It called, in sum, for tactical hyper-alertness and keen strategic acumen from consumers, thus setting them apart totally from their Western counterparts, who typically behave according to the modern capitalist maxim that pronounces the consumer king.

The next section shows that the supply/production side was even more politicized.

Subversion of the Chain of Command: Intrinsic and Extrinsic

Pilfering, shirking, time-theft, and moonlighting were hardly exclusive to Hungary and Poland. Elsewhere in the socialist world, too, economic agents made creative and sometimes ingeniously complex use of their formal structural positions to serve their own interests in contradistinction to the socialist plan.[21] By the early 1980s, Vietnam's State Inspection Commission found that in more than 600 firms investigated, two-thirds of production was "used to generate . . . illegitimate profits," and a majority of consumer goods produced in state-owned enterprises were diverted from the official distribution and trade system, presumably to be sold privately.[22]

Simple, informal market transactions among individuals were even more common. Even in repressive Czechoslovakia, the Economic Research Institute's official survey estimated that by 1988, 75 percent of respondents used bribery and other informal means to obtain retail goods, almost 50 perecent did so to obtain medical services, and about 45 percent to secure repair work.[23] (That this study was undertaken at all is remarkable, since Czechoslovakia's officials admitted that what they called a "shadow economy" even existed only in the last years of the communist regime.)[24]

---

[21] Among the earliest studies of the day-to-day workings of the state-socialist firm were János Kornai's *Overcentralization in economic administration: a critical analysis based on experience in Hungarian light industry* (London: Oxford University Press, 1959), David Granick's *The Red Executive: A Study of the Organization Man in Russian Industry* (New York: Doubleday, 1961), and Joseph S. Berliner, *Factory and Manager in the USSR* (Cambridge: Harvard University Press, 1957).

[22] Porter 1990, 73. It was not until 1988 that the Party officially permitted small private enterprise to function. See the Party's "Resolution No. 16" of July 1988, in Vo Nhan Tri, *Vietnam's Economic Policy Since 1975* (Singapore: Southeast Asian Studies, ASEAN Economic Research Unit, 1992), 202.

[23] Quoted in Wolchick, *Czechoslovakia in Transition*, 254.

[24] Ibid., 233.

The state's approach to informal activity, however, differed widely from one country to another. In Hungary, informal networks of production and exchange not only thrived but actually penetrated the state sector under the thrust of the party-state's economic reforms, engendering functional production and exchange hybrids, and by extension close structural linkages between the socialist and non-socialist economies (Chapter 2). In Poland, by way of contrast, the comparative paucity and incompleteness of reforms from above often blocked the kinds of transformative processes that came to pervade the Hungarian system (Chapter 3).

This key difference between the Polish and Hungarian political economies suggests that whereas informal networks under state socialism always created the *potential* for transformative economic opportunities from below, exploiting and institutionalizing these potential benefits required particular reform policies from above. In Hungary, for example, the 1968 NEM allowed workers to change jobs and relocate, while simultaneously granting state firms greater autonomy in investment and wage decisions.[25] These measures did not create efficient labor markets, but they did allow firms to develop *internal* labor markets as they tried to keep their workers from relocating.[26] Moreover, these internal markets further enhanced state employees' bargaining leverage with firm managers, to the point that much of the Hungarian population gained informal veto power over the application of its own labor rights *on* the shop-floor.[27]

Their Polish counterparts, in contrast, exercised their veto power through far more contentious means.[28] If by the mid-1970s the "Hungarian model" evoked the image of "Goulash Communism" – to borrow a term from the

---

[25] The 1968 reform abolished laws that punished workers for changing jobs, and firms were allowed greater freedom in the management of their labor supply and in the setting of wages. Labor allocation and wage differentials became the subject of overt bargaining between employees and state firms. This created competition for workers – especially skilled workers – among firms whose *overall* wage bill remained static (the "level of earnings for the whole working population and for individual enterprises" were still determined by central economic management). Galasi and Sziráczki, eds., *Labour Market and Second Economy in Hungary*, 14.

[26] Kornai, *The Socialist System*; and János Kornai, *The Economics of Shortage* (Amsterdam: North-Holland, 1980); Galasi and Szirácki, eds., *Labour Market and Second Economy in Hungary*, 15–16; and David Stark, "Rethinking Internal Labor Markets: New Insights From a Comparative Perspective," *American Sociological Review* 51, no. 4 (August 1986): 492–504.

[27] See Gábor and Galasi, "Second Economy, State and Labour Market"; Gábor Kertesi and Péter Sziráczki, "Worker Behavior in the Labor Market"; János Timár, "Strategies and Realities for Employees and Management"; and György Kővári and György Sziráczki, "Old and New Forms of Wage Bargaining on the Shop Floor"; all in Galasi and Sziráczki, eds., *Labour Market and Second Economy in Hungary*. See also Charles F. Sabel and David Stark, "Planning, Politics, and Shop-Floor Power: Hidden Forms of Bargaining in Soviet-Imposed State-Socialist Societies," *Politics and Society* 11, no. 4 (December 1982): 439–475.

[28] See Grzegorz Ekiert and Jan Kubik, *Rebellious Civil Society: Popular Protest and Democratic Consolidation in Poland, 1989–1993* (Ann Arbor: University of Michigan of Press, 1999). Also see Alex Pravda, "Poland 1980: From 'Premature Consumerism' to Labor Solidarity," *Soviet Studies* 34, no.2 (April 1982): 167–199.

journalistic parlance of the West – the Polish political economy evoked images of labor strikes and popular riots. These differences in workers' strategic choices reflected a broader divergence in the two countries' state-society relations. More specifically, if the interaction of state and society in Hungary led to hybrid economic institutions that entangled the state sector and the second economy in a symbiotic relationship, state-society interaction in Poland led to a shifting – at times unstable – political stalemate.

Polish economists asked whether Poland could "become Hungary."[29] But Polish state elites shied away from significant (institutional) economic reform, and the citizenry railed at the political leadership's economic "irrationality." State elites reneged on pacts with workers, and workers increasingly viewed the party-state as an arbitrary task-master. Given the political and economic structure of state socialism, neither side could survive alone. But both were doomed if things remained the same. At stake was an issue that dated back to 1956: how much influence should workers have in the crafting and execution of industrial policy in particular and economic policy more generally? Whatever the answer might be, one of the two sides was bound to incur a relative – and in the case of workers, perhaps even absolute – loss in terms of managerial control.

In both countries, then, workers acquired significant *de facto* veto power over the state's allocation of their labor power. But the *aggregation* of workers' particularistic adaptive repossession strategies – or put another way, labor's veto instruments – differed sharply between the two countries. This difference in labor's veto instruments, it bears repeating, was significantly determined from above. In Hungary, the leadership's reformist experimentation kept citizens' creative energies centered on the second economy, and for this reason, it is precisely in the second economy that we find the key hybrid institutions built inside Hungarian state socialism. Not so in Czechoslovakia, where opportunities for actual private *enterprise* were almost non-existent, since the Party undertook virtually no real economic reform (the serious proposals put forth by Ota Šik foundered with the repression of 1968). And not so even in "reformist" Poland, where the leadership followed an even more politically dangerous path: by delaying and then aborting reform initiatives, the leadership encouraged popular hopes, only to end up replicating the same set of systemic rigidities. The Polish party leadership repeatedly, if unintentionally, tantalized workers, and then dashed their raised expectations. In this way it motivated workers to choose collective action strategies – strikes, work-to-rule – and to aim at the broader realm of economic management.

The Polish authorities' replication of systemic rigidities took place on two levels. First, Poland's extensive second economy was composed of a large, formally private, agricultural sector that was persistently undercut by the state, and an institutionally unsophisticated informal sphere in manufacturing and commerce with scant productive ties to the state sector. This meant that the

[29] Jan Zielonka, "Let Poland Be Hungary?" *SAIS Review* 4 (Summer–Fall 1984): 105–20.

Polish second economy failed to provide the same degree of material relief or entrepreneurial opportunity to the population in general and workers in particular as it was able to do in Hungary. Even more important, Polish workers, like their Hungarian counterparts, had since the mid-1950s perceived the "irrationality" of the economic system and demanded a direct role in setting things right. But if in Hungary the party rejected this demand altogether by the late 1950s (while starting to plan state sector reform in the early 1960s), the Polish party chose a more insidious approach, never really repudiating workers' councils but eviscerating them instead (while failing to carry through with significant state sector reform). The result was the recurrence of Polish workers' bids – articulated both in normative and "rational" terms – to participate in the management of state enterprises and in economic policymaking.

Thus it is not in an increasingly institutionalized second economy, but in workers' outright demands to influence micro and macro policy that we find the origins and logic of the hybrid institutions that the Poles built inside their version of state socialism.[30] Most notably, the origins of Solidarity's complex identity and agenda – a labor union *and* social and political movement – can be traced back to workers' attempts to press demands that appeared at first glance to be consonant with the party-state's agenda, but were in fact a serious challenge to its authority. As in Hungary – although by a different route and with different tangible results – state and society in Poland became entangled in a relationship of mutual vulnerability. The party-state controlled the means of production. But workers' strike capability ultimately gave them veto power over economic policy, a much broader domain than the Hungarian arena of the shop-floor.

The result was that each party-state exacerbated, in different ways, a severe and endemic principal-agent problem. The principal-agent problem multiplied prodigiously because state-socialist systems represented unparalleled attempts to structure entire economies along the lines of a command organization, as well as titanic efforts to capture and channel the political energies of citizens. Not surprisingly, sophisticated analysts have focused on precisely this classic bureaucratic snag: a principal's control over his agent is limited by the agent's superior knowledge of local conditions and possession of specific skills or expertise. Like the state-socialist planners they study, these analysts are primarily concerned with the inner workings of hierarchy: its logic and potential subversions. Steven Solnick, for one, vividly depicts the assault launched from within on Soviet institutions by opportunistic officials, and explains this assault as the outcome of a slippery-slope dynamic: once superiors in a hierarchical chain of command are perceived as irretrievably weakened, they can no longer reassert their authority over subordinates.[31]

[30] Alex Pravda has emphasized the political power of workers in state-socialist systems. See his "Poland 1980: From 'Premature Consumerism' to Labor Solidarity," 167–199.

[31] Steven L. Solnick, *Stealing the State: Control and Collapse in the Soviet Union* (Cambridge: Harvard University Press, 1998), 5–7.

The scope and even the logic of the principal-agent problem, however, varied from one institutional hybrid to another, because Solidarity in Poland and the second economy in Hungary (and to a degree in Poland as well) added different *external* dimensions to the principal-agent dynamic. The *collective* character of labor's veto instrument in Poland naturally inserted Solidarity into the work-ings of hierarchical chains. But Solidarity, though a labor union, did not stand alone, nor was it solely concerned with work issues. Solidarity was also a social movement and an increasingly political force with a complex agenda and influ-ential societal allies. So when Solidarity disrupted the state enterprise – the very fundament of the command economy – it brought to bear the pressure of "extrinsic" actors like intellectuals and the Church on the formal hierarchy of economic command. In Hungary, on the other hand, an increasingly large and institutionalized second economy endowed state employees with *active* leverage over management or, quite often, allowed them to enlist managers as co-conspirators in the erosion of work rules and norms. Hence the ubiq-uity of robust informal networks of production and exchange, and hence the routinization and eventual formalization of accommodative and cooperative arrangements on the shop-floors of state firms.

Transformation in the Hungarian chain of command, moreover, spread beyond the production line to administrative/bureaucratic vectors. As waves of economic reforms became increasingly radical, for example, private entrepreneurs *and* bureaucrats had to cobble together a new regulatory appa-ratus, especially after 1982. Even more interestingly, as private entrepreneurs gained formal rights that same year, it was state-firms' managers who sud-denly found themselves in the strange position of having to seek "equality" of rights *vis-à-vis* the private sector. This was quite a change in a system in which transmission-belt organizations such as the "business associations" were orig-inally intended to facilitate the "inevitable" demise of small private enterprise (Chapter 7).

Thus, societal forces – Solidarity and its precursors in Poland, and an increasingly large and institutionalized second economy in Hungary – helped from "outside" to induce state-firm managers' non-compliance with centralized directives. Firm managers' deviations from planners' instructions, to be sure, also resulted in upward corruption of the plan's overseers. But the *origins* of subversion were partially tied to *extrinsic* dynamics. In fact, the influence of extrinsic forces on hierarchical stability was such that in Hungary, the second economy's links to state enterprises ultimately helped transform the chain of command by giving all parties concerned a stake in mixed forms of produc-tion. In Poland, on the other hand, the growing power of civil society in general and of Solidarity in particular repeatedly strained the chain of command to the point of confrontation.

It follows from this overview that in deploying the principal-agent insight without contextualizing its logic, we run the risk of overdrawing the bound-aries between command hierarchies and society. To minimize this risk, this book builds on the work of the new institutionalists who in the 1980s identified the changing character of state-society boundaries.[32] But whereas the new institutionalists tended to highlight the increased autonomy of "subordinate groups," this book highlights the increasing duality of socialist roles – official, manager, worker, peasant – and by extension, the duality of interests and power in the system. This emphasis on dualism has the additional benefit of preventing us from looking at power as a fixed quantity, an assumption that pervaded those civil society approaches that, in the 1980s, saw the citizenry as ultimately wresting power from the state.[33]

Reformers and Power

Zero-sum power dynamics cannot be assumed even in the most repressive systems.[34] In Hungary, reformers took early steps toward power devolution, and, conversely, entrepreneurs helped reshape and entrench the *formal* apparatus of the socialist state. To the extent that zero-sum dynamics eventually emerge, as in Poland, they need to be examined, just as much as the positive-sum alternative. This means taking a close look at reform patterns and at the enabling conditions and constraints that either enhance or limit the chances, scope, and sustainability of reform.

More often than not, Western political scientists and economists missed the full significance of both informal institutions and economic reforms under state socialism.[35] By the early 1990s, most mainstream Western economists,

[32] See, among others, Szelényi, "The Intelligentsia in the Class Structure of State-Socialist Societies," in Burawoy and Skocpol, eds., *Marxist Inquiries*; Victor Nee and David Stark, *Remaking the Economic Institutions of Socialism: China and Eastern Europe* (Stanford: Stanford University Press, 1989), 22–23.

[33] The following are especially instructive: Andrew Arato, "Civil Society Against the State: Poland, 1980–81," *Telos* 47 (Spring 1981): 23–47; Elemér Hankiss, "In Search of a Paradigm," *Daedalus* 119, no. 1 (Winter 1990): 183–214; Vaclav Havel, *The Power of the Powerless* (New York: M. E. Sharpe, 1985); Tony Judt, "The Dilemmas of Dissidence: The Politics of Opposition in East Central Europe," *East European Politics and Societies* 2, no. 2 (Spring 1988): 185–241; John Keane, ed., *Civil Society and the State: New European Perspectives* (London: Verso, 1988); John Keane, "The Modern Democratic Revolution: Reflections on Jean-François Lyotard's *La condition postmoderne*," *Chicago Review* 35, no. 4 (1987): 4–19; S. Frederick Starr, "Soviet Union: A Civil Society," *Foreign Policy* 70 (Spring 1988): 26–41; and Iván Szelényi, "Socialist Opposition in Eastern Europe: Dilemmas and Perspectives,"in Rudolf Tökes, ed., *Opposition in Eastern Europe* (Baltimore: Johns Hopkins University Press, 1979).

[34] This point has been made eloquently by James C. Scott in *Weapons of the Weak: Everyday Forms of Peasant Resistance* (New Haven: Yale University Press, 1985), and in *The Moral Economy of the Peasant: Rebellion and Subsistence in South-East Asia* (New Haven: Yale University Press, 1976).

[35] In fact, because many Western analysts implicitly accepted communism's definition of the political – which emphasized elites, high politics, and formal institutions – few looked for political struggles in the organization of socialist work. (In general, East European social scientists must be exempted from this characterization, and several important exceptions among Western scholars have also been mentioned in preceding footnotes.) The totalitarian school would simply have noted that labor unions were under the control of the party-state; thus, by definition, no serious labor-management disputes were possible. Interest-group theorists might have conceded

for instance, concluded in retrospect that the deep flaws inherent in the state-socialist model of economic organization were sufficient to explain its collapse. Further, with a few important exceptions, most Western economists dismissed the second economy – which by some estimates in the late 1970s already accounted for more than 20 percent of Hungary's annual GNP and involved the vast majority of Hungarians[36] – as merely the negative print of the state sector, one among many reflections of its weaknesses. Similarly, the principal query most such analyses put to economic reforms was the degree to which they increased the efficiency of state firms.[37] Consequently, a majority of analysts came to agree that efforts aimed either at the improved efficiency of the classical model or at the attainment of some ideal mix of plan and market failed to render socialist economies competitive.

This consensus was compelling, given the abject failure of the model. But it almost completely blocked discussion of the broader ramifications of decades of economic reforms and informal systemic adaptations. Thus, even toward the end of the 1980s, most domestic and foreign observers doubted that Hungary's history of compromises with orthodoxy would fundamentally alter its socialist structures. In the context of this consensus, the historical ubiquity of piecemeal reform seemed to confirm the essential stability of the state-socialist system.[38] Worse yet, this consensus eclipsed crucial differences between state-socialist

---

political struggles amongst the leadership of state-controlled unions, but did not view bargaining between workers and state firm managers as "political."

[36] This figure is in fact understated, since it accounts only for "second-economy activities on which quantified information of any worth [was] available." Gábor and Galasi, "Second Economy, State and Labour Market," 130.

[37] The literature on reform of socialist systems is too extensive to provide even a representative list here. For a summary discussion of the concepts of "partial" versus "comprehensive" reform, or "perfecting" versus reform, see Tamás Bauer, "Hungarian Economic Reform in East European Perspective," *East European Politics and Societies* 2, no. 3 (Fall 1988): 418–432. See also Jan Winiecki, "Obstacles to Economic Reform of Socialism: A Property-Rights Approach," *The Annals of the American Academy of Political and Social Sciences: Privatizing and Marketizing Socialism* 507 (January 1990): 65–71; Barry W. Ickes, "Obstacles to Economic Reform of Socialism: An Institutional-Choice Approach," *Annals*, 53–64; and Jan S. Prybla, "Preface," *Annals*, 9–17. See also Kornai, "The Hungarian Reform Process: Visions, Hopes and Reality"; Kazimierz Poznański, "Property Rights Perspective on Evolution of Communist-type Economies," in Kazimierz Poznański, *ed., Constructing Capitalism: The Reemergence of Civil Society and Liberal Economy in the Post-Communist World* (Boulder, CO: Westview, 1992), 71–96, Poznanski, *Poland's Protracted Transition: Institutional Change and Economic Growth, 1970–1994* (New York: Cambridge University Press 1996), and Poznański, ed., *The Evolutionary Transition to Capitalism.* (Boulder, CO: Westview, 1995); Bartolomiej Kaminski, *The Collapse of State Socialism: The Case of Poland* (Princeton: Princeton University Press, 1991).

[38] This was true not only of understandably cynical Hungarian citizens, but also of many observers and analysts, who, ironically, after 1989, often saw reforms as having contributed to the transformation of socialist systems. For commentary on this tendency, see Andrew Walder, "States and Social Structures Newsletter," Social Sciences Research Council (New York, Winter 1990), No. 12. See also Ákos Róna-Tas, *The Great Surprise of the Small Transformation: The Demise of Communism and the Rise of the Private Sector in Hungary"* (Ann Arbor: University of Michigan Press, 1997), introduction.

political economies. It tended to ignore, for example, the historical-political fact that whereas Hungarian reform economists were the leaders of reformism in Eastern Europe, economists in Poland, actually failed to generate sufficient pressure inside the party-state for meaningful institutional change. Instead, Poland instituted reforms that, though significant by comparison with those of many other state-socialist countries, were neither institutionally radical nor lasting when juxtaposed to those of Hungary.

The failure of Western observers to appreciate these critical differences stemmed from still deeper analytical flaws. The policy reform literature typically starts from the premise that reform requires competent technocrats, who in turn depend on politicians for the necessary political power to make and execute policy. Implicit in this view is the image of technocrats as *users* of delegated power, incapable of generating power resources on their own.[39] But, as Chapter 6 shows, Hungarian technocrats proved quite skillful at leveraging and cultivating their influence over the highest power-holders in the party-state, so much so that power-holders gradually found themselves in a world of mixed institutions whose formal rules and procedures were combined with, and even superseded by, informal arrangements and networks. Several such interlinked networks operated for years even within the formal *political* domain of a party-state espousing communist ideology; its members were widely known to be "market-friendly" technocrats who tended to support and sometimes sponsor economic reform.[40]

The early emergence of this informal network of pro-market officials calls attention to yet another aspect of economic reforms. Reforms are often understood as last-ditch attempts to salvage a system on the verge of stagnation or even breakdown.[41] Yet Hungarian socialism initiated economic reforms when the system seemed most powerful, a fact that some contemporary political scientists miss altogether.[42] Reform economists and technocrats were, of

---

[39] Robert Bates, "Comment," in John Williamson, ed., *The Political Economy of Policy Reform* (Washington DC: Institute for International Economics, 1994), 29–30.

[40] "Piac párti" was the name many of my interview subjects gave in 1988–89 to "market-friendly" technocrats at the Ministry of Finance, in the Planning Office, or elsewhere in the apparatus.

[41] Or as the result of "an abstract desire to improve efficiency." See Ben Slay, "Economic Reform: A Comparison of the Polish and Hungarian Experiences" (Unpublished doctoral dissertation, Department of Economics, Indiana University, 1989), 34. Slay also points out that poor economic conditions cut both ways. Such conditions often serve as the external "shock" that sets a reform process in motion, but can also "dramatically complicate the task of implementing economic reforms. It is thus an open question whether, on balance, economic pressures are a pro- or anti-reform factor," 47, n. 16.

[42] Joel Hellman, for one, confuses cause and effect when he argues that post-communist countries that had more elections and higher turnover ("shorter executive tenures") in the "early stages of reform" . . . are most likely to adopt comprehensive economic reforms. On this logic, Poland, Slovakia, Lithuania, and Bulgaria should have achieved the most impressive reform results in the period studied (1990–97). While Poland fits the bill in terms of its macro-economic reforms and many, though not all, areas of institutional reform, the rest do not – especially in comparison with Slovenia and Hungary, which had, respectively, only one-third and one-half the government turnover of Bulgaria or Poland. Hellman's mistake was the failure to consider the degree of

course, simply trying to improve economic performance. But the precocious-ness and increasingly broad scope of Hungarian reforms also reflected political-ideological shifts, which, as previously discussed, enhanced the possibilities of continuing and deepened reform, whereas in Poland, political-ideological shifts constricted the reform domain.

The State: A Speaking Thing

The capacity of the party-state to respond flexibly to changing conditions hinged on its ability to make legitimate political-discursive adaptations to official ide-ology. As with the actual construction and development of viable economic alternatives, however, analysis of such political discursive adaptations cannot be properly conducted without examining the nexus between state and soci-ety. Specifically, both in Hungary and Poland, state elites and social groups reshaped and contested the meaning and possibility of "economic rational-ity." Through such reshaping, state elites sought additional degrees of free-dom in the formulation of economic policy by manipulating Marxist-Leninist dogma – most notably through discursive elaborations that might justify official "pragmatism."

Societal groups, for their part, manipulated and transformed these elabora-tions still further in order to pursue their own political-economic agendas. In Poland, as Michael Kennedy puts it:

The discourse of the democratic opposition emerged in the late 1970s and established a firm counterhegemony when the public sphere opened in 1980–81. With Solidarity's relative success, this alternative vision developed more strongly there than in the rest of Eastern Europe. This discourse inverted many of the claims of the official ideology. Ideology, for instance, came to be seen as the culprit of illegitimate power, rather than as a reflection of any actor's real interests.[43]

Moreover, as Ray Taras has shown, the emergence of Solidarity "flushed out into the open" the party-state's *intra-muros* debates over major issues.[44] In Hungary, meanwhile, it was not civil society but the party-state itself that became the arena for political-discursive innovation: reformers set out to legal-ize property rights without dismantling the regime, redefining the fundamen-tals of socialist ideology in the process. The Hungarian party-state, in a word, presided over the formal hybridization of the economy, and because of this, the

---

institutional reform undertaken *prior* to 1989 (as opposed to macroeconomic reforms after). One clear implication of the present study is that such early institutional reform – when serious and sustained – is a reasonable proxy for the degree to which communist parties had made peace with their societies. See Joel Hellman, "Winners Take All: The Politics of Partial Reform in Postcommunist Transitions," *World Politics* 50, no. 2 (January 1998): 203–34, especially 205 and table 3, 213.

43 Michael Kennedy, ed., *Envisioning Eastern Europe* (Ann Arbor: University of Michigan Press, 1994), 14.

44 Ray Taras, *Ideology in a Socialist State: Poland 1956–1983* (New York: Cambridge University Press, 1984), 40.

state itself would never be the same. What do these divergent outcomes tell us about the state in general and the communist state in particular?

One way to summarize the most commonly accepted view of the state is simply to echo Charles Tilly's historically grounded definition of states as "coercion-wielding organizations, separate from kinship structures, that exercise[d] priority in *some* regards over all other organizations within delimited territories."[45] Starting from this view, it is a fairly straightforward path that leads to a coherent model of the communist state as distinctive from the state in liberal democracies. As Gianfranco Poggi writes:

> Within a Soviet-type state, the Communist Party has permanently and exclusively vested in it, either expressly or by well-established, unchallengeable convention, constitutional powers of decisive significance. It exercises these powers through its own organs, but in doing so it routinely and bindingly sets the policies, directs the activities, commits the resources of the state.[46]

Andrew Walder identifies the three analytical models of the communist state that held sway in the 1980s. In the first model, partially developed by Konrád and Szelényi, the state is an elite-serving machine whose engine is the system of central planning. Specifically, political elites invoke the state's ideological authority and deploy its coercive puissance in a successful bid to appropriate the role of grand "redistributors" endowed with the power to allocate public resources. It is from the abuse of this power that state elites' tangible privileges flow.

The second model is that of the state as fiscal juggernaut – that is to say, the state as a resolute and even ruthless apparatus bent on extracting surpluses and mobilizing industrial investment. Here, ideology guides the machine and coercion enforces its policies.

In the third model, elaborated most elegantly by János Kornai, the state figures as a particular form of economic administration, whose most striking feature is the mutual dependence between the state and the firm. The state needs the firm to produce goods for consumers and for other firms, to maintain employment, and to contribute to the purse. The firm, in turn, needs the state for investment loans, allocation of centrally controlled inputs to the production process, marginal tax rates, and exceptions to price guidelines. The ceaseless bargaining between "supplicant firms" and the "indulgent state" repeatedly ushers in the redistribution of revenue from the more profitable to the less profitable firms.[47] For more on Kornai's model, see his *The Socialist System*.[48]

---

45 Charles Tilly, "Democracy, Social Change, and Economies in Transitions," in Joan M. Nelson, Charles Tilly, and Lee Walker, eds., *Transforming Post-Communist Political Economies* (Washington DC: National Academy Press, 1997), 403.

46 Gianfranco Poggi, *The State: Its Nature, Development and Resources* (Cambridge, UK: Polity Press, 1990), 149.

47 Andrew Walder, "The State as an Ensemble of Economic Actors: Some Inferences from China's Trajectory of Change," in *Transforming Post-Communist Political Economies* (Washington DC: National Academy Press, 1997).

48 Kornai, *The Socialist System*, 36–50, 71, 361, 388. This is a particularly ironic outcome, since the "regularities" of classical socialism for Kornai flowed from the party-state's monopoly on

The party-state's coercive capabilities, its ideological grounding, its allocative monopoly, and its bargaining functions were all indeed crucial to state socialism.[49] But as Katherine Verdery argues, the party-state also sought to exercise and consolidate systemic control through an "authorized language."[50] And here too it met with contenders. Communist societies were not embedded in a hegemonic political culture in which the party-state identified the "possible" and broadcast it to society while the citizenry passively internalized the official version of "reality" inherent in this vision handed down from above.[51] Rather, as Jan Kubik and Michael Bernhard have shown, alternative political cultures emerged and survived in contradistinction to official political culture. This was most dramatically displayed in Poland in the late 1970s and early 1980s.[52] But even in Russia, presumably the cradle of despotic preferences, democratic aspirations and proposals emerged in the nineteenth century and persisted throughout the twentieth in the face of overbearing official culture.[53]

The potency of the party-state's authorized language and the sway of alternative political cultures were both grounded in political-discursive processes. This was the case in the early 1980s when Hungarian reformers tried "to sell" a sensitive policy package to marginalized but angry hard-liners, to the party as a whole, and to a confused society at large. And it was the case when the Polish authorities and Solidarity confronted one another.

This point obviously goes against Steven Fish's claim that "political opportunity structures" and "political entrepreneurship" can be detached from

---

power, reinforced in turn by the official ideology's juxtaposition of socialist *efficiency* and the wastefulness of market "anarchism."

[49] Prior to the 1980s, however, the most influential theoretical models of communist systems implicitly maintained a somewhat artificial polarity between the two overarching views of politics – the polarity typically posed between the pluralist world-view exemplified by the American political scientist David Easton and that of the German legal and political theorist Carl Schmitt. At one extreme, the object of politics was the defense of collective identity: political decisions being ultimately reducible to the distinction between friend and foe, and political struggle inevitably pitting the two in existential battle. At the other, politics was a pluralistic contest over the allocation of goods and values enforceable by the state. See Gianfranco Poggi, *Development of the Modern State: A Sociological Introduction* (Stanford: Stanford University Press, 1978). This implicit polarization, evident also in analyses of other types of political systems, obscured the true complexity of state-socialist systems, in which both the Eastonian allocative logic and the Schmittian logic of friend versus foe were at work, though one or the other tended to predominate at specific historical junctures in particular countries.

[50] Katherine Verdery, "Theorizing Socialism: A Prologue to the 'Transition,'" *American Ethnologist* 18, no. 3 (August 1991): 431.

[51] On the importance of "fields of imaginable possibility" in political-economic development, see Consuelo Cruz, *Political Culture and Institutional Development in Nicaragua and Costa Rica: World-Making in the Tropics* (New York: Cambridge University Press, 2005).

[52] Jan Kubik, "Who Done It: Workers, Intellectuals, or Someone Else? Controversy Over Solidarity's Origins and Social Composition," *Theory and Society*, 23 (1994): 441–465. Michael Bernhard, "Civil Society and Democratic Transition in East Central Europe," *Political Science Quarterly* 108, no. 2 (Summer 1993): 307–326.

[53] Nicolai N. Petro, *The Rebirth of Russian Democracy: An Interpretation of Political Culture* (Cambridge: Harvard University Press, 1995).

"ideology and culture."[54] If anything, as the post-1956 trajectories of Hungary and Poland show, the uses and misuses of opportunity structures are intimately tied to ideology and culture, and are crucial to the making and execution of policy and to politics more broadly. If state policymakers are to observe John Waterbury's maxim – "the higher the potential political and economic cost of structural adjustment, the greater the premium on obfuscation"[55] – then they had better articulate a rhetorical defense when they first set out to deceive or surprise. After all, the antonym of obfuscation is explication. And since structural adjustment at base rearranges and sometimes even rescinds a multiplicity of compacts between particular groups and the state, adjustment will sooner or later become the subject of interpretive scrutiny. As we will see, state-socialist power-holders and opponents alike understood this well, and acted accordingly by investing considerable time and energy in the crafting of discursive strategies.

Yet discourse is the practice that dare not speak its name too loudly in mainstream social science, even though it underlies both our insights into the most specific maneuvers of state actors and our broadest conceptions of the state. The particular type of modern state that Michael Mann labels "moral-ideological,"[56] for example, could not convey either its reactive or intrinsic powers without deploying discursive authority. Similarly, if Russell Hardin is correct in claiming that the framers of the U.S. constitution intended the document as a device for the coordination of commerce, the obvious fact remains that the framers did resort to principled discourse in order to set compelling organizational parameters on commercial activity.[57] In this book's framework, then, discursive production is a key point of permeable contact at which neither the state nor citizens could unilaterally impose the rules of engagement. In Poland, the party-state produced moral instrumentalism, but societal groups inverted it against its producer. In Hungary, the party-state produced economicism, but societal groups developed its practice to their own advantage.

The infrastructural and despotic powers of the state outlined by Mann remain crucial. They are always, however, conditioned by the state's political-ideological and, by extension, discursive capabilities. Vivien Schmidt, for instance, contends that discourse is more than "cheap talk" – that in fact it can be shown to have independent causative power in the success or failure of welfare state retrenchment in Western Europe.[58] Longtime students of Eastern

54 M. Steven Fish, *Democracy From Scratch: Opposition and Regime in the New Russian Revolution* (Princeton: Princeton University Press, 1995), 200.

55 John Waterbury, "The Political Management of Economic Adjustment and Reform," in Joan Nelson, ed., *Fragile coalitions: the politics of economic adjustment* (New Brunswick, Transaction Books, 1989), 54.

56 Michael Mann, *The Sources of Social Power, Volume II: The Rise of Classes and Nation-States, 1760–1914* (New York: Cambridge University Press, 1993), 44.

57 Russell Hardin, *Liberalism, Constitutionalism, and Democracy* (New York: Oxford University Press, 1999).

58 Fritz Scharpf and Vivien Schmidt, eds., *Welfare and Work in the Open Economy: Diverse Response to Common Challenges in Twelve Countries* (NY: Oxford University Press, 2000).

Europe know that talk was rarely, if ever, "cheap" in state-socialist systems; certainly any discourse that deviated from the official line could be extremely costly, and risky to boot.

Whether in Eastern Europe or elsewhere, in the practice of politics, the strategic deployment of discourse is at the heart of the multiple links between politics and economics – a fact that is today recognized by top business schools in the United States.[59] Consider, for example, the common assumption that property rights develop in order "to internalize externalities when the gains of internalization become larger than the cost."[60] Such a formulation is wholly inadequate to explain the divergence between our two cases, let alone the degree to which property rights developed or failed to develop across the state-socialist world. This theory misses a crucial nexus between politics and economics because it overlooks two questions. First, *when* and *how* – subject to what institutional and political-cultural constraints – do political elites and power-holders come to perceive the "gains" as higher than the "costs"? Second, having once perceived gains to be higher than costs, what means are at their disposal to convince entrenched political-bureaucratic interests to *act* on this perception? Can political leaders find, in the histories they share with wider citizenries, broadly resonant past experiences or intellectual-philosophical resources to deploy against opponents of reform? Or must they undertake to persuade in a context of entrenched enmity and "institutionalized mistrust"?[61] One clear lesson that emerges from the story of state socialism's internal transformation prior to 1989 is that discursive capabilities can prove decisive in determining whether, in the final analysis, state-society relations engender zero-sum or positive-sum power dynamics.

---

[59] A quick perusal of Harvard Business School's web-page for scholars and researchers reveals multiple studies dealing with the power of persuasion, the construction of positive corporate cultures, and the centrality of rhetoric to effective leadership. See http://www.hbsp.harvard.edu/ideas.

[60] Harold Demsetz, "Toward a Theory of Property Rights," *American Economic Association Papers and Proceedings* 57, no. 2 (May 1967): 350.

[61] On the influence that political discourse can exert on trajectories of economic development, see Consuelo Cruz, "Identity and Persuasion: How Nations Remember Their Pasts and Make Their Futures," *World Politics* 52, no. 3 (April 2000): 275–312. On discourse's role in political culture, see Cruz, *Political Culture and Institutional Development in Costa Rica and Nicaragua: World-Making in the Tropics* (New York: Cambridge University Press, 2005).

2

Precocious Reformer

Hungary

> ... there is nothing ... more perilous to conduct, or more uncertain in its success, than to take the lead in the introduction of a new order of things. Because the innovator has for enemies all those who have done well under the old conditions, and lukewarm defenders in those who may do well under the new. This coolness arises partly from the incredulity of men, who do not readily believe in new things until they have had a long experience of them.
>
> Niccolò Machiavelli, *The Prince*, 1513

On January 1, 1982, the Hungarian party-state institutionalized a property rights reform that made private enterprise a citizen's prerogative. Though radically at odds with communist ideology, and unparalleled in the communist world, the reform went largely unnoticed by outside observers. It was easy to miss. Hungarian reformers themselves downplayed the reform's importance. Martial law had been recently imposed in Poland. *Perestroika* and *Glasnost* had yet to appear on the Soviet stage. The Cold War was still on. And the Berlin Wall stood unperturbed, as if facing eternity.

In Hungary, however, the reform seized the imaginations and marshaled the energies of thousands of new entrepreneurs. It also incited resentment in state firms, and prompted resistance in a bureaucratic machinery that could not even fathom the practical, regulatory problems with which entrepreneurs presented them, first in a trickle and then in a flood. Finally, the reform provoked jealousy among a general population unaccustomed to sharp income differentials.

And yet, sooner rather than later, resentment, resistance, and jealousy began to give way to cooperation and imitation. State firm managers saw the benefits of working in tandem with private enterprises, and, more interestingly still, won new privileges on claims for "equal rights" with private entrepreneurs. Technically adept bureaucrats cobbled together regulatory solutions for the entrepreneurs. And increasing numbers of citizens followed their lead, as best they could, into commerce.

The reform, moreover, deepened and accelerated earlier transformative processes. Interest calculations shifted further. A business ethos – a blend of self-serving rationalizations and ethical norms fit for a hybrid economy – developed more fully. Official interest-representation organizations, once intended as the ultimate "liquidators" of the very same private interests they were supposed to "represent," now filled their chambers with authentic business advocates. And the socialist state, no less, began to assume a developmental role not unlike that of some of its capitalist counterparts.[1]

In quick succession, the 1982 reform was followed by others: the 1984 law on enterprise self-governance, which resulted in significant diffusion of property rights within state firms; the beginning of banking reform in the same year; the introduction of individual income tax in 1985 and the VAT a few years later; and the 1988 Corporations Act, which permitted new types of economic associations for both state and private firms, as well as for private individuals (for example, joint stock and limited liability companies). Meanwhile, as early as 1982, the Ministries of Industry and Finance were negotiating some of the large greenfield investments or hybrid acquisitions of several Western companies now operating in the country.[2] And all this long before the drama of regime collapse.

None of it came easily. As we will see, the politics leading up to the 1982 reform were delicate, the outcome uncertain at many points. Fundamental issues of ideology and power were at stake, and redistributional concerns added to the volatile mix. Nor was the 1982 reform Hungary's first important reform; it was simply its most radical up to that point.[3] In fact, Hungary was already well-known as a reform leader. By contrast, in Romania, perhaps the most repressive country in the Soviet bloc, no serious reform was ever implemented. Czechoslovakia's major reform proposals were aborted at the end of the Prague Spring of 1968. Even in Poland, the concentrated reform attempts of the 1970s and early 1980s were essentially short-lived imitations of Hungary's 1968 New Economic Mechanism (NEM). In the Soviet Union, sporadic reforms gave way to more a sustained effort only between 1985 and 1987 under Gorbachev.

Like all of these countries, Hungary suffered under structural economic rigidities that stemmed from its system of centralized production and allocation, reinforced by the division of production within COMECON. But only

---

[1] Or more precisely, parts of the state did so. As will become clear in Chapter 5, the Ministry of Finance was the primary locus of these changes, aided by experts from various branches of academia.

[2] This was true, for instance, of GE and Suzuki; Ford was negotiating with the Hungarian government by the late 1980s. For the case of the multinational car makers, see David Bartlett and Anna Seleny, "The Political Enforcement of Liberalism: Bargaining, Institutions, and Auto Multinationals in Hungary," *International Studies Quarterly* 42 (1998): 319–338.

[3] To draw again on the definition of reform given in Chapter 1, by "radical" reform I mean any reform that alters at least one of the system's defining attributes – ideology, property rights, or bureaucratic coordination. János Kornai, *The Socialist System: The Political Economy of Communism* (Princeton: Princeton University Press, 1992), 36–50; 71; 361; 388.

Hungary had initiated significant economic reforms from above in the mid-1960s – reforms, moreover, that entered into a mutually reinforcing relationship with the ubiquitous second-economy,[4] which began to expand markedly around this time.[5]

From an institutional perspective, in fact, 1960s Hungarian state socialism was beginning to show the impact of impudent builders of informal hybrid institutions that often operated right *inside* the economic organizations of the state sector. By the early 1960s, workers, peasants, and state-firm managers routinely engaged in informal bargaining, which in turn systematized more lenient work-conditions, normalized overtime schemes, and entrenched the practice of granting informal bonuses for "extra"work.[6] More importantly, by the late 1960s, highly skilled workers, technicians, and engineers were able to cultivate informal, mutually beneficial relations with key production centers of the centrally planned economy, and on this basis proceeded to build quasi-private operations that manufactured products ranging from machine tools to plastics.[7]

Here, several things are noteworthy. First, state-socialist economic organizations literally harbored disreputable ideas and practices as quasi-private entrepreneurs found "administrative shelters" inside the formal organizations of work.[8] Second, though quasi-private enterprises were nothing new in Hungary, those of the late 1960s had a "frontier-type boom" quality to them.[9] This new quality was partly due to state-sector reforms interacting with one another and with production structures in unintended ways.[10] The 1968 NEM,

---

[4] Again, the second economy is the sum total of all non-state private economic activity: licensed and informal; legal, illegal, and on the borderline of illegality; both prior to and after its partial legalization. The state sector, by contrast, or "first" economy, encompasses state-owned firms, state-controlled cooperatives, government agencies, and registered non-profit institutions. Definitions of the second economy have varied significantly with the analyst's focus, assumptions, and ideological perspective. The simplified working definition employed here draws on more detailed and comprehensive definitions and categories used by István Gábor and Péter Galasi in their "Second Economy, State and Labour Market" in Péter Galasi and György Sziráczki eds., *Labour Market and Second Economy in Hungary* (Frankfurt: Campus Verlag, 1985); and by János Kornai in both *The Socialist System*, and "The Hungarian Reform Process: Visions, Hopes and Reality," *Journal of Economic Literature* XXIV, no. 4 (December 1986): 1687–1737.

[5] István Gábor explains that the expansion of the second economy in the second half of the 1960s was the result of several factors, including "the relaxation of the policy of isolation from the West," the consequent "consumption-oriented behavior," and "instrumental relationship" to work. István Gábor, "Second Economy in State Socialism: Past Experience and Future Prospects," Paper presented at the 3rd Congress of the European Economics Association (Bologna, August 1988).

[6] István Kemény, "The Unregistered Economy in Hungary," *Soviet Studies* 34, no. 3 (July 1982): 354–355.

[7] Kálmán Rupp, *Entrepreneurs in Red: Structure and Organizational Innovation in the Centrally Planned Economy* (Albany: State University of New York Press, 1983), especially Chapter 7.

[8] Ibid., 1.

[9] Ibid., 2.

[10] A 1967 law enabled agricultural cooperatives to establish industrial sub-divisions with "little explicit regulation." Meanwhile, the broader 1968 New Economic Mechanism (NEM) eliminated a series of barriers to inter-firm trade and voluntary labor turnover, but retained strict

for example, gave workers the freedom to change jobs and relocate, and also granted firms more autonomy in investment and wage decisions.[11] To be sure, serious hindrances to the institutionalization of smoothly functioning labor markets remained: most notably, given full employment and labor shortage, firms persistently tried to satisfy their "labor hunger" by hoarding workers.[12] But in light of the NEM, firms developed *internal* labor markets in an effort to keep their workers from relocating.[13] These internal labor markets further enhanced state employees' bargaining leverage with management, to the point that much of the population gained informal veto power over the use of its own labor.[14]

Third, quasi-private institutions showed unequivocally that informal work-arrangements within state firms could become

stable internal structures. A significant part of the workers adjusted their activities not to the rules laid down by the formal organizations but primarily to the rules of the informal organizations. Formulated from an organizational point of view, this was the phenomenon when workers displayed 'negative' behavior, that is, their activity deviated from the objectives set by the enterprise.[15]

Informality also spread in honeycomb fashion throughout the non-state sector of the socialist system, especially in services and construction. Together with the informal institutions operating inside the state sector, these informal networks of part-time service providers and construction operations brought about an extended *de facto* diffusion of property rights previously controlled solely by state bureaucracies. Finally, since as we will see in greater detail later,

---

wage controls in the industrial sector. The upshot of this combination of relaxation and rigidity was the expansion of this type of entrepreneurial opportunity. Rupp, *Entrepreneurs in Red*, 2–3.

[11] The 1968 reform abolished laws punishing workers for changing jobs, and firms were allowed greater freedom in the management of their labor supply and in the setting of wages. Labor allocation and wage differentials could now become the subject of overt bargaining between employees and state firms. But, "labour market processes could hardly have any influence on the level of earnings since central economic management, by various means, determined the extent and conditions of the increase in earnings both for the whole working population and for individual enterprises." Péter Galasi and György Sziráczki, "Second Economy, State and Labour Market," in Péter Galasi and György Sziráczki eds., *Labour Market and Second Economy in Hungary*, 14.

[12] Kornai, *The Socialist System*; and János Kornai, *The Economics of Shortage* (Amsterdam: North-Holland, 1980).

[13] Galasi and Sziráczki, "Second Economy, State and Labour Market," 15–16; and David Stark, "Rethinking Internal Labor Markets: New Insights From a Comparative Perspective," *American Sociological Review* 51, no. 4 (August 1986): 492–504.

[14] For various perspectives on this and related themes, see Gábor and Galasi, "Second Economy, State and Labour Market"; Gábor Kertesi and György Sziráczki, "Worker Behavior in the Labor Market"; János Timár, "Strategies and Realities for Employees and Management"; and György Kővári and György Sziráczki, "Old and New Forms of Wage Bargaining on the Shop Floor," all in Galasi and Sziráczki, eds., *Labour Market and Second Economy in Hungary*.

[15] Héthy Lajos and Makó Csaba, *Patterns of Workers' Behavior and the Business Enterprise* (Budapest: Institute of Sociology, Hungarian Academy of Sciences, 1989), 9.

many such informal arrangements were formalized through economic reforms, the Hungarian second economy had a robust legal component even *before* 1982.

The interesting point here is the fact that these reforms took place at all, which brings us to a hybrid informal institution that operated right inside the party-state. Specifically, reform-minded technocrats and economists networked back and forth between ministerial and research positions, forming in the process dense personal and professional links that enabled them over a period of almost three decades to seize reform opportunities, survive political reversals, and continue to shape new generations of reformers. Indeed, old- and new-guard reformers were influential enough during reformist peaks and resilient enough during slumps that their coordination capability and their interconnected organizational niches constituted yet another type of informal institution. Among the intelligentsia, its members were widely described as being pro-market, and taken as a whole, this informal institution functioned as a network of "market-friendly" technocrats and functionaries.[16]

Like various quasi-private production schemes operating inside the state firms, the loose confederation of officials who made up the pro-market network, notwithstanding its members' unorthodox embrace of "market-type" solutions to socialist dilemmas, was able early on to find harbor in the temple of socialist orthodoxy. It was this network that one day would seek to harness the dynamism of the second economy by expanding and legalizing private property rights. We will explore that remarkable move in Chapter 5.

In the meantime, the case of the Soviet Union helps to put things in historical perspective. Even more than Hungary's NEM in the 1960s, Gorbachev's mid-1980s campaign for *Perestroika* was originally intended not as a liberalizing measure *per se*, but as a means of forcing state firms to accept some degree of accountability by making them more price sensitive. And although the broader programs of *Perestroika* and *Glasnost* that grew from this more modest beginning are well-known, the origins of the "expert communities" or "specialist networks" that made them possible are not.[17] The main reason is that would-be reformers within the Soviet leadership knew they had to keep these networks well-hidden. After Brezhnev's death in 1982, Andropov moved quietly to create "the permissive conditions" for the mobilization of an expert community "galvanized by a belief in the need for reform," entrusting then Secretary of Agriculture Mihkail Gorbachev and a few other "progressives" in the Party to assemble specialists to work on serious problems across a wide range of issues.

---

[16] If someone was described as being "*piac párti*", it meant that he was friendly to market ideas. In the late 1980s, it was not uncommon to hear academics, entrepreneurs, bankers, and economists in government speak of a network of such individuals as if it were a unified entity, based (mostly) within the Ministry of Finance.

[17] Sarah Mendelson, *Changing Course: Ideas, Politics, and the Soviet Withdrawal from Afghanistan* (Princeton: Princeton University Press, 1998), 10.

By the early 1980s, Gorbachev "and other like-minded members of the Soviet leadership" were discreetly consulting a variety of non-party specialists, and by the mid-1980s, had mobilized some of their ideas in an attempt to transfer the "job of day-to-day economic management" from the Party to the state apparatus.[18] In this respect, then, the Soviet Union of the 1980s might begin to resemble Hungary in the mid-1960s, when Kádár's Alliance Policy also integrated growing numbers of non-party experts into the economic decision-making process. But it was not until the early 1980s that Soviet expert communities succeeded in institutionalizing regularized, open links with the Communist Party leadership. In contrast, the Alliance Policy in Hungary was from the start explicitly and publicly trumpeted, and it was almost immediately instrumental in launching the first of several significant reforms.

How did all this come about, and why only in Hungary? Like elsewhere in the state socialist world, Hungary's citizens protected themselves from the rigidities of the classical bureaucratic socialist economy[19] through their informal economic pursuits. Later, and unlike elsewhere in the state socialist world, these practices were fused with formal structures of the state sector to become hybrid but relatively stable economic institutions. The transformative impact of these on institutions' actors' interest calculations, power relations, and even their social identities was profound. Why did such hybrid institutions evolve in Hungary, and what made them politically sustainable?

To answer these questions, I argue in this chapter, we must take into account the political-discursive adaptations that official power-holders made at critical points in response to the changing reality of the Hungarian political economy. Absent these elite adaptations, the economic reforms that became the hallmark of Hungarian "exceptionalism" would not have been possible. And absent these reforms, the symbiotic and frequently cooperative relationships between the formal and informal sectors would not have developed – as indeed elsewhere in Eastern Europe they did not.

The remainder of this chapter shows how these bottom-up and top-down dynamics came together to create Hungary's most permeable point of contact between state and society – namely, an increasingly mixed economy. The analysis opens with the construction of the state-socialist political economy in the mid-1940s, and then explains how, between 1953 and 1956, Imre Nagy and his inner circle laid the foundations for important later political-economic compromises. It closes with the landmark 1968 New Economic Mechanism.

---

[18] Ibid., 10.

[19] Kornai distinguishes between the "revolutionary-transitional system" (elsewhere often called "war communism"), the classical, or "classical bureaucratic," system, and "reform socialism." In this book, I follow his tripartite division. Kornai, *The Socialist System*, 19. For a detailed analysis of the characteristics of classical bureaucratic socialism, see chapters 3–15 in *The Socialist System*.

Migratory Birds, Climbers, and Small Timers

The construction of East European state socialist systems proceeded in the spirit of the Soviet Union's post-NEP (New Economic Policy) model, and was therefore premised on the argument that rapid economic growth would require massive concentration of capital.[20] The Leninist rallying cry "One Nation, One Factory" conveyed the immensity of the architectonic task at hand – a task that, despite its heroic proportions, the new communist leaders of Eastern Europe embraced enthusiastically. From Hungary and Poland to Bulgaria and Romania, the countries of the region had been latecomers to modernization in the nineteenth century, and except for Czechoslovakia, their various economies were still heavily agrarian in the twentieth.[21] A rapid-growth strategy based on industrialization with a decided accent on heavy industry held an irresistible "leap-forward" appeal for communist leaders who, peering from the outside at the Fordist march of advanced capitalism, were eager to extricate their societies from "obscurity" and "backwardness."

Such a system of large-scale industrial production is not pursued in an ideological vacuum. The foundational rule of classical state socialism held that actors' interests and options are determined by their structural positions. Absent this strict correspondence between structure and politics, workers and peasants could not be relied upon always to behave *qua* workers and peasants. And absent such predictability, state socialism in general, and economic planning in particular, would have made little sense. This basic rule – and its underlying dread of unpredictability – spawned other, more specific rules to manage other fears that haunted the overseers of the classical construct.

The classical bureaucratic system of state socialism made no exceptions to these rules – not even in Hungary.[22] Planners' meticulous regulation of labor mobility reflected their fear that workers, given freedom of movement, might become "migratory birds" flying from one location to another in patterns beyond their grasp. Similarly, severe restraints on individualistic ascent reflected the fear that socialist citizens, if allowed to pursue personal ambitions, would succumb to their climbing impulses without regard for the egalitarian

[20] The model required, for instance, the development of certain key industries like steel, even in countries without iron ore and coal, such as Hungary and Bulgaria. Mikail I. Tugan-Baranovsky, *The Russian Factory in the 19th Century* (St. Petersburg: Nasha zhizn, 1907), reprint (Homewood, IL: Richard Irwin, for the American Economic Association, 1970). On the Soviet Union's NEP, see Stephen F. Cohen, *Bukharin and the Bolshevik Revolution* (New York: Knopf, 1973).

[21] Iván Völgyes, "The Economic Legacies of Communism," in Zoltán Bárány and Iván Völgyes, eds., *The Legacies of Communism in Eastern Europe* (Baltimore: Johns Hopkins University Press, 1995).

[22] In 1940, small-scale industry (under 100 workers) employed about half of all industrial wage earners and provided over a fourth of the industrial product; in addition, thousands were employed in small retail shops or on small private farms. Teréz Laky, "The Hungarian Case," paper presented at the IVth World Congress for Soviet and East European Studies, mimeo (Harrowgate, England, July 1990), 4. Quoted by permission of the author.

objectives of the Hungarian party-state. Mobility and ascent simply had to be controlled. To this end, the crucial institution of centrally administered full employment tied all social benefits except education and health-care directly to state-employment.[23] In addition, work books listing employees' complete work-history had to be surrendered to employers upon demand.[24] Finally, the wage structure was determined by a complex work-classification system that divided manual and non-manual workers, then further subdivided them according to skills, experience, and education.

In this context, the Hungarian Socialist Workers Party (HSWP) redefined work to mean manual labor, and stigmatized non-manual labor as "non-productive." Although in tune with Party ideology, this redefinition was originally also part of the Communist Party's effort to coopt artisans and small producers, whose support it needed after World War II and before the parliamentary elections of May 1949. In the late 1940s, the General Secretary of the Hungarian Communist Party and Deputy Prime Minister Mátyás Rákosi even argued that the Party's expropriation of large industry had *saved* small enterprise, and emphasized the important role of small producers in fulfilling the first Five-Year Plan. And yet, at the same time, the Party blocked small producers' access to credit and material inputs, suspended the operation of independent producers' and retailers' organizations, and made it increasingly difficult to open new private enterprises.[25]

It soon became clear that by "labor" the Communist Party meant *manual labor organized in state firms or state-controlled cooperatives.*[26] This bias

---

[23] Until 1975, full-time artisans or entrepreneurs in the small, licensed private sector that managed to survive after the nationalizations had to pay very high social security contributions in order to receive pensions. And, unless they had a spouse or other family member working in a state firm, they would not be allocated state housing. State employment was not new in Hungary, however: the paternalism and comprehensive nature of socialist state-firms' relationships with their employees was reminiscent of pre-war state employment in mining, transport, and telecommunications. Rudolf Tőkés, *Hungary's Negotiated Revolution* (New York: Cambridge University Press, 1996), 84.

[24] The work book had to be surrendered to employers. Meanwhile, in random street searches, the police routinely reviewed individuals' identification papers, which contained, among other things, current employer's name or the fact that an individual was unemployed, which counted as a misdemeanor. Such a "work-shirker" was labelled a "threat to public safety."

[25] Obtaining permission to open a small private enterprise was a complicated process that included a background check of one's criminal record, and required evidence of political background. If any question arose, there was another level of oversight beyond the police by the local councils of the Independent Popular Front (Hazafias Népfront). Gyula Tellér, Interview with author, Budapest, September 1990.

[26] Because it altered the terms of work and the state's relationship to a dramatically enlarged class of state-employees, this redefinition required a harsh regulatory system to enforce it. For example, from the late 1940s through the mid 1950s, when labor regulation was very strict, work was administratively assigned and individuals were permitted to leave their jobs only in case of grave illness – this despite rising unemployment toward the end of the 1940s (about 9 percent in 1948). See László Bruszt, "The Politics of Private Business and Public Enterprises," EUI Colloquium Papers, Doc. EUI 261/87 Col. 45 (Florence: European University Institute, June 1988).

against small enterprises reflected not only the leadership's conviction that large, vertically integrated enterprises were the superior organizational form of production, but also a deep mistrust of "dangerous forms" of private production. Thus, the leadership hoped that vertical integration would maximize hierarchical control and minimize horizontal contact among economic units, as well as among levels, groups, and individuals within those levels.[27] Amalgamation, in turn, was supposed to prevent the emergence of so-called private interest centers, the logic being that the smaller the firm, the greater the chances it would pursue its own interests at the expense of the collective agenda.[28] By creating a single enterprise for each industry where feasible, the leadership sought to make the interests of "super-firms" approximate those of the entire economy.

The leadership's hand was steady throughout the initial restructuring process. In 1947, banks were nationalized and their capital placed under state control. The consequences of this particular move are neatly summarized by Róna-Tas: "The capital market dissolved. And any private firm seeking credit was now at the mercy of the state."[29] Soon thereafter, the Parliament approved legislation nationalizing all firms with more than 100 employees, with the result that over 85 percent of all employees found themselves suddenly working in state-controlled firms.[30] And just as small firms were merged into state-coops, soon medium-sized and large private firms were amalgamated into still larger enterprises. (All enterprises came under the control of the National Planning Office, which at the time represented the highest level of economic management.)

To bring about the necessary increases in the industrial workforce, the leadership took two crucial steps. One: it mobilized all available labor by using women, the unemployed, the old aristocracy and professional classes, the formerly self-employed and their employees, and (as of 1951) a large portion of the peasantry to feed the process of "mass proletarianization."[31] Two: it imposed

---

[27] Although I am focusing here purposely on a set of administrative-political reasons for verticalization, the *strongest* motivating force behind it was actually shortage: firms that could not secure supplies had to make them in-house. Shortages created high transaction costs (inconvenience, disruption, delays), and one common response in state firms was a "do-it-yourself" attitude. János Kenedi, *Do it Yourself: Hungary's Hidden Economy* (London: Pluto Press, 1981). The other reason is that this kind of verticalization creates monopolies, which function as quasi-state agencies, regardless of what they produce, and are thus easier to control than multiple firms.

[28] Bruszt, "The Politics of Private Business and Public Enterprises," 41.

[29] Ákos Róna-Tas, *The Great Surprise of the Small Transformation: The Demise of Communism and the Rise of the Private Sector in Hungary* (Ann Arbor: University of Michigan Press 1997), 85.

[30] György Ferenc, ed., *Chronology of 20th Century East European History* (Washington DC: Gale Research, Inc, 1994), 237.

[31] In the four years between 1949 and 1953, approximately every seventh agricultural worker took an industrial job. See Bálint Magyar, *Dunaapáti, 1944–1958 (1–3 Kötet) (The Village of Dunaapáti, 1944–1958 (Vols. 1–3))* (Budapest: Müvelődéskutató Intézet, Szövetkezeti Kutató Intézet, 1986).

artificially low wages, which in turn simultaneously compelled everyone to work, and facilitated the rapid absorption of labor into industry.[32]

Labor Hoarding: Reflexive and Managerial

Like other East Europeans, Hungarians responded to the party-state's hegemonic drive by engaging in illegal second-economy activities, even though these entailed high risks that ranged from steep fines to long prison sentences.[33] The simplest strategies and the threat that even *these* posed to the system were captured by Czesław Miłosz as early as 1951.

A worker's wife goes to a nearby town, buys needles and thread, brings them back and sells them: *the germ of capitalism*. The worker himself, on a free afternoon mends a broken bathroom pipe for a friend who has waited months for the state to send him a repair man. In return, he gets a little money, enough to buy himself a shirt: *the rebirth of capitalism*. He hasn't time to wait in line on the day that the state store receives a new shipment of goods, so he buys his shirt from a friend.

[Meanwhile, the wife] has cleverly managed to buy three [shirts] . . . through her friendship with the salesgirl, and now she resells them at a small profit. She is speculating. What she earns . . . in a state factory is not enough to support her three children since her husband was arrested by the security police. *If these manifestations of human enterprise were not wiped out it is easy to see what they would lead to.* A worker would set up a plumbing repair shop . . . The cleaning-woman would become a merchant . . . They would gradually expand their businesses, and the lower-middle class would reappear.[34]

Miłosz was remarkably prescient. Workers *did* set up plumbing-repair shops, and offered services of all kinds, whether from shops or from garages and homes. Cleaning women *did* become merchants. And families routinely expanded their private businesses. In short, a "lower-middle-class" *did* reappear. But prescient as he was, even Milosz failed to perceive how these societal developments would become synergetically tied to the construction of hybrid institutions within the state sector.[35]

The possibilities for such synergy were easy to miss even in Hungary, since the party-state seemed to have been overwhelmingly successful at building the socialist economy. By 1963, only a minuscule portion of the economically active population was still self-employed.[36] And whereas in 1949, employees

---

[32] Salaries remained fixed at 50 percent of their 1938 levels until 1949; between 1949 and 1953, they fell further still. During the same period, salaries in Austria were rising rapidly. István Kemény, "The Unregistered Economy in Hungary," *Soviet Studies* 34, no. 3 (July 1982): 359.

[33] Even in the late 1970s, punitive discrimination was not unheard of in Hungary. See Hegedüs and Márkus, "The Small Entrepreneur and Socialism," *Acta Oeconomica* 22, no. 3-4 (1979), 280.

[34] (Emphasis added) Czeslaw Milosz, *The Captive Mind* (New York: Vintage Books, 1981), 192–193.

[35] Czesław Miłosz. Interview with author, Princeton, October 1994.

[36] In 1963, 1.9 percent outside agriculture, 2.1 percent among peasants. See Rudolf Andorka, "The Importance and Role of the Second Economy For Hungarian Economy and Society,"

of the public and private sectors together accounted for only half the working population, by 1969 the employees of the state- and state-controlled cooperative sector accounted for almost 100 percent of active earners. The changes in the size-distribution of firms were also striking. Successful amalgamation translated into a drastic reduction in the *number* of manufacturing firms,[37] while successful centralization gave *large* enterprises an increasing and ultimately overwhelming preponderance – enterprises with 300 or more employees went from 39 percent of the total in 1956 to 80 percent in 1982.[38] By the end of the 1980s, the size distribution of firms in Hungary was just the opposite of most capitalist countries. In the early years, of course, some very small and scattered private firms managed temporarily to survive the overwhelming forces of amalgamation and centralization. But like the new consumer and industrial cooperatives instituted by the party-state, these remnants of the pre-socialist era were immediately placed under the watchful eye of central agencies with powers roughly analogous to those of the ministries.[39] Formally known as business associations, these agencies were in fact transmission-belt "representative" organizations charged with the task of helping the "lowest" forms of production – small private enterprises – to "wither away."[40]

Suspicion of private enterprise was so marked, in fact, that the policy of centralization that applied to state firms also applied to the oversight agencies themselves, since party-state elites feared that these agencies, too, would prove vulnerable to corruption through contact with dangerous forms of private

---

Unpublished paper (Budapest: Budapest University of Economics, 1990), 4. Although small-scale business was soon repressed, this sector actually grew after the war, partly because of the land reform, which increased the number of smallholders, and partly because after the war, small businesses could get on their feet more easily than large ones. See Ferenc Donáth, *Reform és forradalom. A magyar mezőgazdaság strukturális átalakulása 1945–75* (Budapest: Akademia Kiadó, 1977), 38–45 (Reform and revolution: the structural transformation of hungarian agriculture, 1945–75).

[37] The number of industrial firms declined from 4,000 in 1938 to 1,600 in 1949. György Ránki, *Magyarország gazdasága az első 3 éves terv időszakában* [Y] (The Hungarian Economy in the Period of the First 3-year Plan) (Budapest: Közgazdasági és Jogi Könyvkiadó, 1963); quoted in Péter Galasi and György Sziráczki, "The New Industrial Organization: Review of Developments in the Organization and Structure of Small and Medium Sized Enterprises, Country Report: Hungary." Unpublished paper (Budapest: Karl Marx University of Economics, 1986), 4.

[38] The distribution within this total tells the real story. In 1938, the number of enterprises having 20 or fewer employees was 2,089 (53.4 percent); by 1949, it was 527 (32.3 percent) – 109 (2.8 percent) firms in 1938 had 500 or more employees, and 397 (10.1 percent) had between 101 and 500 workers; by 1949, 173 (10.6 percent) had 500 or more employees, and 433 (26.5 percent) had between 101 and 500. The trend toward firms with between 101 and 1000 employees continued from 1951 to 1956, the number of small (100 or fewer employees) enterprises decreased substantially, and the number of very large enterprises (1,000 or more) continued to grow. Galasi and Sziráczki, "The New Industrial Organization," 3–5.

[39] However, the organizations that oversaw the small remaining formal private sector had less power and lower status than those overseeing state-controlled cooperatives and state firms.

[40] Bruszt, "The Politics of Private Business and Public Enterprises," 17.

production. Agency officials, after all, might develop a certain sympathy for small producers, and perhaps even enter into informal deals with them.[41]

This logic of suspicion was not unsound; it was simply misdirected. For it was precisely *within the plan itself* that economic agents would quickly identify the first opportunities for particularistic repossession of their own labor power and labor time. To begin with, labor-discipline, in a full-employment economy was not easily enforced, despite the Stakhanovite movement and the cooperation of the National Council of Trade Unions.[42] As in the rest of Eastern Europe, absenteeism was soon rampant, the quality of production suffered visibly, and labor turnover accelerated – a problem that was reduced but not eliminated when leaving one's assigned job "arbitrarily" became a criminal offense in 1950.[43]

Labor *turnover*, though serious, was less problematic than reflexive labor *hoarding* – workers hoarding their own labor time and power for application in the second economy – since managers exercised limited control over the effort workers actually *expended* in the production process. Three factors limited managers' sway. First, there was the difficulty of controlling individual or small-group behavior, especially in a system set up to deal directly only with peak organizations. We can think of this as the classic principal-agent problem magnified through multiple bureaucratic levels. Second, labor shortages – induced as early as 1949 by intensive investment in industry and rapid absorption of previously unemployed groups into the industrial labor force – turned even sub-standard workers into precious assets.[44] And third, managers had few incentives to offer workers. Not only were firms' wage-funds centrally set, but housing, vacations, and other benefits were also allocated quite strictly according to centralized guidelines, thus leaving managers only minimal discretion in the manipulation of rewards.

---

[41] In this, communist theorists and state practitioners prefigured our own awareness of the possibilities for regulatory capture. For an excellent discussion of the topic more generally, see Cass R. Sunstein, "Deregulation and the Hard-Look Doctrine," *Supreme Court Review*, 1984 Chicago, University of Chicago 0-226-46436-9/84/1983-0046.

[42] Moreover, the Soviet experience of the late 1920s ought to have alerted the Hungarian leadership to this fundamental problem. See Stephen F. Cohen, *Bukharin and the Bolshevik Revolution*. For the role of the Stakhanovite movement and the unions, see Sándor Balogh, ed., *Nehéz Esztendők Krónikája, 1949–1953, Dokumentumok* (Chronicle of Difficult Years, 1949–1953, Documents) (Budapest: Gondolat, 1986).

[43] Some of these cases were severely punished, though in others the miscreants simply received fines. In the early 1950s, thousands of cases were tried in the courts. György Belényi, "Önkényesen Kilépett" ("Arbitrarily" Resigned), *Kritika*, no. 3 (1984):14–17.

[44] The actual dynamic originates in state firms' *overdemand* for labor, a systemic feature of state-socialism that results in labor shortage. Other systemic characteristics, such as the lack of price-responsiveness, the "expansion drive," and "investment hunger" of firms, fuel the tendency of firms to hoard labor. For a full explanation of the lines of causality among these phenomena, see Kornai, *The Socialist System*; and Kornai, *The Economics of Shortage* (Amsterdam: North-Holland, 1980).

These specific constraints were reinforced by the broader institutional reality of ineffectual collective bargaining. Workers could act in league only through the official trade union controlled by the state, which for all intents and purposes was just another transmission-belt. Indeed, since citizenship had been effectively defined as state-employment, no theoretical argument in favor of a different arrangement could be articulated – not even in the face of profound tensions between individuals' rights as *citizens* and their rights as *workers*.

Formal constraints thus locked workers and managers into a relationship of mutual dependence mediated by *informal* bargaining. Managers needed the goodwill of their workers in order to keep productivity from plummeting on the shop-floor. Managers also needed workers' goodwill if they were to satisfy the party-state's explicit preference for conflict-free enterprises.[45] Workers, in turn, needed managers' collusion in order to implement the strategies that enabled them simultaneously to reshape work norms on the shop-floor and to engage in second-economy activity outside (or inside) the state firm. The bargaining outcome typically involved more lenient work-conditions, overtime schemes, and informal bonuses for "extra" work.[46]

Hybrid Practices: Origins

In all state-socialist countries, skilled workers in heavy industry were particularly well-positioned to take advantage of bargaining opportunities. The economy-wide wage classification system,[47] for instance, tacitly recognized their special rights to income. But just as importantly, this implicit recognition reflected and reinforced an almost taken-for-granted preferential culture that both emboldened skilled workers to devise particularly generous overtime schemes and inclined managers to acquiesce more willingly. Such overtime schemes generally functioned as follows. By working very slowly or hardly at all during regular hours, workers exceeded the prescribed length of time in performing standard tasks. Managers, for their part, agreed to pay for this "overtime" work at between 25 percent and 100 percent above the designated wage – depending upon the number of hours, and whether evenings and weekends were involved. Moreover, because workers doing overtime work *a fortiori* spent more hours on the job, additional compensation was necessary to make the scheme worthwhile. There were several ways to compensate. Workers used regular working hours to run errands, make calls, and depending

---

[45] Jan Adam, *Why Did the Socialist System Collapse in Central and Eastern European Countries?* (London: Macmillan Press, 1996), 60–61.

[46] Kemény, "The Unregistered Economy in Hungary," 354–355.

[47] In 1975, the *Unified Classification System of Occupations* was introduced, and organized thousands of occupations according to a uniform code that described the job and specified its place in the system of wage-classification.

upon the nature of the work, complete outside second-economy projects *at* the workplace.[48]

Completing second-economy projects at the workplace of course required more than the initial bargain between management and labor. It required trust and mutual masking. Workers trusted managers to keep their part of the deal and turn a blind eye; managers trusted workers to exercise prudential judgement in selecting their clients. By faithfully rehearsing time and again the entire "overtime" formality, both workers and managers routinized the additional precaution of mutual masking. The circle was completely closed as state-firm managers themselves – whose expertise and training were not typically in high demand in the informal sector [49] – took on legal second jobs that often shaded over into informal work. Thus at every point along the line, skilled workers, state managers, and others exploited their positional duality by transferring capabilities and resources from one position to another.[50] And at every point, both workers and managers showed a keen concern with "reputational utility" – that is to say, they showed an "abiding interest" in one another's preferences.[51]

The same was true of less highly skilled workers, even though their private work effort was more heavily focused on the "outside." Workers in the service sector, for example, came into direct contact with customers. This in turn rendered managerial supervision all the more difficult. Thus workers could develop particularly dense informal networks with customers: networks that workers could then use to operate safely in the unregulated parts of the second economy. Not surprisingly, it was precisely in the service sector that second-economy activity expanded most rapidly and visibly. Of course, less highly skilled workers also benefited from the transforming effects of the constant bargaining between skilled workers and management, since the more ubiquitous and entrenched this informal practice became, the more the *formal* incentives provided by the state

---

[48] The picture of informal economic activity sketched here holds less well for more repressive ex-socialist countries, like Romania under Ceauçescu. See Katherine Verdery, "Theorizing Socialism: A Prologue to the 'Transition,'" *American Ethnologist* 18, no. 3 (August 1991): 422. It is similar to the Polish informal economy, and at least in some respects, to that of the Soviet Union. See, for example, Janine Wedel, *The Private Poland* (New York: Facts on File, 1986); and Gregory Grossman, "The 'Second Economy' of the USSR," *Problems of Communism* 26, no. 5 (September-October 1977): 25–40.

[49] However, many professionals could transfer their skills. A language teacher could always find pupils; so could almost any teacher willing to spend spare hours helping students prepare for entrance exams – and this was so widespread that it amounted to a kind of Hungarian SAT-preparation service. Nor was it beneath many state-firm managers to have a household plot in the city, and grow enough produce to make it worth his wife's time to market it. For more detailed examples, see Kemény, "The Unregistered Economy in Hungary."

[50] For a remarkable sociological study of the "hiding places" or "parking orbits" in which "people with entrepreneurial aspirations could resist the pressure to become fully proletarian," see Iván Szelényi et al, *Socialist Entrepreneurs: Embourgeoisement in Rural Hungary* (Madison: University of Wisconsin Press, 1988), 19.

[51] Timur Kuran, *Private Truths, Public Lies: The Social Consequences of Preference Falsification* (Cambridge: Harvard University Press, 1995), 42.

actually came to operate *within* the *informal* framework imposed by workers on the enterprise.[52] Finally, less highly skilled workers derived bargaining leverage from the simple fact that in the institutional environment of the soft-budget constraint, and in the broader context of a resource-constrained economy,[53] firms hoarded workers regardless of their skill or productivity.

A partial list of the reasons why firms disliked losing *any* workers would include the following: (1) Extra workers helped in periods of storming: non-stop, intensive work to meet quotas and/or deadlines. (Storming was itself the result of a vicious cycle: supply-bottlenecks caused underutilization of firm-capacity, which in turn later had to be at least partially recouped.) (2) Extra workers represented a hedge against future shortages of labor. (3) Extra workers helped protect managerial bonuses, which were linked through a complicated formula to profits and also to firm-size.[54] And (4) in an economic culture where size was an important determinant of political leverage, extra workers helped firms increase their prestige and bargaining power with ministries. In short, even sub-standard employees, who in a capitalist system might be seen as "redundant," became valuable assets for management.

The result was that workers' implicit but growing power altered labor-management relations, and the balance of interests began to shift throughout the system. Caught between the workers' *de facto* influence over the pace and quality of shop-floor activity and the ministries' demands for fulfillment of the plan, managers tried simultaneously to bargain *up* workers' productivity and to bargain *down* the planners' requirements.[55] Furthermore, in order to bring up productivity, the typical state firm manager – not only in Hungary but also in Poland – had to show real respect for workers' preferences. That is to say, he had to bear in mind that from the workers' perspective, as Jan Adam puts it, "a good manager" was able to extract from the authorities

an easily fulfillable plan with the allocation of sufficient inputs, including labor, and an increase in the wage bill which would guarantee an increase in the real wage without the need of much greater intensity of labor. If the employees felt that their manager was not successful in protecting their interests because he was indifferent or because he wanted to balance the interests of the workers and the economy, or if they suspected that he did not have the needed skills (political and professional) for bargaining with the authorities, his popularity necessarily declined.[56]

The relative weakness of managers, however, did not mean that the enterprises were themselves weak. On the contrary. Party leaders, as we have seen, had initially feared the emergence of "private interest centers" in small, decentralized

---

[52] See Kemény, "The Unregistered Economy in Hungary"; and Miklos Haraszti, *A Worker in a Worker's State* (New York: Universe Books, 1978, c1977).

[53] Kornai, *The Economics of Shortage*; and Kornai, *The Socialist System*, especially chapter 11.

[54] See Károly Attila Soós, *Terv, Kampány, Pénz szab ályozás és konjunkturaciklusok Magyarországon és Jugoszláviában* (Budapest: Közgazdasági és Jogi Könyvkiadó, 1986).

[55] On plan-bargaining, see Kornai, *The Socialist System*, 121–124, and 244.

[56] Adam, *Why Did the Socialist System Collapse in Central and Eastern European Countries?* 61.

state (and especially private) firms. But, in fact, it turned out that all over the state-socialist world, it was the large *public* enterprises that became independent power centers, gaining strategic importance and bargaining power as a result of the concentration of resources in a limited number of firms. These enterprises often managed to reallocate incomes for themselves via central institutional channels. And eventually the need for a small, relatively open trading economy such as Hungary's to meet export obligations meant, in effect, that the state became hostage to the monoliths it had created. Even Party reformers who wanted to see them broken up had little leverage with which to accomplish this kind of mammoth reorganization.[57]

This combination of relatively weak managers and powerful enterprises ultimately worked to enfeeble the very core of the plan's hierarchical administration. Along with collective and state farms, for example, industrial enterprises routinely made "tributary" payments to administrative agencies for "their general benevolent attitude and protection." Enterprises, in a word, purchased administrative laxity in hopes of gaining "greater flexibility and freedom from the burden of unnecessary regulation."[58] And so, administrators' interest calculations, too, effectively shifted away from defending the integrity of the plan.

Hungarian Realism: Between Orthodoxy and Pragmatism

In the late 1940s, when Hungary began its first collectivization campaign, the country still had a large number of private farms.[59] (East European countries had launched waves of land reform after both world wars, and Hungary undertook its most ambitious program beginning in the spring of 1945, when it redistributed agricultural holdings that exceeded 575 hectares among the poorer peasants.) But as in the case of industry, the party leadership proved resolute in its efforts to restructure agriculture. Deploying all means at its disposal – from naked propaganda and the pressure-tactics of party zealots known as "teachers of the people" to outright coercion – the leadership pursued its goal of establishing Soviet-style *kolkhozy*, or collective farms.

---

[57] This should not be misconstrued to mean that state firms were so successful at exporting that the leadership became dependent upon them. To the contrary, socialist firms had to be administratively forced to export to any country with quality-control standards higher than those they faced domestically. See Kornai, *The Socialist System*, chapter 14, esp. 348–49. But, having organized the economy into mammoth firms, the party-state was caught in dilemmas of its own making. Among these were the need to meet export obligations even if it meant making larger-than-usual concessions on supplies, credit, investment, and other inputs to firms earning hard currency or meeting CMEA obligations.

[58] Rupp, *Entrepreneurs in Red*, 97.

[59] In the early 1950s, roughly 1.5 million farms remained in private hands. Starting in the late 1940s, however, the independence of private farms was severely curtailed by strict production and delivery obligations that aimed to substitute centralized redistribution for market mechanisms and ensure agricultural exports to the Soviet Union. See Iván Pető and Szakács Sándor, *A Hazai Gazdaság Négy Évtizedének Története, 1945-1985 (The History of Four Decades of the Domestic Economy)*, Vol. 1 (Budapest: Közgazdasági és Jogi Könyvkiadó, 1985), 37, 40.

If the large, vertically integrated enterprise was believed to be superior to other forms of industrial organization, then the *kolkhoz* was believed to be the most advanced model of agricultural production.[60] Central regulation of the *kolkhozy* nevertheless was deemed imperative. In fact, central planners went beyond instructing state farms and cooperatives on matters regarding investment, development, and marketing decisions. They also told them precisely the number and kinds of animals to raise, what and where to plant, how to transport agricultural produce for delivery to the state, and even the "ways in which individual phases of the work should be performed."[61]

As in industry, suspicion and dread of dangerous ideas and practices played a significant part in agricultural restructuring. This was most evident in the case of the cooperatives. For instance, the cooperatives' *members* were "nominally the owners," and as such bore the risks of production,"[62] yet it was the *collective* that owned the land, livestock, and equipment *de facto*. Moreover, whether as individual members or as collective entities, cooperatives saw the fruit of their labor dissipate into the hands of the state. For it was not until year's end – after the cooperative had subtracted overhead costs, investments, taxes, and compulsory deliveries – that its total income was divided proportionally according to members' earned units.[63] Incentives for labor productivity, then, were negligible. And the peasants soon discovered that by hoarding their own labor-power and labor-time, they could redirect – without need of overt collusion – the productive energies of entire families toward whatever private use they could devise.

Measured by standards of productivity, agricultural collectivization and rapid industrialization was a dismal failure. In fact, against the troubling backdrop of workers' strikes in Budapest's industrial suburb of Csepel and in the large industrial centers of Eastern Hungary, the decline in agriculture prompted the Kremlin in June 1953 to summon key Hungarian officials for "consultations" in Moscow. At those meetings, the Soviet leader Georgii Malenkov and his colleagues criticized the "high-handed and domineering style" of Hungary's prime minister and First Secretary of the Hungarian Workers Party (HWP),[64]

---

[60] For a description of other forms of agricultural cooperatives ("termelöszövetkezeti csoport" and the "szakszövetkezet") see Donáth, *Reform és forradalom* (*Reform and Revolution*).

[61] In the early 1950s, approximately 400,000 farmers went to jail or paid fines for violating some part of these regulations – especially those having to do with compulsory deliveries to the state. Ferenc Donáth, "Hungarian Agriculture: Achievements and Problems," *Journal of Rural Cooperation* XIV, no.1 (Budapest, 1986): 7.

[62] Donáth, "Hungarian Agriculture: Achievements and Problems," 9–10.

[63] Gyula Tellér (expert on agricultural cooperatives and then MP for the Alliance of Free Democracts). Interview with author (Budapest, September 1990).

[64] The Hungarian Workers' Party (*Magyar Dolgozók Pártja*) was the result of a "merger" between the Hungarian Communist Party and the Social Democratic Party, when the latter, weakened and decimated, was in fact absorbed by the former. At the end of October 1956, the Political Committee of the HWP dissolved the old Hungarian Socialist Workers' Party (which, until it was disbanded in 1928, had been the legal cover for the banned Hungarian Party of Communists).

Mátyás Rákosi, and blamed him for the "countless mistakes and crimes" that had "driven Hungary to the brink of a catastrophe."[65]

The Kremlin did allow Rákosi to remain First Secretary but also instructed him to relinquish the post of prime minister. The Soviets intended Rákosi's demotion as a major departure from established policy on two interrelated counts.[66] First, they transferred the position of prime minister, still regarded as the most important in the hierarchy, to Imre Nagy. The choice of successor was key because Nagy – a former minister of agriculture – was widely perceived as a "peasant advocate."[67] Second, the Soviets charged the succeeding prime minister with the delicate mission of charting a "New Course," which Nagy promptly outlined in his July 4, 1953, speech to the Hungarian parliament.[68]

The New Course not only allowed peasants to leave cooperatives but also permitted the dissolution of cooperative farms.[69] In no time, peasants deserted coops *en masse*. In industry, meanwhile, the New Course loosened state policy toward small private firms and, in the first of numerous swings between orthodoxy and reform, partially reversed the earlier attempt to abolish small-scale industry. Most notably, workers were now given the opportunity to resign from industrial cooperatives, and private artisans were allowed to apply for licenses. The response from artisans was immediate and substantial: in a year and a half, more than 60,000 such licenses were requested and issued.[70]

These liberalizing measures were meant to address the practical need – recognized by the Soviet leadership – to "rationalize" the state's "unbalanced heavy industry policy."[71] The small firms that had been merged into industrial cooperatives, for example, had become so vertically integrated into the state sector

---

In 1956, the HWP's Political Committee founded a new party of the same name: the Hungarian Socialist Workers Party (*Magyar Szocialista Munkáspárt*, or MSZMP in its Hungarian acronym).

[65] Mark Kramer, "New Evidence on Soviet Decision-Making and the 1956 Polish and Hungarian Crises," in *Cold War International History Project Bulletin*, 8/9 (Washington DC: Woodrow Wilson International Center for Scholars, 1996/97), 362.

[66] Bill Lomax, *Hungary 1956* (London: Allison & Busby, 1976), 19.

[67] Gale Stokes, ed. *From Stalinism to Pluralism: A Documentary History of Eastern Europe Since 1945* (New York: Oxford University Press, 1991), 81.

[68] The Soviet Union, with a dismal record of its own in collective agriculture, also announced *its* New Course in 1953. But instead of easing control over *kolkhozy* (cooperatives) and *sovkhozy* (state farms), Soviet leaders tightened it; instead of decentralizing, they *re*centralized. The harshness of policy enforcement was also striking. In 1954, for instance, Soviet state-farm employees' compulsory labor contribution and obligatory meat deliveries to the state were increased substantially; and a shortfall by *any member of a household* brought a 50–75 percent surcharge on the households' tax, or even imprisonment. Gregory Grossman, "Soviet Agriculture Since Stalin," in *RussiaSince Stalin: Old Trends and New Problems, Annals of the American Academy of Political and Social Science* 303 (January 1956), 63, 70.

[69] Martha Lampland, *The Object of Labor: Commodification in Socialist Hungary* (Chicago: University of Chicago Press, 1995), 157.

[70] András Hegedüs and Mária Márkus, "The Small Entrepreneur and Socialism," *Acta Oeconomica* 22, no. 3–4 (1979): 275.

[71] Stokes, "The Hungarian Revolution," in Stokes, ed., *From Stalinism to Pluralism*, 81.

that they were producing almost exclusively for the large state enterprises, and as a result were unable to meet the population's demand for consumer goods.[72]

But the New Course would turn out to be more important for its *unintended* consequences than for its deliberate thrust at structural rationalization. To begin with, in the face of strong internal opposition from orthodox party-state functionaries, the justification and execution of the New Course required rhetorical as well as tactical adaptations on the part of its proponents. Such adaptations, in turn, provided the basis for specific political-institutional legacies that one day would serve as transformative resources for future reformers.

On the rhetorical front, the New Course gave rise to an official discourse that bowed to Marxist-Leninist principles while simultaneously articulating a vision of pragmatic realism. In his early presentations of the New Course, for example, Nagy took pains to embed his reform policies in the rhetorical framework of Lenin's NEP. This meant rehearsing a particular vision of socialist construction as a process that unfolds in stages and through grand compromises. The line of argumentation that flowed from this premise was far from novel, but it was controversial nonetheless because it tied Hungary to the gradual pace of pragmatic realism. That is to say, Hungary would have to pass through a transition period during which the principal task of the Communist Party was simply to lay the economic foundations of socialism. Moreover, given the "large number of small peasants" present in the Hungarian setting during this period, the New Course would have to serve as the key transformative instrument.

The New Course – like the Soviet Union's NEP – was a repudiation of past excesses associated with ultra-industrialization, which between 1949 and 1953 threw relations of production completely off balance in Hungary. To help rectify this imbalance, the New Course would emulate the NEP on a number of fronts, most notably by easing the rate of heavy industry development; accelerating the production of light industrial goods with an eye toward consumer needs; intensifying agricultural investment and slowing or even partially reversing collectivization; allowing private enterprise in retail trade and small business; and finally, allowing the "market exchange" of goods between socialist industry and private agriculture.[73]

Although these new policies relied for ideological justification on the Soviet NEP, the ways in which local actors organized their struggles around the future of New Course policies were partly Hungarian innovations. The Nagy government, for example, began to "restore" economic research institutes, where ideological dogma was now displaced by "scholarly discourse."[74] By October of 1954, government experts and other economists were engaged in pioneering discussions of the Hungarian *economic mechanism* and its problems – well

---

[72] Galasi and Sziráczki, "The New Industrial Organization," 8.

[73] Lomax, *Hungary 1956*, 58–59, 60–61.

[74] László Számuely, "Establishment and Erosion of the Soviet Model of CPE as Reflected in Economic Science in Hungary, 1945–1980" (Frankfurt [Oder]: Discussion Paper 1/96, Frankfurt Institute for Transformation Studies, European University-Viadrina, 1996).

ahead of their counterparts in Poland, the GDR, and the USSR. This difference in timing, as László Számuely notes, indicates that Hungarian economists were not borrowing ideas from abroad, as they had been prone to do in the past, but were instead squarely focused on the home front's micro- and macro-economic dilemmas.[75]

In approaching these dilemmas, Hungarian economists studiously avoided open ideological confrontations while putting forth unorthodox proposals. On the one hand, they proposed shifting the emphasis from production of quantity to quality, "narrowing" the range of centrally approved plan indicators, and promoting "healthy competition" among enterprises. On the other hand, they argued that economic efficiency and profitability in no way threatened such inviolable tenets as the "basic laws of socialism," "the power position of the working class," and the proletariat's "alliance with the toiling peasantry."[76]

In so doing, Hungarian economists helped promote the idea that the economics profession was unencumbered by "dogma." Moreover, from this privileged position of objective detachment, reform-minded economists deployed empirical evidence in order to articulate arguments that were unacceptable elsewhere in the Eastern bloc. Pointing to the rapid growth of small-scale business and its beneficial effect on output levels of consumer goods, for example, reform economists argued that the active encouragement of the small-scale private sector could promote "flexibility" in the economy as a whole. The precociousness of the reform economists' argument was remarkable, and the argument itself, while insufficient to avoid further restrictions on the small-scale private sector in the short term, would one day be used by reformers for more radical purposes.

Beyond the articulation of pragmatic realism and the "professionalization" of economics, the New Course left yet another intangible but crucial legacy: the effective deployment of political activism through informal networking. Part of the impetus for informal networking came inadvertently from Nagy himself, since his structural re-equilibration agenda was accompanied by a seemingly innocuous but equally radical pronouncement of faith in the "creative power of the masses."[77] Implicitly, this pronouncement of faith justified a crucial shift in the power of everyday decision-making and market transactions from the party-state to workers and peasants. This potential shift rallied both friends and foes of the New Course, alarming recalcitrant functionaries while seizing the imagination of independent-minded journalists, writers, and intellectuals in ways unanticipated by Moscow, and perhaps by Nagy himself.

Of course, Nagy realized that party functionaries deliberately tried to sabotage the implementation of the New Course. This is why he reorganized the non-party People's Patriotic Front in an effort to garner broad popular support,

---

[75] Számuely, "Establishment and Erosion of the Soviet Model," 16.
[76] Ibid., 16–18.
[77] Lomax, *Hungary 1956*, 61.

and established a special Government Information Office to publicize the New Course policies. Nagy even defended the New Course before the Party's Central Committee in 1954, after that body had passed a resolution condemning the reform's re-equilibration policies. By arguing that economic hardship was the result not of the New Course but of the party's resistance to its policies, Nagy actually forced the Central Committee to delete the first resolution and pass a new one, "restating the New Course and calling for an end to resistance among party functionaries."[78]

The profound impact of the new resolution can hardly be overstated. Nagy's speech was discussed at lower party organs throughout the country. And after Nagy rewrote his speech as an article – published in the newspaper *Szabad Nép* (Free People) on October 20, 1954 – the intellectual community came to life. As Bill Lomax writes:

A junior reporter working on the city's evening paper *Esti Budapest* recalls that on that day 'everyone in the corridors was waving Nagy's article.' Three days later, Imre Nagy reached the height of his precarious victory at the opening congress of the People's Patriotic Front, where he was enthusiastically and rapturously acclaimed amid scenes reminiscent of Lajos Kossuth's reception by the Hungarian Parliament in July 1848.[79]

The cause of the New Course was embraced most effectively and spontaneously by sympathetic journalists in the *Szabad Nép*. They operated on two fronts simultaneously by blending informal networking with political activism. On the one hand, they deployed their contacts among second-rank members of the Central Committee in order to push for implementation of New Course policies. On the other hand, they debated the October resolution, called for an end to opposition to the New Course, and argued for democratization of the party itself. They also promoted similar debates in other newspapers, including the *Népszava* (The People's Voice) and Budapest Radio, as well as in universities. And they circulated minutes of the *Szabad Nép* debate at the Journalists' Club, where future tactics were planned.

All these actions were carried out through a wide network of personal contacts, rather than a central organization, thus making it difficult for the authorities to repress the activists involved.[80] Even the reversals suffered in 1955 – when Rákosi and the Central Committee expelled Nagy from the Politburo and the Central Committee, and later dismissed him as head of the government – proved temporary. For that same year, the Soviet leader Nikita Khrushchev rehabilitated Yugoslavia's Marshal Tito, thus giving pro-Nagy forces new impetus in Hungary.

Once more, informal networking and political activism came together. Following Nagy's expulsion in March 1955, his "brain trust" spread his ideas

[78] Ibid., 23.
[79] Ibid., 23–24.
[80] Ibid., 24.

among supporters, who in turn pressured the decision-making bodies of the party. As one New Course supporter recalled:

We had a regular "adult education" campaign. In the evening the council of war would meet somewhere, exchange information gathered since we had last seen each other, and then divide the tasks . . . Through contacts and threats we exerted influence on the party and received excellent information.[81]

These informal networks thrived in part because its members had at their disposal a clear line of argumentation that drew on Nagy's "scientific Marxism-Leninism," which he restated between 1955, when Rákosi forced him out of his post as prime minister, and 1956, when he was brought back in the midst of the Hungarian Revolution. Specifically, Nagy argued in writing that the "New Course must not be liquidated but, rather, should be fully realized, eliminating its shortcomings and paying great attention to those specific tasks that are necessitated by specific conditions in Hungary."

The overall argument hinged on two rhetorical moves. The first was the general point made by Lenin that

the concrete ways and means of achieving [a socialist economy] are necessarily very diverse and they must so remain, since they depend upon [local] conditions . . . All these local differences, as well as the characteristic forms of the economy, the ways of life of the population, the degree of their preparedness, and all the plans directed toward realizing the road to socialism must be reflected in attempts to bring about socialism.

Nagy's second rhetorical move consisted of a series of recommendations for future application of Lenin's counsel to Hungary's reality. These recommendations, which reflected the political learning that flowed from the experience of the New Course itself, ranged from the specific to the general – from "the establishment of increasingly closer relations in the exchange of goods between the city and the village, and between socialist industry and the system of small holdings producing for the market," to "giving the green light" to the "creative initiatives of the masses."[82]

Informal activism thrived even after official repression temporarily managed to isolate and disperse journalists and intellectuals between the autumn of 1954 and the spring of 1955. Part of the reason, once again, was a fortuitous Soviet move – Khrushchev's denunciation of Stalin. The post-Stalinist thaw, for example, led to the startling transformation of Hungary's Petőfi Circle. A small discussion group created in 1954 as a forum for the Communist Youth League, the Circle now turned into an opposition "movement of young Hungarian intellectuals, including all the professions, teachers, economists, physicians, engineers." By 1956, the Circle had formed a network of personal contacts among party intellectuals that was so extensive and reliable that Stalinist leaders

---

[81] Ibid., 31.
[82] Imre Nagy, "Reform Communism," 1955–56, in Stokes, ed., *From Stalinism to Pluralism*, 83–84, 86, 87.

described it as the country's "second political center." Indeed, the Circle went so far as to openly denounce Rákosi's Stalinist excesses.

The Circle's bold activism, coming on the heels of the Poznán riots in Poland and workers' strikes in Hungary, alarmed Moscow, where CPSU leaders referred to the Petőfi Circle's meeting as "an ideological Poznań without the gunshots" – an experience they did not want repeated in Hungary. In July 1956, the Soviet minister Mikoyan arrived unannounced in Budapest, where he proceeded directly to the Central Committee – then in session – and demanded Rákosi's resignation.[83]

Partly because Rákosi was replaced by Ernő Gerő, who was perceived as no more than an ineffectual extension of his predecessor, the political situation in Budapest deteriorated further. As one English communist observer put it:

It would be wrong to think that there was any such organization as 'The Party' any longer, with a unified control. It was breaking up into its component parts – the tiny, rigid core surrounding Ernő Gerő, and the mass of members who were in varying degrees drawn into the tide of the opposition, criticism and independent action.[84]

Within this context of "latent revolt," the opposition sought power niches in the administration and gained influence in the Budapest City Party. And the Petőfi Circle, though officially banned, began holding meetings again, and established a wide network of debating circles.[85] The brashness of the opposition, in fact, became alarming even to Nagy and his inner group. But by then, Nagy's apprehension was overshadowed by his own rhetorical legacy, and the dissertations he had authored after his ouster from power in 1955 now replenished the opposition's ideological arsenal.

The central weapon in this arsenal was a simple yet powerful proposition: *the final goal of socialism is to raise the standard of living of the people.* From this proposition, there flowed a series of practical steps that Nagy himself had outlined. First, in order to achieve a higher standard of living, it was imperative to strike the proper balance between the production of industrial goods and consumer goods. Second, striking such a balance required the promotion of agriculture. Third, in the context of the Hungarian reality, it would be impossible to achieve collectivization and industrialization simultaneously, nor was it possible to attempt collectivization and increased agricultural production at the same time. Fourth, to try to do all this at once was simply to put at risk workers' living standards. Fifth, a more moderate tempo, rather than immediate collectivization, ought to be the government's highest priority. Sixth, while agricultural collectives should be encouraged, this ought to be done solely on the basis of free choice. Seventh, socialism must be built within the framework of a cooperative political alliance with the peasantry.[86]

---

[83] Lomax, *Hungary 1956*, 33–34.
[84] Cited in ibid., 40.
[85] Ibid., 40–43.
[86] Ibid., 57–59.

The development of this potentially disturbing discourse – with its emphasis on raising popular living standards, on moderately paced structural transformation, on state-society cooperation, and on free-choice collectivization – finally peaked in the political arena. In October of 1956, the Hungarian Workers' Party (HWP) Politburo readmitted Nagy into the party, and soon thereafter, demonstrators in Hungarian cities clamored for national independence and the government's resignation. Amidst increasingly violent conflict, Nagy was restored to power.

Nagy's restoration, to be sure, did not stop the spiraling process of radicalization that broke out into rebellion on October 23. But even after Soviet forces entered Budapest and fighting escalated on the 24th, and even after János Kádár replaced Gerő on October 25, indecision reigned in Moscow as rifts within the CPSU intensified. In fact, Moscow unified behind the motto "We cannot and will not retreat" only temporarily, after Nagy himself became increasingly radicalized. On October 28, he embraced the Revolution as a "great national and democratic movement." And on the 30th, he announced the abolition of a one-party system, formed a multi-party cabinet in which János Kádár represented the Communists, and proclaimed Hungary's unilateral withdrawal from the Warsaw Pact.

Moscow's ambivalence in the face of such defiance can be explained by the Soviet leadership's recognition of Hungary as a potential quagmire. The Revolution had already caused many deaths on both sides. And Kádár – and even the radicalized Nagy – began to look like exemplars of socialist moderation when compared with oppositionists bent on overthrowing the entire regime. Thus, by October 30, the Soviet Presidium had reached a consensus: to follow the path of "troop withdrawals and negotiations." Moscow, in fact, issued the "Declaration of the Principles of Development and Further Strengthening of Friendship and Cooperation between the USSR and Other Socialist Countries."

The Declaration was too little too late. Hungarian politics careened out of control, and the CPSU Presidium, fearful of a "spillover effect," reversed course in favor of intervention on October 31. At the same time, however, Moscow secretly brought in Kádár for consultations in early November. Kádár conveyed to the Soviet leadership both the depth of antipathy evoked by Rákosi among the Hungarian population and the country's undeniable rightward drift.

The subsequent Soviet invasion of November 4 brought up the thorny issue of leadership succession. The Soviets consulted with Yugoslavia's Tito, who recommended Kádár to succeed Nagy, because of his anti-Stalinist credentials. Tito also insisted that the Soviets make sure that the new provisional government denounce the Rákosi era and undertake reforms to garner popular support. That the Soviets agreed with Tito on these points shows the extent to which Khrushchev in particular was already thinking of a postinvasion attempt at co-optation and compromise. Kádár himself, once installed as prime minister, kept open the idea of a coalition government into late November.

It was not to be. As Henryk Szlajfer wrote in the pages of the Polish underground publication *Krytyka*, the Kádár regime spent the next six years "brutally dismantling" the "revolt syndrome."[87] This was a major task. During the Revolution, the Party's control apparatus had disintegrated, a multiplicity of political parties had emerged, and industrial workers had spontaneously instituted workers' councils – a direct repossession move based on workers' claim that as producers they had the right to participate in enterprise management.

More profoundly, the councils were arguing for a division of labor between the political and economic realms. As labor representative Sándor Báli put it in a speech before the Hungarian Parliament on November 25:

The workers' councils cannot be political organizations . . . We do not want to commit the same error as that of the Communist Party in the past, which regarded itself at the same time as both the ruler of the country and the factories, and the only organization to represent the interests of the workers. If we should make the same mistakes, we'll be back just where we started. We want the workers' councils to run the country's economic affairs, and the trade unions to have the right to call strikes and deal with all matters concerning the protection of the workers' interests.[88]

The idea that a line could in fact be drawn between political and economic interests was one which, as we shall see in the next chapter, the Polish leadership under Gomulka did not repudiate flatly. In fact, Gomułka initially fed the illusion, only to turn around and eviscerate the councils gradually but surely. The Kádár regime, by contrast, acted quickly and resolutely in its November 1957 decree of the councils' dissolution. The Hungarian regime also instituted a legal framework "designed to prosecute and punish all acts of political opposition and non-cooperation with the regime." This framework "included a whole range of preventive measures that gave the security authorities virtually a free hand in using any repressive strategy."[89]

The effects were grim. After the bloody November clash, in which approximately 22,000 Hungarians and 2,300 Soviet soldiers died or were wounded, there followed two years of intensive "normalization" based on purges, arrests, deportations, and executions. By the time it was over, more than 100,000 people had been arrested, 35,000 had been tried for "counterrevolutionary acts," nearly 26,000 had been sentenced to prison, and as many as 600 had been executed.[90]

The Kádár regime also restored central planning and launched a second collectivization campaign, which succeeded in reintegrating agriculture into the directive management system (albeit in a looser fashion than industry and with some new flexibility compared with the 1949–1953 period). And yet, despite the brutal repression and partial resurgence of orthodoxy, Kádár would soon

---

[87] Henryk Szlajfer, "Under the Military Dictatorship: Between the 'Freeze Frame' and 'Restoration,'" in Michael Bernhard and Henryk Szlajfer, eds., *From the Polish Underground: Selections from Krytyka* (University Park, PA: Pennsylvania State University Press, 1995), 13.

[88] Lomax, *Hungary 1956*, 200.

[89] Grzegorz Ekiert, *The State Against Society: Political Crises and Their Aftermath in East Central Europe* (Princeton: Princeton University Press, 1996), 76–78.

[90] Kramer, "New Evidence on Soviet Decision-Making," 376.

emerge as the archetypical post-Stalinist leader. As Andrew János put it, in the post-Stalin era,

the patterns of leadership, and the symbols surrounding it, reflect[ed] [a] more pragmatic and limited view of social engineering. The leader [was] no longer expected to perform miracles or superhuman tasks; hence he [was] no longer under subtle pressures to vest himself in the garb of omniscience and divine grace. Rather than cultivating the image of a miracle man and scientific genius, the new type of Communist leader attempt[ed] to base his personal prestige on skills in the mundane arts of administration and economic management.[91]

Kádár was not the only one to fit this image, to be sure. Gierek in Poland, for example, would also try his hand at the "mundane arts." But while Kádár began in the early 1960s to pursue a strategy of compromise, Poland's Gierek rose to prominence a full decade later. More importantly still, while Kádár helped forge stable collaborative relations between state and society in an effort to create a measure of economic rationality, Gierek failed miserably in his attempt to rationalize the Polish economy. The next chapter explores the reasons for this failure. But what explains the relative success of the Kádár regime? I have argued that Kádár succeeded in part despite himself – specifically, because he was unable to destroy the legacies of the New Course the way Stalin had destroyed the NEP. In fact, the thread of continuity between New Course policies and those of the Kádár regime was evident in Kádár's initial concessions.

In an attempt to coopt the peasantry, for example, the new regime lived as best it could with the break-up of many of the agricultural cooperatives, and even temporarily accepted the fact that the remaining cooperatives lost nearly half of their membership.[92] The result was that by 1959, the number of small private farms approached the pre-collectivization figure.[93] In addition, each individual who was a full member of an agricultural cooperative[94] was now permitted to keep a household plot for private production and consumption, and was thus given the opportunity to keep up with the living standard of

---

[91] Andrew C. János, "Systemic Models and the Theory of Change in the Comparative Study of Communist Societies," in Andrew C. János, ed., *Authoritarian Politics in Communist Europe: Uniformity and Diversity in One-Party States* (Berkeley: University of California Press, 1976), 20.

[92] See Ákos Róna-Tas, *The Great Surprise of the Small Transformation*, table 3.2, 51.

[93] It is worth noting that in 1958, more than 40 percent of economically active Hungarians still worked in agriculture. See Hanz-Georg Heinrich, *Hungary: Politics, Economics and Society* (London: Pinter, 1986), 159. See also Ákos Róna-Tas, "The Social Origins of the Transformation of Socialism in Hungary," Paper delivered at the American Association for the Advancement of Slavic Studies (Chicago, November 1989), 17.

[94] A pensioner, for instance, who could no longer work the land but was a full member of the cooperative would receive a plot, and other family members could work it in addition to their other plots. Frequently, families followed a two-track strategy: women were full members of the cooperative and men went to work in industry. See Rudolf Andorka, "The Importance and Role of the Second Economy For Hungarian Economy and Society," unpublished paper (Budapest: Budapest University of Economics, 1990), p. 4; and Donáth, *Reform és forradalom* (*Reform and Revolution*).

the industrial wage-earner. Members could also retain vineyards and gardens, and peasants were allowed to raise many more animals privately than in other socialist countries.[95] Moreover, starting in 1956, work-units – the basis of cooperative members' pay – were now denominated in money, fixed in advance, and guaranteed. Finally, in what was a truly radical move at the time, the Kádár regime did not reverse Nagy's abolition of compulsory deliveries of agricultural produce to the state. (It would be many years before other countries followed suit; in Poland, for instance, mandatory deliveries continued until 1972.)

Continuity with the New Course, however, while immensely significant, was not assured. If anything, the fate of Hungary's political economy stood on a knife's edge. By the late 1950s, the regime confronted a strategic dilemma – namely, the choice of exit path out of the "freeze frame," to borrow Henryk Szlajfer's apt term. For as Szlajfer points out, the intensity of the initial shock did not guarantee an "innovative restoration." Restoration based on liberal reformism depended on two additional factors. One was the availability of realistic alternatives to orthodox economic policy. The other was the sway that reform held over both the population and power-holders.[96]

Out of the Freeze: Innovative Restoration

The Kádár regime hedged its bets for as long as possible. On the one hand, it established in late 1956 an array of expert commissions to work out a strategy for economic consolidation and development, so that by 1957, Hungary had a coordinating Economic Commission composed of high government officials and academics studying "the economic mechanism." On the other hand, the regime used the weekly *Economic Spectator* to condemn in advance the proposals on which the Commission was still working.

There were powerful reasons for such ambivalence. The Soviets – now embarked on a campaign against Yugoslav revisionism – gave Hungary

---

[95] By comparison, Andorka pointed out that in the Soviet Union, it was only "each cooperative peasant family" on a *kolkhoz* that was allowed a single household plot; thus the Hungarian policy was considerably more generous. (Andorka, "The Importance and the Role of the Second Economy for the Hungarian Economy and Society.") Only 14 percent of the private farms avoided collectivization by 1962. Indications that the state would have to coopt peasants, and that dependence would run both ways, appeared early on, and contributed to the expansion of the second economy. For instance, allowing peasants to keep a larger number of animals was crucial to productivity, because they sometimes slaughtered their cattle rather than give them up to forced deliveries. Iván T. Berend, *Gazdasági Utkeresés 1956–1965* (Searching For the Economic Path, 1956–1965) (Budapest: Magvetö, 1983), 287–288. In fact, between 1950 and 1951, the number of cattle decreased by almost 10 percent and the number of pigs by 22 percent. However, this was not wholly determined by the system of forced deliveries: animals were also secretly killed in these years simply as the result of food shortages. [Figures are calculated from data in Iván Pető and Szakács Sándor, *A Hazai Gazdaság Négy Évtizedének Tőrténete, 1945–1985 (The History of Four Decades of the Domestic Economy)*, Vol. 1 (Budapest: Közgazdasági és Jogi Könyvkiadó, 1985), table on p. 210.]

[96] Henryk Szlajfer, "Under the Military Dictatorship: Between 'Freeze Frame' and 'Restoration,' " in Bernhard and Szlajfer, eds., *From the Polish Underground*, 13.

substantial aid, which enabled the Kádár regime to stabilize the economy without implementing the expected reforms. In addition, ideological aversion to private property remained strong among the Hungarian leadership. Gradualists fully expected private and quasi-private forms of agricultural production to disappear eventually; conservatives could barely tolerate even temporary private production, which represented a "serious concession of principle" as well as evidence of the "survival of capitalist tendencies" in the countryside.[97] As for the large informal sector, the authorities considered it, at best, a transitional nuisance to be minimally tolerated until the economy matured into socialism, and at worst, a dangerous virus that, unchecked, could kill socialism altogether.[98]

In fact, as far as the second economy was concerned, the logical step for the regime would have been to resort to the formula I call "revocable permissiveness" – a formula favored by communist party leaderships across the world.[99] The formula was simple: as shortages became more severe and social pressures increased, governments permitted a limited amount of private or semi-private production in agriculture and services to provide an escape valve, but once the crisis eased or second-economy activity threatened to grow too visible, they reimposed earlier restrictions or created new ones, and decreed still tougher punishments.

Revocable permissiveness, in short, was precisely what the Kádár regime seemed to need after 1956: a formula for balancing ideological principle, political prudence, and practical exigency. Yet, whereas the Polish authorities wavered between neglect and restriction of the informal second economy, in Hungary the leadership ultimately accommodated and integrated it. And in the early 1960s, the Kádár regime finally opted for the most "consistent" and "liberal" economic policies in the East European bloc.[100]

Three interrelated factors brought about this startling outcome. First, once the regime was consolidated, the informal legacies of the New Course came

---

[97] László Bruszt, "The Politics of Private Business and Public Enterprises," 25. Also, Ákos Róna-Tas, focusing on the debates about consumerism, colorfully recounts conservatives' critiques of "refrigerator socialism," 188–190.

[98] This view was widespread among most communist party leaderships. And fifteen years after the East European revolutions, Fidel Castro remains keenly aware of the loss of political and economic control that can result from giving private enterprise freer scope to operate. Domestic private enterprise in Cuba is still severely curtailed even as a two-tier economy permits foreign capitalists to invest in the economy and to hire socialist workers – as long as their wages are paid directly to the state bureaucracy. See Consuelo Cruz and Anna Seleny, "Reform and Counter-Reform: The Hungarian and Cuban Paths to Market," *Comparative Politics* 34, no. 2 (January 2002). See also Jorge F. Perez-Lopez, *Cuba's Second Economy: From Behind the Scenes to Center Stage* (New Brunswick, NJ: Transaction Publishers, 1995), and Susan Eckstein, *Back from the Future: Cuba Under Castro* (Princeton: Princeton University Press, 1994).

[99] As we will see in the next chapter, this describes Polish policy as well. And Castro, for example, followed such a formula. See Cruz and Seleny, "Reform and Counter-Reform."

[100] Ben Slay, "Economic Reform: A Comparison of the Polish and Hungarian Experiences" (unpublished doctoral dissertation, Department of Economics, Indiana University, 1989), 277–78

into play, thus providing Szlajfer's "additional requisites" for the *possibility* of "innovative restoration." Key legacies included the practice of informal networking among intellectuals and functionaries, and the discourse of pragmatic realism that had suffused these networks. Potential reformers – both inside and outside the state apparatus – could now draw on the lessons that socialist revolutionaries had gleaned from the truncated experiences of the 1953 New Course and the 1956 Revolution. In fact, such lessons were inscribed in a two-part pamphlet formally entitled "On a Few Lessons of the Hungarian National-Democratic Revolution," also known as *Hungaricus*.

The first part of *Hungaricus* appeared in December 1956, the second in February 1957. The pamphlet, in essence, followed the discursive thread of pragmatic realism by targeting the irrational imbalances that threatened Hungarians' "standard of living."[101] Among these imbalances, *Hungaricus* identified the disproportion between working citizens and party-state watchdogs: it took a bureaucratic apparatus of almost 1 million to watch over a general population of (then) about 9 million individuals with an active labor force of 3.5 million. *Hungaricus* also identified the bureaucratic concentration of the centrally planned economy as the fundamental reason for the emergence of an "anti-socialist socialism."[102]

Important as the lessons incorporated in *Hungaricus* were, they were not the only legacies available to the reform-minded leaders of the 1960s. Reformers also could now safely point to the fact that prior to 1956, toleration of the small private sector had yielded increases in production and that, as economists had then reasoned, the sector could increase the flexibility of the larger socialist economy. In this connection, would-be reformers could also safely echo Nagy's formal "Marxist-Leninist" argument concerning the need to respect "local conditions" and the advantages to be derived from unleashing the masses' "creative initiatives" while in pursuit of mature socialism. Indeed, the "realism" that suffused Nagy's "balanced" transitional strategy was now revived in Kádár's claim that a "rapid transition to 'full socialism' in twenty years" – as advocated by some at the 1962 Party Congress – was "unrealistic."[103]

Around the time of the Congress, Kádár appointed Rezső Nyers[104] as the Central Committee Secretary for Economic Policy, and charged him with the task of reforming the system of economic management. The emphasis on

---

[101] By 1953, *Hungaricus* stated, the standard of living was 17 percent lower than four years before. Lomax, *Hungary 1956*, 187.

[102] Ibid., 187–188.

[103] Tőkés, *Hungary's negotiated revolution*, 94–95.

[104] Rezső Nyers was not only one of the main architects of the NEM of 1968, but would remain active in future reform programs, as well as in the effort to find a workable middle road between communist orthodoxy and economic pragmatism. His *Útkeresés-Reformok (Searching for a Path – Reforms)*, published in 1988, "maintained that the tenets of infallible Marxism must be replaced by self-actualizing Marxism." Mária Széplaki and Raymond Taras, "Hungary," in Raymond Taras, ed., *Handbook of Political Science Research on the USSR and Eastern Europe* (Westport, CT: Greenwood Press, 1992), 115.

technical expertise that had been so prominent in the development of a non-dogmatic economics profession under Nagy now took a more explicit and comprehensive shape, as Kádár opened the entire field of policymaking to "experts." The Kádár regime's new and defining Alliance Policy was itself an invitation to economists and technocrats to advise the government and even hold positions of power in it. Most importantly, the Alliance Policy formally and publicly stated a pragmatic approach to political-economic dilemmas – "Marxism must be turned and twisted until the truth is wrung from it"[105] – and in this sense, it also represented an openness to reform projects.

This brings us to the second, decisive factor that helped bring about innovative restoration: the lesson – derived from past experiments – that economic pragmatism was both effective and politically non-threatening. Here, the tried and true household-plot model proved key, since it showed the possibility of "organically" integrating private production into the state socialist model without causing political disequilibrium. This experience helped shift the political calculus in favor of innovative restoration.

Finally, the third factor behind innovative restoration flowed partly from the other two, and partly from the structural rigidities of the planned economy – namely, the particularly acute mutual dependence of state and citizens *qua* producers. In industry, we have already seen, managers and workers jointly set the *de facto* terms of production. In agriculture, the mutual dependence of state and peasants was even more glaring. On the one hand, cooperatives and state farms by 1961 held 90 percent of the land, and 94 percent of farm-workers belonged to cooperatives. On the other hand, the productivity of the household plots continued to rise considerably. Even as the percentage of the agricultural workforce decreased and that of the industrial workforce increased,[106] the labor-intensive household plots supplied much of the country's vegetables, fruits, and meats.[107] And even counting food grown for the peasants' own consumption, the income produced by household plots in the first half of the 1960s exceeded income produced by the cooperatives.[108] Viewed from a macro perspective, the importance of these and other reforms in agriculture was that by 1961, agricultural yields had recovered from the trauma of collectivization, and agricultural goods would soon be plentiful at home despite significant and growing agricultural exports.[109]

---

[105] Ervin Lászlé's 1966 study, *The Communist Ideology in Hungary*, quoted in Széplaki and Taras, "Hungary," 115.

[106] Gábor Révész, *Perestroika in Eastern Europe: Hungary's Economic Transformation, 1945–1988* (Boulder, CO: Westview, 1990), 46.

[107] Bruszt, "The Politics of Private Business and Public Enterprises," 25–26. See also Andorka, "The Importance and Role of the Second Economy for Hungarian Economy and Society," and Donáth, "Hungarian Agriculture: Achievements and Problems," 17.

[108] By 1966, household plot farming comprised one-third of all time invested on cooperative farms to raise "hoed plants." Révész, *Perestroika in Eastern Europe*, 47.

[109] Éva Ehrlich and Gábor Révész, "Coming in from the Cold: The Hungarian Economy in the 20th Century," *Hungarian Quarterly* XLI (2000): 5–6.

Corresponding shifts in the balance of interests also became apparent. By 1966, household plots, auxiliary production, and private farms generated *over 35 percent of total agricultural production*. In other words, peasants remained embedded in the state sector, but were now in a position gradually to turn urban centers into the dependent consumers of private farming.[110] The imminent reform of 1968 would both reflect and accentuate these shifts in outlook, interests, and power relations.

The Reform of 1968: The New Economic Mechanism

By the mid 1960s, reform was high on the Hungarian national agenda for all the reasons that it was being discussed in nearly every COMECON country. As the import and investment-intensity[111] of production rose, growth slowed; shortages of consumer goods, raw materials, and intermediate and capital goods became more serious; and inventories of unsold goods accumulated. The planning process proved too slow and inflexible to accommodate the quickened pace and changes in the composition of public and state consumption. The growth in real wages fell behind the rate of increase in production, causing tension in factories, and to make matters worse, as Soviet crude-oil production shifted from the area near the Caspian Sea to Siberia and became more expensive, the cost of energy to its East European satellites rose.[112]

But if reform was discussed in other state-socialist countries in the face of these structural and conjunctural exigencies, significant changes occurred only in Hungary. These changes occurred in – and partly because of – an already liberalized context. In fact, the reforms instituted by Hungary were sufficiently radical at the time to evoke objections – even "heavy, ideological attack"[113] – from the USSR, the GDR, Czechoslovakia, Poland, and Romania.[114] This reform – the New Economic Mechanism (NEM) – was above all an attempt to come to terms with the fact that by the late 1960s, all available labor had been absorbed,

---

[110] By the 1980s, as Donáth noted, "... virtually half of Hungary's population engage[d] in small-scale [private or quasi-private] production activities [and] the total number of working hours spent in small scale production exceed[ed] that in the large scale farms." Donáth, "Hungarian Agriculture: Achievements and Problems,"16.

[111] Import-intensity refers to the proportion of imported intermediate goods required to produce final goods; investment-intensity refers to the investment required to increase national income by a given percentage. See Révész, *Perestroika in Eastern Europe*, 57. See also János Kornai,"Transformational Recession: A General Phenomenon Examined Through the Example of Hungary's Development," in *Economie Appliquée* XLVI (1993 no. 2): 181–227, especially Table 6, 192.

[112] This was a particular problem, since as in other socialist countries, the energy-intensity of production in Hungary was widely acknowledged to be "irrationally" high (socialist countries utilized far higher proportions of both material and energy inputs than capitalist countries at comparable levels of development). Ibid., 58.

[113] Éva Ehrlich and Gábor Révész, "Coming in from the Cold: The Hungarian Economy in the 20th Century," *Hungarian Quarterly* XLI (2000): 6.

[114] Tőkés, *Hungary's negotiated revolution*, 22.

but firms' demand for labor continued to increase. Stated more generally, the NEM was the socialist reformers' response to the end of possibilities for extensive growth, and amounted to a concerted attempt to make the transition to intensive methods of production.

The NEM brought changes both in economic policy and in management. It abolished mandatory planning – the all-encompassing system of compulsory plan directives and centralized resource allocation. Enterprises were formally declared to be autonomous with respect to short-term input and output plans. Public ownership would remain dominant, but according to the new policy, there would be room for the further development of other property forms. Cooperative and private forms of production were declared "permanent" and "organic" parts of the economy.[115] Enterprises would be autonomous and profit-oriented; goods would trade freely between state firms, and between the latter and the population, bypassing state distribution centers.

The NEM also increased the autonomy of non-branch ministries – the "functional ministries," or "central state agencies" – responsible for economic equilibrium. Agencies such as the planning office and the price office gained some decision-making latitude, while branch ministries and county Party committees lost much of their direct control. The result was yet another compromise: firms achieved increased autonomy in day-to-day operations, but the basic political-institutional system remained unchanged, as did the basic *institutional* system of management. Between firms and state agencies, bargaining over regulations and parametric measures replaced bargaining over compulsory plan targets.[116]

The idea of the reformers – who wanted more than just to "perfect" the existing system[117] – was that the state's directive role should be limited to macro-aggregates plus the largest investment projects: in other words, "market-socialism." In principle at least, the state would control the supply of money and credit, develop infrastructure, and establish wage and employment policy.[118] In

---

[115] As already mentioned, the official policy on cooperatives until 1968 had been that they, too, would disappear, evolving into more verticalized and more fully "socialist" forms of production.

[116] See Kornai, "The Hungarian Reform Process," for a detailed description of the 1968 NEM; and Bruszt, "The Politics of Private Business and Public Enterprises."

[117] "Perfecting" usually referred to simplifying plan directives; allowing enterprises *limited* control over the investment of state credits; giving more importance to profits; and so on. Révész cites the Kosygin reforms in the USSR and various measures undertaken in Hungary in the decade following 1956. Révész, *Perestroika in Eastern Europe*, 58. See also Tamás Bauer, "Reforming or Perfecting the Economic Mechanism," *European Economic Review* 31, no. 1–2 (February–March 1987): 132–138. Compared with such reforms, 1968 was "radical," though Kornai argues that it was conceived by "naive" reformers and reserves the term "radical" for later conceptions that no longer accepted the viability of an ideal mix of plan and market elements. On this and on the origins of conceptions of market socialism, see Kornai, "The Hungarian Reform Process," 1724–1730. On the evolution of economists' proposals away from market-socialist conceptions, see also Tamás Bauer, "Two Remarks on Socialism and Reforms," in Ota Šik, ed., *Socialism Today? The Changing Meaning of Socialism* (London: Macmillan, 1991).

[118] Here again is an example of the centrality of political learning in the development of Hungarian reform programs. The intellectual roots of the 1968 proposals also reach back to the 1950s,

practice, although enterprises were no longer given detailed annual instructions, and had more independence in making decisions about employment, investment, and product-mixes, they remained dependent on the central budget, and the state still controlled market entry and exit, as well as all major reorganization, such as mergers. Successful firms still saw their profits redistributed to loss-making enterprises, so "cost-insensitivity and over-demand for resources" remained the norm.[119]

Despite these limitations, however, a quasi-market price system did emerge with the 1968 reform. And despite the complex, hybrid nature of labor markets and the high level of subsidization and soft credit throughout the system, the NEM created a degree of transparency in the Hungarian socialist system that was unknown elsewhere in the communist bloc.[120] To put the NEM in perspective, it is useful to recall that Gorbachev's own *khozraschet* (roughly, "self-financing") proposals for industry – which came to be known as *Perestroika* – did not go nearly as far as the Hungarian reforms of two decades before.

Further Concessions in Agriculture: Building on the Household-Plot Model

The reforms of 1968 greatly increased productivity in state-controlled agricultural cooperatives, as the latter were placed on "equal footing" with enterprises in most respects, and members began to receive both a monthly wage and participate in profit-sharing schemes.[121] In practice, though, agricultural cooperatives actually achieved considerably *more* independence than most state-owned enterprises in other sectors.

During the NEM period, many restrictions on the millions of small agricultural household plots were also eased. In what amounted to ideological flattery, household farming was officially reclassified as "part of the cooperative rather than private sector." This was a revealing shift in official discourse.[122] Recall that these very same household plots were supposed to have been vertically

---

notably to the writings of György Péter and János Kornai. See Péter, "Az egyszemélyi felelős vezetésről" (On Management Based on One-Man Responsibility), *Társadalmi Szemle* 9, no. 8–9 (August-September 1954): 109–124; Péter, "A gazdaságosság jelentőségéről és szerepéről a népgazdaság tervszerű irányításában" (On the Importance and Role of Economic Efficiency in the Planned Control of the National Economy), *Közgazdasági Szemle* 1, no. 3 (December 1954): 300–324; Kornai, *Overcentralization*; and Kornai, "The Hungarian Reform Process," 1689.

[119] Galasi and Sziráczki, "The New Industrial Organization," 14; János Kornai and Ágnes Mátits, *A Vállalatok Nyereségének Bürokratikus Ujraelosztása* (*Bureaucratic Redistribution of Firms' Profits*) (Budapest: Közgazdasági és Jogi Könyvkiadó, 1987).

[120] See István Dobozi, "The Price Sensitivity of the Economy," in Roger A. Clarke, ed., *Hungary: The Second Decade of Economic Reform* (Harlow, Essex: Longman Group UK, 1989), 139.

[121] Donáth, "Hungarian Agriculture: Achievements and Problems," 10.

[122] Róna-Tas, *The Great Surprise of the Small Transformation*, 201. Revealing on two counts: first, it was a clear "promotion" in the socialist hierarchy. At the same time, the "reclassification" guarded against hardliners' sensitivity to an alternative "private sector" classification.

integrated into the agricultural cooperatives (the so-called MGTSZ, into which the small plots would be subsumed and so ultimately disappear). Now the peasants who worked the plots were actually encouraged to market their produce either directly or through the MGTSZ, which frequently supplied the necessary inputs and technical advice, lent equipment, and often shared profits from the sales of privately produced goods. The upshot was that soon the finances of the MGTSZ and the private peasant producers became inextricably intertwined in a substantial symbiosis.[123] The cooperatives helped to coordinate small-scale production by providing seeds, fertilizer, and machinery, and help with transport, advice, and marketing assistance. (By 1979, the agricultural coops employed 1,300 economists "expressly for the organization of household production and marketing.")[124] A division of tasks evolved whereby coops and state farms concentrated on products that could be most efficiently made by large-scale operations while the household plots focused on labor-intensive products.

The number of cooperative-members' plots and those of workers not employed in agriculture started to expand rapidly in the late 1960s.[125] But more importantly, the symbiosis between the state agricultural coops and the private household plots meant that there was less financial exposure and political risk for private producers. They could now be supplied with resources and legal protection as the result of their association with coops, and they could more easily sell their products. As a result, the percentage of plots producing purely for their own consumption declined from 77 percent to 43 percent between the mid-1960s and the mid-1970s, while that of commodity producers increased to 57 percent – an increase that was the most rapid in the household plots of *non*-agricultural workers. (Hungarian sociologists called this "repeasantization.")[126] By 1976, the net value of the output of *workers'* household plots equaled that of agricultural cooperative members' household plots, and "between 1970–75 their gross return from sales increased one and a half times."[127]

---

[123] To take just one common example: calves born in the cooperative were sometimes sold to individual members who raised them on private household plots. The cooperative later bought them back, and sold them to a state enterprise. Because the cooperative was considered part of the socialist sector – though nominally in cooperative ownership, it functioned essentially as a state-owned unit – it received a slightly higher price for the cattle than the peasants' private plots would, had the calves been sold directly to a state firm without the mediation of the cooperative. The state cooperative farm typically received the premium and split it with the individual cooperative members who had raised the cattle on their household plots. Rudolf Andorka, interview with author (Cambridge, Massachusetts, May 1990).

[124] Bruszt, "The Politics of Private Business and Public Enterprises," 33.

[125] Ibid., 24–27.

[126] Iván Szelényi, *Socialist Entrepreneurs: Embourgeoisement in Rural Hungary* (Madison: University of Wisconsin Press, 1987), 72. See also Bruszt, "The Politics of Private Business and Public Enterprises," 34. On some of the more explicitly political and cultural aspects of this phenomenon, see Lászlo Kurti's *The Remote Borderland: Transylvania in the Hungarian Imagination* (Albany: State University of New York Press, 2001), esp. 150–153.

[127] Bruszt, "The Politics of Private Business and Public Enterprises," 34.

Another important outgrowth of the NEM reforms was the so-called "joint secondary plant," or "auxiliary production" of agricultural cooperatives, which could now undertake non-agricultural ventures. The idea was that these non-agricultural businesses within the cooperatives would produce goods related to agriculture – from canned fruits and vegetables to goose-down pillows and comforters. They did this, but they also supplied much-needed industrial products. Moreover, "many subcontracted with large state companies to manufacture spare parts, and quite a few began business in construction." And in a broader example of the symbiosis between private and state enterprise, the state coops sometimes served as fronts for private businesses not located in the cooperatives at all, but in nearby villages or in Budapest.[128]

The twin phenomena of "repeasantization" and "auxiliary production" on agricultural cooperatives are just two examples of how informal and formal second-economy production helped to shift the boundaries of social categories upon which the socialist system rested, and they are part of an already-familiar pattern. Earlier we saw that workers' instrumentalization of their structural positions in factories resulted in a kind of dual existence – state-employee and part-time entrepreneur – in the structure of production. This duality was almost always lived out simultaneously, and became a regular institutional feature of state-firm operations. In agriculture, such dual positions had been *formally* institutionalized by the late 1960s. Now many industrial workers were becoming city peasants, while rural peasants became entrepreneurs.

Early Expansion of the Possibility Frontier

The NEM brought relatively little fundamental change in the treatment of private forms of *industrial* production, but it followed clearly from the logic of the reform to question the complete dominance of the state in *any* sector.[129] We have seen that state-controlled agricultural cooperatives, for instance, were treated more leniently in this period, and not only members but craftsmen, engineers, and others could start quasi-private auxiliary or joint secondary plants in their local cooperatives.[130] State-sector employees and pensioners could legally work part-time in private small-scale industry from 1968 on. And some of the more prohibitive tax-rules for private enterprise were also eased.[131]

---

[128] Róna-Tas, *The Great Surprise of the Small Transformation*, 204–205. Róna-Tas also explains that such auxiliary production would make use of local resources, help to absorb idle labor in the winter months, and employ wives and other family members for whom "many jobs in the collective were considered unsuitable...but as social welfare support was tied to employment...could not receive maternity benefits or pensions unless they were employed." Pál Juhász (1988). "Zsákutcában van-e a magyar mezőgazdaság?" (Is Hungarian agriculture on a dead-end street?) *Medvetánc* 1:197–211, quoted in Róna-Tas, *The Great Surprise of the Small Transformation*, 203.

[129] Bruszt, "The Politics of Private Business and Public Enterprises," 31–34.

[130] Rupp, *Entrepreneurs in Red.* Also Kémény, "The Unregistered Economy in Hungary," 56.

[131] These selective concessions to the legal non-agricultural private sector were not enough to motivate large numbers of people to engage in full-time, formal private enterprise. One hundred

The NEM had an enormous impact on the "possibility frontier" of future reform in Hungary. Consider the relationship that NEM policies fostered between state-controlled and private agriculture. The government's acceptance of the institutional symbiosis between the state agricultural coops, on the one hand, and household plots, family-share farming, and auxiliary production on the other, meant that private production had become generally less precarious. This signal – announcing risk-reduction to the average Hungarian – had a ratchet effect, and increasing numbers of people entered the second economy in agriculture and in "auxiliary" forms of production at cooperatives.

The NEM reforms, and the more liberal atmosphere surrounding them, also signaled the rehabilitation of consumerism, as the regime began to place greater emphasis on the production of consumer goods to alleviate increasing shortages. This ideological message had enormous systemic consequences, both direct and indirect. On the one hand, the citizenry's orientation became decidedly more "consumerist." On the other hand, ailing state-firms could not keep up with consumer demand, and in any case, consumers' needs and preferences had a very weak influence on the composition of the supply of goods and services on offer by the state sector.[132] This contradiction, in turn, gave further impetus to the second economy both at the societal level and at the level of state elites. Average citizens without access to special *nomenklatura* stores or foreign exchange had to produce or purchase many of their own supplies through the second economy. And in order to relieve some of the pressure on state firms, the leadership generally turned a blind eye when the population decided to trade its leisure time for higher consumption levels achieved through second-economy work.

Finally, and most fundamentally, the NEM intensified the second-economy's tendency to blur the social categories – the identities – of the state-socialist system. Peasants, initially stereotyped as creatures of habit tied to vestigial methods of production, were by the late 1960s the principal agents in what hard-liners described as the "threatening development of agricultural capitalism." The category of "urban worker" also changed, as did the structure of actual production. By the mid-1970s, *worker* households in the aggregate derived more extra income from marketing their small-scale agricultural production than did members of agricultural cooperatives. In fact, because of previous liberalizations, the "repeasantized" worker now occupied an explicitly dual position in the socialist system – he was at once a farmer and an urbanite consumer of his own and others' agricultural produce.

In this context of deepening structural duality, the 1968 reforms inadvertently hastened social change by lifting most administrative barriers to changing jobs. The result was that labor turnover increased considerably and employers

percent of registered artisans/entrepreneurs worked full-time in 1960; 53 percent worked full-time in 1985. István Gábor, "A második gazdaság és környéke Magyarországon," Bulletin N. VI. (Budapest: HSWP Central Committee Social Science Institute, 1985), 126.

[132] Kornai, "The Hungarian Reform Process," 1720.

began to compete more intensely for available labor.[133] This exacerbation of labor shortage was just one of the consequences of NEM reforms that ran counter to the interests of large state enterprises. Parts of the vast bureaucracy – for instance, the branch ministries that were slated for elimination – were also threatened by their loss of direct control.

The radical implications of these developments were plain to losers and potential losers. In 1971, directive agencies that wanted to reinstate their privileges of unmediated intervention joined with the large public enterprises wishing to stabilize their monopolistic positions to launch a counterattack on the NEM. They presented this policy reversal as a defense of the workers. Hard-liners tried to equate the size of enterprises with the interests of industrial workers, dredging up the highly charged issues of relative wages, income distribution, "profiteering," and speculation. They argued that peasants were now *better off* than industrial workers, because the freer scope for business activities in agricultural cooperatives and the expansion of small-scale agricultural production was tantamount to "rural capitalism."

Thus, between 1972 and 1974, the Party imposed restrictive measures on the agricultural second economy. These measures, which caused a drop in output and disrupted food supplies to urban centers, represented more than an error of economic policy on the part of hard-liners. By fixating on the peasants' proto-capitalist tendencies, hard-liners had failed to grasp the structural duality that had made many urban workers into quasi-peasants, too. And so they failed to see that recentralization attempts worked doubly to the detriment of workers. As urban consumers, workers paid higher prices for agricultural produce along with everyone else as supplies were reduced, and as urban agricultural producers, they actually stood to lose even more income. Furthermore, hard-liners failed to understand that the history of informal bargaining and socialist reform had deeply altered the power relations linking the agricultural sector to the larger political economy. Not only had a powerful agricultural lobby emerged, but the "legal umbrella" of state farms and cooperatives provided considerable "political protection" to private production forms.[134]

As a result of all this, hard-liners were able to slow down but could not actually stop the commercialization of private small-scale agricultural production and auxiliary production in rural cooperatives.[135] By the late 1970s, the hybrid model of state-controlled, semi-private, and private farming in Hungary had attained the character of relatively advanced agro-industry, a fact that

---

[133] See Károly Fazekas and János Köllő, "Fluctuations of Labour Shortage and State Intervention After 1968," in Galasi and Szirácki, eds., *Labour Market and Second Economy in Hungary,* especially 57–59.

[134] Pál Juhász, "Hungarian Agriculture: In the Right Direction, or Toward a Dead End?" (Budapest: Cooperative Research Institute, 1987), 19, quoted in Slay, *Economic Reform,* 279.

[135] On the attempt to restrict the agricultural second economy, see Andorka, "The Importance and Role of the Second Economy for Hungarian Economy and Society," 5. On the process and socio-political significance of its commercialization, see Iván Szelényi, *Socialist Entrepreneurs: Embourgeoisement in Rural Hungary* (Madison: University of Wisconsin Press, 1988).

heightened party leaders' ambivalence toward private enterprise. Party elites, for example, sought still greater concentration in the state industrial sector by reorganizing smaller state-firms into larger enterprises and mammoth trusts. But the old fear of private enterprise as a potential center of *"particular"* – as opposed to *public* – interest was not the official rationale used to justify recentralization. Rather, the argument now was that the bureaucratic chain of command would be *simplified* and macroeconomic planning *rationalized*, since consolidated firms would not compete against one another or duplicate productive efforts.[136]

There were other signs of ambivalence. For instance, it was in this comparatively repressive period that the government issued the first regulations authorizing joint ventures with Western firms.[137] Moreover, party leaders not only recognized that private contracting was profitable to all concerned, but they also began to grasp the politically unsustainable incongruence between the economy's actual structure and the party-state's ideological pronouncements. Partly for this reason, the second economy was allowed to expand still further, even during this brief, relatively illiberal period.[138]

Conclusion

Reflexive and managerial labor hoarding and positional duality so thoroughly permeated the structure of Hungarian state socialism that informal shop-floor bargaining and compromises in agriculture became standard procedure in state

---

[136] Many agricultural, industrial, and consumer cooperatives were once again re-amalgamated, and in 1972, a high-level decision granted special treatment to the fifty largest public enterprises. Some cooperatives and smaller state enterprises were even incorporated into larger enterprises suffering particularly severe labor shortage. At this point, the largest firms employed 39 percent of the entire workforce, held 59 percent of all assets, and accounted for 49 percent of the total gross production value. Erzsébet Szalai, "The New Stage of the Reform Process in Hungary," *Acta Oeconomica* 29, no. 1–2 (1989), 25–46, and Bruszt, "*The Politics of Private Business and Public Enterprises*," 36.

[137] The regulations were issued in 1972 and strengthened in 1977. Slay, Economic Reform. 279.

[138] This expansion continued despite the increased risks to individuals, as occasionally in this more repressive period, property was confiscated, heavy fines levied, and people sent to jail for terms of several years duration. András Hegedüs and Mária Márkus cite two cases in the early 1970's from the newspaper *Népszabadság* (People's Freedom). "An entrepreneur in Budapest who had not been granted an artisan's license agreed with four cooperatives to run his screw-making machines under their auspices [auxiliary production]. 27 million forints worth of goods were turned out over the years and sold as products of the cooperatives. The cooperative managers shared in the profits. The small entrepreneur was sentenced to three-and-a-half years' prison and confiscation of property worth 100,000 forints." In another case, "the chairman of a cooperative farming on poor quality land introduced herb production (the court acknowledged his merits in this field). However, a [small] group within the cooperative, including the chairman, produced camomil[e] in their household plots but harvested and processed it with the equipment of the cooperative. They distributed between themselves nearly 1 million forints collected for the essential oil. The chairman was sentenced to two year's prison and a fine of 10,000 forints." Hegedűs and Márkus, "The Small Entrepreneur and Socialism," *Acta Oeconomica* 22, no. 3–4 (1979), 280.

firms and cooperatives. Moreover, "standard procedure," interacting with formal structures of production, developed into hybrid economic institutions, such
as overtime schemes on the shop-floor and commercialized household plots in
agriculture. These institutions not only transformed the power relations and the
configuration of interests of the planned economy, but also blurred the social
identities and structural roles of "worker," "peasant," and "entrepreneur."

Hybrid economic institutions were also at the root of the expanding second
economy, which burgeoned further in the shadow of the 1968 NEM. Reform,
however, was not inevitable. No other state-socialist nation undertook anything
nearly as radical. Instead, other states managed similar economic exigencies in
a variety of ways. The Polish party-state "tolerated" private farming in order to
avoid food shortages and peasant unrest, while strangling the sector in myriad
ways. Other communist regimes temporarily diffused social pressures by opening – then restricting – the second economy. But in Hungary, once the Kádár
regime extirpated the "revolt syndrome," state elites were able to avail themselves of the political-discursive legacies of the 1953 New Course.[139] Hungary's
success in economic reform cannot be explained by Kádár's superior leadership,
better-trained economists, or any other straightforward factor. A large part of
Kádár's – and Hungary's – success was due to the fact that after 1956, he was
unable to destroy the legacies of the New Course as Stalin had destroyed the
NEP.

A particular combination of social pressures from below and reforms from
above focused state-society relations on economic settlements, so that over
time an implicit "consumerist pact" between regime and citizens emerged as
the hallmark of the Hungarian political economy. This "pact" rendered the
Hungarian regime acutely vulnerable to the pressures of the socialist "social
contract," which claimed the citizenry's loyalty on the promise that "the state
would provide." Most East European states were unable to provide a reasonable
level of goods and services for their populations, and all failed to sustain the level
of social welfare that had been the system's claim to superiority.[140] As late as
1990, food shortages in the Soviet Union were so severe that many goods were
rationed.[141] But in Hungary by the early 1980s, consumers' frustrations posed

---

[139] Chapter 5 of the present book analyzes a reform vocabulary constructed from the political
bargains struck between hard-liners and reformers within the party-state apparatus and in
academic circles. For a comprehensive study of the individuals associated with reform and
a detailed examination of the views espoused by various reformist-groups, see János Mátyás
Kovács, "Reform Economics: The Classification Gap," *Daedalus* 19, no. 1 (Winter 1990):
215–249.

[140] Nigel Swain, *Hungary: The Rise and Fall of Feasible Socialism* (New York: Verso, 1992), 13–
14. By the late 1980s, it had become common practice to refer to this sort of "social contract"
in Hungary, but obviously there can be no *true* contract, given that the citizenry did not enter
into it freely. The term is generally used, and is used here, as a short-hand for the *quid pro quo*
on which Hungarian state socialism was based, and which functioned somewhat analogously
to a social contract in a framework of doubtful legitimacy.

[141] William Moskoff, ed., *Perestroika in the Countryside: Agricultural Reform in the Gorbachev
Era* (New York: M.E. Sharpe 1990), *ix*. Moskoff recounts several jokes then circulating in the

a threat to regime legitimacy. Public opinion research, for example, showed that the citizenry was losing confidence in the government's ability to solve the economy's problems and achieve socialist targets. The Poles had long since lost confidence, as the next chapter shows. Moreover, as subsequent research has demonstrated, this failure significantly weakened the Party's moral and practical authority to limit individuals' private efforts to provide for themselves and for others.[142] Chapter 5 explains how the Hungarian leadership met this challenge while maintaining state-society relations focused on "purely" economic issues. But first, we examine how a radically different focality developed in the case of Poland.

Soviet Union. Among them, a "starkly empty food shelf in an absolutely empty food store bears a sign that says: 'Food for Thought'"; and "Question: 'Is it possible for an elephant to get a hernia?' Answer: 'Yes, if it tries to lift Soviet agriculture.'"

[142] Swain, Hungary: *The Rise and Fall*, 13.

3

Injustice

Poland 1948–1980

In Poland, as in Hungary, state socialism generated systemic dysfunctions and individual adaptive responses, which in turn subverted the internal logic of the plan and altered the microfoundations of the economy. Consider the following chain-reaction on the supply side. Planners imposed either exacting production quotas or output targets on state firm managers, which the latter tried to meet by assiduously collecting both material inputs and workers. But workers responded by hoarding their own labor power. Doubly constrained in this way, managers perpetually sought to bargain *up* workers' productivity and to bargain *down* planners' exigencies.[1] Now consider consumption. Chronic shortages of goods and services led consumers to seek relief in informal structures of market exchange. These informal structures, however, could only be effective if protected by participants from the punitive power of a disapproving state. Participating economic agents minimized this peril by creating and entrenching networks of complicity, trust, and mutual masking. In so doing, they altered the very foundations of the economic system by replacing the mass of selfless, passive consumers envisioned by the party with dense groupings of day-to-day tacticians.

In these profound ways, the Polish and Hungarian stories of internal transformation are quite similar. But if in Hungary, citizens' adaptations from below interacted with increasingly liberal state policies to foster a differentiated second economy, in Poland, orthodox (or at best highly contradictory) state policies actually debilitated private agriculture, fomented the largely speculative character of the illegal non-agricultural economy, and left both the illegal and legal segments of the second economy poorly integrated with the state sector. One by one, these contradictions and failures buttressed the charge of irrationality and ultimately injustice that workers leveled against the party-state.

---

[1] Jan Adam, *Why Did the Socialist System Collapse in Central and Eastern Europe?* (London: Macmillan Press, 1996), 61.

Pyramids and Islands

To illustrate the contrast between the Polish and Hungarian second economies, it may be useful to think of pyramids and islands. By the late 1960s, the second economy in Hungary resembled a three-layered pyramid. The broadest layer – the base – was made up of an entirely informal and largely hidden private sector. The middle layer was composed of quasi-private, borderline legal activities often found inside the state sector. Finally, the smallest layer, or the apex of the pyramid, was occupied by the formal private sector, which was licensed and controlled by the state. In Poland, on the other hand, the second economy resembled not a pyramid but rather two large islands that were in many ways isolated from each other. One island was the formal sector, composed mostly of small private farms.[2] The other was the informal sector.[3] Largely missing from the Polish second economy were the state-sanctioned nodes of entanglement that in Hungary come together to form the nexus of the state and the informal private sectors.

Missing, too, was the history of unintended successes from which the Hungarian leadership drew practical lessons for reform. Recall here that in the late 1950s, the Hungarian leadership set out to coopt the peasantry by temporarily allowing quasi-private forms of agricultural ownership. Recall also that tactical cooptation turned into structural change, as these quasi-private forms became entwined in a highly productive symbiotic relationship with socialized agriculture. Recall, finally, that in time the Hungarian leadership began deliberately to foment this symbiosis.

All this, it bears repeating, had profound systemic implications. The informal methods of production that had gradually infiltrated state firms and state-controlled cooperatives proved to be the precursors of the so-called "intra-firm work partnerships,"[4] as well as specialized groups (in cooperatives) that would be institutionalized by the early 1980s. And two decades before that, as we have seen, social identities and economic roles shifted in ways wholly unintended by the Hungarian state. Peasants, for example, outperformed the stereotypical expectations attached to a "backward class": they became reliable suppliers of produce to urbanites, and thus solidified their position in the increasingly important business of consumer satisfaction. (By comparison, of $21 billion

---

[2] To be sure, by 1968, one could occasionally find shoe-repair shops, specialty food shops, and the like in most towns. Thinking back to the late 1960s and to the decade of the 1970s, economist Tomasz Charanzkiński pointed out that such firms were scarce and "always [had] a political anchor in the state administration." They were politically motivated, "to show that not everything is suppressed in Poland," and almost always, the owner(s) were themselves members of the *nomeklatura*, or at least prominent in local administration. Charanzkiński recalled that in smaller towns, these links were often quite easy to see. Tomasz Charanzkiński, author's interview, Warsaw, October 1995.

[3] Later in the chapter, we will see that this second "island" also had around it small atolls of formal private firms that the state permitted after 1956 and increasingly in the mid-1980s, as well as scattered joint-ventures called *Polonia* firms.

[4] VGMK in its Hungarian acronym.

TABLE 3.1 *Share of social sectors in gross agricultural output – Hungary* (percentage distribution)

Year	State farms	Cooperative farms	Private sector*
1975	——	——	31
1981	——	——	32
1982	——	——	31
1983	——	——	34
1984	——	——	——
1985	15.8	50.3	34.0
1986	15.5	49.1	35.5
1987	15.2	48.3	36.4

* Household plots on cooperatives, private farms, and gardens and plots of persons employed.

Source: 1975, 1981–83: Nancy J. Cochrane, "The Private Sector in East European Agriculture," *Problems of Communism* (March–April 1988), p. 48–49. 1985–1987: EIU Country Profiles, *Hungary* (1986–89).

Poland borrowed from the West in the 1970s, "fully $6 billion were siphoned off to pay for food imports, despite the fact that 25 percent of the population was engaged in food production.")[5] As a result, by the 1970s in Hungary, the increasingly diversified second economy also foreshadowed a new politics of work and consumption.[6] More importantly for our purposes, by the mid-1970s, the success of Hungarian agriculture provided vivid proof that hybrid forms of agrarian production (like the private household plots cooperating with state cooperative farms) could meet supply/demand exigencies without posing a serious threat to the political order (see Table 3.1). In Poland, on the other hand, the size of the private agricultural sector was large enough to pose both a practical and an ideological threat to the authorities (see Table 3.2).

So why islands and not pyramids in Poland? The simplest answer is that at least until the mid-1980s, the Polish leadership oscillated between neglect and willful restriction of the second economy. Most notably, non-socialized agriculture – the largest formal sector of the Polish second economy – was the permanent object of official discrimination. Partly for this reason, participants in Poland's second economy were simply unable to follow the path of

---

[5] Roman Laba, *The Roots of Solidarity* (Princeton: Princeton University Press 1991), 93.

[6] Nigel Swain writes, for instance, that the Hungarian sociologist Elemer Hankiss's work on the "second society" resonated so strongly with Hungarians precisely because "in their daily lives people were experiencing the schizophrenia of the institutionalized dualism of the first and second economy." Nigel Swain, *Hungary: The Rise and Fall of Feasible Socialism* (New York: Verso, 1992), 13. István Kemény goes further, characterizing the "hidden economy" as a means of "de-statification" and a form of resistance. Kemény "The Second Economy in Hungary," in Maria Łoś, ed., *The Second Economy in Marxist States* (New York: St. Martin's Press, 1990), especially 63.

TABLE 3.2 *Share of social sector in employment – Poland*
(percentage distribution)

Year	State	Private	
		Total	Agriculture
1980	72.0	28.0	24.5
1981	70.9	29.1	25.3
1982	69.2	30.8	26.7
1983	69.3	30.7	26.1
1984	69.5	30.5	25.4
1985	69.5	30.5	25.2
1986	69.9	30.1	24.5
1987	69.9	30.1	23.9
1988	69.6	30.4	23.4
1989	66.7	33.3	23.2
1990	65.9	34.1	21.6*
1991	45.9	54.1	25.8*
1992	41.5	58.5	25.8*
1993	39.4	60.6	26.5*
1994	39.4	60.6	——
1995	37.6	62.4	——
1996	——	——	——
1997	31.5	68.5	——
1998	29.3	70.7	26.8
1999	27.7	72.3	27.1

* EIU estimates
Sources: 1980–1989: Ben Slay, *The Polish Economy: Crisis, Reform and Transformation* (Princeton: Princeton University Press, 1994), p. 76; 1990–1994: Economist Intelligence Unit *Country Profile: Poland;* 1995–1999: Central Statistical Office (GUS) Yearbook, 1999–2000.

their Hungarian counterparts, who increasingly over time – despite irrational and sometimes punitive regulations common in Hungary too – thrived in the shadow of reform waves aimed at the state sector. But this answer, though satisfactory from a purely structural perspective, raises deeper questions about official attitudes and policies, and it is here that the political-ideological interaction between state and society comes to the forefront.

To begin with, Poland did not experience an innovative restoration from above. In the spring of 1956, Bolesław Bierut, the general secretary of the Polish United Workers Party (PUWP) died, bringing to an end the rule of the "Muscovites."[7] Then, on June 28 in Poznań, over 18,000 workers marched on the city. Their work-stoppage and demonstration soon encompassed the

---

[7] Gale Stokes, "Marxian Opposition in Poland," in Stokes, ed., *From Stalinism to Pluralism: A Documentary History of Eastern Europe Since 1945* (New York: Oxford University Press, 1996), 107.

whole city in a "spontaneous violent uprising."[8] As a result of the 1956 crisis, the Polish state bowed to pressures that erupted from below by explicitly ratifying workers' demands for direct participation in industrial management. This initial accommodative response from above solidified a positive "structure of expectations" – to borrow Alain Touraine's apt phrase – regarding the state's willingness to pursue economic "rationality." Indeed, many of the "most dedicated worker-activists placed their hopes in a reformed trade union and council movement."[9] But by 1957, the leadership had begun to renege on its promises; it would eventually extinguish altogether the hopes it had fostered. First, Stanisław Matya, a prominent figure in the 1956 revolt who had been elected to lead a workers' council, was fired along with other activists. Finally, Roman Laba explains, the council movement was "brought to heel as the government swamped the movement with 'ringer' councils from more passive factories."[10] The gap between societal expectations and actual state policies thus gave rise to the popular perception of the state as untrustworthy and irrational.

The perception was not divorced from the hard facts of life. State-socialist systems, after all, were expected to provide for the material well-being of the entire population. Indeed, as Mira Marody points out, because socialism "inhibited" real politics, the economy was "the main arena for articulating and negotiating social interests. The frequent overlapping of political and economic crises demonstrates the economy's importance in establishing the system's credibility."[11] And whereas material hardship was common throughout the East European bloc, in most periods it was quite keen in Poland compared with Hungary. This can be traced, in the first instance, to Gomułka's economic strategy, which in practice had little in common with his powerful rhetoric against the Stalinist model of development at the Eighth Plenum of the PUWP in October 1956. Throughout virtually his entire tenure as first secretary, Gomułka's focus remained on natural-resource extraction and capital-intensive development, to the serious neglect of consumer goods and foodstuffs. He tended to distrust intellectuals, including economists arguing for economic reforms, ignoring prominent Polish economists such as Michal Kalecki, who warned in 1964 of the pressing need to improve standards of consumption.[12] At the same time, Luba Fajfer points out, the conservative party *apparat* supported

[8] Laba, *The Roots of Solidarity*, 103.

[9] Ibid., 103.

[10] Ibid.

[11] Mira Marody, "From Social Idea to Real World: Clash Between New Possibilities and Old Habits," in Kazimierz Z. Posnański, *Constructing Capitalism: The Reemergence of Civil Society and Liberal Economy in the Post-Communist World* (Boulder, CO: Westview Press, 1992), 162.

[12] Luba Fajfer, "December 1970: A Prelude to Solidarity," in Jane Leftwich Curry and Luba Fajfer, eds., *Poland's Permanent Revolution: People vs. Elites, 1956–1990* (Washington DC: The American University Press, 1996), 60, 68. See also Nicholas Bethell, *Gomułka: His Poland and His Communism* (London: Longman Press, 1969).

Gomułka because of his distinct lack of enthusiasm for economic reform. And yet another factor exerted a powerful influence. In contrast to Kádár's *Alliance Policy* and the relatively free flow of professional exchange that it promoted among scholars, technocrats, and politicos, the flow of information in Poland was tightly curtailed. Those, like Wlodzimierz Brus at the 1964 Fourth Party Congress, who dissented even in their professional capacities as economists, were rebuked or even "severely punished."[13]

But just as importantly, the Party in Poland had committed itself in 1956 to something quite specific and radical – namely, the active and significant inclusion of workers in the economic determination of the Republic. The Party's failure to honor this commitment magnified its credibility problem and entrenched its image as a capricious taskmaster whose industrial and agricultural policies harmed not only workers but society as a whole.

The Party's image was in part the result of its very real inability to escape the constraints of state-socialist orthodoxy. But this image was a political-discursive artifact as well. For as we will see, when the leadership demonstrated political-discursive incompetence – as it frequently did – workers seized the upper hand. Specifically, workers were able to articulate a credible vision of "economic rationality," and just as importantly, they were able to endow this vision with normative significance – although the steps leading to this outcome were not always clear at the time.

Throughout the post-Stalinist thaw and into the 1970s, Polish workers returned time and again to the justice and soundness – the *just rationality* – of a straightforward idea: workers' active participation in economic decision-making. In this way, activist workers were able to perpetuate the plausible claim that there existed a viable alternative to the state's dismal managerial performance. To put it differently, in this crucial area, *Polish workers often assumed a political-discursive role similar to the one that in Hungary was generally played by reformers located in the economics profession and in the state itself.*

Of course, unlike the Hungarian reformers, Polish workers lacked the institutional resources that might have broken, Hungarian-style, Poland's much more starkly self-limiting pattern of reform and counter-reform. What Polish workers *did* have was the post-1956 period. This was more than a moment in history when the Party leadership made promises to workers that it later failed to keep. It was also a moment when the country's opportunity structure expanded in tandem with looser geopolitical parameters only to close down again, and when popular expectations responded positively to a seemingly liberalized party-state that soon reverted to dogmatism. In other words, this was a *national* moment marked not by a full-blown revolution to be crushed (as in Hungary), but rather by a spike in collective hope that was soon overwhelmed by collective disappointment. In the Poland of 1956, the potential for a clearly articulated, unified political vision to emerge from civil society, though certainly not foreordained,

---

[13] Fajfer, 61.

remained. By contrast, civil society in Hungary was systematically dismantled prior to the innovative restoration discussed earlier.[14]

With this tangible commitment from the party-state broken, labor emerged as the most palpably aggrieved actor in Poland. Hence the high clarity of its voice early on, and ultimately, worker-activists' search for a unifying vocality. But it is easy to forget, in retrospect, that until the late 1970s, no one could have been certain that the grievances of the labor movement would be able to aggregate the unspoken grievances of *the nation as a whole*. In the event, the political-discursive moves discussed in this chapter enabled workers to link their own grievances to those of other societal groups. This is why the transformation of Poland's independent labor movement into a social movement is in many ways a chronicle of the political-discursive moves through which workers crafted a frame of reference for the *nationalization* of their normative grievances: a chronicle of how, together with intellectuals, they ultimately fashioned an easily communicable understanding of violated commitments. It was this communicable understanding which, powered by the theme of *just rationality*, helped workers defeat the party-state in the political-discursive battles of the 1970s and 1980s, even as they were violently suppressed. Indeed, we will see how the party-state eventually managed to forge a Polish version of pragmatic realism, only to see the construct's internal contradictions used against it by society. It is here that we can locate the origins of Poland's most salient hybrid: Solidarity.

The First Phase: The Politics of Economic Rationality

Even before the 1953–55 *New Course* interlude in Hungary, a significant wing of Poland's communist leadership envisioned key modifications to the prescribed Soviet model. Notable among these revisionists was General Secretary Władysław Gomułka, who argued that forced collectivization of agriculture would be a mistake given the country's highly agrarian structure. But this and other "deviations" led in 1948 to Gomułka's imprisonment and to the truncation of the deviationist "Polish Path to Socialism." The new leadership – supported by Stalin and in the name of a "sharp class struggle" – nationalized the industrial sector, liquidated most private trade and crafts, relegated unions to the task of enforcing labor discipline in state enterprises, sanctioned the overly ambitious production targets set by central planners for heavy industry, and resumed collectivization efforts in the agricultural sector, though with scant success. Between 1948 and 1956, the state managed to collectivize no more than 23 percent of the cultivated land. However, to understand the intensity of Poles' anger at food shortages (beginning in 1956 and continuing cyclically through

---

[14] See, for instance, Zvi Gitelman, "Is Hungary the Future of Poland?" *East European Politics and Societies* 1 (Winter 1987): 135–59, and Bill Lomax, *Hungary 1956* (London: Allison & Busby, 1976), as well as Grzegorz Ekiert, *The State Against Society: Political Crises and their Aftermath in East Central Europe* (Princeton: Princeton University Press, 1996).

the 1980s), it is important to note that despite the *overall* failure of collectivization in Poland, some branches of agricultural production in which private
production would have been "especially advantageous such as butchery, trade
in most foodstuffs and sales of inputs to peasants, were thoroughly socialized
in Poland *unlike* in other East European states. . ." Even the Soviet Union had
large private meat markets.[15]

In the context of rapid industrialization and limited collectivization, agriculture in general and private agriculture in particular became targets of
official discrimination. Socialized agriculture received insufficient investment
resources. And although the Party leadership eschewed unnecessary clashes in
this period, it still harbored the prejudices that in time would crystallize into a
view of private farmers as "ideologically retarded" and unworthy of "political
recognition": "second-rate" citizens who should be kept "deliberately in a state
of extreme insecurity."[16]

Even so, the authorities treated private agriculture much more gingerly than
other forms of private enterprise. By mid-1947, over the objections of the non-
communist minority opposition, the Sejm (lower house of the Polish parliament) passed legislation requiring all private tradesmen to register with the
state, which would decide whether to grant licences; firms doing business with
foreigners or in wholesale, for instance, were almost never granted licences and
were soon eliminated altogether. Private businesses of all kinds were subjected
to exorbitantly high taxes and end-of-year lump sums "against allegations of
unrecorded sales"; retailers often received fines and even jail sentences for selling at "speculative prices (higher than cost plus a standard profit margin)."
There was no legal recourse.

The result of these and related measures was that from 1946 to 1950, the private sector share in retail trade fell from 78 percent to 15 percent, while private
industry and handicrafts declined from 21 percent of total output to 6 percent
in the same period.[17] Between 1947 and 1953, the absolute number of non-
agricultural private enterprises declined by more than 60 percent, and employment fell even more dramatically.[18] And by the mid-1950s, private industry
(excluding handicrafts) accounted for less than 1 percent of total industrial output.[19] The upshot was a system plagued by deteriorating imbalances. On the one
hand, forced industrialization led to significant increases in national income.

---

[15] Anders Åslund, *Private Enterprise in Eastern Europe* (New York: St. Martin's Press, 1985),
47, emphasis in original. This is diametrically opposed to the Hungarian policy of permitting
private and quasi-private production of all agricultural products that required the application
of intensive labor, such as the cultivation of grapes for wine; dairy, hog, rabbit, and other meat
production; and most vegetable cultivation.

[16] Łoś, "The Dynamics of the Second Economy in Poland," in Maria Łoś, ed., *The Second Economy
in Marxist States*, 27–28, 34.

[17] John Michael Montias, *Central Planning in Poland* (New Haven: Yale University Press, 1962),
54.

[18] Åslund, *Private Enterprise in Eastern Europe*, 42, table 2.4.

[19] Montias, *Central Planning in Poland*, 82.

Between 1946 and 1950, agricultural and industrial production more than doubled. On the other hand, agriculture's share of national income declined in only four years from 70 percent to 60 percent as a result of resource reallocation away from agriculture to industry; this trend only continued more dramatically in the 1950s. Consumption's share of national income fell drastically relative to investment, and the slow growth of consumer goods production, combined with price controls, led to chronic shortages and low-quality goods.[20] Polish economists interviewed after 1956 admitted openly that planners treated consumer goods and private handicrafts as the economy's "buffer sectors." Only the crisis of 1953 – when real wages fell below the "political danger point" – forced a partial reappraisal of the policy. This occurred at the Ninth Plenum of the Polish United Workers Party's (PZPR) Central Committee in October of that year.[21] Even then, however, it was not the tiny remaining industrial private sector (the "inferior social forms") that benefited, but state firms producing consumer goods.

This timid change in policy was not Hungary's New Course of the same year: indeed, it would be misleading to conclude that 1953 in Poland brought anything like a comprehensive shift in policy, especially considering the variety of direct and indirect administrative measures the Polish party-state routinely employed in support of its prioritization of industrial investment over consumer goods and services. To mention just one: after 1952, only organizations specifically exempted from paying "retail" prices were authorized to purchase material inputs at "procurement" (wholesale) prices. This was no small distinction: from 1953 to 1955, for instance, "retail" prices could be more than five times greater than wholesale prices.[22] Even the state-controlled consumer services cooperatives, for instance, were ineligible to purchase at wholesale prices, despite the fact that in Poland as elsewhere in the state-socialist world, these cooperatives differed little in practice from state-owned firms.[23] And this is to say nothing of the meager allotments of inputs for the tiny remaining legal private sector that planners blamed for "extortions" against which they had to protect state firms – which in this case they did through the differential price system. This system simply reinforced a *status quo* in which "only state firms received quotas of materials at all commensurate with their needs." Thus, even during periods of modest loosening of plan targets for industrial development, the authorities used parametric and various administrative measures to control the production of consumer goods and, especially, services.[24]

---

[20] Ben Slay, *The Polish Economy: Crisis, Reform, and Transformation* (Princeton: Princeton University Press, 1994), 25.

[21] Aslund, *Private Enterprise in Eastern Europe*, 45.

[22] Montias, *Central Planning in Poland*, 211 n.53.

[23] That is, they differed not so much in administration but mostly in name and in some legal details of their founding constitutions. The difference was ideological: they were, of course, considered to be inferior to state-owned farms.

[24] The only private organization known to have received "special dispensation" from these rules was the "'progressive' Catholic organization *Pax*, which was supported by the regime" and

By the early 1950s, declining real wages and increasing shortages also began combining with political pressures. The population harbored a strong anti-Russian sentiment, and after the death of Stalin in 1953, pro-decentralization and democratization voices emerged in the Sejm and among the rank and file of the PUWP. Further, riots broke out in Poznán in June 1956, and workers started to elect enterprise councils and demand control over management. Amidst this spontaneous multiplication of councils, the Party brought Gomułka back to power in October 1956.

Only a year earlier, opinion among party leaders had split over the publication of Adam Wazyk's *Poem for Adults*. The reasons for the controversy are telling. The poem was penned by a communist, and appeared in an official literary journal. Moreover, the poem called on the party to heed the voice of "burning reason" and change its failed policies.[25] As if responding to this urgent call for rationality, Gomułka promptly recognized the workers' councils, shifted to an emphasis on consumer goods production, and put a formal end to agricultural collectivization. More importantly still, the Seventh Plenum of the Central Committee actually outlined the mechanisms for the "systematic transfer" of industrial management to the working class. This task was to be carried out by workers' councils.[26]

These measures seemed to enhance an already expanded structure of expectations, which Alain Touraine captures forcefully by placing it in comparative perspective:

At the end of 1956 Hungary and Poland seemed to be going in opposite directions. Hungary had been invaded, its political leaders had been imposed by the Soviet Union, and the principal figures of the revolution executed, imprisoned or forced into exile. In Poland, on the other hand, hopes were running high: the peasants had been freed from forced collectivization, the Primate had been released from prison, and the Church was no longer persecuted. The intellectuals were now free to express themselves and to maintain contacts with the West; workers' councils were active and the population in general placed great hopes in Gomułka, whose return had meant a break with Stalinism.[27]

The Polish party's commitment to workers' participation in industrial management was underscored by the state-sponsored *Economic Council*. An institutional arena for intellectual debate on the roles of the market and centralized planning, the *Council* finally produced a consensus embodied in the *Polish Theses of 1957*. Though in no way a challenge to the fundamentals of state socialism, the *Theses* nevertheless argued that "democratizing the management of the

---

"carried on certain industrial and commercial activities." Montias, *Central Planning in Poland*, 210–211.

[25] Warren Lerner, *A History of Socialism and Communism in Modern Times*, 2nd edition (Englewood Cliffs: Prentice Hall, 1994), 175.

[26] Raymond Taras, *Ideology in a Socialist State: Poland 1956–1983* (New York: Cambridge University Press, 1984), 58–59.

[27] Alain Touraine, *Solidarity: Poland 1980–81* (New York: Cambridge University Press, 1983), 26–27.

national economy [called] for the active participation of employees, workers' councils, local authorities, and Parliament in the development of the Plans."[28]

To assess the potential significance of the *Theses* and, more importantly, Gomułka's recognition of robust workers' councils, we need only think back to a crucial point in the history of U.S. business-labor relations. In 1945, the United States' National Labor Management Conference failed to carve out a zone of business decision-making that might "fall within the scope of unions' legitimate interests." The reasons for this failure throw light on Gomułka's Poland. From the American unions' perspective, the attempt at zone designation was futile at best and counterproductive at worst. As the unions' representative put it: "We cannot have one sharply delimited area designated as management prerogatives and another equally sharply defined area of union prerogatives without either side constantly attempting to invade forbidden territory, thus creating much unnecessary strife." From the vantage point of management, the attempt at zone designation was a dangerous slippery slope that was bound to end in the "joint management of enterprise." Indeed, the president of General Motors later remarked that the "union leaders" would be "running the economy of the country," and "have the deciding vote in all managerial decisions," or at least, would "exercise a veto power " that would stop "progress."[29]

Now consider Gomułka's dilemma. After having recognized the Workers' Councils, after having committed himself to the systematic transfer of industrial management to workers, and after having accepted the Economic Council's *Theses*, Gomułka was left to ponder the potential threat these concessions posed to the party's "leading role." The threat, of course, was enormous. The Party had actually accepted as the *starting point* of Polish industrial relations the very scenario that General Motors had feared as an *end point* – that is to say, "workers running the economy," or at a minimum, exercising "veto power." Put yet another way, the deal offered by Gomułka to Polish workers meant that the latter would not even have to contemplate the compromise arrangement that their American counterparts had rejected as unsustainable, because in Poland there would be no substantial territory that was "forbidden" to labor.

If in Hungary, by contrast, workers' councils would gain (lesser) powers only in 1984, in the Poland of the late 1950s, Gomułka had implicitly forfeited the state's exclusive claim to economic leadership. This was a strategic mistake he soon set out to correct. First, he made it clear that the workers' councils were neither political nor administrative entities. Lest any doubts remain, the resolutions of the Eleventh Plenum and Fourth Congress of Trade Unions emphasized the councils' subordination to the party.[30] By 1957, the councils were once again under the supervision of official trade unions. And after formally recognizing

---

[28] Bernard Chavance, *The Transformation of Communist Systems: Economic Reform Since the 1950s* (Boulder, CO: Westview Press, 1994), 37–38.

[29] David Granick, *The Red Executive: A Study of the Organization Man in Russian Industry* (Garden City, New York: Anchor Books, Doubleday & Company, Inc., 1961), 189.

[30] Taras, *Ideology in a Socialist State*, 58–59.

workers' crucial participatory role in enterprise management, the party-state proceeded to dilute the meaning of "participation," thus divesting workers of their managerial role. Taras outlines the process of divestment:

> In 1956, workers' councils constituted the chief mechanism through which such participation was channeled; in 1959, workers' self-management committees became the most important institution in workers' 'co-management' of workers' enterprises; by the mid-1960s, the trade union organization was deemed to be the most appropriate agent through which workers exerted influence; and by the late 1960s 'workers' self-management' became a more abstract (though no less emphasized) concept which referred to a conglomerate of workers' institutions through which they might participate, largely, it seemed, for participation's sake.[31]

Divestment of the right to participatory management was a grievous violation of the initial terms of state-society engagement: labor would support the party-state, and in return the party-state would recognize and respect workers' direct control over their own labor. This violation, moreover, combined with a deepening popular perception of the regime as hopelessly tied to habits of economic irrationality. The party-state, to be sure, made tactical adjustments. In the aftermath of 1956, for example, it responded to workers' demands for rationality by recruiting enterprise managers in accordance both with *nomenklatura* rules *and* standards of technical competence. But at the same time, the party-state left the strategic field unchanged. Technical staff, workers, and even managers could barely understand – let alone reshape – the opaque logic of state enterprises. Indeed, this opacity was one of the offending attributes that kept labor strategically engaged. And for good reason. Investment decisions, for instance, were acts of political obedience, and capital flowed in the direction of influential provincial and municipal officials seeking the prestige that came with such inflows.[32]

There were other signs of "untrustworthiness" and "irrationality." Between 1956 and 1970, the party leadership seemed caught in a cycle of "rather spurious" reforms of the "socialized" sector – that is to say, reforms were supposedly aimed at "limiting" central command while simultaneously "extending parametric state management."[33] The result was an accumulation of economic failures under Gomułka's leadership – failures that in 1968 led the government to declare the pursuit of individualistic ambitions "compatible" with society's welfare.[34]

---

[31] Ibid., 126.

[32] Touraine, *Solidarity: Poland 1980–81*, 94–95. Of course, here we are focusing on *perceptions* of irrationality and of broken agreements, since the *reality* was not so different in Hungary. Indeed, it was the norm in state-socialist economies. For a more detailed explanation of investment patterns in state socialism, see Kornai's *Political Economy of Socialism*, and Bartołomiej Kamiński, *The Collapse of State Socialism: The Case of Poland* (Princeton: Princeton University Press, 1991).

[33] Łoś, "The Dynamics of the Second Economy in Poland," 28.

[34] Taras, *Ideology in a Socialist State*, 60–80, 103–107.

But this declaration notwithstanding, the fact remained that state policies continued to restrict the economic opportunity structure of the citizenry far more dramatically than either political rhetoric or structural-economic factors would have suggested. By 1969, Gomułka had reversed course and embarked on a number of ambitious, strongly centralizing – even coercive – economic strategies. To be sure, some of his plans might have benefited the Polish economy overall – though if the party *apparat* had not blocked them, they certainly would have come up against the workers' considerable veto power. Gomułka targeted certain industries for "selective development" and others for decreased emphasis; he even considering closing down some shipbuilding and aviation firms and creating a large pool of unemployed workers. Such drastic measures never came to pass, of course. In the event, the party used its unions and other "administrative and managerial means to squeeze more labor out of its workers." A new wage policy cut wages and overtime, while raising work-norms. The party assiduously tried to limit absenteeism as well. All this increased the workers' frustration, and caused arguments at factory meetings. In effect, as Roman Laba put it, "the party's policy of 'broadest possible consultations' " mobilized workers throughout the country.

And in agriculture, the leadership's "particularly acute" ideological disdain for private enterprise led to a concerted attempt to "starve" the large private agricultural sector. This disdain was all the more intense, the economist Bartołomiej Kamiński insightfully points out, because collectivization was never completed.[35] At least until the late 1970s, private farmers had no access to "family allowances, health insurance, pensions, and other services reserved for ... state employees." And many private farmers lived in constant fear of expropriation, some even as late as 1983, despite the formal guarantees extended by the state in 1982 (see Chapter 4). Moreover, access to supplies, farm implements, and technical assistance was centrally controlled and sharply limited, and the district administrations (*powiaty*) distributed scarce agricultural equipment, fertilizers, and services "according to highly politicized criteria."[36]

Polish agriculture – once the breadbasket of Europe – declined to the point that the country became a net food importer. This decline looked all the worse in comparison with the success of Hungarian agriculture. By the 1970s, Hungary exported in excess of one-third of its agricultural output; and by the mid 1980s its *per capita* production value was the highest among the Council for Mutual

---

[35] Kamiński, *The Collapse of State Socialism*, 93 n. 24.
[36] Wiesława Surazska, "Between Centre and Province. The Pendulum of Power in Communist Poland: 1944–1989 (unpublished doctoral dissertation, Oxford: Wolfson College, Oxford University, 1990), 101–102; 163–165. Private farmers' access to fertilizers, technical assistance, machinery, and so on was under the exclusive control of the so-called Agricultural Circles, which in turn were controlled from above by the *powiat* authorities (which were strengthened at the VIIIth Central Committee Plenum in 1961). The Party's long-term goal was to force small farms to enter collectives, and although it was unable to achieve these "doctrinal ends ... neither were the peasants given opportunities to develop their private farms."

Economic Assistance (CMEA, aka COMECON) countries. In Europe as a whole, it was second only to Denmark's.[37] By contrast, in Poland – where nearly half of workers' income was spent on food[38] – increases in food prices led to dramatic waves of workers' strikes in Gdańsk, Gdynia, and Szczezein during 1970 and 1971. The party responded with brutal repression, using 61,000 soldiers in over 100 operations to massacre scores of protesters.[39] All of this culminated in a deep crisis, during which the ailing and discredited Gomułka was replaced by Edward Gierek.

The Second Phase: The Politics of Unity

Following the crisis, and in response to workers' demands, the government made several "concessions" on paper. These, however, were so vague as to be virtually worthless. Just as workers in the Warski Shipyard in Szczecin were about to strike again, Gierek

> addressed the nation and presented himself as a new kind of chief executive, one promising sweeping reforms. He not only promised consultation with the working class and intellectuals, but also asserted that ill-considered policies would be reversed with immediate financial compensation for the least well-off, and for working women.[40]

Over the next several days another twenty five factories stopped work, but Gierek's promises broke the strike in the Warski Shipyard. Nevertheless, throughout January 1971, a "rolling wave of strikes buffeted the entire coast," especially after the police beat a Warski worker to death, on Christmas Day. So important was the appearance of serious "consultation" with workers that Gierek authorized a "demand-gathering campaign." But as Laba points out, this campaign

> succeeded merely in affording workers an opportunity to reflect on the state of Poland. Despite the constraints implicit in public discussions conducted under the close supervision of the party . . . a wide-ranging debate and discussion now went on in the factory shops.[41]

What happened next gave the lie to Western governments that at the time mistakenly saw the Gierek regime as more liberal than other East European regimes or previous Polish ones. Even in contemporary accounts and academic discussions, Gierek is sometimes portrayed as a clever technocrat who, given

---

[37] Ferenc Donáth,"Hungarian Agriculture: Achievements and Problems," *Journal of Rural Cooperation* XIV, no. 1 (Budapest, 1986): 4–5.
[38] Laba, *The Roots of Solidarity*, 18.
[39] Ibid., 71.
[40] Ibid., 76.
[41] Ibid., 79.

more time, would have modernized Poland's economy much sooner.[42] In fact, Gierek was "contemptuous of workers . . . and under a veneer of technocratic competence and prosperity based on Western loans, party politics in Poland continued as before."[43] If Gierek differed at all from other Communist rulers, it was in the depths of deception he practiced with workers.

The events at the Warski Shipyard are an example. When he undertook a campaign to increase productivity, Gierek toured factories across the country in a bid for support from workers. As Laba explains, this was

. . . a reprise of an exotic custom found in socialist countries . . . voluntary compulsion. In such a campaign, the party leadership, having increased production targets without increasing capital or labor, would gather workers in selected plants and pressure them to pledge voluntary overtime. A normal dictatorship would have issued orders to work. A socialist dictatorship wanted workers to say they agreed wholeheartedly.[44]

The government managed to extract such pledges from workers, including Wałęsa in Gdańsk, but not from the Warski shipyard, which would have been a "large trophy," as Laba puts it, for the government to show in the media, which was daily trumpeting the production campaign. Receiving no cooperation, the government sent the state radio and TV to the factory, and

in an empty meeting hall decorated with banners and posters supporting the voluntary overtime campaign, technicians filmed a handful of party activists who pledged that the thousand workers of Shop W-4 would work that Sunday . . . That night the Warski workers, to their utter bewilderment, saw themselves on national television cheering for Gierek and promising to work the following Sunday. The government had spliced old footage of a festive meeting in the shipyard from three years before with footage of the banner and party activists. In this surrealistic fashion, the most combative and irreconcilable workers in Poland saw themselves cheering for Gierek on national television at the very moment they were agitating for a strike.[45]

This time, the party managed to placate the workers of Szczecin and Gdańsk with patriotic appeals. But it was facing continued strikes among the textile workers of Łodz in central Poland. When party officials traveled there to attempt the same appeals that had worked on the Baltic coast, they met with a large assembly of strikers. It was the women of Łodz who refused to allow the focus to be shifted away from the price increases, and would not give in. Finally the government had to rescind the price increases that had started the December 1970 wave of strikes. In February 1971, food prices returned to their levels of mid-December 1970.[46]

---

[42] Adam Przeworski, for instance, in public discussion after a presentation at Princeton University in 1993, insisted that if Poland had only continued with Gierek's economic policies of the 1970s, it would have become a classical export-led economy.

[43] Laba, *The Roots of Solidarity*, 80.

[44] Ibid., 79.

[45] Ibid., 80.

[46] Ibid., 80–82.

The Gierek period, then, was not about innovative reforms. Rather, its real significance lay in the political elite's renunciation of "the principle of economic disinterestedness." Specifically, whereas Gomułka had consistently demanded political loyalty on the principle that power is its own reward and that no substantial economic reward was necessary,[47] the Gierek leadership actually embraced political-ideological *pragmatism* as a central "value."[48]

As in Hungary, Polish pragmatism was tied to a "realism" that was itself anchored in tactical adaptations of Marxism-Leninism. But if in Hungary pragmatic realism provided a coherent value scale in which dogma was demoted to make room for developmental success, in Poland, official pragmatism amounted to little more than an instrumental amalgamation of ideological and developmental objectives. In effect, dogma retained its high ranking, even as it came to be seen as an instrument for the promotion of economic development.[49]

The short-term benefits of this new view were obvious to the leadership. The party-state, for example, could now take the position that while materialistic values had to be eliminated, material rewards for "people of good work" were not only acceptable but desirable.[50] Thus the state could set its own particular standards of "good work" and, on this basis, could also introduce and enforce incentive differentials. The costs of such instrumentalism, though less obvious than its benefits, were perhaps even more crucial. By proclaiming the "inseparability" of material and moral motivations,[51] the party-state created a kind of moral instrumentalism in both rhetoric and practice. This meant that it had to reward citizens' contribution to the nation's welfare with tangible benefits. And, in fact, Gierek gave Poles the most liberal travel policy in the bloc after Yugoslavia's. He also allowed a flourishing dollar economy, developed through energetic economic tourism, and along with it, a growing hidden economy of "alternative employment."[52] (It was also "technically possible" to open a private business, but the administrative requirements were onerous and permission was granted rarely and erratically.)[53] Even managers of state firms could often earn more through illegal transactions in foreign currency than through their enterprise positions.

But moral instrumentalism was also accompanied by the displacement of the discourse of class struggle, and by the concomitant emergence of a corporatist,

---

[47] Jacek Kurczewski, "Poland's Seven Middle Classes," *Social Research* 61 (Summer 1994): 401.

[48] Taras, *Ideology in a Socialist State*, 120. For a more general assessment of the Gierek period, see Abraham Brumberg, *Poland: The Genesis of a Revolution* (New York: Vintage, 1983).

[49] Taras, *Ideology in a Socialist State*, 121–124. In this respect, Poland resembled its more orthodox state-socialist counterparts than Hungary.

[50] Ibid.

[51] Ibid.

[52] Kurczewski, "Poland's Seven Middle Classes," 401–402.

[53] If in a particular area, the need for a given service or good was extremely pressing, permission might be granted (and just as easily taken away later); there were also cases that would be hard to explain except as acts of political expediency: a dissident from 1956, for example, who was allowed to open a restaurant after he came out of hiding in hopes that he would abandon politics. Tomasz Charańzkinski, author's interview, Warsaw, December 1995.

almost organic discursive theme: the "moral-political unity of the nation."[54] This emphasis on the nation's moral-political unity privileged the value of social harmony while leaving the party's leading role intact. By declaring himself a "friend of the common man," Gierek accentuated the solidaristic strain of the new official discourse. Thus Gierek agreed to hold prices constant for a five-year period in exchange for a cessation of factory strikes, and his "New Development Strategy" stressed consumerism and "international integration" through the importation of Western investment goods (to be financed largely by debt).[55]

Both the sustainability of frozen prices and the success of the New Development Strategy, however, hinged on a reform plan aimed at transforming state firms into modern, efficient "socialist corporations." This was the 1973–75 WOG program – *wielka organizacja gospodarcza*, or "large economic organization" – Poland's putative answer to Hungary's 1968 New Economic Mechanism (NEM). The Party technocrats who designed the reform intended to replace the center's direct control of firms with "indirect financial instruments" (which, as we saw in Chapter 2, was one result of Hungary's NEM, though not, in fact, its stated goal). In institutional terms, this was to have been achieved through a major administrative and bureaucratic reorganization that lessened the power of industrial ministries and subordinated groups of state enterprises to the WOGs instead. In the context of the WOG's new incentives (for example, limited permission to set new product prices and to retain profits), these managing organizations would presumably treat the enterprises as "divisions within a large corporation."[56]

The party-state's emphatic praise of industrial efficiency and its open quest for modernization proved compelling to Western lenders. (The latter liberally financed Poland's burst of investment without understanding that in state-socialist systems, most large investment projects were driven not by any clear economic rationale but by a combination of bids for political prestige and firms' attempts to integrate vertically in order to control resources in shortage economies.)[57] But for all the short-term stimulating impact of capital inflows on production and consumption, the WOG initiative remained fatally flawed in two ways. First, it was acutely vulnerable to resistance among branch ministries. Second, it was plagued by the inherent contradiction between a decentralizing mandate and "increased organizational concentration."[58] In fact, Gierek now emphasized the shipbuilding and aviation behemoths that Gomułka had tried to curb. In addition, he supported the construction of the new Katowice Steelworks – yet another politically showy but economically

---

[54] Slay, *The Polish Economy*, 36–37.
[55] Ibid.
[56] Slay, *The Polish Economy*, 38–39.
[57] See Kornai on the strong incentives built into state-socialist systems to allocate investment goods to highly visible and politically prestigious projects, as well as on the more general phenomenon of "investment hunger." Kornai 1992, chapter 9.
[58] Slay, *The Polish Economy*, 38–39.

irrational investment.[59] The result was rampant institutional incoherence and a patent failure to increase industrial output, both of which unleashed a vicious cycle of rising trade deficits, mounting foreign debt, drastic cuts in capital investment, and abandoned industrial projects. Meanwhile, agricultural production continued its seemingly inexorable decline, and the combination of price freezes and wage expansion engendered inflationary pressures. With no alternatives left, the leadership resorted in 1976 to "economic streamlining": a strategy that relied on "improved cost efficiency through a decrease in subsidies and an increase in prices."[60]

The streamlining strategy not only shredded the party-state's proclaimed ties of solidarity with society, it also highlighted its growing ideological incoherence and, by extension, its inability to carry out the mission attached to its self-proclaimed identity as guardian of the nation's moral-political unity. Indeed, years before this policy reversal, Gierek's moral instrumentalism – originally intended to satisfy functional as well as ideological exigencies – had begun to reveal serious internal contradictions. To begin with, the speculative character of the informal dollar economy and the hidden economy's lack of cooperative institutional linkages with the state sector closed off the kinds of entrepreneurial activities that, by generating new economic opportunities, could have significantly broadened the scope of upward mobility among the citizenry, and allowed the credit for such opportunities to accrue to the government. Yet those with the right skills and connections did enrich themselves through the informal economy, and income inequalities were suddenly highly visible. They were also beyond the party-state's direct control. And they came at a time – the early 1970s – when 80 percent of Poles associated a "good social system" with the provision of "equal chances" for the general population.[61] This association had not changed much by the late 1970s, when, due partly to a shortage of foreign currency, the government permitted foreigners of Polish descent to establish firms or joint ventures with state firms. Known as *Polonia* firms, these firms and the obvious income inequalities they promoted became a "real source of hostility" toward the government.[62]

Beyond the resultant inequities within society, moral instrumentalism also caused a direct alienation between state and society, as it became increasingly obvious that the leadership would set the limits of moral instrumentalism arbitrarily. This was most apparent in agricultural policy. In 1972, for example, Gierek responded to civil strife over living standards by finally putting an end, at

---

[59] Laba, *The Roots of Solidarity*, 93.

[60] Jack Bielasiak, "Poland," in Sabrina P. Ramet, ed., *Eastern Europe: Politics, Culture, and Society Since 1939* (Bloomington: Indiana University Press, 1998), 139.

[61] Raymond Taras, *Consolidating Democracy in Poland* (Boulder, CO: Westview Press, 1995), 85.

[62] This resentment only grew later in the 1980s when the small number of *Polonia* firms increased as Jaruzelski's government lifted the nationality restriction and "liberalized laws regarding size and field of operation." Andrzej Bloch, "The Private Sector in Poland," *Telos* 66 (Winter 1985–86): 128–133.

least nominally, to compulsory deliveries in agriculture[63] and allowing "minor expansion" of the legal private sector in services and trade. These measures, in turn, resulted in rapid increases in private farm production of goods for market (up 30 percent between 1971 and 1973). Meat production, in particular, rose in a five-year period "by as much as it had . . . over the previous twenty years."[64] But despite its success, Gierek moved in 1975 to *reverse* this more lenient policy toward agriculture and toward the second economy as a whole: he closed the land market again, and began an "unpublicized" collectivization campaign that led to a 10 percent loss of privately held agricultural land by 1980.[65]

Had the success of private Polish agriculture during this brief "golden period" been allowed to continue, it would have increased pressure on the government to extend long-term loans and to "mobilize supply industries (particularly to provide small-scale equipment) and food processing industries." In essence, growing private-sector success would have siphoned off resources from the state sector and created an additional "obstacle to direct State ownership of agriculture in the future."[66] Such an outcome was intolerable. The reform was reversed.

Frozen since 1971, food prices were hiked in 1976. As in 1970, workers retaliated with hundreds of strikes all across Poland. Workers also relearned an old historical lesson. As in 1956, they learned again not to trust the party-state's "promises of reform."[67] If anything, they now expected the party-state to act not only as an unreliable agent of reform, but as an arbitrary task-master. Hence the severity of the 1976 strikes and riots, which forced the authorities quickly to rescind the price increases. To be sure, the party would soon attempt to liberate itself from the veto power of extrinsic actors, launching a campaign of targeted reprisals in the form of "dismissals, arrests, and trials" against activists involved in the 1976 events.[68] In fact, it was the brutality of the party's reprisals that gave rise to a novel development: the state now came up against a variety of social groups prepared to rally around the workers' self-vindicating agenda. Most significantly, opposition intellectuals in Warsaw formed KOR (*Komitet Obrony Robotnikow*, the Committee for the Defense of the Workers) to help with medical and legal assistance for the victims and their families.

---

[63] Although compulsory deliveries came to an end (in all but milk products), the administrative measures put in their place amounted to coercion by other means. Jean-Charles Szurek, "Family Farms in Polish Agricultural Policy (1945–1985)," paper presented at the conference on "The Effects of Communism on Social and Economic Change: Eastern Europe in Comparative Perspective," Bologna, June 23–28, 1986.

[64] Szurek, "Family Farms," 22–23.

[65] Ibid. For a description of several other administrative means the state used to discriminate against and limit private agriculture, see also Bloch, "The Private Sector in Poland," 129.

[66] Szurek, "Family Farms," 23–24.

[67] Gale Stokes, *Three Eras of Political Change in Eastern Europe* (New York: Oxford University Press, 1997), 169

[68] Jack Bielasiak, "Poland," in Ramet, *Eastern Europe: Politics, Culture, and Society Since 1939*, 135.

There were several reasons for the focalization of societal energies around the workers' movement. First was the depth of consumer discontent. The party-state's "policy of deliberate neglect" of agriculture resulted in serious shortages of food.[69] These had become chronic by the late 1970s, and together with the low efficiency of industry in general and the balance of payments crisis in particular, they created a full-blown economic disaster. In the context of an economy now rife with shortages of consumer goods and saddled with an onerous foreign debt, workers were the one group capable of exercising veto power over state policy. Indeed, caught in a structural bind common to all state-socialist systems, the Polish party-state, unlike most others,[70] had often *publicly* yielded to this veto power, thus informally institutionalizing a contentious mechanism for political bargaining. (Hungarian leaders yielded too, but tacitly, in their prioritization of consumer goods and treatment of the private and quasi-private enterprise.) Second, even when workers were not demanding vindication of labor's old claim to participatory management, society still perceived vindication of this claim as a plausible solution to the "irrationality " of the party-state's economic policies. Third, participatory management could address the party-state's credibility deficit by formally incorporating labor as an honorable voice in the conduct of affairs that affected the entire Republic. Fourth, by 1976, the party-state's commitment to the nation's "moral-political unity" had been so discredited that dissident groups could actually transpose the official discourse of moral instrumentalism. Specifically, dissidents could invert the party-state's self-image as the architect of organic welfare by rendering it as a thoroughly destructive force, and just as importantly, dissidents could readily avail themselves of a natural protagonist for the collective drama of moral outrage. In a word, they could turn to the workers.

This was a momentous political-discursive shift. Dissident intellectuals had previously operated in a grey strategic zone from which workers in particular, and society more broadly, were missing. For dissident intellectuals, the party-state was both presumptive interlocutor – their partner in dialogue – and a target for "normative suasion." Simply put, dissident intellectuals had traditionally aimed to "chastise" the authorities into addressing a series of "grievances." In 1965, for example, two graduate students at the University of Warsaw – Jacek Kuroń and Karol Modzelewski – submitted their argument in favor of worker-managed socialism not to the workers or peasants but to official power-holders. The title of their reformist essay – "Open Letter to the Party" – succinctly illustrates this crucial point.[71]

---

[69] Bloch, "The Private Sector in Poland," 130.

[70] Yugoslavia is the exception, since there firms were managed by workers, and a different dynamic prevailed. Susan Woodward, *Socialist Unemployment: The Political Economy of Yugoslavia, 1945–1990* (Princeton: Princeton University Press, 1995)

[71] Michael Bernhard, "Civil Society and Democratic Transition in East Central Europe," in *Political Science Quarterly* 108, no. 2 (Summer 1993): 307–326. Kuroń and Modzelewski argued from a Marxist perspective for a true revolution of the working class and for workers' councils to "set the goals of social production." They wrote, further, that "only the workers sense the need

It would not be until the 1970s, after years of state unresponsiveness to dissident voices and after the 1968 repression of intellectuals and students demanding democratic reform, that intellectuals moved from dissidence to opposition. This is not to say that early dissidents risked less: Kuroń and Modzelewski went to prison for that essay. Like the workers, Kuroń – who twenty five years later would become Labor Minister, and Modzelewski, who became a member of Parliament in the first post-communist government – highlighted the need for rationalization through workers' councils that would manage factories and oversee the plan.

This was the thread that connected all the episodes of opposition in Poland and brought dissidents a step closer to the workers. Rather than telling the "party-state authorities how to act," dissident intellectuals now looked to society "as the basis for resistance."[72] But even this opposition strategy remained rooted in Leszek Kolakowski's hope for a "reformist" line of action, meaning "a belief in the possibility of effective, gradual, and partial pressures, exercised within the framework of a long-term perspective of social and national liberation."[73] Hence the strategic vision of "The New Evolutionism" advanced by Jacek Kuroń and Adam Michnik:

> Such a programme of evolution should be addressed to independent public opinion and not just to the totalitarian authorities. Instead of acting as a prompter to the government, telling it how to improve itself, this programme should tell society how to act. As far as the government is concerned, it can have no clearer counsel than that provided by social pressure from below.[74]

The massive firings and selective criminal proceedings that followed the 1976 strikes accelerated the evolutionists' proposed shift in orientation toward "society." Intellectuals and professionals created the Committee for the Defense of Workers (KOR) for the specific purpose of providing accused workers and their families with financial and legal assistance. Despite taking the risky step of "ostentatiously publishing the names, addresses and telephone numbers of the founding members,"[75] KOR not only survived but fostered cooperative relations between workers and intellectuals. Moreover, in 1977, KOR expanded its scope of action and changed its name to Committee for Social Self-Defense: KOR-KSS. Soon thereafter, other dissident organizations began to

---

for abolishing the bureaucracy." Michael Bernhard, *The Origins of Democratization in Poland* (New York: Columbia University Press, 1993), 112–113.

[72] Bernhard, "Civil Society and Democratic Transition in East Central Europe," 307–326.

[73] Ibid.

[74] Ibid.

[75] Sarah Terry, "June 1976," in Jane Curry and Luba Fajfer, eds., *Poland's Permanent Revolution: People vs. Elites, 1956–1990* (Washington D.C.: The American University Press, 1996), 133. One reason for this was that the founding members of KOR wanted workers and others who were arrested to be able to call them or tell others to do so. It was not uncommon, as the security police were arresting someone, that he would shout at open windows or to anyone on the street who might hear: "Call Kuroń: tell him they've taken me!" Jacek Kuroń, author's interview, Princeton, September 1996.

emerge – most notably the Movement for the Defense of Human and Civil Rights (ROPCiO, *Ruch Obrony Praw Czlowieka i Obywatela*), the Confederation of Independent Poland (KPN), and various Catholic and student associations, as well as the "Flying University" (TKN, *Towarzystwo Kursow Nankowych*).[76]

The second political-discursive shift occurred with the opposition's rhetorical inversion of the official organicist theme. Precisely because the party had exalted the nation's moral-political unity, now the opposition proceeded to seek social unity against the party by emphasizing its destructive bent. Consider KOR's 1978 "appeal" to society. In this rallying cry for a united society, the organized opposition depicted the state as an arbitrary, deceitful power-holder whose policies threatened every aspect of the Republic's life. To render this terrifying specter credible, however, KOR had to meet several rhetorical objectives. The first was to unmask the party-state's duplicity. Here, KOR claimed that the party-state was engaged in a deliberate attempt to dupe society on the matter of price increases by "hiding" upward trends under cover of new labels and dubious official data. The second objective was to show the extent of the damage inflicted on society by the party-state. Here, all KOR had to do was recite a litany of obvious grievances. Meat was not only scarce, but the logic of meat rationing was unclear; health services and housing were both shamefully inadequate.[77] Finally, KOR would have to establish the fact that state policies were both widely harmful and grievously offensive to the principle of unity. To do so, KOR highlighted three fundamental contradictions.

The first contradiction had to do with the integrity of a self-declared workers' state. Simply put, workers in this workers' state were actually the first victims of economic irrationality because the authorities sought not to correct the economic "disorganization" they had brought to the Republic but merely to compensate for it by intensifying the "exploitation" of workers.

The second contradiction related to the systematization of inequality by a self-declared egalitarian state. KOR depicted a society in which "earnings [were] overly differentiated without much regard for qualifications," a society, moreover, in which the politically powerful had managed to establish an exclusive "system of privileges." Worse yet, this system of privileges was taking on alarming features: in a context of material scarcity, said KOR, the beneficiaries were reduced to an ever smaller minority; and in a context of politicized allocation, benefits were becoming inheritable.

The third and final contradiction referred to the deleterious effects of the "usurpation" of party-power. Free from restraints and accountable to no one, the leadership could implement the discriminatory agricultural policies that were leading to "the destruction of family farming;" allow "violations of the

---

[76] Bielasiak, "Poland," in Ramet, *Eastern Europe: Politics, Culture, and Society Since 1939*, 135.
[77] "KOR's Appeal to Society," October 10, 1978, in Stokes, ed., *From Stalinism to Pluralism*, 194–95.

rule of law" by police and security service; and indulge in the "preventive censorship" that put Polish science and culture in peril.[78]

KOR's dissection of the party-state's arbitrariness – and of the threat such arbitrariness posed to the whole of Polish society – dismantled and then transposed Gierek's avowed commitment to the nation's "moral-political unity." But in constructing this discursive negation of the party-state's commitment to unity, KOR did more. It effectively established a practical dichotomy. On one side stood the party-state with its irrational policies. On the other side stood a viable alternative – a program of radical reform unimpeded by official trade unions in "blind" compliance with the party-state's directives.[79] Stated positively, *the viability of radical reform was once again perceived as hinging on the autonomy of workers.*

This last requisite was fulfilled that same year of 1978 when the first committee of free trade unions was formed at Katowice: the workers of Gdańsk – Lech Wałęsa among them – founded their Free Trade Union. The founding's context was by now familiar. Predictably, official trade unions failed to represent effectively the workers' interests,[80] while the party-state's "irrational" industrial and agricultural policies led to constant shortages that hit workers particularly hard. Even groups of workers that were relatively better off, such as the miners, felt "exploited," and "denounced the spuriousness of official figures and mistakes in investment and planning."[81]

Meanwhile, farmers, angered by the government's new pension scheme, which they "perceived as little short of confiscation of their land," and also by the "manner of its adoption (featuring a media campaign and 'consultations' that glossed over its onerous financial implications), provided the catalyst for a rural opposition movement . . . the nucleus for the Rural Solidarity Movement that would emerge in 1980–81."[82] Since by 1980, more than a quarter of the labor force was engaged in private farming, this was a significant potential challenge to the state.

All the pieces were now in place for a broad, *political* response from society to the next "attack" from the party-state. This came in July of 1980, when the government increased meat prices. August saw several major occupation strikes on the Baltic coast and the formation of an inter-factory strike committee in Gdańsk and Szczecin, which set forth a list of demands. The strikes spread to

---

[78] "KOR's Appeal to Society," 196.

[79] "KOR's Appeal to Society," 199.

[80] The Central Council of Trade Unions (CRZZ) sought to benefit workers by influencing decisions concerning, among other things, bonuses and fringe benefits, but it could not negotiate wage claims with state enterprises. And although the CRZZ unions could protect workers against charges of low productivity and absenteeism, they could not shield strikers from official retaliation. The fact that Solidarity had nearly 10 million members very soon after its creation was further proof that the CRZZ had failed to champion the workers' interests effectively. Taras, *Consolidating Democracy in Poland*, 62.

[81] Touraine, *Solidarity: Poland 1980–81*, 32.

[82] Terry, "June 1976," 135.

other cities, which extended their support for the Gdańsk and Szczecin strike committees.

Interestingly enough, workers did not initially call for plant-based representation. Instead, they pressed for a reallocation of resources from heavy industry to consumer goods. But soon the unions' factory committees began demanding control over managerial decisions. This was 1956 with a twist.

Gdańsk: 1956 Revisited

To appreciate the degree to which this new critical juncture was a complicated extension of 1956 – and of course, of 1970–71 and 1976 – consider the premise, the stakes, and the formal outcome of the 1980 negotiations between striking workers and the party-state.[83] Both parties to the negotiation acted on the assumption that they were "condemned to get on together" in order to avoid the Hungarian catastrophe of 1956.[84] Hence the workers' recognition of (a) the PUWP's "leading role," and (b) the "existing systems of international alliances." Nevertheless, the negotiations yielded state concessions that exceeded expectations within the non-negotiable parameters of realpolitik. Notably, by late September, the Warsaw Provincial Court was already starting to register new labor unions, and as a million or more workers in approximately 800 factories continued to strike, the party replaced Gierek with Stanisław Kania. More importantly, the logic workers used to extract and justify such concessions flowed directly from the grievances that the Gomułka regime left outstanding and its successor Gierek aggravated.

The Gdańsk agreement, to begin with, tied the "necessity" for independent trade unions to the "failure" of official trade unions, which had proved either unwilling or incapable of defending the "social and material interests" of workers. Though leveled at the official trade unions, the charge was also an implicit but unmistakable indictment of Gomułka's divestment strategy. Indeed, the fact that the Gdańsk agreement left open the possibility for "cooperation" between the new independent trade unions and their official counterparts only underscored what might have been if in 1957 the party leadership had honored its commitment to the principle of workers' self-management. So too did the fact that the new unions now agreed not to play the role of a political party, and to respect the socialization of the means of production. In so doing, they underscored the point that workers remained focused on the very same role they had secured for themselves in 1956, and which Gomułka had subsequently vitiated.

The shadow of 1956, in fact, loomed large throughout the entire Gdańsk agreement. The effective exercise of the trade union's role meant that the new unions, as was also stipulated in the agreement, would be able to participate in decision-making processes relating to the "conditions of the workers": to have

---

[83] The signatories were a government commission and workers' representatives from Gdańsk and Szczecin.

[84] Touraine, *Solidarity: Poland 1980–81*, 67.

a voice in matters ranging from the division of national assets between consumption and accumulation to the setting of wage and price policies; from the allocation of investment resources to the economic plan itself.[85] Here, workers were actually formalizing the structure of expectations that had emerged in 1956 and which they had kept alive since then.

At the same time, however, common sense dictated that the fulfillment of these expectations now required guarantees aimed at addressing the long-standing grievances that flowed from those unmet expectations. The recurrent demand for economic rationality, for example, partly accounts for the stipulated creation of a "research center" under the enterprise committee: a research center whose general mission, the Gdańsk agreement stated, would be to conduct "objective analysis" of workers' and employees' conditions. Similarly, mistrust of the party-state helps explain some of the center's more specific tasks, such as providing the "information" and "expertise" necessary for the crafting of price and wage policies. And, of course, the perception of an "arbitrary" party-state reinforced the need to codify the right to strike as part of a new trade-union law, which the Sejm passed in October.[86]

The Gdańsk agreement provided for this, too. The agreement, however, could not solve everything. Most ironically, at this new critical juncture, the agreement could not solve the contradiction inherent in its own terms. For how could workers remain apolitical if they now held the fate of society in their hands? How could they have a say in the uses of national assets or price policy and not affect their fellow citizens? Indeed, could workers claim that the party-state's incapacity to manage the economy threatened their survival and not claim that it threatened Poland as a whole?[87] Finally, how could workers, or any other group for that matter, ignore the terrifying argument – so vividly articulated by opposition intellectuals – that the party-state was as thoroughly destructive as it was irrational?

Conclusion

Scholars of Polish state socialism have generally acknowledged that the crisis of the late 1970s, which culminated in the eruption of Solidarity onto the national scene, stemmed from a broadening process of economic, political, ideological, and even "spiritual" decay of the-party state.[88] The foregoing analysis adds a dimension to our understanding of the unlikely, often tortured, yet undeniably transformative socio-political reconstruction that occurred alongside – indeed helped bring about – the party-state's "decay." The well-known events of 1980–81 understandably captured the imagination of scholars, journalists,

---

[85] "The Gdańsk Agreement," August 31, 1980, in Stokes, ed., *From Stalinism to Pluralism*, 205–208.

[86] Ibid., 205–206.

[87] Touraine, *Solidarity: Poland 1980–81*, 90–91.

[88] Ekiert, *The State Against Society*, 227–229.

and observers the world over. But the transformative process that gave rise to Solidarity actually centered on the 1956 structure of expectations. This transformation proceeded in two phases, each characterized by political-discursive contestation over the meaning and practice of economic rationality.

The first phase, corresponding to the Gomułka era, witnessed the following dynamic. On the one hand, the party-state's incapacity to transcend ideological dogma led to official policies that simultaneously produced severe material hardship and divested workers of their right to participate in the economic determination of the Republic. On the other hand, workers redeployed the political-discursive theme of economic rationality in order both to buttress their *de facto* veto power over state economic policy and to voice grievances rooted in the party-state's violation of the 1956 agreements.

The second phase, corresponding to the Gierek years, built directly on the experiences of the first. The party-state leadership sought a more pragmatic statecraft by applying the logic of moral instrumentalism to the pursuit of organic national unity. This move, however, proved counterproductive precisely because the internal contradictions of moral instrumentalism seemed to erode rather than foment harmony among the citizens of the Republic. Indeed, dissident intellectuals exploited this official failure in order to transform the regime's political discourse into its own riposte. Specifically, by assembling a vision of the state as broadly and inexorably destructive, intellectuals appealed successfully both to the normative sensibilities and the rational fears of diverse social groups, thus rallying potential opposition forces around the workers movement.

The upshot of all this was the emergence of Poland's defining hybrid institution, Solidarity: the Independent Self-Governing Trade Union (NSZZ), officially registered by the Supreme Court on November 10, 1980. At once a labor union and a social movement, Solidarity enabled Polish citizens to reclaim in unison the promises of 1956, which the party had so often cynically repeated to workers in the 1970s. The compound yet cohesive character of Solidarity now shifted power relations sufficiently to force the party-state to engage with society's representatives on the political plane.

4

Poland

From Solidarity to 1989

> The question at the center of intellectual life in the last thirty six years is discourse.
>
> *Magyar Fuzetele*, 1981

> We ought not to allow our language to turn into a litany of fixed formulations, for frozen language leads to frozen thought.
>
> Alfred G. Meyer, 1960

The second economy in Poland, as we just saw, is best understood as having been divided into two large islands, whereas in Hungary it increasingly resembled a pyramid at whose center were a variety of informal and – increasingly – formal institutional links with the state sector.[1] The metaphor of separate islands would have appealed to Poland's great classical sociologist, Stefan Nowak, who understood *all* of Polish society analogously. For him, the family and its immediate social circle were pitted against the communist state; in between was an enormous "social vacuum."[2] But in fact, during the 1980s especially, a richly complex civil-social sphere emerged in Poland. If in Hungary by the early 1980s we see a dense institutional landscape in the economic sphere, in Poland we see a proliferation of voluntary associations, particularly after Jaruzelski's military coup at the end of 1981.

---

[1] Of course, even if the institutional links were largely missing, there were other kinds of connections between the informal economy and the Party in Poland. These involved mostly the families of *nomenklatura* who, as Poznański noted, provided a "convenient camouflage for 'second economy' activities steered by party members themselves." Kazimierz Poznański, "Institutional Perspectives on Postcommunist Recession in Eastern Europe," in Poznański, ed., *The Evolutionary Transition to Capitalism* (Boulder, CO: Westview 1995), 12. Anecdotal evidence suggests that such links were also common in Hungary, although for those interested in running real businesses, they became increasingly unnecessary as legal possibilities for private enterprise evolved.

[2] For a useful summary and critique of Nowak's model, see Janine Wedel, ed., *The Unplanned Society: Poland During and After Communism* (New York: Columbia University Press, 1992), 9–15.

By the mid-1980s, these associations constituted an incipient civil society. Already, just two weeks after martial law was imposed, the Committees for Social Resistance (KOS) emerged. A dizzying array of informal activities soon proliferated. There were sophisticated underground publishing houses supported by a range of sources, from Solidarity members' contributions and proceeds from the sale of books, stamps, and even stickers, to donations from Western organizations. There were also more quirky organizations, such as the private chimney-cleaning company established by journalists who were also alpinists.[3]

A kind of syncretic creativity went into the construction of these civil networks of trust. By 1986, there was even an insurance fund for underground publishers. Created to assist those who were the subject of police brutality, or whose publications and equipment were confiscated, the fund nevertheless drew on the experience and know-how of Western insurance companies, so that by design, it was an ingenious blend of communitarian loyalty and capitalist spirit. The fund, for example, set premiums on the basis of each organization's "safety record" – meaning "the frequency of police related accidents in the past."[4]

Civil networks of trust, moreover, were supple enough to allow for adaptive redirection. By the end of the 1980s, many Poles began to abandon involvement in explicitly political affairs, refocusing their energies on the task of "reclaiming control of their lives in business, housing, education and the environment." Both in the second economy, and especially in the sphere of social activism, hundreds requested, and some obtained, government registration so that they were able to organize and conduct their operations in the light of day.[5]

Chapter 3 demonstrated that workers' opposition in Poland arose, in the first instance, from the party-state's betrayal of the expectations to which it gave rise in 1956. This chapter makes two additional but closely related arguments. First, by the late 1970s, both the party-state and labor unions were attempting, yet again, to solve the stalemate by now embedded in the system's points of permeable contact. Workers at times sought to achieve this goal by offering compromise and cooperation in the factory in exchange for a measure of inclusion in matters of economic policymaking, and the party-state, for its part, tried its hand occasionally at a sort of moral suasion. But in the end, the party-state failed at this too, and resorted to repression, whereas workers and intellectuals succeeded at *jointly* creating an opposition discourse, which, endowed with both political clarity and flexibility, could bring together disparate societal forces. Thus, as Hungarian reformist officials began to explore a radical property-rights reform, in Poland the distinction between "us" and

---

[3] Marta Toch (pen name), *Reinventing Civil Society: Poland's Quiet Revolution 1981–1986* (New York: U.S. Helsinki Watch Committee, 1986), 25. See also Piotr Gliński, "Acapulco Near Konstancin," in Wedel, ed., *The Unplanned Society*.
[4] Toch, *Reinventing Civil Society*, 65.
[5] Wedel, ed., *The Unplanned Society*, 11.

"them" was becoming the central referent of political discourse.[6] And whereas in Hungary the party-state and society engaged in a continual, albeit at times tacit, renegotiation of their consumerist pact, much of Polish society now stood explicitly in direct opposition to the communist authorities.[7]

From this oppositional stance, workers would mount strikes, then bargain with the state. And from this opposition-driven bargaining, strategically unsustainable compromises emerged. This did not preclude the effective tactical use of such compromises, however. Indeed, it was precisely in order to exploit the *legal* opportunities generated by specific bargains that intellectuals insisted on a relatively flexible political attitude that might temper the discursive clarity that the workers so avidly sought. Through this combination of clarity and flexibility, they ultimately gained much more than they had bargained for.

This demand for clarity stemmed in part from collective outrage caused by accumulated historical grievances and, relatedly, from cycles of material hardship. We have already seen that direct confrontations between citizens and the party-state were usually set off by price increases on foodstuffs and other consumer goods. In Poland as in Hungary, struggles over the share of national income allocated to consumption versus investment were key to state-society relations. The crucial difference was that in Poland in 1956, 1970, and 1976, these struggles had turned into full-blown clashes. And though the party-state authorities beat, imprisoned, and even murdered citizens, they subsequently felt compelled to rescind the price increases, and then to make promises about reforms, which they subsequently carried out incompletely or not at all.[8]

Increasingly, then, price hikes were the last straw for a society that was distrustful of the state and was becoming radicalized. Already in 1970, fully ten years before the emergence of Solidarity, a worker protesting in Gdańsk recalled,

I didn't think I was protesting just the price rise, although that is what sparked it – it had to do with an overthrowing, at least in part, of everything we hated.[9]

---

[6] In an attempt to understand the structure and attitudes underlying the Polish crises, a team of Polish scholars undertook a series of four detailed surveys that were completed over the course of the decade (1980, 1981, 1984, and 1988). These provide clear evidence of the "us vs. them" cleavage. See Władysław Adamski, ed., *Societal Conflict and Systemic Change: The Case of Poland, 1980–1992* (Warsaw: IfiS Publishers, 1993), Table 1, 37.

[7] Jan Kubik, "Who done it: Workers, Intellectuals, or someone else? Controversy over Solidarity's origins and social composition," *Theory and Society*, 23 (1994): 441–465. See also Roman Laba, *The Roots of Solidarity* (Princeton: Princeton University Press, 1991).

[8] In fact, one study shows a correlation between investment cycles and political upheavals. Another, which measured the "satisfaction of economic and social needs of the population" from 1955–1980 using variables such as the "share of private consumption in total consumption, the ratio of marriages to newly built dwellings, the previous year's growth rates in final agricultural output, [and] real wage index," found that the "bottom turning points" were 1956 and 1980. Other low points also "coincided with cleavages within the ruling elite that eventually led to the changes in the leadership of the PUWP." Bartłomiej Kaminski, *The Collapse of State Socialism: The Case of Poland* (Princeton: Princeton University Press, 1991), 127–28.

[9] Laba, *The Roots of Solidarity*, 39.

By the early 1980s, the opposition's discursive projection of flexible clarity in civil society led the Polish party-state to seek a return to "normalcy" – a return to the days when the shared fear of Soviet encroachment on Polish sovereignty had helped assuage domestic antagonisms.

The chapter's second argument is that this attempt to restore the *status quo ante* had the unintended consequence of injecting the full force of a now deeply mistrustful societal opposition onto the shop-floor of state firms and, as worker discontent spread across the country, onto the national stage. Put yet another way, the party-state unwittingly restored the central cleavage of Polish politics to its point of origin, and strengthened the hand of the original protagonist: Polish labor.

The Discourse of a Delicate Balance

The forces underlying this cleavage in the Polish political economy varied in visibility and degrees of institutional strength. At one end of the spectrum, there were spontaneous, grass-root tendencies toward polarization. Ethnographic accounts suggest, for example, that even in obscure villages such as Wola Pławska, Poles used the word "friend" not only in opposition to the external "foe" – the Soviet Union – but also to the internal enemy embodied by the "communist state." For this reason, the party-state's use of the word "friend" to describe the Soviets was an especially grievous affront to villagers' sensibilities. And for this reason, too, villagers considered the words "communist" and "farmer" to be mutually exclusive. As one long-time resident of Wola Pławska put it in the late 1970s, "We are not Communists, we are farmers."[10] At the other end of the spectrum, at a highly visible and institutionalized level, the Polish Church developed a "socio-political discourse" that enabled citizens to recast "socialist sovereignty" as "slavery" and protest action against the regime as a "struggle for freedom."[11]

Between the socio-cultural heights commanded by the Church and the less authoritative multiplicity of villages stood opposition intellectuals and workers, who now joined in the pursuit of a common political agenda. Finding a shared discourse that could serve as a vehicle for that agenda was the first step during the Solidarity period – August 1980 to December 13, 1981 – when opposition intellectuals began to sharpen their own discourse in a self-conscious effort to satisfy workers' demands for communicative transparency. As one of the editors of *Wezwanie* (*"The Call"*) explained:

[Prior to 1980, workers] would come back to us and say, What do you mean here? This is too hard. You have to work too hard to understand it. *Can't you just say what you mean?* We [intellectuals] were forced to see how the density of our language – which we

---

[10] Carole Nagengast, *Reluctant Socialists, Rural Entrepreneurs* (Boulder, CO: Westview Press, 1991), 128.

[11] Jan Kubik, *The Power of Symbols Against the Symbols of Power* (University Park: Pennsylvania State University, 1994), 128.

had developed as a kind of adaptation to repression – itself *served* repression, since it kept us separate from our natural allies among the workers. *So one of the great labors [after] 1980 [was] the invention of a language that [was] clear and yet flexible and intelligent.*[12] [emphasis added]

Clarity did, in fact, become the hallmark of opposition discourse, even in relatively esoteric essays. In 1981, a renowned Catholic intellectual was able to articulate in the journal *Tygodnik Powszechny* (Universal Weekly) a view of Solidarity as Polish society's "concrete" attempt to resist "objectification" by the communist state. On this view, state authorities posed a lethal threat to the agency of citizens by seeking to deprive them of their role as the "subjects" of their own history. Of course, workers had been saying the same thing even earlier, explicitly valorizing the ability "to shape actively their fate" as members of a "larger human community."[13]

The Szczecin strike committee, for instance, had declared in December 1970:

. . . we cannot be treated by a group of irresponsible people like an unconscious mass, fit only for submission to decrees.[14]

From the summer of 1980 on, state-society relations would be widely and explicitly understood as a profound struggle for survival: were Poles to be merely passive extensions of a party-state that was irrational and destructive? The answer was obvious. Workers' historical memory in particular reflected this broadening scope of action. Referring to the strikes of 1970 and 1971, for example, the Solidarity Program of October 1981 stated retrospectively:

What we had in mind was not just bread and butter . . . but also . . . the repair of the republic.[15]

This retrospective view was accurate: recall the repeated demands of workers in Gdańsk, Gdynia, and Szczecin for rationality in economic governance and for accurate information about the state of the economy. In fact, some workers in Gdynia seized on the broom as their symbol to signify that Poland needed a "'good cleanup.'"[16] And it was in the Lenin Shipyard at Gdańsk that the Council of Striking Workers first formulated the demand for free trade unions. As Roman Laba writes:

Here, six years before the appearance of intellectual opposition in Poland, which is almost universally held to have taught the Polish workers the demand for a free union independent of the party, is the first point of the 1980 Gdańsk Accord, the fundamental demand of Solidarity.[17]

---

[12] Lawrence Weschler, *The Passion of Poland: From Solidarity Through The State of War, The Complete New Yorker Reports on Poland* (New York: Pantheon Books, 1984), 150.
[13] Kubik, "*Who done it,*" 446.
[14] Laba, *The Roots of Solidarity*, 73.
[15] "Solidarity's Program," October 16, 1981, in Stokes, *From Stalinism to Pluralism,* 209.
[16] Laba, *The Roots of Solidarity*, 39.
[17] Ibid., 45.

But in 1981, the demand for free trade unions was only the first in a long list of demands. Now, Solidarity called for the creation of a "self-governing republic," a goal that the party could only perceive as a threat to its own "leading role." The perception was not unfounded. If anything, the threat was all the more real because this time around, the party faced a workers' movement well-schooled in the art of resistance. The workers of the Lenin Shipyard, for example, drew on the 1971 experience of the coastal dock workers of Szczecin, and reinvented

the tactics of the occupation strike and the interfactory strike committee. The workers' movement, in other words, was now endowed with a 'creative basis.'[18]

The party, moreover, now faced an internally diversified workers' movement that was nevertheless able to retain its coherence by focusing on the ideas of self-management and economic rationality. During the crucial year of 1981, for example, the various strands of Solidarity were able to agree that, through self-management, workers would be "liberating the management of industry from the Party and the *nomenklatura*" and, by extension, would also make space for "economic rationality," particularly at the enterprise level.[19]

To be sure, by the time the Solidarity National Congress met in September 1981, there were also major disagreements – even the beginnings of rifts – within the union. But by focusing its attention largely on the enterprise, Solidarity could plausibly claim that its intent was not the party's overthrow. Rather, its claim was that the liberation of at least a part of civil society would flow from the liberation of the enterprises. In this sense, to borrow from Touraine, Solidarity finally came face to face with "its own enhanced power." But the different groups of Solidarity – from Gdańsk to Warsaw – still shared the conviction that the movement must avoid a clash with the party and the Soviet Union.[20] Indeed, the "self-limiting" character of Solidarity was clearly evident in the transcript of the National Congress.[21]

This was a delicate balance for Solidarity to maintain. Ironically, the longer it managed to do just that, the more Solidarity brought out into the open discussions of major issues that had been previously confined to meetings of party

---

[18] Raymond Taras, *Consolidating Democracy in Poland* (Boulder, CO: Westview Press, 1995), 85; and Stokes, *Three Eras of Political Change in Eastern Europe*, 171.

[19] Touraine, 94–95.

[20] Touraine, 94–98, 135.

[21] See George Sanford, *The Solidarity Congress, 1981: The Great Debate* (London: Macmillan, 1990), Introduction, especially 11–12 and 14–17. The most obvious reason for this strategy was the inescapable fact of the party-state's overwhelming power (and behind it, the ever-present fear of Soviet intervention). But the legacy of Poznań in 1956, and Gdańsk, Gdynia, and Szczecin also left Solidarity activists fearful of manipulation and suspicious of generalized, sweeping promises of reform. Hence the intense struggle at the Congress over proposed compromises with the Sejm on the Self-Management Law. Sanford, *The Solidarity Congress*, 12, 101–124, and 128–134.

organs.[22] And the longer Solidarity managed to hold its focus on economic rationality, the more the party-state lost control of the production apparatus. Union and party negotiations produced new laws that allowed for the creation of democratically elected workers' councils with the power to veto appointments of enterprise directors and to vote on their retention. In addition, major strategic decisions by the firm would require the approval of the enterprise council, though the state insisted on exempting a variety of enterprises from this arrangement on grounds of national security.

Maintaining a balance between strategic struggle and instrumental compromise, it soon became apparent, called for the crafting of the discourse that the *Wezwanie* editor quoted earlier had said ought to be clear, yet flexible and intelligent. The politics underlying the construction and deployment of such a discourse proved volatile and complicated. On this point, the proceedings of the Solidarity Congress are illuminating. To begin with, many delegates to the Congress felt that Wałęsa and three other members of the Solidarity National Coordinating Commission (KKP, *Krajowa Komisja Porozumiewawcza*)[23] had compromised too much on self-management, and that in a decision "taken autocratically," they had, in fact, been outfoxed by the authorities. In particular, the Łódź, Lower Silesian, and Sieć delegates worried that the KKP had conceded too much in the procedures for the nomination of enterprise directors.[24] There was also some internal suspicion: the audience cheered when one delegate from Lower Silesia suggested that

. . . certain individuals [were] setting out their electoral programmes [for positions in the national union] at [the workers'] cost, at the cost of self management.

The compromise took the form of the "Self Management of Staffs of Enterprises Act" of September 1981. Worker self-management was institutionalized in such a way that it left to central decision-makers the necessary prerogatives to control the economy at the national level. At the same time, the Act moved Poles closer to the goal of a democratized enterprise management, and transferred some decisions and responsibilities from the higher to the lower echelons.[25]

But worker-delegates remained skeptical, and many were even hostile to the compromise. One point of contention between the Party (represented by Sejm Committees) and Solidarity was the appointment of enterprise directors and the right to recall them. Although Solidarity did gain some control over

---

[22] Raymond Taras, *Ideology in a Socialist State: Poland 1956–1983* (New York: Cambridge University Press, 1984), 40.

[23] The KKP consisted of delegates from MKZs: the regional Solidarity Inter-Factory Strike Committees. See Timothy Garton Ash, *The Polish Revolution: Solidarity 1980–82* (New York: Vintage, 1985), 76.

[24] Sanford, *The Solidarity Congress*, 23.

[25] Barbara Gaçiarz, "Employee Self-Management in the 1980s," in Jerzy Hausner and Tadeusz Klementewicz, eds., *The Protracted Death Agony of Real Socialism* (Warsaw: Institute of Political Studies, Polish Academy of Sciences, 1992), 111.

appointment and recall of directors, the Party retained a majority of seats on the so-called "competition committee," which would have final say over such matters. As Grzegorz Pałka, delegate from Łódź, explained:

. . . if any of the new existing self-managements wanted to choose its director, then it would stumble across [the] composition of the competition committee which [guaranteed] the Party and the social organizations in its control a majority on it. And the Council of Ministers [would] decree the final course of procedure of this committee, in other words this [meant] the blocking of all self-managements, and not only those in the large workplaces.[26]

Although the final decision could always be appealed to the Supreme Court, several delegates pointed out the court was neither truly independent nor impartial. Andrzej Gwiazda, a prominent Solidarity leader from Gdańsk, opined that the single achievement of the Act was the debate it provoked in the Sejm on the subject. Gwiazda gave voice to a complaint shared by many delegates and repeated frequently in the transcripts: that the Union's Presidium was instrumentalizing the rank-and-file membership, and that it had

stopped talking to the people; it [talked] only to the government, *in a language understandable to the authorities, paying completely no regard to how this [was] received among members.* [emphasis added]

This statement was met with cheers. Because instead of the Union going to "Holy War" with the authorities, it now

turned out that there was nothing to talk about, that everything [was] in full agreement, that we did not really want [true self-management].[27]

Part of this lengthy and often acrimonious debate centered on Wałęsa's autocratic methods, but most of it was grounded in delegates' acute fears of manipulation by what seemed to them an almost infinitely cynical party-state. Their fears were fully justified, and arose, of course, from workers' memories or experiences of Poznań 1956; Gdańsk, Gdynia, and Szczecin 1970; and Radom and Warsaw 1976. Some had even more personal reasons to distrust anyone who, by virtue of party membership and service at high levels of the government, could be seen as complicit in the Soviet domination of Poland. As a child, Andrzej Gwiazda, for instance, had been one of more than a million Poles whom the Soviets deported to Siberia in 1939, fewer than half of whom were ever to return. In May of 1978, the engineer Gwiazda became one of the founding members in Gdańsk of the "Free Trades Unions on the Coast"; two years later, in August 1980, he would be among the leaders of the strike at the Lenin Shipyard, and along with Wałęsa and several others, producing the publication *Robotnik Wybrzeża ("Worker on the Coast").*[28] Speaking in the

---

[26] Sanford, *The Solidarity Congress,* 108.
[27] Ibid., 110–111.
[28] Garton Ash, *The Polish Revolution,* 4, 24.

public negotiations at the shipyard that August about political prisoners and the citizenry's right to freedom of conscience, Gwiazda gave eloquent voice to his widely shared skepticism of the governments' promises:

We live in a land where national unity is imposed by the police truncheon . . . We would like to know what guarantees there are, what solid guarantees, that such things will not occur again. On paper our laws are splendid, but the practice is far removed from them.[29]

Gwiazda's words prefigured the debate that would ensue at the Solidarity Congress. In August, addressing concerns about whether the new unions would be "totally free," he had reminded the workers in the shipyard of "the simple truth" that the workers had learned in 1956: "Our only guarantee is ourselves . . . We know that hundreds of thousands, millions of people think the same as us. . . . The word 'Solidarity' will survive."[30]

Timothy Garton Ash points out that whereas some of Solidarity's leadership was at times more prone to compromise, Gwiazda was "not a natural practitioner of the art of the possible"; Garton Ash also notes, however, that at times Gwiazda was "more closely in tune with the mood of the workers than the counselors of caution." Karol Modzelewski, on the other hand, a Congress delegate from Lower Silesia, felt that even though the compromise law did not achieve all of Solidarity's original aims, the Congress should accept the compromise on self-management, or risk the self-defeating internal tensions that the Union would likely face. Modzelewski conceded that accepting the compromise was not easy, because the membership had expected Solidarity's leadership to launch a frontal attack on the issue of self-management. The leadership's choice not to do so, Modzelewski reasoned, naturally came as a shock to the members. After all, he explained, leading activists like himself had repeatedly told the people that

the most important and fundamental . . . struggle [is] for self-management. [That they would] go like a battering-ram, [and would] not give way a millimeter . . . .

So Modzelewski was not surprised by the delegates' skepticism. As he put it,

I appreciate how difficult it is for the majority to accept what I am saying, [that we] should pass a resolution which will give this Law a binding interpretation for the future Union authorities.

But he also insisted on strategic prescience.

. . . we have to make all our members aware . . . that the struggle for self-management has moved to another dimension, although it [does] continue.[31]

---

[29] Ibid, 60.
[30] Ibid, 65.
[31] Sanford, *The Solidarity Congress*, 115.

At all costs, Modzelewski exhorted the delegates, they should avoid the

transference of the conflict from the front between us and the Sejm, between us and the government and administration, to [the front] within the union itself.

And he reminded them that the Presidium members who had agreed to this compromise with the Sejm

mainly counted on the Law on Self-Management, which [was] not a bad law and which [was] in conflict with the Enterprise Law, giving [Solidarity] a formal basis for creating *faits accomplis* by appointing directors (. . . written down in the Law on Self-Management) before the list of exclusions [had] any binding force. Because the list of exclusions [could not] arise during the next six months without [the councils'] agreement. And in the meantime, *if the foundries, coal mines, the large metal-works were to have directors appointed by the workers' councils, what power would take away what they had already gained?* [emphasis added]

Solidarity KKP Secretary Andrzej Celiński took another tack to try to convince the delegates. He emphasized that the Union's main goal had not been compromised, emphasizing in explicit detail two central claims. The first had to do with programmatic consistency. The thrust of his argument was that the Union's goal from the start had been to make economics, not politics, the governing principle of enterprise operations. Allowing politics into the enterprise at the expense of economic rationality, he reminded his audience, invariably had brought losses to the "national economy" in the past. From his perspective, avoiding a repetition of this costly historical mistake had been the main concern driving the decision of the KKP Presidium.

The Secretary's second claim was tactical. That is to say, did the Presidium's decision hinder or help attain the goal of restored economic rationality? In answering his own question, the Secretary argued that in reclaiming the economy, success would be achieved through a seemingly oxymoronic combination of cold and hot: dispassionate struggle.

Does this decision facilitate the achievement of this aim or does it push it back? . . .It is an obvious fact that the government in spite of passing this law will attempt to force through its standpoint and that the text of the document, article 34 of this law, will not make it easier for it. It is obvious that this time, the government in defending *nomenklatura* will be acting against the legally binding Sejm law. And that is the most important fact. Our task, the task of the Union, is to make use of this law as an instrument of struggle for the Union's aim . . . . It would be political stupidity not to use this instrument. *Emotions are not appropriate companions in the struggle for the economy. One needs courage, but intelligent courage* . . . . We already have [the instrument we need] . . . in our hands.[32] [emphasis added]

Many delegates were not mollified. Jerzy Ciepiela from Dąbrowa-Silesia won applause when he countered that accommodation had been reached under the sway of government propaganda. Even more tellingly, Ciepiela expressed the

---

[32] Ibid., 119–120.

fear that Solidarity was ceding too much ground, and that, as if on a slippery slope, the upshot of it all would be that someone in the Union's leadership one day would dissolve it, using "experts" to persuade the membership that dissolution was simply a ruse to "confuse the enemy."[33]

Solidarity, which had originated and thrived through civic networks of trust, now was threatened by internal political suspicion. One delegate even charged that the crux of the problem was collaborationism with the Warsaw *apparat* by some Union leaders, which is why, he further claimed, "the whole affair had been choreographed." Yet another accused everyone of telling "half-truths." The truth in full, he claimed, was that "in agreeing to the compromise, we gave our hand to the Sejm, who took it, and bit the fingers off."[34]

The fear of betrayal, which originated with the Party's doublespeak of 1956, was never far away. Tadeusz Romanowski from Lower Silesia opined that Wałęsa and the others had made a fundamental a mistake with the compromise law, and that the consequences of this mistake would be catastrophic for the Union:

In place of a struggle, at one blow, for all the enterprises we allowed ourselves to be led into various individual conflicts . . . which we [feared] so much. . . .[those] who sit here do not have the right to use the cheap demagogy of the 1950s. Because many of the speakers before me presented exactly this style, and I lament over this [applause]. On the other hand, we have the right, and even the obligation, to make use of our powers. Making use of them we can annul the KKP Presidium decision, we can also punish those individuals who took it. We can also not agree to this law.[35]

Several other delegates echoed the fear that the government would successfully employ a divide-and-conquer strategy.[36] But in many ways, this debate was also an existential one for the Solidarity delegates. This was so in part because it involved crucial issues such as the power of workers' councils versus the state; the degree to which the law changed the "bureaucratic method of directing the economy," as one delegate put it;[37] and the number and kind of firms that the state would exempt from the Self-Management Act on grounds of "national security."

But the debate also had an existential dimension because another struggle was taking place simultaneously: the struggle *within* the Union itself over centralization versus decentralization, as well as fundamentalism versus pragmatism. And this, too, was often grounded in deep mistrust of power *per se*, and the fear that their own leaders would turn out to be little better than the

---

33 Ibid., 120.
34 Ibid., 134.
35 Ibid., 121.
36 For example, ibid., 128.
37 R. Jarmuszkiewicz from Łódź. Sanford, *The Solidarity Congress*, 126.

Party. Delegates deplored the development of

a power elite . . . some sort of *nomenklatura*" [in the Union]; [and of] centralized power . . . which could be justified at the beginning; however, one should gain guarantees that this would not be turned against Solidarity members.[38]

Yet some participants in the debates also showed an awareness of how the conditioning of the past negatively affected present attempts to act. Leopold Zgoda (from the Little Poland region) noted:

It is unfortunate that 'compromise' is for us associated with 'conformism.' It teaches us hatred, and hatred does not tolerate compromise. One should struggle with hatred. There is an element of risk in negotiations but it is a creative risk.[39]

For others, the matter was not so clear. Toward the end of the second round of the Congress's meetings, Jan Rulewski, a radical from Bydgoszcz, drew a distinction between broad political compromises and concrete compromises that might actually work – compromises that would render enterprises more efficient and productive. He then urged the assembly to "talk the workers' language" and, by logical extension, to choose concrete compromises. In an impassioned speech, he touched on the recurrent themes of betrayal and the absence of just rationality:

We must throw off the forms of betrayal of our factory which up til now have led to economic and social degradation . . . We are now at a stage when people do not dream of [attending] . . . theater performances but of a piece of bread and a beef-bone . . . The motor for realization of economic reform is not the worker . . . the lack of any built up system of incentives [is basically at] fault. However, the Sejm spread cancer into our laws and poisoned not only authority in the enterprises but the shape of this enterprise.[40]

There is little doubt that the proposals on self-management advanced by Solidarity would have had

much wider and deeper social and economic consequences than . . . those advanced by political elites and the experts. Since their aim was to transfer rights from the state to groups of worker-managers, the conceptions of self-management undermined, above all, the hitherto unquestioned principle of the primacy of state property as the foundation of the system.[41]

Reaction

Political leaders and expert advisers did chip away at the set of faculties and powers that workers were seeking, but Solidarity had come out of the contentious debates on the compromise in one piece. A subtle yet fundamental change was already in place: just as the party had done in 1956, the government

---

[38] Sanford, *The Solidarity Congress*, 163–65.
[39] Ibid., 126.
[40] Ibid., 195.
[41] Barbara Gaçiarz, "Employee Self-Management in the 1980s," 110.

had reached agreements with Solidarity in August of 1980, raising hopes for real change. A survey carried out in 1981 by the Solidarity Center for Social Studies showed that the members of the trade union considered economic reform to be of paramount importance, according it an even higher level of priority than the country's sovereignty.[42]

The survey's results notwithstanding, the party leadership, internally divided on political decentralization and economic reform, seemed unsure about how to treat Solidarity. Some early tactics were familiar: admit to certain excesses under Gierek and remove those who were especially unpopular or resented in the firms, regions and in the top leadership. Thus Gierek was out and Stanislaw Kania was in.

This circulation of elites achieved little. Kania – and Jaruzelski, who replaced him – had held high positions under Gierek. It was a pattern by now familiar to Poles, and as Marjorie Castle points out, this time the workers and the population in general were indifferent to the change in leadership. Even the fact that Kania had been in charge of the police and had overseen "unpopular Church policies" went unopposed.

Poles neither protested the appointment of the man who had supervised two of Poland's most contentious institutions nor rallied around him, as they had around Gierek when he criticized the party and called for reform.[43]

Increasingly, as individuals from outside the old party and government "establishment" assumed positions vacated by disgraced Gierek cronies, and as "attacks on corruption swept out ever larger circles of party and state leaders," party leaders lost control of the state administration. In early 1981, party progressives began to

consider reforms that involved paring down the party and state administrative and economic bureaucracies that had grown under Gierek. All of this, given the bureaucracy's sense of its power in the 1970s, resulted in a dramatic split and distrust between many policy makers and administrators.[44]

Meanwhile, the leadership at times appeared to treat Solidarity as having some legitimacy, a legitimacy that Solidarity derived, the leadership acknowledged, from having emerged as an independent force at a time when old trade unions had lost their authority. This acknowledgment turned out to be merely tactical. The Gdańsk Accords had committed the authorities to recognize Solidarity and its right to strike, and yet, in November 1980, the court, in the process of registering the Union, unilaterally and without advance notice introduced a provision asserting the Union's obligation to recognize the party's

---

[42] Zbigniew Drag and Jerzy Indraszkiewicz, "Change in the Political and Economic Consciousness of Polish Society," in Hausner and Klementewicz, eds., *The Protracted Death Agony of Real Socialism*, 97.

[43] Marjorie Castle, "The Solidarity Crisis, 1980–81," in Jane Leftwich Curry and Luba Fajfer, eds., *Poland's Permanent Revolution: People vs. Elites, 1956–1990* (Washington DC: American University Press, 1996), 174, note 10.

[44] Castle, "The Solidarity Crisis," 175.

supremacy.[45] And although many state administrators joined Solidarity – especially those operating in the economic bureaucracy – they tended to support only those Union platforms that did not threaten their prerogatives. As Marjorie Castle explains:

Below the roughly two hundred people holding positions in the top central party and state elite and the rest of the entrenched party apparatus, the party membership lived its own life between August 1980 and March 1981.

Some party members in the larger urban industrial centers, including Torun and Krakow, "held their own unsanctioned elections for new officers and delegates to a special party congress" – a congress that party leaders had promised but not yet announced. By the winter of 1981, these "horizontalists" – so called because they bypassed the centralized structures and procedures of the party – had begun to spread among the lower echelons. While the more liberal party leaders "flirted" with the horizontalists, hard-liners saw them as a threat to the party and to national security.[46] But under pressure from its membership base, the party called the Ninth Plenum of the PUWP Central Committee at the end of March 1981, and

began the process of setting up the election machinery for the Extraordinary Congress. This opened the doors for local party bodies to hold secret-ballot elections and negotiations over most of the seats at the congress. At the same time, party leaders ordered party members not to join or remain in Solidarity. This marked a clear shift from treating the union as a problem created by the Gierek era to be incorporated or co-opted into the existing party system, to treating it as a threat to the system whose faults were caused by the 'anti-system' KOR intellectuals.[47]

The Ninth Plenum followed on the heels of the first instance of state violence against protesters since the Gdańsk Accords: the Bydgoszcz events,[48] where police beat farmers demanding to establish their own union. It took a strike by Solidarity, protests from the Church, and warnings of a full-blown national strike for the authorities to admit to the beatings, though they did not admit that any directive had come from the center.[49]

Initiative Denied

During the Gdańsk Accords and in the months immediately following, the Party had claimed that the 1980 strikes were directed not against socialism

---

[45] Ibid., 174.

[46] Ibid., 176.

[47] Ibid., 179.

[48] On March 8, students at the University of Warsaw held a rally commemorating the student protests of 1968, which was followed by the farmers' strike that took over the Provincial Headquarters in Bydgoszcz. After Solidarity's four-hour warning strike and the announcement of a general strike to protest police beatings of the farmers at the Provincial National Council meeting in Bydgoszcz, the authorities and the union reached an agreement that ended the conflict.

[49] Castle, "The Solidarity Crisis, 1980–81," 179.

but against its "deformities."[50] The growing instability, however, soon gave the lie to this stock formulation. In October 1981, Kania had to resign, and General Jaruzelski assumed power. Within weeks, Solidarity occupied the Fire Fighting Academy in Warsaw, and two days after the occupation, Army Operational Groups were deployed in all the provinces. On November 27–28, the Sixth Plenum of the Central Committee discussed implementation of economic reform, and acknowledged that the growing social tensions might threaten national security.

The government's new slogan for the so-called "first stage" of economic reform in 1981 was "initiative." Its central concern, however, was economic equilibrium. This was not surprising, since the government was caught between the imperatives of the higher living standards demanded by the population, and its onerous debt service to Western creditors. The Gdańsk Accords further constrained the government. The party not only had agreed to an independent trade union and its right to strike and to participate in meetings pertaining to economic reform, but also to a series of specific measures: limit price increases; raise the minimum wage and pensions; lower the retirement age; shorten the working week to five days; export only products that were not in short supply domestically; and provide three-year paid maternity leaves. Such measures, certain to overwhelm an economy already weakened by Gierek's follies and in recession since 1979, now resulted in worsening balances and further inflation. In fact, these problems were so severe that they took the attention of party leaders away from discussions of economic reform itself.[51]

During the months after the Gdańsk Accords, the party looked as if it might split between those willing to cooperate to some degree with Solidarity, and hard-liners who called for control through repression of the Union. Meanwhile, the party's own lower ranks were pressing for greater openness. This internal division, however, resulted merely in delays and reversals when it came to the implementation of the Gdańsk accords.[52]

The macro-economic context for the launching of this first reform effort of the 1980s could hardly have been less auspicious. The economic decline that began in 1979 worsened in 1980–81, and national income and investment declined precipitously (by 24 and 45 percent respectively from 1979 to 1982, in real terms); consumption fell by 2 percent. This was brought on by a 54 percent fall in the volume of hard-currency imports – which in the 1970s had been the Polish economy's steady diet – and by an increase in retail prices of 169 percent. Meanwhile, the inflationary overhang – "the difference between the population's money holdings and the nominal value of the goods available in the official economy" – was growing.[53] Adding to this volatile mix were Solidarity's claims in a context of deep societal mistrust; the USSR's concerns

---

[50] Sanford, *The Solidarity Congress*, 12.
[51] Slay, *The Polish Economy*, 51–52.
[52] Ibid., 51.
[53] Ibid., 52.

about the radicalization of Polish society; and from Western creditors, worries about Poland's increasingly erratic payments of its debt service.

The economic reform debates of the 1980–81 period generated professional analysis and public discussion, including the first of several unofficial reform proposals put forth by economists working under Leszek Balcerowicz at Warsaw's Central School of Planning and Statistics. But neither Kania nor Jaruzelski was willing to cede much control over the debate. Ben Slay notes that the official Committee for Economic Reform was composed of a "leviathan" – 500 members with 14 separate working groups that took more than a year to produce the official reform blueprint of 1981.[54] This blueprint was introduced between 1981 and 1983.

Like the "naive" Hungarian reformers of 1968,[55] in the autumn of 1981 the Polish government and probably many Solidarity delegates hoped that the draft proposal for economic reform would indeed awaken the "initiative" of managers and workers in state-owned firms and thus rescue the economy from the depths of lethargy. Central to the reform was the slogan of the "Three S's," which were : self-reliance and self-financing of enterprises, and self-management by the workers.[56]

The reform also called for a major reduction in the number and prerogatives of branch ministries. Clearly, its authors borrowed a page from the book of the Hungarian NEM, although they did not go as far in a number of respects. The rhetoric of the Polish reform, however, was considerably more radical. The fundamental cause of the economic crisis, it was asserted, could be traced back to the political system, and the solution to the crisis would require the democratization of the planning and policymaking processes. However, these assertions led nowhere, thus confirming Poland's nice fit at the far end of what Peter Murrell called a reform-rhetoric continuum, where rhetoric was high but accomplishments scarce.[57]

---

[54] Ibid., 54.

[55] On "naive" reformers, see János Kornai, "The Hungarian Reform Process: Visions, Hopes and Reality," *Journal of Economic Literature* XXIV, no. 4 (December 1986); and Andrzej Bloch, "The Private Sector in Poland," *Telos*, no. 66 (Winter 1985–1986), 128–133.

[56] Slay, *The Polish Economy*, 54–55. Enterprise managers and workers' councils (to which managers were supposed to be accountable) were to design their own production plans and arrange their own supply and distribution networks without obligatory physical targets from the central authorities. Managerial and worker incentive systems were to be linked to yearly enterprise profitability. The compliance of enterprises with the central plan was to be influenced through financial instruments whose magnitudes would be determined both administratively and by market forces; this element implied major changes in the role and scope of central planning. . . . Approximately 75 percent of total investment was to be decentralized to the enterprise level, while 25 percent would be devoted to completing the unfinished central investment projects left over from the 1970s.

[57] Murrell found a continuum between a country such as Mongolia in 1991, "with a rhetoric higher than anywhere in the world" but few actual reforms to show for it, and the "Kosygin reforms, with little rhetoric and no accomplishments." In between are several countries that in the early 1990s had "much lower levels of ambition and are much more advanced in matters such as the development of the new private sector, the establishment of secure property rights, and the

Like the Hungarian NEM, the reform was internally inconsistent, only considerably more so, because it failed to provide the institutional mechanisms that might align stated principles and actual behavior within the party *apparat* and the state administration. Private farmers, it is true, were finally given guarantees of their "secure position" and income parity with urbanites, as well as improved access to loans and agricultural equipment. But unlike the NEM, for example, the Polish reform did not even entertain the renunciation of central planning or a reconsideration of private ownership.[58]

In addition, the Polish government lacked the luxury of Hungary's stable polity and cooperative society, as well as its institutional residue of earlier reform successes and the credible discourse that was part of that legacy. To the contrary: "reform," which in Poland by 1980 had come to be associated with a cynical and untrustworthy party-state, was by 1982 accompanied by large price increases on consumer goods. In the context of martial law, these were "price increases imposed at gunpoint."[59] Finally, though Hungary would later amass a large *per capita* foreign debt as well, debt service was not yet a pressure Hungarian reformers faced in 1968, nor were the economic sanctions that followed the imposition of martial law in Poland.

But even in Hungary, the NEM achieved its objectives of decentralization and price responsiveness only incompletely, and then, as we have seen, in part as the result of its indirect effects on the private and quasi-private sectors.[60] What, then, was the outcome of the 1980–81 reforms in Poland? Very few of its provisions were fully implemented, and others were reversed in practice within a matter of two years. Despite many pieces of impressive reform legislation passed by the Sejm, by December 30, 1981, the reform's self-management provisions were suspended,

further [deepening] Polish workers' cynicism and mistrust toward economic reform and [removing] another important player from the pro-reform camp.[61]

The State Speaks and Society Replies: Organicism Shattered

If the crisis of governability that the party-state suffered in the early 1980s was a more intense version of previous crises, the imposition of martial law by Poland's new leader, General Wojciech Jaruzelski, represented a recognition of the party-state's highly diminished sense of control. Whether an accurate

---

establishment of the rule of law." Peter Murrell, "Reform's Rhetoric-Realization Relationship: Mongolia," in Poznański, ed., *The Evolutionary Transition to Capitalism*, 93.

[58] Slay, *The Polish Economy*, 55.

[59] Ibid., 56.

[60] A few economists, however, take a more positive view of the NEM. Jan Adam, for instance, suggests that the NEM took the "Hungarian economic system beyond the framework of the traditional system" and made it "qualitatively different." Jan Adam, *Why Did the Socialist System Collapse in Central and Eastern European Countries? The Case of Poland, the Former Czechoslovakia and Hungary* (London: Macmillan, 1997), 128–129.

[61] Slay, *The Polish Economy*, 59.

reflection of sincere beliefs or a self-serving manipulation of the facts, Jaruzel-ski's discourse nevertheless depicted a besieged party-state bent on "normaliz-ing" the public affairs of the nation. Consider the explicit reasoning he deployed to justify what was in essence an abrogation of the Gdańsk Accords. First, he argued that the nation – rent by "hatreds," "controversies," "interminable con-flict," "strikes," and "protest actions" – was facing nothing less than imminent anarchy. Second, continued instability would lead to "poverty and hunger" – a dreadful scenario that the "severe winter" would surely make worse. Third, Solidarity itself had "openly" announced a "confrontational" program that threatened to revisit "tragedy" on Poland. Indeed, by planning mass gatherings to commemorate December 1970, Solidarity was courting a repetition of those "tragic" events.[62]

For most Polish workers, the significance of the events of December 1970 to January 1971 was clear. The government's violent suppression of strikes and protests – including massacres of unarmed workers in the Lenin Shipyard at Gdańsk on the morning of December 16 – was the turning point in their rela-tions with the party-state, and remained a central "focus of political action for the next ten years."[63] But from the leadership's perspective, December 1970 had been a critical moment because it had led to the replacement of Gomułka by Gierek amidst deep crisis, or, put more directly, it had led to a highly tur-bulent change of guard at the apex of the party, in the context of the USSR's unwillingness or inability to send troops to restore order.[64] So now, the question arose: could the party withstand similar turmoil? And if it could, was there any hope that the Party would be able to perform any better – economically and politically – than it had under Gierek? The imposition of martial law and the planned restoration of "normalcy" aimed to push precisely such questions to the margins of politics, while privileging the agenda of national "salvation" – the stated purpose of the Military Council of National Salvation (WRON).

Underlying the creation of WRON in December of 1981 was the old iden-tification of the party's domestic supremacy with the preservation of Poland's sovereignty, the one point of unity traditionally shared by state and society, the one point on which the party, by drawing on a shared prudential view of

---

[62] Jaruzelski creates the Military Council of National Salvation (WRON). Declaration of Martial Law, December 13, 1981. Stokes, *From Stalinism to Pluralism*, 214–215. See also Garton Ash, *The Polish Revolution*, and Jack Bielasiak and Maurice Simon, *Polish Politics: Edge of the Abyss* (New York: Praeger, 1984).

[63] Laba, *The Roots of Solidarity*, 44.

[64] I leave aside here the provocation thesis, raised by Fajfer: the possibility that the 1970s workers' protests "resulted from a carefully orchestrated provocation by political forces within the ruling elite to achieve changes in the leadership, including the ouster of the first secretary." Luba Fajfer, "December 1970: a Prelude to Solidarity," in Jane Leftwich Curry and Luba Fajfer, eds., *Poland's Permanent Revolution: People vs. Elites, 1956–1990* (Washington DC: American University Press, 1996), 58–59. True or not, the strikes of December 1970-January 1971 soon proved to emanate from an even wider and more energetic base of worker resistance. Any purposeful involvement of Party functionaries in sparking the unrest for instrumental political purposes would only underscore the depth of their miscalculation.

Soviet power, had at times been able to set to its advantage the terms of state-society engagement. On all other matters of substantial importance, both the party-state and society had been forced to operate within the *points of permeable contact* that riddled state-socialist systems. As we have seen in the case of Hungary, these were points at which, despite an undeniable power asymmetry between the party-state and society, neither one could unilaterally dictate enforceable terms for either bargaining processes or conflictual encounters.

Such points of rough equality were endemic to the economy. State enterprises and the agricultural sector were the dominion of neither state nor workers and peasants. The entire economy belonged to no one. The state produced mostly shortages, and consumers could barely adapt. And while workers exercised *de facto* veto power over official economic policy, the party-state retained its grip on the decision-making process. The Gdańsk Accords, in fact, were at base an attempt on the part of the unions to transcend this stalemate by stipulating and formalizing a set of prerogatives for workers and party-state alike. Jaruzelski's agenda, in turn, was an attempt to transcend the stalemate by different means: to reclaim unilaterally the party-state's role as the leading agent of organic unity.

The result was counterproductive, to say the least. If the state demanded "loyalty oaths" of disaffected workers, then the Catholic Church countered by salving the conscience of those who bowed and took the oath. (Church Primate Jozef Glemp formally stated that coerced oaths were not binding.) If the underground opposition developed a mutual-help discourse – a simple yet fully articulated "solidarity" ethos – in the face of massive firings of workers, then the state vilified the opposition as a movement corrupted by "radical intellectuals" and "extremists" pushing the nation toward "civil war." The upshot of all this was that by January of 1982, many Poles already perceived themselves as being in a state of war.[65]

Intellectuals tapped into this perception, drafting a discursive chart that simultaneously fomented a climate of foreign occupation – with the regime in the role of occupier – and indicated to working citizens the subtle weapons at their disposal. Soon after the imposition of martial law, for example, the Warsaw underground issued its "Basic Principles of Resistance." Consider Principle No. 6:

Work slowly; complain about the mess and incompetence of your superiors. Shove all decisions, even the most minor ones, into the laps of commissars and informers. Flood them with questions and doubts. Don't do the thinking for them. *Pretend you are a moron.*[66] [emphasis added]

This call to purposeful idiocy was but one way in which Solidarity, a broad social movement presumably extrinsic to the production chain of command,

[65] Lawrence Weschler, *The Passion of Poland: From Solidarity Through The State of War: The Complete New Yorker Reports on Poland* (New York: Pantheon Books, 1984), 112–115, 117–120.

[66] Weschler, *The Passion of Poland*, 107.

was now involved in the strategic manipulation of the principal-agent problem that pervaded state-socialist systems. No wonder, then, that when in early
1982 the military government again tried to increase industrial output through
reform, it was to no avail. In fact, gross economic output fell by almost 8.5 percent (more in the production of consumer goods), further increasing popular
mistrust of the government and economic discontent. In response, the government "expanded the rationing of consumer goods and, in the spring of 1982,
introduced sharp price increases, which raised the average cost of living by
56.6 percent." This was followed by the public's demand for higher wages to
keep pace with cost increases – demands to which the government ultimately
acceded, creating an inflationary spiral and even more severe disequilibrium in
consumer goods markets.[67]

Although private enterprise had again been restricted after the 1981 coup,
now, in a desperate attempt to meet consumer demand, the government liberalized a number of "administrative, fiscal and credit policies for privately-owned
business." But decades of ineffectual and aborted reforms had created structural
conditions that severely limited the possibility frontier of serious institutional
change precisely at a time when the possibility frontier of political action had
been expanding for workers and their societal allies. Food was being rationed,
agricultural policy "returned to its emphasis on the socialized sector," and
the Council on Small Scale Manufacturing, "which had previously served as a
spokesman for the interests of the legal private sector," was dissolved.[68]

Once again, regulation was eased for a brief period in 1981–82. But apart
from this hiatus, the laws governing the formal, non-agricultural private sector
were considerably stricter in Poland than in Hungary, and legislation formally
promoting the development of the private sector was not passed until 1989.
The impact of restrictions on the scope of the Polish second economy and its
importance to the daily lives of citizens compared with the Hungarian case is
hard to ascertain, for a variety of reasons. Very few estimates of the overall
size and growth of the second economy in Poland are available; fewer still
have been published. And they vary significantly depending upon the methods
used.[69] The available estimates suggest that the Polish non-agricultural second
economy was smaller on a *per capita* basis: one estimate puts it between 10 and
22 percent of personal incomes in 1986; another between 17 and 24 percent.
The foremost expert on the second economy in Hungary placed the second
economy conservatively at 30 percent of incomes around the same time.[70]

What *is* known is the following. First, few participants in the incipient civil
society described at the outset of this chapter earned any significant portion of
their living from their politically motivated informal activities; most worked

---

[67] Bloch, "The Private Sector in Poland," 130.
[68] Slay, 280.
[69] Kamiński, *The Collapse of State Socialism*, 183, and author's interview with Marek Bednarski,
Warsaw, November 1995.
[70] Kamiński, *The Collapse of State Socialism*, 183, and author's interview with István Gábor,
October 1989, Budapest.

on underground publications in their free time, and only a few "professionals" – employed mainly at "widely-circulated publications" – were paid, as were the printers when printing had to be commissioned.[71] Second, while the Polish second economy, particularly its informal components, did grow in the 1980s, especially during the crisis,[72] the sector was dominated by arbitrage transactions aimed at exploiting the differentials between state-controlled and market prices, and between domestic and international prices.[73] The largest part of non-agricultural second economy activity, in fact, was comprised of economic tourism and currency speculation. The first brought goods from abroad in scarce supply at home, to be resold a profit. The second hinged on the fact that the złoty was considerably more overvalued than the Hungarian forint, making currency speculation a lucrative endeavor in Poland.[74] Third, informal services also proliferated, but tended to be concentrated in the repair of automobiles, televisions and household appliances, and so on. Fourth, unlike in Hungary, informal private traders and entrepreneurs faced very high barriers to entry into the legal private sphere until 1989.[75] Fifth, private and quasi-private institutions comparable with those in Hungary either did not develop at all before the late 1980s, or were briefly allowed to develop and were then dramatically restricted (for example, the *Polonia* firms owned by foreigners and Poles residing abroad).[76]

This meant that the second economy could neither significantly help to absorb the creative power of a frustrated citizenry nor could it substantially ameliorate the ever-mounting pressures generated by the systemic "irrationalities" already targeted by workers in 1956. The party-state's historical inability to loosen its own ideological constraints, rather than ignorance of a viable

---

[71] Toch, *Reinventing Civil Society*, 49. It is also worth noting that while acknowledging the "role of the private sphere and small groups," many of the Polish sociologists who wrote about the informal sphere in Poland emphasized the social-activist, community-building, and "democratiz[ing]" aspects of what Andrzej Rychard called society's "adaptive processes" in the face of the monostate. Author's interview, Warsaw, October 1995. For a brief review of these studies, see Andrzej Rychard, *Reforms, Adaptation and Breakthrough* (Warsaw: IFiS Publishers, 1993), 79, note 2.

[72] Kamiński, *The Collapse of State Socialism*, 183.

[73] Ibid., 183.

[74] During the 1980s, the gap between official and unofficial exchange rates in Poland was between 350 percent and 450 percent, while in Hungary it was between 20 percent and 25 percent. Slay, *Economic Reform in Hungary and Poland*, 282.

[75] Kamiński, *The Collapse of State Socialism*, 183.

[76] A 1976 decree permitted small-scale foreign investment in Poland by Poles living abroad, but by 1982 there were only 144 such *Polonia* joint ventures, a number that grew considerably over the next few years. But soon the Polish government imposed restrictions on these firms that mirrored, in spirit and partly in substance, the sorts of restrictions it placed on private agriculture (for example, requiring *Polonia* firms to "sell 50 percent of their export receipts to the treasury at the official exchange rate)." The result was that by 1989, there were only forty joint ventures operating in Poland (compared with eighty five in Hungary, where small-scale joint ventures had been authorized since 1972 and large-scale ventures since 1977). Slay, 284 and 256–257; Marer, 1986a, 250–51.

alternative to the *status quo*, was at the root of this failure. After all, Polish authorities and professional economists alike had been aware for decades of Hungary's successful accommodation of the private sector. In a telling anecdote from an interview with the author, the Polish economist Tomasz Charanziński recalled an invitation to Novosibirsk in 1973 to discuss ways to improve Soviet agriculture. One of the principal researchers at the host institute and several of the other visiting Poles floated an idea: allow 10 percent of state farms to try out the Hungarian household plot model. As in Hungary, the peasants working these plots would have access to machinery and assistance from the state farm. "Of all the East Europeans present," Charanziński recalled further, "only the Polish 'boss' stood up, and on the spot, pronounced the idea 'ridiculous.'" Charanziński mused: "We were not invited back."[77]

Polish authorities and professional economists were well aware of the political benefits generated by an accommodative policy towards the private sector. Once again, Charanziński was an involved witness. He recounted conversations in which Hungarian economists, while in residence as visiting fellows at the Institute on Agriculture of the Polish Academy in 1974, had made it plain that by allowing Hungary's private sector to develop, the government provided an escape valve for the "guilt and resentment" associated with 1956.[78]

More opportunities would be missed. In the late 1970s, as Hungary launched a new, more radical wave of reforms, Poland remained hesitant at best. Charanziński observed: "Nothing comparable to Hungary's 1982 reform happened here. Some things looked similar, but they were quite different in practice."[79] Hesitancy might have paid off if the Polish party-state had been able to find its own viable alternative. The opposite occurred. The workers' self-management movement was temporarily halted by martial law, but the terms of the debate had changed completely: the old forms of centralized management based on the "command-and-quota system typical of earlier years" were gone for good.[80] In their stead, however, all that emerged was a pattern of barely controlled incoherence that manifested itself in a multiplicity of untenable distortions and contradictions.

There is some disagreement among economists familiar with the Polish reforms about what was actually achieved. Poznański is the most optimistic, arguing that virtually all changes, however small, moved the cause of reform forward. Most analysts are considerably more skeptical, and emphaisze multiple distortions and contradictions. Despite some bureaucratic reorganization and shifting of responsibilities, for instance, the branch ministries managed to shape these changes to their own ends. A freer price system was introduced, but the categories of items to which it applied were progressively reduced over time,

---

[77] Author's interview with Tomasz Charanziński, Warsaw, November 1995.

[78] Author's interview with Charanziński, 1995. See also Jan Zielonka, "Let Poland Be Hungary?" *SAIS Review* 4 (Summer–Fall 1984): 105–20.

[79] Author's interview with Charanziński, 1995.

[80] Gaçiarz, "Employee Self-Management in the 1980s," 119.

and in 1983 and 1984, price freezes were also imposed. When compulsory plan targets re-emerged in 1982, devolution of wage determination to enterprises also went by the wayside. The export incentives offered to firms were too weak to overcome inflationary tendencies, the adverse effects on competitiveness of insufficiently rapid devaluations, and domestic shortage, which ensured high demand in local markets for virtually all goods. Exporting enterprises were given foreign exchange accounts for the first time, but since firms were not permitted to keep more than 20 percent of their export revenues, another fundamental incentive to export was missing.[81]

The political consequences of all this for the regime were as profound as they were intractable. On the one hand, in the period between 1983 and 1985, the regime once again had to resuscitate workers' councils and the idea of self-management. The councils' relegalization was an "indispensable element of [the regime's] legitimation of their policy of economic reforms." On the other hand, virtually all the councils

> identified with Solidarity, tried to carry out its proposals, and assumed the role of the sociopolitical representation of staffs . . . . employee councils were a public continuation of the then illegal Solidarity movement . . . . the years 1983–85 were above all a period of *an obstinate struggle for the enforcement of the legal prerogatives of employee councils* . . . in particular in the personnel policy and strategic decisions pertaining to investments, membership of the enterprises in branch associations, and changes in the form of ownership.[82] [emphasis added]

The unresolved issue of ownership forms also affected the small formal private sector. This sector, to be sure, initially enjoyed some benefits of the reform. In January 1982, the authorities had given only 144 production licences to *Polonia* firms; now the 1976 law was liberalized and a three-year income tax holiday was granted. These changes brought much-needed foreign currency from the Poles living abroad who set up *Polonia* operations; by 1984, such firms comprised 9.8 percent of the output of small-scale manufacturing, and by mid-1985, 736 licences had been granted. But in 1983, as soon as Poland's immediate economic crisis had passed, the 1982 law was modified to require the *Polonia* firms to sell half their export receipts to the treasury at official exchange rates: to receive the income tax holiday, investors had to reinvest a third of their profits into the firm, and the tax rate that would be applied after the tax holiday expired would be 50 percent higher than originally planned. In 1985, the initial investment requirement was increased to $100,000. Little surprise, then, that when the income tax holiday ended, the *Polonia* firms' export share started to fall; in 1984 and 1985, the number of these firms also declined.[83]

One can only surmise what reform economists and sincere reformists within the party felt when Prime Minister Messner announced in late 1985 that the

---

[81] Slay, *The Polish Economy*, 62–64.
[82] Gaçiarz, "Employee Self-Management in the 1980s," 120.
[83] Slay, *The Polish Economy*, 64.

reform had been "completed." Nevertheless, at the Tenth Party Congress in 1986, work began on the "second stage" of the reform. Ben Slay points out that several factors had converged to make possible discussion of proposals that had been "beyond the realm of the politically possible since 1981." Among these were the rise of Gorbachev in the Soviet Union, Poland's readmission to the IMF and the World Bank, and "the failure to fulfill the 1986 plan for hard-currency exports." Thus, in 1987, the Central Committee approved the Economic Reform Commission's 174 *Theses*, which emphasized, among other things, "socialist entrepreneurship," self-finance, decentralization, reform of the foreign-trade mechanism, increasing the independence of the banking system, and – once again – "support for worker and local government self-management." Because the reform proposed sharply reduced subsidies and price increases required for enterprise self-financing, the government called for two referenda: one on the pace of the reform's implementation, and a second on the "desirability of 'far reaching political reforms.'" The referenda were held in November 1987.

By then, however, the workers' councils had achieved the status of a

partner in management *vis-à-vis* the management [sic] and the administration of enterprises. This period also witnessed a qualitatively new situation, marked by intensifying contradictions between the interests of . . . enterprises and the state, which wanted to prevent a financial disaster. This led to alliances between employee councils and managers, alliances kept together by the common interests of the enterprise and its staff, [both] menaced by the policy of the government.[84]

And by then, too, the opposition – understanding the public's profound disillusionment with what many saw as a cyclical charade of economic reform, and hoping to embarrass the government by invalidating the referendum – had advised citizens to boycott it. Consequently, although two-thirds of those who voted favored the reforms, voter turnout was too low to validate the results.[85]

The government was becoming even more reactive to Solidarity's initiatives in the *selection* of core conflicts and specific *modes* of core-conflict resolution. As defined in the Introduction to this book, *selection of core conflicts* is the articulation and prioritization of stakes contested by state and societal actors, whereas *mode of core conflict resolution* is the institutional mechanism deployed by agents in the settlement of clashing political and economic visions and programmatic action.

The years 1986–1989 were . . . a period of renewed development of the self-management movement, which took . . . the form of regional agreements and clubs, and also conferences on the national scale. The movement was at first oriented toward practical purposes, such as the organization of legal and economic advice for the employee councils. *Gradually, however, the movement came to be dominated by sociopolitical goals*

---

[84] Gaçiarz, "Employee Self-Management in the 1980s," 121.
[85] Slay, *The Polish Economy*, 69.

connected with the endeavour on the part of the self-managing bodies to participate in the shaping of systemic visions of the transformation of the Polish national economy.[86] [emphasis added]

It was in this context of increasing boldness on the part of Solidarity that in 1988, the Messner government significantly raised prices on consumer goods, rents, and fuel, causing waves of protests and strikes to erupt. Demands now went beyond wage hikes to keep up with prices; calls for the re-legalization of Solidarity were soon heard. The government placated strikers by hiking nominal wages, which resulted in a nearly 14 percent increase in real wages in 1988. The elusive goal of economic equilibrium was further than ever from realization, and after another strike wave in the summer, the government resigned. The strikes and subsequent negotiations had a more subtle yet crucial outcome as well.

As the talks began, the union's factory committees reemerged on the shop floor, reinvigorating previously dormant employee councils or electing new ones. The councils, in turn, began to exercise their legal prerogatives over firm decisions, often in an effort to combat the managerial appropriation of state assets. Indeed, by early 1989, the communist property regime had completely collapsed: on the one hand, state firms had come to own themselves, with workers and managers vying for control. On the other hand, around the edges of state enterprises an increasingly open but unregulated private sector was thriving on the economy's overall shortages.[87]

And it was also after the 1988 negotiations that the Polish non-agricultural private sector began to flourish most visibly. Although the formal private sector remained small compared with its counterpart in Hungary, especially on a *per capita* basis, this period was significant for a select group of Polish entrepreneurs who got an early start. For example, of the one hundred richest owners of businesses in Poland in 1994, a majority "began their private enterprises before 1989, taking advantage of economic liberalization under the last Communist governments."[88] As in Hungary in the late 1980s, some in the party-state apparatus also used their political connections to open businesses, becoming part of a trend sociologist that Jadwiga Staniszkis dubbed the "enfranchisement of the *nomenklatura.*" Jeanine Wedel nicely captures the irony of the fact that as some officials traded political capital for economic capital, Solidarity activists newly released from prison under martial law often switched from "risky political to economic activity," establishing companies that "trade[ed] computers, electronic equipment and information." But she also points out that the "*nomenklatura* men" had a definitive advantage: many started in business

---

[86] Gaçiarz, "Employee Self-Management in the 1980s," 122.

[87] Levitas, unpublished manuscript, 38.

[88] Ákos Róna-Tas, "Post-Communist Transition and the Absent Middle Class in East-Central Europe," in Victoria Bonnell, ed., *Identities in Transition* (Berkeley: University of California Press, 1996), 37.

by appropriating state property – "including entire factories" – or selling them at deep discounts to "cronies."[89]

Spontaneous privatization, as this type of corruption came to be called, was common in Hungary too, at least until the first post-communist government, fearful of the potential for revenue loss to a state budget perpetually in deficit, imposed much stricter controls in 1991.[90] By all accounts, it was even more dramatic in Poland, if only because both the PUWP and the state administration were in considerably greater disarray by the late 1980s. But no reliable measures of comparative degrees of spontaneous privatization are available, and although "successful" spontaneous privatization schemes must at times also have required entrepreneurial talents, such schemes were neither a sound nor a sufficient basis from which to develop a thriving private sector in an incipient market economy, as the Russian example clearly shows.

To be sure, the last communist government, headed by Mieczysław Rakowski, who became prime minister in September 1988, did pursue a variety of reform proposals, though from a somewhat different angle. In December of 1988, legislation was passed liberalizing the law on joint ventures, legalizing the underground trade in foreign currency and introducing partial convertibility, reducing subsidies and price controls, and easing restrictions on the establishment of private firms. The legal private sector grew rapidly in 1989 as a result. It is estimated that 294,000 private firms were established – a doubling of the number of such firms in one year. And as many as 500,000 people may have been "engaged in various forms of unregistered but legal trade, especially of the informal, street variety."[91]

What had changed? The power asymmetry that characterized relations between state and society under communism still obtained, both in terms of actual coercive capabilities and people's broad vision of the possible. This is why the regime in Poland seemed as deeply entrenched as it did in Hungary. Party-state rule, everyone still believed, was as much the future as it was the past. But within this context of power asymmetry, the rough equality that had for decades stalemated state and society finally had been altered – for two reasons. First, Solidarity managed effectively to harness disparate societal forces for long enough to apply significant political pressure on the party-state. Second, and just as crucial, the party-state's historical failure to find a reform path "out of the freeze" – to borrow Szlajfer's term yet again – left it in an ironic position: liberalize the private sector swiftly, or risk an economic debacle whose political ramifications it could not possibly control. The Polish economist Mirosław

---

[89] Wedel, ed., *The Unplanned Society*, and Jadwiga Staniszkis, *The Dynamics of the Breakthrough in Eastern Europe: The Polish Experience* (Berkeley: University of California Press 1991), quoted in Wedel, 125.

[90] It would, of course, be naive to imagine that all forms of spontaneous privatization ceased in Hungary as a result of better-specified and controlled privatization plans; indeed, there is ample anecdotal evidence that many forms of corruption in the privatization process continued, albeit on a smaller scale, and that some new forms of corruption were born.

[91] Slay, *The Polish Economy*, 77.

Zeliński makes a similar point in terms of lessons learned. By 1989, Zeliński suggests, the regime finally understood that it was preferable to "direct" people toward business activities than to have them strike.[92] This is why the Polish party-state now made it easier to obtain administrative permission to open and run the kind of businesses that for decades had absorbed so much of the time and energy of the Hungarian citizenry.

The regime, however, was not alone in facing a deep irony. A surprise was in store for workers, too. As the privatization of the economy gained acceptance and momentum in 1989 and 1990, the salience of workers' councils began to decline.

It turned out, with an almost brutal force, that the relative strength and attractiveness of employee self-management had its source in its political functions, and also in a structure of the political system in which management was dependent upon extra-economic factors that required bargaining between social and political forces. The removal of the barrier to reform of the political system resulted in the progressive elimination of the elements of political bargaining from the processes of management. In that situation, employee self-management became an institution artificially rooted in the management of enterprises.[93]

Nevertheless, workers' councils would continue to exert their influence in state firms for some time to come, often slowing privatization.

Conclusion

After the strikes of 1976, workers at the Radom and Ursus factories were arrested and put on trial. This was the impetus for a variety of groups of individuals to band together to help defend the accused. In founding KOR, these groups not only bridged "the fatal gulf between workers and intellectuals" as well as "some deep divides within the critical intelligentsia"; they opened the way for a renaissance of civil society in Poland. As Garton Ash points out, the fact that the Gierek regime permitted these developments when repression was unquestionably "technically feasible" suggests that "the 'high-ups,' notably Gierek himself . . . thought that this flowering of intellectual opposition would not amount to a serious political threat, while tolerance might win them a broader measure of co-operation from the intelligentsia."[94]

Gierek could not have been more mistaken. The year 1976 was a moment when "socialist intellectuals" and the Church were starting to craft a common vocabulary of self-defense and defense of the workers against the state. By 1979, this would become "a tacit alliance of workers, intelligentsia and Church

---

[92] Author's interview with Mirosław Zeliński, Warsaw, November 1995.

[93] Gaçiarz, "Employee Self-Management in the 1980s," 122.

[94] Garton Ash, *The Polish Revolution*, 18–19. Certainly, other factors, also mentioned by Ash, such as detente and the increasing power of the Church, played a role. The latter factor only lends support, however, to the thesis that societal actors' understandings of the limits of possibility were blurring in Poland, and the former does not negate it.

unprecedented in Polish history, unique in the Soviet bloc, [and] unseen in the West."[95]

An analogous discursive consensus could be found in Hungary only among party-state reformers and their academic allies, who struggled continually to expand their shared understandings to include more and more party "hard-liners." At that time, many dissident intellectuals in Hungary – sociologists, philosophers, and other writers – still faced considerable constraints even as reform economists, who had already achieved significant leeway and since 1963 had increasingly influenced government policies, were given even more oppor-tunities to travel and to write freely.

Moreover, in Poland after August 1980, "even those who knew there were limits," Garton Ash observes, "did not know exactly what those limits were. The impossible, after all, had already happened" in the course of what Jacek Kuroń ironically dubbed Poland's "evolutionary revolution."[96] Now it was a matter of how far the opposition could push for *clarity*, for *explicit* rules, for rationality, and above all, for independence not only for workers and groups in civil society, but for the nation as a whole.

In Hungary, "self-limitation" appeared, at least, to succeed, but in Poland, continuing attempts at a self-limiting revolution ultimately failed. These failures seem to buttress the claim that "the overwhelming majority of Polish society, and therefore of Solidarity, was from the start profoundly "radical."[97] And yet, in January 1971, after Gierek's marathon speech at the Warski Shipyard in Sczeczecin, the workers cried out "*Pomozemy!*" – "We will help you! We will help you!" in your plans to reform the system and to reconstruct the country. This they offered despite the government's brutality toward unarmed workers in the Lenin Shipyard at Gdańsk on the morning of December 16, 1970, just a little over a month earlier. Even a decade later, in March of 1981, union leaders briefly entertained a cooperative stance, provided workers were "fully informed about the country's economic position." If treated as rational eco-nomic agents, they were willing to "work a six-day week," and if economic conditions warranted it, to "go to work on *Sunday*! Even if the priest shouts at us!"[98]

It was not to be. A decade and a half later, Privatization Minister Janusz Levandowski said that "the arena of struggle in Poland was the state firm."[99] He was partly right. The firm was *the* original, most important point of perme-able contact between state and society, but labor's struggles with the party-state transcended the firm, and permeated and reshaped broader state-society con-flicts. This is what made Solidarity a unique hybrid. Indeed, the infusion of

[95] Garton Ash, *The Polish Revolution*, 20, 25.

[96] Ibid., 88.

[97] Ibid., 86.

[98] Wojciech Kamiński, leader of the Warsaw Transport Union, and Lech Wałęsa, quoted in Garton Ash, *The Polish Revolution: Solidarity*, 137.

[99] Author's interview with Janusz Levandowski (first Privatization Minister in post-communist Poland), Princeton, 1994.

Solidarity into the factory allowed Polish labor to exercise its collective veto power so effectively. Labor was able partially to repossess not only the state firm but also economic management, and to hold on to some of those gains even after party-state leaders and plan bureaucrats had ceded the stage to elected politicians and market-oriented privatizers.

Yet the outcome might have been different had the regime been able to stretch and bend its own ideological constraints. In this important sense, the key struggle took place on the discursive field where labor and the party-state had engaged with increasing intensity since 1956.

5

Hungary

Property Relations Recast

Words are also deeds.
V. I. Lenin[1]

The history of Hungarian reformism suggests that Lenin was right. We need only recall how reformist leaders, particularly during the period of the New Course, manipulated Marx's and Lenin's own words in order to justify official deviations from socialist dogma. But *how* words become deeds is neither a linear process nor a matter of pure political will. As Douglass North has argued, any attempt at purposeful change of a system must build incrementally on the "mental models" already embedded in the organizations comprising that system's broader institutional framework.[2] At the same time, agents of innovation must also exploit windows of opportunity that can close as swiftly as they open. If innovators move too quickly or brazenly, they are likely to provoke countermoves that block or even reverse their agendas. If they move too slowly or timidly, they risk wasting advantageous circumstances that might never again present themselves. A political-discursive strategy that gives reformers a hold on both the scope and pace of change is an essential part of success.

In 1982, Hungarian reformers managed to bring about a broad institutionalization of private entrepreneurship precisely because they devised and

---

[1] In "Dve taktiki sotsial-demokratii v demokraticheskoi revoliutsii" ("Two Tactics of Social-Democracy in a Democratic Revolution"), *Polnoe sobranie sochinenii*, Vol. 11 (Moscow: Gosudarstvennoe izdatel'stvo politicheskoi literatury, 1960): 59.

[2] Douglass C. North, *Transaction Costs, Institutions, and Economic Performance* (San Francisco: International Center for Economic Growth, 1992), 16. In fact, North equates true revolutions with institutional "gridlock," and finds that these rare "revolutionary" cases have generally been less truly revolutionary than they appear at first glance. On purposeful change in state-socialist systems, and for a detailed discussion of the concept of reform, see János Kornai, *The Socialist System: The Political Economy of Communism* (Princeton: Princeton University Press, 1992); and János Kornai, "The Hungarian Reform Process: Visions, Hopes and Reality," *Journal of Economic Literature* XXIV, no. 4 (December 1986): 1687–1737.

successfully deployed just such a political-discursive strategy. By drawing on the legacies of prior reform experiments, they set out to reinterpret the official ideology's building blocks, thus taking a seemingly "incremental" approach to the transformation of the dominant "mental model." In the beginning, for example, reformers denied that this was a "reform" at all, insisting instead that it simply represented the perfecting or "further development" of the planned economy.[3] Moreover, once the process was underway, "old" terms and procedures inherited from previous reform waves enabled reformers to discuss safely what in other countries was considered dangerous at that time, and, as late as 1991, was viewed by many in the Soviet Union as "subversive."[4] (In fact, no comparable reform was undertaken by any other state socialist country before the political transformations of 1989–90, and in some cases, not even then.) In the end, the 1982 reformers redefined ideological tenets like "full employment" and "exploitation," as well as the norms that governed work.

At the same time, however, highly placed key actors accelerated the tempo of this piecemeal transformative process by deploying a tried-and-true "coup-like" method. In the past, officials contemplating unorthodox policy packages had typically conducted and contained struggles within the party-state apparatus through this method, "circumvent[ing] the bureaucratic system" and "exercis[ing] bureaucratic power."[5] Mini-coups occurred, for example, during economic crises, particularly when new and unconventional "centralized measures" considered "of great political importance" were under serious consideration.[6] In 1982, reformers fought amongst themselves and with conservatives over the constitutive terms of socialist ideology, but they were careful to place their early battles within discrete institutional and rhetorical parameters. And it was only as reformers gained momentum by imposing their reinterpretation of those key terms on conservatives, that they moved to "sell" this reinterpretation to the larger groups within the Party apparatus. Ultimately, the reformers

---

[3] Tamás Bauer, "Hungarian Economic Reform in East European Perspective," *East European Politics and Societies* 2, no. 3 (Fall 1988): 418.

[4] In 1991, one could easily find articles appearing almost daily in the Western press showing evidence of repression of so-called "speculation" and "black market" activity in the Soviet Union, forced exchange of ruble notes above a specified denomination to lessen opportunities for private economic activity, and the like. One article mentions an old woman in prison for manufacturing bootleg vodka, and the criminality of raffling soap in scarce supply ("A Ural Spring Thaw, an Ideology Clog," *New York Times*, April 4, 1991); another reports the practice of sentencing fishermen to ten years in jail for trying to compete with the state monopoly in caviar harvesting ("Astrakhan Journal: Hotel for Young Lovers? Perestroika Turns Pale," *New York Times*, July 8, 1991); yet another states that "cooperative workers can be equated with bandits and black marketeers" ("As Soviets Wait Tremulously, Ailing Economy Struggles On," *New York Times*, July 14, 1991).

[5] Judit Fekete described various stages in the life of a socialist reform as similar to a "putsch,"or a "coup" – and ultimately, as a "campaign." Judit Fekete, "'Coup' As a Method of Management: Crisis Management Methods in Hungary in the Eighties," *Acta Oeconomica* 42, no. 1–2 (1990): 55–72. For the original conception of "campaign" as used by Fekete, see Károly Attila Soós, *Terv, Kampány, Pénz (Plan, Campaign, Money)* (Budapest: Jogi és Közagazdasági, 1986).

[6] Fekete, "'Coup' as a Method of Management."

managed to create new and stable cognitive expectations about their country's socialist future. Put another way, they institutionalized a hybrid "mental model" that simultaneously built on and altered the one already "embedded" in the Hungarian state-socialist system.

In this political-discursive struggle over cognitive expectations and institutional change, risk-mediation and manipulation of potential adversaries were certainly a concern for reformers. But risk-mediation and manipulation, while crucial, were not the only objectives. The political-discursive formations associated with the reform also greatly enhanced the capacity of state elites to reconcile socialist ideology with capitalist practices, and altered the attitudes of a population long accustomed to an institutional structure that appeared to be fixed even as it was changing internally.[7] Indeed, as if molded by North's insight, the reform's discursive reconstructions rendered a radical program all but conservative – a reform program, in fact, that appeared to bolster existing belief systems in the very act of systemic transformation.

It is no small matter that this veil of immutability – torn apart a mere seven years after the 1982 reform – was preserved intact by key actors' ability to conciliate socialist ideology with capitalist practice and by their minimization of hazard and rivalry through political discourse. For it was precisely these components of "Hungarian pragmatism" that muted the kind of discord emblematic of Polish politics. Here we need only recall that just as reformist party-state officials began to explore a property-rights reform in Hungary, in Poland the distinction between "us" and "them" was entrenched once and for all as the central referent of political discourse. It is also worth recalling that whereas the Hungarian party-state and society engaged in a continual, if tacit, renegotiation of their consumerist pact, Polish workers, peasants, and intellectuals came to stand as one – "the people" – in direct normative opposition to "the communist authorities."[8]

Nevertheless, although Hungary's repertoire of institutional economic reform was much greater than Poland's, it too adopted debt-led growth as one among several strategies for maintaining the consumerist pact with the population. Thus the *immediate* impetus for the Hungarian reform was provided by a sharp deterioration in the external balance and its worrisome implications for payment of the growing debt-service. Hungary, like Yugoslavia, the GDR, and Poland, initially responded to the oil crises of the 1970s and ensuing trade-account imbalances by stretching its long-standing model of extensive growth. But since domestic inputs of labor, capital, and raw materials had already been fully mobilized, the country now turned to external credit. By 1978, however,

---

[7] This apparent "fixity" was bolstered not only discursively, but also by a certain indeterminacy built into the 1982 reform, which did not unequivocally revise property rights throughout the economy, and by the fact that such rights were in some cases left purposely vague even within the expanded private sector.

[8] Jan Kubik, "Who done it: Workers, Intellectuals, or someone else? Controversy over Solidarity's origins and social composition," *Theory and Society*, 23 (1994):441–465.

in the context of rising interest rates and deteriorating terms of trade,[9] the debt service could only be met by taking drastic measures on the domestic economic front.

Thus a new wave of reform measures began in 1979, attempting to bring domestic (mostly non-agricultural) producer prices in line with world market prices. The new policy, which also meant the reduction of numerous subsidies on producer and consumer goods, was implemented as part of a larger effort to reduce foreign indebtedness through the restriction of domestic demand. This in turn led to a fall in real wages, consumption, and expenditures on social services, and eventually to a trade surplus that helped reduce slightly the country's considerable foreign debt.[10]

And in another attempt to address the deeper institutional causes of inefficiency, a number of large monopolies were now once again reorganized into smaller firms, while other large plants were decentralized, so that some 300 "new" state-owned firms were established between 1980 and 1983. In a pattern repeated in Poland and elsewhere, large capital projects undertaken in the 1970s by mammoth enterprises and partially paid for with Western credits failed to produce the hoped-for hard-currency earnings. The Hungarian sociologist László Bruszt noted that in 1982, "75% of the losses were incurred by 10% of the enterprises," and that in fact much of the national budget deficit and the stock of corporate losses could be traced back to these projects.[11]

But whether indebted or not, virtually every state-socialist country faced similar – or worse – returns from equally large and lumpy investment projects.[12] In Hungary, however, the poor showing of these large investment projects strengthened the position of reformers arguing for a re-thinking of official ideology toward private enterprise. The painstaking process of ideological revision

---

[9] Due to increased world energy prices, Hungary's increasing import-intensivity, and loss of market-shares to the NICs.

[10] Galasi and Sziráczki, "The New Industrial Organization," 22. Paul Hare explains that in the early 1970s, Hungary, hoping to upgrade its industrial plant, accepted the Western credits that banks were offering on easier terms in the context of their massively increased liquidity in the form of petrodollars. But a vicious circle of problems ensued. Energy-intensive investments meant that the investments made with the credits were less profitable than they might otherwise have been. Together with the fact that much of the debt was not used for investment at all, but for maintenance of domestic consumption levels, this led to the accumulation of a still larger hard-currency deficit in the context of the second oil crisis of 1979. In the early 1980s, some of the sizable payments came due just as the Polish debt crisis and effective default intensified the banking community's worries about the creditworthiness of both Poland and Hungary. In late 1982, Hungary was for a time unable to negotiate new credits with Western banks, and only "severe domestic restraint" restored the confidence of the banking community. Paul Hare, "Industrial Development of Hungary Since World War II," paper presented at the 1986 ACLS/SSRC Joint Economic Committee on Eastern Europe Conference (February 1986), 29.

[11] László Bruszt, "The Politics of Private Business and Public Enterprises," EUI Colloquium Papers, Doc. EUI 261/87 Col. 45 (Florence: European University Institute, June 1988), 41.

[12] János Kornai, "Transformational Recession: A General Phenomenon Examined Through the Example of Hungary's Development," *Economie Appliquée* XLVI (1993, no. 2), 181–227, Table 6, 192.

that ensued hinged most crucially on a particular reading of past reforms' signals as *positive indications of reformism's politically non-threatening character*. Not surprisingly, this revision was hotly contested at several points. Still, an early indication that radical reform might be possible came when even conservatives started to take the new line that *large state enterprises* – and *not private firms*, as Leninist ideology held – had turned into "vehicles of particular interest [that] obstructed the assertion of general economic interests, especially the efforts to improve the balance of payments situation."[13] By 1980, as the economic crisis deepened and the foreign debt assumed alarming proportions, reformers turned to the sector the Party had for so long tried unsuccessfully to repress. In fact, HSWP (Hungarian Socialist Workers Party) leaders convened a committee of (mostly non-Party) experts to discuss the advisability of formally integrating second-economy activities into the larger economy. In particular, they charged the committee with finding ways to harness the second economy to increase the productivity and efficiency of state firms. The final outcome was far more radical. A little more than a year later, the HSWP recognized the rights of Hungarians to engage in most forms of private enterprise, to employ others in their businesses, to form joint ventures with foreign firms, to import and export – in short, to conduct most economic activity normally associated with commerce and manufacturing. Such rights were no longer to be granted selectively and arbitrarily at the discretion of municipal councils or party officials. Private enterprise – though subject to various legal regulations and to an ever-loosening series of size limitations – became simply a *citizen's* prerogative.

Natural and Logical: Points on the Possibility Frontier

If, by the early 1980s, polarization seemed "natural" in Poland, in Hungary the 1982 property-rights legislation that followed the reform initiative of the late 1970s might have appeared to be a "logical," almost inevitable outcome, given the confluence of endogenous rigidities, external shocks, and the legacy of reforms. The immediate background for the 1982 reform, after all, was a period of intensifying economic crisis that had become grave enough by 1978 to warrant increasingly open debate within the Party apparatus.[14] Most notably, party and government officials responsible for economic policy were alarmed by declining investment, slow growth, and stagnating living standards.

---

[13] Bruszt, "The Politics of Private Business and Public Enterprises," 41.

[14] In addressing the question of why radical reform could not be implemented under less pressured circumstances, many analysts of socialist systems have noted the reactive nature of the economic decision-making process, central planning notwithstanding. By its very nature, crisis is usually handled reactively in any system, and is everywhere exacerbated by delayed government action. But Fekete mentions the "conditioning" favoring late action on the part of socialist bureaucracies that equated stability not with the management of problems, but with the semblance of "no problems. Thus, [socialist] bureaucracies do not take notice of existing conflicts" until they are forced to do so by "phenomena which in [their] own judgement . . . endanger political stability . . ." Fekete, "'Coup' as a Method of Management," 58, n. 4.

The concern for living standards, however, was not the only reform legacies exerting pressure for change. The legacy of undogmatic, *professional* economics also came into play. Specifically, the economics profession in Hungary by and large felt free to point out the core inconsistency in the methods employed theretofore by central economic management: recentralizing on the one hand, while attempting to impose world-market discipline on the other.[15] Moreover, whereas political-discursive adaptation in Poland served polarization, in Hungary it seemed destined to enhance reformist compromise. Full employment, for example, had once meant that almost "every able-bodied person had to be employed in the state sector." But by the late 1970s – in the context of an expanding second economy and against a historic backdrop of reforms – the State Wage and Labor Office began to emphasize that employment was *not* the exclusive business of the state-firm and state-cooperative sectors. By the beginning of the 1980's, for example, the concept of full employment was understood to include "all those employed in 'socially useful' activities, including [those] in the second economy, in households, etc." As for the government's role: its responsibility was "to create the conditions that would allow the *economy as a whole* to supply employment opportunities."[16]

Despite this powerful combination of economic pressure and reformist legacies, the intra-party debates preceding the adoption of the 1982 reform package contradict the impression of an inexorable march toward a radical policy shift.[17] Opposition to the proposal was strong enough that it could have been turned around at several points prior to its implementation. And although Hungary's reformist legacy did facilitate political-discursive moves toward accommodation, the construction of reform discourse in general and reform policy in particular remained an ongoing and complex process punctuated by struggles whose outcomes were far from preordained. In fact, it is precisely because reformers recognized the political perils inherent in the reform proposal that they proceeded from the start in a "coup-like" fashion.

---

[15] The economists Péter Galasi and György Sziráczki point out that two types of reforms occurred simultaneously. On the one hand, attempts were made to recentralize control over state-firms' investment-funds and imports while issuing directives aimed at increasing their exports. On the other hand, price and currency reforms were implemented (for example, uniform forint exchange rate), as well as the decentralization of some large enterprises, as mentioned earlier. See Péter Galasi and György Sziráczki, "A Review of Developments in the Organization and Structure of Small and Medium-Sized Enterprises: Hungary." Budapest: Karl Marx University of Economics, 1986. Unpublished paper.

[16] István Gábor, Péter Galasi, and György Kővári. Interview with author, Budapest, September 1991. Gábor, Galasi, and Kővári reaffirmed the views they offered here and elsewhere in the book in subsequent rounds of interviews with the author. Budapest, summer 1994, fall 1996.

[17] These debates are characterized here on the basis of interviews with Anna Székács, one of the architects of the reform who was also its major spokesperson after it became law; former Deputy Minister of Planning and later Minister of Finance István Hetényi, who was responsible for the original reform conception; and Professors István Gábor and Péter Galasi, who were participants in the first expert commission to discuss the second economy.

The internal coup was meant to involve only a trusted few. In addition, it was geared toward informal consultation at various levels of the party-state apparatus, and it was designed to minimize internal acrimony for as long as possible. The process unfolded roughly as follows. The Deputy Director of the National Planning Office, who was also a State Secretary, first assembled a group of government officials and scholars to debate whether and how the informal sector might be used to ease the difficulties of the state sector and of the economy more generally. His staff then drafted a document purporting to synthesize the group's divergent opinions concerning the appropriate role of the private sector in a socialist economy. The State Secretary presented this document to the Central Committee's Economic Sub-Committee,[18] which, having approved it, set in motion a two-year process of negotiation with ministries, trade unions, and other representative organizations.

This protracted effort was orchestrated by a special inter-agency task force and was spearheaded by a small team in the Ministry of Finance, which produced a reform proposal that ultimately became the subject of official debate at the highest levels of the Party before it was put to a vote and approved. Reformers ultimately won the day, and the reformist "coup" culminated in a successful "campaign" to educate lower-level Party and government institutions and agencies as well as the public about the need for the new private and quasi-private partnerships. But as we are about to see, if the country's deep history of reform and its legacies mattered greatly to this outcome, so did actors' tactical skills, political imagination, and discursive struggles.

Intellectual-Ideological Background of Reform

In a resolution passed in April 1978, the Central Committee of the Hungarian Socialist Workers' Party (HSWP) identified a number of areas of economic activity that could be developed to improve living standards. These were "disciplined work, the utilization of leisure time, the relations of distribution, and the development of services."[19] Some months later, the National Planning Office began a study of income distribution, and in this framework, a survey of the second economy. The study aimed to answer two questions: how did participation in the informal economy affect income distribution, and how could such activities be harnessed to the possible benefit of the state sector?[20]

The study, subject to the normal bureaucratic process, moved slowly. So in order to "take the initiative" in the guise of an "outsider," State Secretary and Deputy Minister of the National Planning Office István Hetényi established an

---

[18] This committee was not a sub-set of the Central Committee (as opposed to the Political Committee). The Economic Sub-Committee was chaired by a member of the Central Committee, but also had outside members.

[19] See the resolution of the HSWP's Central Committee: "On Work Performed Since the 11th Congress and the Tasks of the Party (April 28–29, 1978)," in *Az MSZMP Határozatai És Dokimentumai, 1975–1980 (Resolutions and Documents of the HSWP, 1975–1980)* (Budapest: Kossuth Kiadó, 1983), 764–71.

[20] Fekete, "'Coup' as a Method of Management," 64.

expert commission to examine the problem. In this way, the work was speeded up outside of normal channels, and the Deputy Director was able to mitigate any potential political risk involved in the introduction of a reform proposal at the end of almost a decade of "anti-reform mentality."[21] By late 1979, Minister Hetényi was able to convene a meeting of government and academic experts to discuss the role that private economic activity might play in revitalizing the Hungarian economy.

Drawing on the dense informal networks that had linked scholars and party functionaries since at least the early 1960s, the Ministry asked thirteen individuals to attend this meeting in their personal and professional, but *not* institutional capacities. Professors István Gábor and Péter Galasi of the Karl Marx University of Economics – subsequently renamed Budapest University of Economic Sciences and Public Administration[22] – were among those present. Individually, and with Galasi, Gábor had written seminal articles on the second economy, particularly on the need to integrate it into the official economy and expand its operational possibilities. Approved and funded since 1977 by the Social Science Institute of the Central Committee of the Hungarian Socialist Workers Party (MSZMP/KB Társadalom Tudományi Intézet) – the Party's research institute – Gábor's work had been officially debated at the Institute and even in the Academy of Sciences. Now his work was about to provide a central referent for the thirteen members of the committee as they engaged in critical readings of available research, commentary, informal discussions at high levels, and various rounds of official debate.

That this debate could take place at all in 1979–80 was remarkable. It bears repeating that neither the relative openness demonstrated in 1977 by the party's Social Science Institute nor the Planning Office's 1979 initiative can be explained solely by economic pressures, since these were equally or more severe elsewhere. Nor is it sufficient explanation that the second economy was particularly large and diverse in Hungary – its dimensions, after all, were far from negligible in other state-socialist countries.[23] Even the fact that István Gábor was publishing pathbreaking research on the informal economy cannot account for the interest shown by the Social Science Institute and the Planning Office. For instance, why would any typically risk-averse party-member willingly associate himself with the "second economy " – the term Gábor used – when the term itself was controversial precisely because many of the informal sector's activities were not

---

[21] Ibid.

[22] In September 2004, the Budapest University of Economic Sciences and Public Administration was officially renamed the "Corvinus University."

[23] See, for example, Gregory Grossman, "Sub-Rosa Privatization and Marketization in the USSR," Berkeley-Duke Occasional Papers on the Second Economy of the USSR, no. 17 (Department of Economics, Duke University, 1989). See also Łoś 1990, Aslund 1985, and Wedel 1986. On the Hungarian second economy, see Iván Szelényi 1988; Gábor 1989, 1988, 1985; Sik 1994, 1988; David Stark, "Coexisting Organizational Forms in Hungary's Emerging Mixed Economy"; Andorka 1990; Kenedi 1982; Róna-Tas 1989, 1995, 1998. In any case, as this study has shown, the fact that Hungary's second economy was more institutionally and sectorally diverse was due not to any "natural" development, but to a unique history of economic reform.

only illegal but officially regarded as inherently "shady"? And indeed, when Gábor's earliest research was formally debated at the Academy of Sciences and at the Party's Social Science Institute, many commentators praised the originality and thoughtfulness of the work, but emphatically distanced themselves from what they perceived to be its political implications.[24] During the 1978 debate at the Party institute, a professor of political economy from the Party College (Párt Főiskola) summed up the implications of the research with his exasperated exclamation of protest: "But . . . this means that socialism has to throw in the towel!"[25]

So how to explain the idea to liberalize the second economy? Minister Hetényi's response sheds some light on the processes and institutional linkages behind the incipient reform concept.

Q: How was the idea itself born?
A: In Hungary there was a close connection among academic researchers, on the one hand, and the Ministry of Planning and the Party Central (Párt Központ), on the other. If someone was working on a particular topic . . . we were aware of it. So the idea [of liberalization] was in the air . . . The [route] that ideas tended to follow was more or less like this: researchers would write an article, the Ministry of Finance would encounter a particular tax issue or problem, which in turn somehow would reach the Party's Social Science Institute, and then the Central Committee. There someone might say: we ought to do something about [this problem]. Someone has got to decide that . . . the state should occupy itself with [this problem]. Finally, someone [would ask] the Minister of Planning to put together some materials telling [the Central Committee] what to do.
Q: If you had not made this your project, is it possible that nothing would have been done?
A: No. Someone [from above] told us to do 'something,' even if they didn't specify exactly what this 'something' had to be. In determining what was to be done, we [at the Ministry] played a role. But obviously, the idea of doing 'something' was discussed in the Party Central. Maybe TTI [the Party's Social Science Research Institute] put out a study and Havasi[26] decided it would be debated the following year in the Economic Subcommittee. This was enough so that [the study] would be written into a work-plan, and then we [were] told to prepare the necessary materials.[27]

---

[24] For many, the main problem was that Gábor and Galasi viewed the second economy as structurally embedded in the socialist system and intimately linked to labor shortages (itself a structural feature of the system). The main argument against this view was that policy mistakes or historical accidents had caused the phenomenon. (Two exceptions in the debate at the Academy of Sciences were János Kornai and János Timár, who both accepted Gábor and Galasi's analysis.) Gábor, interview with author, Budapest, October 1991; and typed transcripts of the Academy of Sciences debate, unpublished mimeo (Budapest: Department of Human Resources, Budapest University of Economics, 1979).

[25] The professor was Jenő Rövő, and he meant that certain systemic features of the second economy could undermine Hungarian socialism, for example: that income disparities between earnings in the state sector and the second economy held serious implications for work morale. Gábor, interview with author, September 1991.

[26] Ferenc Havasi, then head of the Economic Subcommittee of the Central Committee of the HSWP.

[27] István Hetényi, interview with author, Budapest, October 1991. Hetényi reaffirmed the views he offered here and elsewhere in the book in subsequent rounds of interviews with the author. Budapest, summer 1995, fall 1996.

Despite the political opportunity provided by the green light from above, then, Hetényi and his team were under no obligation to champion any *particular* proposal for easing the economic crisis, and someone else in his position might have avoided the ideas he espoused. Nor did the Central Committee's decision to study the potential contribution to the state sector of the informal economy guarantee that the 1982 reform would emerge at all, let alone in the form in which it eventually did. It would have been much simpler on every level, for example, to stop at the liberalization of the small extant private sector (allowing more employees, launching special credit-schemes, placing greater emphasis on leasing.)[28] Furthermore, without at least one minister supporting the idea wholeheartedly, and lacking a hard-working alliance of economists and government technocrats to hash out the regulatory framework, the proposal could never have been elaborated. This required a group of highly qualified people who truly believed in the proposal to fight for it against opposing ministries and the larger party apparatus.[29]

Here, too, several reform legacies proved essential to success. The first was the relative openness on the part of influential politicians and technocrats to foreign intellectual currents and to the ideas of pro-reform economists and sociologists at home. In the late 1970s, some Hungarian intellectuals were intrigued by the "Small Is Beautiful"[30] fashion raging abroad, and by the growing interest in small-scale enterprise and appropriate technologies. From this perspective, they came to see Hungary's second economy, though resource-poor, as a way of motivating individuals and mobilizing the energies of the population. In addition, Hungarian economists were influenced by the work of their Western counterparts and, perhaps most profoundly, by János Kornai, who is today widely regarded as the preeminent analyst of state-socialist and post-socialist economic systems.[31]

The second reform legacy had to do, not surprisingly, with informal networks. Despite the controversy it aroused, Gábor's research was ultimately supported by the Party's Social Science Institute because of the personal influence and connections of the head of his department at the university, János Timár,

---

[28] Simpler, that is, relative to the complexity of the requisite economic and legal regulation, not to mention political infighting.

[29] Several reasons for commitment to a reform of property rights emerged from my interviews with members of the core group of officials associated with this reform. They ranged from personal background (parents or grandparents who had been self-employed artisans or entrepreneurs) to the learning-curve associated with the experience of other reforms such as the 1968 NEM, and a general conviction based on such learning that further liberalization was needed.

[30] Ernst Friedrich Schumacher, *Small Is Beautiful: Economics As If People Really Mattered* (New York: Harper and Row, 1973).

[31] Evidence for this claim is provided by a detailed analysis of articles published in the late 1980s by the party-sanctioned journal of economics. This quantitative study compares Kornai's influence with that of Marx, Lenin, and other foreign and Hungarian and economists. See György Such and István János Tóth, "A Magyar Közgazdaságtudomány a Közgazdasági Szemle Tudománymetriai Vizsgálatának Tükrében" (Hungarian economics as reflected by a scientometric analysis of articles published in *Közgazdasági Szemle*), *Közgazdasági Szemle* 36, no. 10 (October 1989): 1163–1241.

a well-respected and audacious long-time Party member who a decade later
would publish a comprehensive study of time-use in the second economy versus the first.[32] Timár, a close friend of István Hetényi's, then Deputy Director
of the National Planning Office, had at one time also worked under him there.
Timár remembers calling Hetényi's attention to Gábor's research findings on
the nature and extent of the second economy, and telling him that "this [was]
something we [the Party] could use; that *this could fit in the state line.*"[33]

The third legacy involved Hungarian "realism" and its "pragmatic" bent.
Timár, for example, operated on the premise that the country's state-socialist
system had really already begun to "fall apart" during the New Course in the
early 1950s. It was at that critical point, he felt, that the key elements of the
Hungarian "difference" had been established, so that by the late 1970s and
early 1980s, the prevalence of a kind of socialist *laissez-faire* allowed "people"
to look for ways to "downsize the regime" (*"leépíteni a rendszert"*: literally,
"build down"). By "people," Timár meant pro-reform officials and influential
scholars whose opinions had to be accommodated somehow by the party-state
apparatus. Indeed, it was this accommodative imperative that in Timár's esti-
mation explained his own ability to get Gábor's research proposal accepted
and funded by the Party's Social Science Institute.[34] Timár mused in retrospect that "fear lived longer than anything that could reasonably cause it";
that the system's increasing political elasticity outstripped actors' awareness of
change.

But while the New Course had in fact marked a critical juncture, it clearly
had not predetermined the outcome of future reform attempts. Timár himself
had waged significant and costly ideological battles. In the 1960s, he had fought
repeatedly for his "right" to hire "bourgeois intellectuals" instead of individuals
with peasant or proletarian backgrounds who were judged more suitable by his
superiors. Although he was censured for his defiance of orthodoxy, in 1974 he
went on to argue with hard-liners at a meeting of the Party's Labor Committee
over whether or not it was permissible to talk about a "labor market" and
"unemployment." This time he was severely reprimanded for using terms like
"unemployment" and "market" – and such "reprimands" could and often did
hurt a professional's career. Even so, in the end, Timár won ground. At least one
of the previously disreputable expressions – "labor market" – did appear in the
document subsequently produced on the basis of that Committee meeting.[35]

---

[32] János Timár, *Idő És Munkaidő* (Time and Worktime) (Budapest: Közgazdasági és Jogi
Könyvkiadó, 1988).

[33] Timár and Hetényi were "old sailing buddies" who trusted one another implicitly. János Timár,
interview with author, Budapest, October 1991.

[34] Ibid. Timár was thinking not only of the thaw that ensued with Stalin's death, but more specifically, of the critical fact that – uniquely in Hungary – in 1952–53, peasants were relieved of the
heavy burden of mandatory deliveries to the state. See Chapter 2 of the present book.

[35] Ibid. In response to my queries about whether his ideological skirmishes had produced any
appreciable effect, Timár recalled this incident as an ideological win for his side in a protracted
battle with orthodox bureaucrats and party hacks. He confirmed the then highly significant

The enabling legacies of reform history – the receptivity of intellectuals to foreign and novel ideas, the sociology of informal ties, and the inter-subjective factor of the Hungarian "difference" – helped Timár negotiate a highly ambiguous political terrain.[36] More specifically, these legacies helped him negotiate his way between two broad parameters. On the positive side, in Hungary, unlike Czechoslovakia or even Poland, few reform-minded party members or researchers were labeled "revisionist," lost their positions, or were exiled after the mid-1960s.[37] On the negative side, as Timár himself stressed, challenges to the construction of socialism at home were not tolerated, and many researchers and people in unrelated walks of life saw much of the 1970s as a politically oppressive time. István Gábor, for example, was only able to "name" and study the second economy thanks to well-connected and helpful superiors and to a friendly ideological micro-climate in his department at the university. Even so, as a young researcher embarking on his career, he was taking a significant risk.

Between these two broad parameters lay a field of action that had been rendered increasingly hazy by the frequent alternation between repressive periods, on the one hand, and periods of liberalization and reform, on the other. Looking back on the late 1970s, Gábor asked rhetorically: "Did the Party really exist? Did it exist if being a conformist was not even worth the effort because one never knew what to conform *to*?"[38] The rules of the game were sufficiently blurred that even the "cadres" – the unquestioning "regime-robots," as one researcher called them – could be caught off-guard by a new reform wave.

Meanwhile, non-conformist researchers – typified by Gábor – and pragmatic party members and sometime high-ranking government officials like Timár,[39] were able to talk to one another *officially* because both knew what could *not* be

---

fact of being permitted to include the term "labor market" in the document by showing me the twenty-year-old transcripts of the meetings, which he dug out from his files during the interview.

[36] Numerous factors influenced the degree to which an official could go against the prevailing party line. To name just a few: high position, especially experience in the Party Central; informal connections among colleagues, especially but not exclusively close connection to Kádár; similar pre-socialist cultural, ethnic, religious, and social backgrounds among colleagues; for a select few, holding the "order of the defense of the socialist homeland" (*socialista hazáért érdemrend*), awarded to those who had distinguished themselves in fighting the Nazis and/or, later, in their efforts to quell the 1956 uprising. If an individual or even his/her father had received this award, then access to housing, acceptance to university, and the purchase of automobiles out of queue were assured; but more to the point, it rendered the recipient (and to a lesser degree, even his immediate descendants) essentially beyond reproach within the Party. Other kinds of decorations could also provide some protection, as might special (publicly recognized) talent or expertise, fame abroad, and so on.

[37] However, a number of prominent sociologists and philosophers were forced to leave the country or were prohibited from publishing or acting as principal investigators in the mid-1970s: notably Agnes Heller, György Márkus, and Iván Szelényi. Thus cyclical repression remained a feature of a system that, on the whole, was becoming increasingly flexible.

[38] Gábor, interview with author, September 1991. Though none put it as eloquently, variations on this attitude prevailed among many of the academic researchers whom I interviewed on research trips between 1989 and 1996.

[39] Timár had earlier been head of a department in the Planning Office.

said. Adhering to this one clear rule, non-conformist scholars and technocrats – party members and non-party members alike – pushed the limits of permissible speech while trying to maintain a distance from policy issues (or in the case of officials, to support suggestions with technical, "neutral" arguments). The pragmatists, for their part, learned to live with increasing contradiction, and, when the failure to resolve systemic contradiction became too noticeable, listened to the non-conformists, provided that they refrained from openly attacking or criticizing the regime or its policies.[40]

In addition, non-conformists and pragmatists were able to communicate *unofficially* because of informal ties developed during prior reform waves. In a common pattern of professional development, for instance, both Hetényi and Timár held research posts at various times during their careers. Moreover, like many of the handful of scholars who had dedicated themselves to studying the second economy, both came from social backgrounds characterized by colleagues as "bourgeois-professional," which may have influenced their support of an expanded private sector. Indeed, among researchers and technocrats closely involved with the reform, a number had parents or other relatives who had been entrepreneurs or artisans.[41]

The ability of non-conformists and pragmatists to communicate both officially and unofficially enabled them to read economic and political signals and to exploit opportunities for reform in a relatively *coordinated* fashion. By 1976–77, for example, a variety of circles began "to think and speak about new possibilities."[42] These circles proved crucial in 1979, when the party-state publicly acknowledged the need for adjustment of the system – or "perfecting of the economic mechanism." The public acknowledgment signaled a potential

---

[40] It sometimes did happen, however, that a study that simply reported the evidence as researchers found it caused them serious problems. One of the better-known cases is that of the sociologist Iván Szelényi, who had many difficulties with the Party and the political police between 1970 and 1975 because of studies that grew out of his national rural surveys, particularly a paper about the negative effects on small villages of the 1971 Regional Development Plan. His work was not published for ten years, and, unable to continue his research, he emigrated in 1975. But it is further evidence of the cyclicality of repression in Hungary that by 1981 it had become clear that the Hungarian authorities might be willing to reconsider their positions: by 1982, Szelényi traveled back to Hungary on a Hungarian passport and continued his research. See Iván Szelényi, *Socialist Entrepreneurs: Embourgeoisement in Rural Hungary* (Madison: University of Wisconsin Press, 1988).

[41] Anna Székács, interview with author, Budapest, October 1990; and Gábor, interview with author, September 1991.

[42] Székács, interview with author, October 1990. Székács was referring to what she called a "fine intellectual workshop" within the Ministry of Finance. This group included, among others, Andrea Deák, Sándor Ferge, László Antal, István Kolárik, József Lukács, Györgyi Várhegyi, and Péter Medgyessy (who later became Finance Minister and who, after the transition, became Prime Minister when the Socialist Party won the 2002 elections. It was revealed that he had also been working as a counter-intelligence agent for the Ministry of the Interior while he was in the employ of the Ministry of Finance, and he resigned after intense disagreements with the junior coalition member of the government, the Free Democrats (SZDSZ). For additional details, see Chapter 8.

opening, something that was quickly picked up at the Ministry of Finance, the institutional shelter for many members of the well-known 1968 "reform-guard." Since 1972 it had been relegated to a defensive position, and its role had largely reverted to the handling of day-to-day issues.[43] But in 1979, this informal "market-friendly" group within the Ministry – so called because the individuals associated with it tended to push for market-type solutions to economic problems – was reactivated. The Ministry as a whole was ready to seize the moment, because its pro-reform officials had kept abreast of novel ideas, and had continued to cultivate informal relations with scholars through discussion circles that articulated new possibilities. Its influence was pervasive in part because it continued to draw on larger networks that had developed within universities, research institutes, and bureaucracies. Among the latter, for instance, was the Ministry of Foreign Trade, where Minister Gyula Horn – who later became the first post-transition Prime Minister – presided over the liberalization of foreign trade regulation. Meanwhile, in the universities and research institutes, unorthodox economists like Gábor and Galasi shaped the thinking of colleagues and students. New configurations of this network, in fact, could appear anywhere, and at the most opportune times: the meetings on the possible liberalization of the private sector, for example, were organized by a young man whose thinking had been formed by professors Gábor and Galasi.[44]

Legitimizing the Coup: The Expert Committee

Ensuring the credibility of the expert committee was vital to the coup's success. No one knew this better than its architect, Minister Hetényi. To be taken seriously by high-level party-state officials, the Committee's membership would have to include both champions and critics of second-economy liberalization. But Hetényi also knew that for the coup to succeed, the Expert Committee would have to avoid acrimony for as long as possible. It was a delicate operation.

To achieve the goal of credibility, the minister assembled a group representing a wide spectrum of opinion. At one end stood the sociologist Pál Juhász, who had long stressed the need to rehabilitate small entrepreneurs and to expand the private sector, and was one of the most optimistic about the prospects for achieving these goals.[45] At the other extreme was Gyula Varga, the deputy head of the Agrarian Economic Research Institute. He believed that the large state-controlled agricultural cooperatives[46] should remain central and dominant, and

---

[43] Ibid.

[44] And he could hardly have been the only one of their former students who joined the Party or went to work in government bureaucracies. István Kalász had recently earned his degree from the Karl Marx University of Economics, and spent an additional year working with Gábor and Galasi before joining the Planning Office as an assistant to Hetényi. Gábor, Galasi, and Kővári, interview with author, Budapest, December 1991.

[45] After 1989, Juhász became an MP representing the Alliance of Free Democrats.

[46] MGTSZ, in its Hungarian acronym.

the most he was willing to accept was that the household plots be allowed to develop, provided they were "appropriately integrated." More specifically, he envisioned a private sphere kept well in hand by the large agricultural cooperatives. In fact, Varga argued strongly that "chaos" would ensue if the large concerns failed to "control" the household plots.[47]

The danger of acrimony among these experts was real. Varga's view was no mere individual opinion: it represented the official agrarian policy, as well as the line prevailing at the Agrarian Economic Research Institute, which he headed. Similarly, the opposing view, advanced by Juhász, represented the prevalent line of the Cooperatives Research Institute (*Szövetkezeti Kutató*), which also studied agricultural issues and where Juhász worked as a researcher. Divergent economic interests further compounded these political-institutional oppositions. Liberalization, after all, would impinge on the state budget in general and the distribution of state subsidies in particular.

To prevent uncontrollable battles from breaking out among the committee experts, Minister Hetényi deliberately selected individuals with sharply different viewpoints who, for the most part, nevertheless shared a common point of reference: a conviction that only pragmatic policy changes could mitigate the economy's problems. A few idealists believed that the introduction of a considerably expanded private sector would not cause serious contradictions in the economy and in society. Others were convinced that the advantages of liberalization would far outweigh any problems that might result from the coexistence of a growing private sector with the socialist economy. And still others chose to de-emphasize the complex forces they consciously proposed to release from what had theretofore been regarded as a kind of Pandora's box at best, and at worst, a profound corruption of the socialist way of life.[48] Many, however, shared the belief that if only "politics" would not interfere, liberalization and legalization of the second economy could harmonize macro-economic requirements and social goals: competition among private producers would hold down incomes, which in turn would ease the social conflicts that might otherwise be expected to result from higher second-economy incomes.

Gábor and Galasi, however, took a more complex view. Like many serious academics, both had kept their distance from the regime's internal politics. Although their writing and research implied the necessity of structural change and occasionally made specific policy suggestions, neither expected to contribute to a concrete outcome. Now both argued that existing restrictions on scale should be lifted to allow private enterprises to grow, and that the scope of the second economy should be expanded dramatically. At the same time, they maintained that this expansion would unavoidably cause severe contradictions and pressures.

Consider their view of material incentives. If people were "split in two," they argued, it would affect the economy in general and create problems in

---

[47] Gábor, Galasi, and Kővári, interview with author, September 1991, Budapest.
[48] Ibid.

the workplace, especially if the second economy were to be incorporated into state firms, as was later done in the case of the VGMK's, or intra-firm work partnerships. Workers would clearly have much greater incentive to put their energies into private and quasi-private endeavors than into their primary, or "first-economy" jobs (whether those were physically located in state firms or outside them). While strongly supporting liberalization of the second economy, both researchers were completely unconvinced that this liberalization would result in the "self-correction" of the larger system. Gábor was particularly insistent that even if the state were to make much larger concessions toward the second economy than anticipated at the time, it would not be enough to solve existing economic contradictions.[49]

The economists, in fact, were highly skeptical of what they perceived to be an effort to "mislead the politicians" by presenting liberalization of the second economy as a solution to the country's systemic crisis. They suspected that their concerns would be glossed over in the document that would be produced at the expert committee's first meeting. But the document, distributed and rehashed at the second meeting, actually attempted to mesh the divergent opinions of the individual committee members. After this second meeting, the committee adjourned, never to reconvene. Gábor found this strange. He believed that a third meeting was necessary if the final document were really to "synthesize" participants' views.[50]

The coup method, however, now demanded the exclusion of the expert committee. It was Hetényi and his immediate aides who would synthesize the Committee's debates, and only they would see the final document that was sent to the Political Committee of the HSWP. The document, edited by Hetényi, unambiguously endorsed liberalization of the informal sector, making no mention of implementation details or of possible new economic forms.[51] But for the substance of the endorsement – and the arguments later to be employed in its defense – Hetényi drew from the deliberations of the expert committee.

Legitimizing Content: Reform Discourse

One of the thorniest issues regarding liberalization of the second economy had come up prior to the experts' meetings. It had to do with the term "second economy" – a term that had been attacked as insufficiently neutral and as discrediting socialism by *Társadalmi Szemle* (*"Social Review"*), the Party's main theoretical journal of social science.[52] In the "second economy," Gábor

---

[49] Ibid. Gábor and Galasi. In other words, took a position they later characterized as professionally consistent but politically "unfortunate," in the sense that "most of the others would have preferred to sweep conflicts under the rug, as if all problems thus far had been the result of purely political errors."

[50] Ibid.

[51] Hetényi, interview with author, October 1991, Budapest.

[52] See Lajos Héthy, "A Második Gazdaság: A Gazdaság és Társadalom" ("The Second Economy: Economy and Society"), *Társadalmi Szemle (Sociological Review)* 40, no. 7 (1980). Another

included all non-state economic activity without regard to its character.[53] But following years of cyclical repression and propaganda aimed at "speculators" and "black marketeers," the term naturally carried negative connotations for many people, or was at the very least not intuitively clear.

The ideological charge could not be ignored, since Minister Hetényi's principal task was to make the second economy "fit" into socialism. Often understood to exclude small manufacturers or shopkeepers working with a permit, the second economy was equated with "black, informal activities." But for Hetényi, the basic distinctions were "large" versus "small," "primary job" versus "secondary job," and "legal work" versus "non-legal work."[54] He recalled discussions on the subject with his colleagues, as he tried to decide how to phrase the proposal to the Central Committee's Economic Sub-Committee:

I asked: 'what is the first economy if there is a second?' After all, no one talked about a *first* economy. So we agreed that the *first* would be the socialist economy, which in practice meant the large firms (though this wasn't completely clarified, either). The *second* would be the private economy, the 'small economy' . . . The point I stressed was the *economic* nature of the second economy. That is to say, cheating and pure speculation . . . not linked to economic activity [sic] were explicitly excluded. I admit that this was conscious and purposeful. The essence of getting the reform accepted was *to define* it in such a way that things that clearly should be condemned were under no circumstances to be included. Tax-evasion . . . prostitution, which were previously understood as second economy, were simply unlawful. So this left the second economy as an *economic activity*, to which we added that exploitation was not allowed, and so it became acceptable as a term . . . The researchers wrote it down: it was on the record. The job of the Planning Office, our job, was to decide what the state's relationship to the second economy would be.[55] [emphasis added]

The definition chosen by the Planning Office was clearly politically bounded. To read it as a strictly economic definition would be absurd: it would entail, among other things, accepting that currency speculation, for instance, was not an economic activity. Political constraints, however, could not be ignored. In the academic debate mentioned earlier, the editor of the Party's theoretical journal *Társadalmi Szemle*, who was an opponent of the term "second economy," suggested "helper economy" or "completer economy" as alternatives. This was, as Hungarians like to say, the language of the political "salon"[56]: such terms were

objection made in other forms by the same critic – who at the time was the editor of the Party journal – was that Gábor had exaggerated the structural differences between socialist and non-socialist second economies. Gábor, interview with author, October 1991.

[53] István Gábor, "The Second (Secondary) Economy: Earning Activity and Regrouping of Income Outside Socially Oriented Production and Distribution," *Acta Oeconomica* 22, no. 3–4 (1979): 291–311.

[54] Hetényi, interview with author, October 1991, Budapest.

[55] Ibid.

[56] "Szalonképes kifejezes" actually refers to any expression deemed appropriate for polite society; in this context, however, the "szalón" in question was the political arena, in particular the Central Committee.

acceptable because they emphasized harmony and labor-exchange between the state and its "helper" sectors, and carried the reassuring implication that the latter was self-limiting.

In addition, specific interests were sometimes tied to the use of particular terms: the agricultural lobby was concerned, for instance, that the term "second economy " would incriminate household plot activity, which was seen as "organic" and socialist in nature, since the plots were integrated into large state-agricultural cooperatives. Gábor was attacked by the National Council of Agricultural Cooperatives, which felt that it was "unconscionable that he had mixed up 'stealing' with household plots."[57]

Thus the attempt to redefine the second economy was an effort to divide it between "integratable" and "unacceptable" parts, while simultaneously stressing the self-limiting character of the legalized second economy. The legacy of the Hungarian reform experience helped in this effort at critical points. Although the agricultural lobby was concerned about the "contamination" of household plot activity by association with the term "second economy," it was precisely the example of the household plots that Hetényi and his reform group in the Planning Office (and later in the Ministry of Finance) used to legitimate the "new" second economy. They billed the proposed intra-firm work partnerships (VGMK's) as the "household plots of industry" – and as part of a self-limiting helper economy of small manufacturing firms and service establishments operating outside state firms. More generally, Hetényi and his associates took to asking repeatedly of critics and opponents: "if it exists in agriculture, then why not in industry?"

The effort to rehabilitate a number of second-economy activities by redefining them as socialist was crucial to the larger party-state apparatus's acceptance of the reform, especially because a number of the organizational forms that were instituted in 1982 were not much more than formalizations of previously informal and largely illegal activities. It could be said of the VGMKs, for example, that they amounted to little more than legalized versions of earlier informal subcontracting and overtime schemes within state firms. However, the goal, according to Hetényi, was the new and more productive application of such activities within state firms. "Informal private work in factories existed from the start, but here there was the definite aim to develop and extend, not just to legalize existing activities." Though the VGMKs' record between 1982 and 1989 is mixed,[58] the 1982 reform also created completely new property forms, among them two that were unambiguously private partnerships – the economic work partnership and the civil law partnership – and a third that was nominally cooperative but functioned as a private partnership – the "small cooperative."

[57] Gábor, Galasi, and Kővári, interview with author, December 1991.
[58] See David Stark, "Coexisting Organizational Forms in Hungary's Emerging Mixed Economy," in Victor Nee and David Stark, eds., *Remaking the Economic Institutions of Socialism: China and Eastern Europe* (Stanford: Stanford University Press, 1989).

Asked about the difficulties he and his team encountered in winning acceptance for these new property forms, Hetényi again emphasized discursive reconstruction:

Because of the various political considerations, great juggling and wizardry were needed
to find the new socialist forms which would be appropriate for small-scale private
production . . . small cooperatives, for example. We explained that this socialist – or a
little bit socialist, or half-socialist – type of activity was not alien to socialism. Certainly,
capitalist organization was not included here [sic]. By labeling these new forms "partnerships," "small cooperative," and so on, we gave them a socialist patina, and sent the
message that [they] harmed no one.[59]

It is not immediately obvious how should we understand the statement: "capitalist organization was not included." The economy, of course, remained organized largely along socialist lines – strictly speaking, until 1990, when the first
post-socialist government sought openly to create "full-fledged capitalism." But
again, several of the property forms instituted in 1982 were fully private. No
formal limits on investment were set, though some of the partnership forms
restricted the number of partners or employees. And while no capital market
existed yet, private entrepreneurs could obtain loans from Hungarian banks,[60]
or failing that, informal loans and the monetary overhang common to a number
of socialist countries would fill the gap.

Here is how Hetényi handled this fundamental issue:

Q: Did you ever think that you might have been, in a way, starting to 'deconstruct' the
system?
A: We could solve [everything] by the *forms* we chose and by emphasizing that the
reform really provided opportunities for the workers. This eased the fears of [many]
politicians. It was not about capitalism, or about *capitalist* entrepreneurs. It was about
tens of thousands of workers being able to . . . earn additional income.[61]

This rationale amounted to a description of the Party's continued efforts
to maintain nominal conformity with an inoperative ideology: the 1982
reform provided opportunities not for *capitalist*-entrepreneurs, but for *worker*-
entrepreneurs.

It is tempting to interpret such statements as the thoughts of a reformer
who was a capitalist in socialist guise, or to conclude that the guardians of the
socialist regime had been reduced to image-keeping. But in fact, the motivations
of reformers were more complex.

---

[59] Hetényi, interview with author, October 1991.
[60] The banks had little incentive to lend to private businesses, given the size of the loans they were
accustomed to making to state firms and the attached implicit government guarantees (hence
portfolios of 100 percent compliant, performing loans). The banks were not, however, in any
way prohibited from providing capital for the private businesses, and a few special banks were
set up specifically with the purpose of making small loans to private entrepreneurs.
[61] Hetényi, interview with author, October 1991, Budapest.

When asked whether he had been thinking in larger terms about the direction in which the reform might be taking the system, Minister Hetényi shrugged, smiled skeptically, and replied:

A: If someone says that they saw a private market economy in this reform, or a mixed market economy – well, perhaps. But it was not of the order of a system-change, although in retrospect this is not so clear. *What was clear even then was that in Hungary politics were highly pragmatic* . . . Of course, we had to respect the rule that there should be no exploitation, meaning no private firms employing large numbers of people [sic]. But as to the rest, why should it not fit into the system? We could always try to sell it to those who really needed to be sold on it . . . with phrases like 'at present, our productive forces and our socialism are not so strong . . . this [proposal] will still fit [in the system] . . . and if you think that in ten years it will no longer fit . . . that is another matter, about which we don't have to [worry right now].' It was also obvious that the second economy was developing rapidly 'in black' . . . and the only question was: 'why does it have to be clandestine? After all, it is spreading, and there is nothing we can do against it.' Besides, there were many phenomena about which one said: '*why* do we have to do anything against it?' . . . '[If we legalize it] the range of activities will be broader . . . more responsible, perhaps we will get some taxes out of it' . . . *In short, we searched for ways to say about a variety of things: 'this too is socialism.'*[62] [emphasis added]

Here, then, was a reformer trying to reconcile the conflicting goals of a system he believed he served best by trying to improve from within.[63] But there is one additional factor to consider: the system had moved far enough away from its original blueprint that officials could easily hold competing interpretations of its essential nature – and how far it could be reformed without changing that essence – at any given moment. Timár could look back and reflect that the system began to undo itself in 1952–53; on another day he might have said 1956–57. For Hetényi and his co-workers in the Planning Office, the 1968 NEM was the historical turning point. For this particular group of reformers, though fully aware that the NEM had not achieved all of its stated goals in practice, the reforms that followed in the 1980s were the NEM's natural heirs.

Q: When you say that it doesn't matter what happens in ten years, aren't you implicitly thinking about what might happen in ten years? And with this reform, didn't many of the fundamental, previously hidden contradictions of the economy suddenly become the legal responsibility of the Ministry of Finance . . . are there not countless concrete examples of this?
A: Yes. This is true. But it was not such a major step, because if in 1968 we were able to declare that the engines [for] state firms were profit and demand, and not plan indicators, then it became simpler to declare that this was also the case for individuals. The real issue was: did [private] activities fit into socialism or not?

---

[62] Ibid.
[63] Anna Székács, who worked closely with Deputy Finance Minister Villányi under Minister Hetényi from 1980–86, spoke often of this conviction, which represented an ongoing dilemma for her and for many of her colleagues under Hungary's socialist system. Székács, interview with author, October 1990.

And they did. They fit because by 1968 we had turned away from the Leninist conception of socialism as one large factory; what remained was that this wasn't an exploitative society. So everything that was not exploitative – such as private firms employing large numbers of people – was already included in the definition of socialism, or somehow got included.[64]

For Hetényi, neither the legalization of the informal economy, nor the liberalization of existing legal private businesses, nor the introduction of new private partnership forms to the socialist system was particularly remarkable, let alone "revolutionary." Hungary, after all, had long since gotten past the idea that "large firms" were the only ones that could be considered "socialist." Moreover, in a predominantly socialist system that was "not exploitative," small private firms could not, by definition, be exploitative. "Exploitation" had, in fact, become just one more redefined term among many: it was enough that there should be "no private firms employing large numbers of people." Nothing needed to be said concerning working conditions, pay, unions, and so on presumably because people enjoyed some form of security in those areas at their state jobs.

So if it was incorrect to equate socialism with large firms, socialism had to allow for the inclusion of small firms (and the less said about the distribution of property rights in such firms the better), but then implicitly, capitalism, or at least capitalist exploitation, was equated with large private firms. What was insufficient to define socialism became, at least for a time, a serviceable definition for capitalism – even as the 1982 reform undermined it by formalizing and expanding the incipient capitalist sector of the Hungarian economy. And precisely because Hetényi and all those working with him were aware that firm-size was a slippery issue, it, too, was reduced to an operational problem:

. . . This was just a practical question: whether a private entrepreneur could have two, ten or thirty employees or partners. We had already committed the sin; now we were just arguing about how big it was going to be.[65]

Some of this may reflect the tendency of problems to diminish in hindsight. At the time, size was still a politically charged issue. A year or two after the reform had been passed into law, the spokeswoman on private firms for the Ministry of Finance, who had worked closely with Hetényi, accepted an invitation to appear on a popular television show about crime that was sponsored by the Ministry of the Interior. Her story shows that not only was firm-size very much an issue, but that private firms *in se* were still somewhat suspect.

I had to appear on the 'Blue-Light Show,' the monthly TV show about crime where they usually featured a prostitute or a killer . . . it was not the most comfortable situation; people might think I'd become involved in some sort of shady business, and I didn't much want to go, especially since the Ministry of Interior was foreign to me. But I had no choice, because the State Secretary had assigned it . . . [This] program was always

---

[64] Hetényi, interview with author, October 1991, Budapest.
[65] Ibid. Heténji reconfirmed his news in a subsequent interview in June 1995.

carefully edited in advance; they showed you what film inserts would be included, and they rehearsed for an hour in advance. I had never known why the participants looked into the TV screen so fixedly. It's because they were reading a prepared text in front of them, from which they never diverged, [perhaps] because of the sensitivity of the subjects under discussion.

So at any rate this particular program dealt with the fact that somebody was engaged in fairly large-scale commercial activity, the resale of something or other . . . and so the police had imprisoned him. It was my job to discuss whether laws and regulations had in fact been broken. But the program director suddenly diverged from the prepared text and asked me whether or not I thought it was conceivable, in theory, that private individuals would ever undertake large-scale commerce in Hungary. Well . . . I started to make a spontaneous presentation about what how great it would be if individuals could in fact get involved in large-scale private commerce. Then after a while, [the show's hosts] started to say that well, maybe it wouldn't be such a good idea, and anyway the population would not have money for it, etc. From then on, no matter how hard I tried, I wasn't allowed to speak again.

The next day the Council of Ministers of the Ministry of Domestic Commerce held a special meeting and declared that private commerce on a large scale was out of the question, and that it was a political error that I had ever said such a thing, and how dare I? Fortunately, István Hetényi was still Minister of Finance, and when the Minister of Domestic Commerce called him, Hetényi turned on the charm, saying, 'yes, I saw her, and she was . . . so nice, and didn't she speak well; I thought you were going to want to hire her away from us, and anyway she didn't say that she was expressing the opinion of the Ministry of Domestic Commerce or of the Ministry of Finance or of the Party; she spoke as a private individual. Besides, you've all made mistakes in your time, so let's forgive her this one . . . '

And they did. But this was in 1983, and you can see more or less what the atmosphere was like.[66]

The Budapest Party Meeting: Close to Victory

Once Hetényi received formal approval for his draft proposal from the Economic Policy and Political Subcommittees of the HSWP's Central Committee, a complex two-year process of negotiation with the various branches and organizations of the government followed. This government-wide "negotiation" involved, among other things, soliciting the opinions of the branch ministries and making each feel that it was an integral part of the process, while limiting its actual involvement to technical matters insofar as possible. Each ministry assigned an individual to produce a position paper and report to a government coordinating committee, which was to have met frequently. But after a

[66] Székács, interview with author, September 1990, Budapest. In a June 1993 follow-up interview, Székács elaborated on the gravity of this incident, pointing out that the extraordinary meeting of the Council of Ministers of the Ministry of Domestic Commerce had explicitly recommended to the Ministry of the Interior that she be fired from the Ministry of Finance, as well as prevented from working elsewhere in the state apparatus.

few meetings, the coordinating committee was not reconvened. Instead, the responsible individuals from the Ministry of Finance and the Planning Office met individually with the ministries. The coordinating committee consisted of fifty or sixty people and was unwieldy, especially given the Central Committee's insistence that the plan be elaborated quickly. But the decision not to reconvene may also have been another "coup-like" tactic intended to limit dissent: to divide powerful Ministries that were opposed to the plan lest they join forces in an attempt to stop or dilute the reform.[67]

In 1980, at the beginning of this process, Hetényi became Finance Minister, and assigned responsibility for the reform of the second economy to his deputy, Miklós Villányi, who in turn worked closely with Chief Department Head Péter Medgyessy, Department Head István Kolárik, and his immediate subordinate, Anna Székács.[68] The latter was most closely involved with the elaboration of the reform and the subsequent campaign to familiarize lower-level party and government institutions and the public with it. Székács was a passionate supporter of the reform (known to advise personally would-be entrepreneurs by the hundreds in addition to her policy-related and public-relations duties), and became the Ministry's official spokesperson on the private sector.

After two years of both behind-the-scenes and open negotiation with ministries and other government organizations, as well as extraordinary (and not wholly successful) efforts to fit the new regulations into the highly rigid existing regulatory framework, Hetényi's team in the Ministry of Finance faced another trial. In the late autumn of 1981, they had to inform the district party secretaries and the other high-ranking members of the Budapest Party Committee about the draft regulations. Approximately 200 people attended this meeting.

The presentation – to be made by Villányi – was crucial because among those in attendance were several influential hard-liners, including László Marothy, the First Secretary of the Budapest Committee. Villányi skillfully emphasized the non-threatening character of the reform, and managed to sway the First Secretary. Anna Székács remembered:

We were all extremely anxious about how the party apparatus would react. But after the presentation, László Marothy argued that regarding this very important political and economic issue, the Party should not fear for itself; it was necessary to take responsibility for this – to stand by it courageously.

---

[67] Opinion expressed by economist Péter Galasi in author's interview with Gábor, Galasi, and Kővári, Budapest, October 1990. Gábor felt, however, that this was a straightforward effort to avoid time-wasting.

[68] Many others were directly involved with the ongoing work in the Ministry of Finance, notably István Csillag, who later moved to the Financial Affairs Research Institute. It would be impossible to list all those involved at the Ministry of Finance and the Planning Office (under whose auspices, for instance, István Kalász also continued to play a role), let alone the many researchers and scholars who served as formal or informal advisers.

The battle, however, was far from over. Székács recalled:

[After Marothy spoke] there was a short intermission, and then the reaction began. A former university classmate of mine, who was then the President of the Budapest KISZ (Communist Youth League), grabbed me and said: "you cannot do this; it is politically unacceptable – intolerable; an outrage!" He warned me that if a single KISZ member were to get involved with such private businesses, he would expel them from the KISZ immediately.

When the meeting then resumed in the auditorium, the first speaker was the director of the state firm Orion.[69]

He insisted that what was being prepared was a political crime and . . . should not be permitted; that in his firm there would be no VGMK or anything of the kind. Many others spoke in a similar vein.

Then a Party Secretary from one of the outer districts of Budapest – Emil Peják, a major figure in the workers' movement – rose to his feet to make a plea. His intervention mattered greatly because

[Pejak] actually lived in a workers' district and so . . . he really felt the terrible tension that existed in workers' circles. He declared with some emotion that he would vote for this new law 'with two hands.' He stressed that the Party had to understand that people were increasingly dissatisfied . . . that people felt that they just worked and worked and never got anywhere, and had no opportunities. And he explained just why it was that these small businesses were so needed.

The impassioned plea of the labor leader emboldened Marothy to speak out again.

He said that if the entrepreneurial spirit could take off, [it] would do the economy a great deal of good. Entrepreneurs were unlikely to upset the political apple-cart because political and economic stability are of fundamental, existential importance to the entrepreneur; these are the essential elements of his existence.[70]

The association of an old idea (the primacy of political stability) with a new one (the entrepreneur as promoter of stability) proved key to the reform proposal's survival at this point. By persuading the Budapest Party Committee that entrepreneurs would help reshape the economic system without subversive intent or consequences, Marothy managed "to appease the politicians."

Once this fundamental issue was resolved, Marothy could address two additional concerns. The first had to with the politicians' concern about the likelihood that people would end up working after their official working hours.

---

[69] Székács noted further that this man was "called Köteles, [and that he] later became some kind of secretary of the Budapest Party Committee, and then director of the Post Office" – just one example of how, in a typical pattern of circulation of elites, hard-liners and reformers continued to co-exist after 1982. Székács, interview with author, September 1990.

[70] Ibid.

Marothy countered that if after-hours work was well organized, it could only have positive feedback effects, resulting in increased output. Moreover, this kind of behavior might even have a beneficial demonstration effect: the rest of the society could learn something about how to "organize and be organized from a person working after hours."[71] The politicians' second concern was that workers in private firms would not be "represented" by a labor union, nor would there be party activities in the private workplace.[72] Marothy replied that this was not to be feared, because if party activities were merely a formality, then "why keep them up?" And conversely, if party activities were in fact substantive, then people would participate regardless, because "it would remain an ambition that they would want to fulfill alongside their work."[73] Looking back on Marothy's entire political career, Székács came to the conclusion that "on balance" the hard-liner's "influence" had not been positive. But she also stressed that on this particular occasion, it had proved "crucial" to the acceptance of the proposed reform regulations.[74]

The week following the late autumn 1981 meeting, another 200 or so middle-level party directors met, and during this debate held by László Békesi, a secretary of the Budapest Party Committee, a calmer mood prevailed.[75] But the "campaign" was just beginning. Over the next two years, Székács would give hundreds of presentations and make numerous television appearances to try to educate the public and lower-level party and government organizations about the new regulations. When the first of January 1982 arrived, most of the new regulatory framework was in place, but the only informational material that had been published was a guidebook to orient municipal officials, with the specific intent of preparing lawyers and others who would have dealings with the new entrepreneurs. The directors of the provincial municipal councils had been briefed, as had the directors of the lawyers's cooperatives. But no one had actual experience with the new regulations, and would-be private businesspeople were sent from office to office in the bureaucratic and procedural confusion. Székács was the only person with a grasp of the totality of the new regulations who

---

[71] Székács, interview with author, September 1990, Budapest.
[72] Here the concern was not, of course, truly representation of workers' interests, but the state's ability to control workers, to which the official trade union had been key.
[73] Székács, interview with author September 1990, Budapest.
[74] Ibid. There are many possible reasons why a so-called "hard-liner" might support this legislation: Marothy was known as a "party careerist" and for moving with the party-line. Indeed, he was regarded by some as a possible successor to Kádár. He was a special favorite of both Kádár and his wife. In any case, whether Kádár was personally a strong supporter of the reform or not, Marothy could not have been strongly opposed, since it received the support of the Central Committee. Perhaps, at the Budapest Party meeting, Marothy was speaking as Kádár's voice. But in any case, the distinctions between "hard-liners" and "reformers" were rarely completely clear. It was, for instance, possible to be a "hard-liner" on foreign policy but a "reformer" in domestic economic policy, like Kádár himself; or "independent" in foreign policy but brutally hard-line in domestic politics, like Romania's Ceauçescu.
[75] Székács, interview with author, September 1990, Budapest.

could answer questions and give advice about which of the new organizational forms was best suited to particular needs.

During the next two years . . . people stood in line in front of my door at the Ministry to ask for advice. I [also] tried to accept every invitation to speak, since the need was so great, and I held large presentations, for example, at the Law Faculty, where they organized courses. Three or four hundred people would show up. These presentations were advertized at state firms, not in newspapers; of course people still worked almost exclusively in the firms and institutes. Then lawyers, economists, technical directors attended; or the locksmith came because he thought he might want to start something.[76]

Conclusion

The 1982 reform would have profound regulatory and socio-political effects. As one of the reform's main architects put it:

The 1982 reform had the effect of transforming peoples' thinking. The whole idea of entrepreneurship, of working in non-state organizations, was a major change, and it certainly didn't happen in Czechoslovakia, Poland, or the USSR. The 1982 reform had a social effect we failed to anticipate. The economic effects were not negligible, but developed differently than we thought . . . In theory, a socialist firm need not be large; but in practice it tends to work out that way. So the socialist/non-socialist sector divide had come to be seen as large/small. The significance of what was explicitly said at the time – which is always quite different from what happens in the end – was that it was written down that the large socialist firms could not solve the problems of the economy; could not supply the population's needs . . . Eventually all private work-partnerships became fully a part of the collective consciousness.[77]

Did any of this imply a significant transformation of the socialist system? Like many others, Hetényi preferred to think of it as a straightforward continuation of a process of "decentralization." But as we saw in Chapter 2, there was no linear process of decentralization, the last *re*centralizing period being the one between roughly 1972 and 1979. Once again, reformers redefined a concept. Although some did speak of "deconstruction," Hetényi's fixed point of reference remained 1968, when the "real deconstruction" occurred. At the same time, however, he observed some of the more concrete effects of the reform.

There was serious opposition in the Ministries and in State Management, which in the final analysis is explained by the fact that the reform decreased their power, as did everything which it was permissible to do without them . . . [The private sector] was not controllable like the large firms, which could be controlled even after '68, after the abolition of command planning. [And] . . . in certain cases expansion of the private sector meant competition for the large [socialist] firms. But this was a different kind of opposition, [which] had already appeared in the earlier case of the specialized groups of the state agricultural cooperatives, even though this was an accepted socialist form. But if

---

[76] Ibid.
[77] Hetényi, interview with author, June 1995, Budapest.

construction and machine industries started up in the cooperatives, the ministries didn't like it. So less than an ideological battle, it was a struggle between various branches of power whose authority [was] being chipped away.[78]

For Hetényi, the fact that the 1982 reform chipped away at the power of some bureaucracies did not signify part of a systemic change; it was merely something that had happened before on a smaller scale – just another type of internal opposition to be managed. Ultimately, this reformer came to the conclusion that he had no real ideological adversaries; if anything, he had only "tactical" enemies, and they were within the regime, not in society.

As to deconstructing the regime . . . I didn't experience it that way. The fact that profit-motivated activity [was] allowed in a small sector, when we already said there was profit motivation in the large sector,[79] . . . one felt that we were taking a step toward the undoing of the classical, monolithic system. But I wouldn't like to say that we knew that with this move we were turning socialism into a market economy . . . because from the political standpoint we didn't really know . . . it was a step in the process of decentralization. And there were other steps which we should've taken at the same time . . . for example the banking system. In 1980, we should've done at least what we managed only by 1987. But the National Bank defended its position fiercely, and even in '87 it was the Ministry of Finance that had to execute the bank reform. Back in 1978, when growth slowed, mostly we achieved macroeconomic, not institutional changes, except for the 1982 reform. No bank reform, no capital market, no transformation of the structure of production, breaking up of monopolies . . .[80]

If Hetényi had managed to bring about such changes in the early 1980s, perhaps he would have characterized them, too, as no more than a matter of "decentralization." Clearly, the Hungarian socialist system by the late 1970s had reformed itself frequently enough that agents of change could press for radical shifts without thought of revolution. By then, the system had become identified with its long history of pragmatism, and the possibility of revolution seemed remote – as remote as the possibility of actually naming a part of that system unsocialist. For "non-conformist" intellectuals, all the institutional fixed-points had vanished: the essential character of the system had become so indeterminate that if there was nothing it was truly possible to conform to, it was also difficult to decide precisely what to "revolt" against. "Pragmatic" reformers, in turn, were there simply to address economic problems within extant structures.

The case of former Minister Hetényi – a prominent example of such pragmatists – reveals the contradictions that bound these reformers – contradictions inherited from previous reforms and reform-attempts, and which they

---

[78] Ibid.

[79] Although in the preceding quote, Hetényi himself has drawn attention to the fact that the 1968 reform did not achieve all its goals, here he speaks as if a *declaration* that state firms should be profit-motivated could be compared with the structural incentives for profit-oriented behavior associated with personal risk and ownership of private partnerships instituted in 1982.

[80] Hetényi, interview with author 1991, Budapest.

encountered over long careers spent serving the system even as they became agents of its transformation. In the effort to win acceptance for the 1982 reform, Hetényi and other pragmatic insiders redefined terms and recast ideologies until what had once been central became marginal, and the unimaginable became possible. Moreover, accustomed to the shifts in intra-party politics, these pragmatists found nothing out of the ordinary in their own actions, all the more so because it was primarily in words that they could be "revolutionary" – words whose full import is frequently understood only in retrospect, and which in daily memoranda or conversation appear only as the tools for solving immediate conflicts and problems.

These actors, whose identities and tactics had been shaped by previous reforms, introduced an ambitious property-rights reform proposal in coup-like fashion, then forged in the early 1980s a new discourse of property-rights that recast the socialist mandate by redefining it piecemeal. Loaded tenets and concepts like "full employment," "exploitation," and "entrepreneurship" were defused one by one, and made to "fit." As a result, no one had to confront the issue of whether socialism was being "refined," "improved," or altered beyond recognition. Given the history of Hungarian reform, the "turning point" could always be located in the past or in the future; it never had to be the particular reform under discussion.

This political-discursive approach to change allowed "non-conformists" and "pragmatists" to overcome opposition from "hardliners," and to carry through the radical liberalization of the second economy with virtually no reference to ownership or property-rights *per se*. In this shared vocabulary, the points of common understanding among intellectuals, reformists, and conservative officials focused on what would remain *unsaid*. It was clear to all that they could construct new worlds, but could not explicitly "speak attempts" against socialism. The result, however, was not silence: academic and party-state reformers subtly employed a circumscribed but specific and shared vocabulary to defy established maxims. The construction and reconstruction of reform discourse allowed reformers to take further "pragmatic action" and to work within a regime characterized by cyclical transformation without saying what would have been understood as revolutionary. In the case reviewed here, this was that the 1982 reform in fact represented much more than the liberalization of supplemental earning-possibilities for workers. What remained unsaid – and, thanks to entrenched habits of obfuscation, unperceived by most – is that the new regulations amounted to an institutional reform of property-rights with far-reaching socio-political effects potentially leading to the deconstruction of the socialist regime, and certainly signifying further transformation of the socialist economic system.

In the end, party-state leaders who once were geared toward constant vigilance against existential enemies, were now either uninterested in distinguishing "friend" from "foe," or unable to do so. Ultimately, they proved capable of accommodating champions of radical reform. Six years after the 1982 reform, and one year before the 1989 "collapse," the President of Hungary's Council of Industrial Policy could openly claim that

the socialist market economy has no precisely formulated and described model covering all details. Anyway, it cannot be anything fundamentally different from that of the up-to-date market economy.[81]

Political actors involved in the reform process had once again shifted the possibility frontier of Hungarian socialism while appearing to merely move along its points.

---

[81] Béla Csikós-Nagy, "Situation and Prospects of the Hungarian Economy," in *Hungarian Business Herald* 3, 1998, 14.

6

Schumpeter by the Danube

From Second Economy to Private Sector

> The function of entrepreneurs is to reform or revolutionize the pattern of production.
>
> Joseph A. Schumpeter

The socio-political ramifications of the 1982 property-rights reform, which institutionalized private entrepreneurship in Hungary's state-socialist system, were complex and profound. Pre-reform informal entrepreneurs, accustomed to an old set of rules, suddenly found themselves in a strange new world. They now operated in a hybrid economy in which enhanced legality and heightened competition was an irrevocable fact. Anyone doubting this had only to look at the new entrepreneurs who began to emerge into the light of day. Some – albeit a clear minority – were bold enough to leave the state sector entirely. Some even became legislators *avant la lettre*, lobbying and petitioning state bureaucracies to such a point that they forced the broadening of existing regulations and, in successive rounds, the enactment of new, more liberal ones. A few became so well-versed in the laws affecting them that they advised the state through the "representative" organizations that had originally been created to oversee and control the tiny pre-1982 private sector of craftsmen and shopkeepers. Still others set out to harness the politics of entrepreneurship, and founded an independent representative organization, the National Association of Entrepreneurs (VOSZ).[1]

Like their informal predecessors in industry and services or their counterparts in agriculture, these new entrepreneurs began collectively to change their environment, even as they remained convinced that they were merely functioning as best they could within the confines of micro-universes carefully constructed to ward off outside interference. Like the reformers we met in Chapter 5, these new entrepreneurs saw themselves as pragmatists. They learned the law simply because they wanted to make their businesses successful in a difficult and

---

[1] See Chapter 7 for more on VOSZ and the state representative institutions with which it competed.

confusing environment. And although they were aware that they might exercise some influence over discrete state decisions, they did not imagine that the incremental concessions they had won would contribute to a wholesale systemic transformation.

But contribute they did, at a time when the insertion of private property-rights into socialism opened up new political-economic possibilities. At first glance, many of the challenges and requirements for the success of the new private and quasi-private enterprises in post-1982 Hungary appeared to be the same as those that in earlier years had applied to firms in advanced capitalist countries.[2] This impression stemmed from the fact that state-socialist systems – despite marked variances in reform histories – implemented their own version of a mass-production/extensive-growth model. State socialism and capitalism, in fact, shared a Fordist tradition.[3] Moreover, socialist systems held to this model much longer than the advanced capitalist countries.

Upon further examination, however, it becomes clear that features specific to state-socialist macro-economic organization presented Hungarian private firms with markedly different opportunities and problems – chief among them, the double-edged sword of shortages.[4] On the one hand, many of the early entrepreneurs enjoyed guaranteed demand for their products and services. On the other hand, at least in manufacturing, they also faced near-certain dependence on state firms for raw materials. The same was true of the vast labor pools still embedded in state firms. Entrepreneurs needed to draw on those pools without alienating the state-firm managers on whom they relied for their supply of inputs.

The upshot of all this was that the emerging private sector, favored by pent-up demand, could now begin to compete with state firms, but entrepreneurs could do so only with a measure of cooperation from those self-same state competitors. In negotiating this delicate situation, entrepreneurs required a business ethic that would accommodate their special practical needs. And they needed networks that conveyed "deep information" about economic agents – information about their goodwill, trustworthiness, skills, and technical knowledge.

A Kafkaesque regulatory framework and remaining biases against the private sector also rendered robust contact networks and a hybrid code of ethics essential. If sophisticated entrepreneurs were to effectively circumvent and/or sway bureaucratic officials on a quotidian basis, they needed a normative logic to keep them from sinking – in their own eyes and those of society – to the level of vulgar profiteers. And they needed the contacts to help them identify

---

[2] Requirements such as experience in a relevant field; customer-oriented production and service; willingness to take growth-oriented risks; concern for excellence; and persistence. See, for example, Jeffrey A. Timmons, *The Entrepreneurial Mind* (New York: Brickhouse, 1989).

[3] See Michael Piore and Charles Sabel, *The Second Industrial Divide* (New York: Basic Books, 1984).

[4] Janos Kornai, *The Economics of Shortage* (Amsterdam: North-Holland, 1980).

the avenues and propitious circumstances for circumventing and overcoming official obstructions.

That self-described pragmatic entrepreneurs would go to all this trouble is puzzling, especially if we take at face value the widely held assumption that individuals worked in the second economy simply in response to their need to supplement incomes or, later, out of a drive for conspicuous consumption.[5] However, the puzzle dissolves once we include the sociopolitical motivations behind the entrepreneurs' pragmatic drive for what can only be described as capitalist success. Though few of the entrepreneurs had any sense of political mission *per se*, for some, second-economy activities had been a form of covert opposition to the socialist system of work and consumption even before 1982, and provided a sense of personal and professional agency. For others, second-economy work represented the perpetuation of family traditions of craftsmanship or enterprise, or simply the challenge of competition. For all, second-economy work became the foundation of new socio-economic relations as entrepreneurs made a place for themselves in a still-hostile system by turning innovation, efficiency, and competition into a source of both pride and profit.

This chapter looks at socio-economic change from the ground up, conceived as the "cumulative effect of individuals' reinterpretations of their roles."[6] It explores the strategies entrepreneurs used to function in a hybrid economy, and analyzes some of the ways these strategies worked to transform both their identities and the institutions of socialism. Although I briefly profile a prototypical informal entrepreneur, the chapter is largely devoted to post-1982 "success stories" in manufacturing. In the late 1980s, highly successful manufacturers exporting to the West were still not to be found on every street corner in Budapest or any other Hungarian city, though they were far more common than some among the Hungarian intellectual elite – former dissidents included – believed.[7] Three entrepreneurs receive special notice here, not because they are

---

[5] While most second-economy activity was certainly motivated by the need to supplement income, this chapter demonstrates that individuals soon experienced other rewards and realized broader possibilities. Tibor Kuczi found that only 17 percent of a sample of 389 legally employed private artisans and retailers cited purely material reasons for their choice of profession. Kuczi, "A legáalis kisipar" ("Legal small enterprise"), in Kovách, ed. *Gazdaság es rétegződés* (*Economy and stratification*), (Budapest: Institute of Social Sciences, 1984).

[6] See Lucy Mair, *Anthropology and Social Change* (London: LSE Monographs on Social Anthropology, no. 38, 1969).

[7] During a visit to Boston and a meeting of the "Harvard Kör" (Harvard Circle, a group of Hungarian expatriates in Boston), Gábor Demszky, the invited speaker, member of the Free Democrats and soon-to-be Mayor of Budapest, scoffed at the idea that there were any "real" entrepreneurs, let alone successful manufacturers in Hungary. That I claimed to be interviewing such individuals was apparently unpersuasive. The second economy, he confidently declared, was populated only by "thieves" and fly-by-night small-timers whose only interest was in short-term profit-taking, most of whom did little besides "patch tires or sell sunflower seeds on corners." This sentiment was typical; it was echoed, if not always so categorically, by the majority of non-specialist Hungarian intellectuals with whom I discussed my work between 1988 and 1990, and also by a few professional economists and sociologists.

unique – though each is in some respects remarkable – but because they serve as exemplars of the thriving manufacturers I interviewed, and because they represented the future of Hungary's economy.[8] The manufacturers profiled were also chosen because, though successful by any reasonable criteria, they were nevertheless not among the most famous or wealthiest; they did not appear in the media, as did a handful of the best-known 1980s private entrepreneurs. Other than pre-existing connections from school years or from previous workplaces, their social and political links to the party-state bureaucracy were forged largely in the course of running their businesses, and were not unusual; nor did they receive any special political favors.[9] As such, these three entrepreneurs appeared to possess no unusually great advantages that would render them inappropriate illustrations of the opportunities and obstacles faced by many others starting a manufacturing firm at the time. Like John W. Kiser III, the businessman-researcher who studied many of Hungary's innovative joint ventures between state-owned and foreign firms in the 1970s and 1980s and faced similar concerns when profiling firms and individuals, I am convinced that these cases possess a "generic significance . . . much greater than any statistical sampling would provide."[10]

To place these new or "modern" entrepreneurs in historical perspective, I first sketch the prototype of the more "conservative" entrepreneurs who chose to remain informal even after the 1982 reform. Like our prototype, these tended to be in retail and services rather than manufacturing. The modern and conservative "types," however, should not be seen as polar opposites. To be sure,

---

[8] Of the more than 100 interviews conducted for this book, 57 were with private entrepreneurs. The majority were done between November 1988 and October 1991, and were followed by numerous in-depth interviews and correspondence between 1991 and 1996 with those profiled here. Of the original 57 interviews, approximately 25 were of a quality and depth that warranted direct or indirect incorporation in the specific or general findings presented in the book. Several interviews were repeated two or three times, and in numerous cases I spoke later by telephone with entrepreneurs whom I had interviewed in person. Due to the timing and nature of my research and the sensitivity of the questions asked, it was not possible to distribute questionnaires or even to ask the same questions in each case. As a result, when drawing comparisons or general conclusions, I relied for corroboration on the scholarship of several Hungarian social scientists cited at various points throughout the book, especially István Gábor, Péter Galasi, Teréz Laky, Mihály Laki, Endre Sik, László Bruszt, Elemér Hankiss, Csaba Makó, Róbert Manchin, and István Tóth. Corroboration came also from the larger data sets of Tibor Kuczi and Ágnes Vajda, presented in English in "The Social Composition of Small Entrepreneurs," *Acta Oeconomica* 42, no. 3–4 (1990), as well as from the early statistical studies of Ildikó Ékes of the Hungarian Statistical Office. In the United States, I drew also on the earlier published and unpublished research of, and invaluable conversations with, Iván Szelényi, Ákos Róna-Tas, and József Böröcz.

[9] A few of these very famous entrepreneurs were also interviewed as background for this study, perhaps best-known among them János Palotás, founder of VOSZ (the National Association of Small Entrepreneurs) and founder of Kandeláber, the firm that made most of the streetlamps on Castle Hill in Budapest.

[10] John W. Kiser III, *Communist Entrepreneurs: Unknown Innovators in the Global Economy* (New York: Franklin Watts, 1989), 4. Kiser is president of Kiser Research in Washington DC, and was working to discover advanced technology in the Soviet bloc for possible acquisition by Western firms.

the personal characteristics, educational background, and business strategies I found among the new entrepreneurs represented the wave of the future, and a large-scale statistical survey confirms that the attributes of this generation of entrepreneurs were indeed the hallmark of those who came after them.[11] But the post-1982 entrepreneurs had attributes in common with older second-economy entrepreneurs who began their activities in the 1960s or 1970s. These attributes, however, were obscured by the limited number of official organizational forms available before 1982, and by the intensity of oversight and regulation to which registered artisans and retailers were subject in previous decades. Other factors also contributed to a lack of transparency: the greater need for discretion, and even secrecy, in some areas of endeavor; and in the case of agriculture, the complex symbiotic relationship between the entrepreneurs and their state-controlled cooperatives that we saw in Chapter 2. In fact, only in the late 1980s did it become feasible for outsiders to carry out in-depth studies of socialist entrepreneurs, and to acquire a fuller understanding of their impact on the larger system.[12]

Roads to Transformation: Tradition and Innovation

Prior to the 1982 reform, informal entrepreneurs almost always kept one foot firmly planted in the state sector. Mechanics, electricians, window-washers, chimney-sweeps, and masons all worked for state firms during official hours, and then turned to moonlighting. A representative case is Miklós,[13] a plumber who, since 1956, worked in a state plumbing firm, and informally repaired and even installed entire plumbing systems for his private customers. Decades of this heavy double-shift took a toll: at the age of fifty, he looked like an old man. By the time of the property-rights reform, however, he was able to cut back; and for larger jobs, he employed an assistant.

The 1982 reform, as this entrepreneur fully understood, meant that he could start a legal business much more easily than before, and still more easily by the end of 1988, when I met and first interviewed him. But he declined to do so.[14]

---

[11] Tibor Kuczi and Ágnes Vajda, "The Social Composition of Small Entrepreneurs," *Acta Oeconomica* 42, no. 3–4 (1990).

[12] A superb study of sanctioned and often formal entrepreneurship in agriculture was done by Iván Szelényi *et al.*, *Socialist Entrepreneurs: Embourgeoisement in Rural Hungary* (Madison: University of Wisconsin Press, 1988).

[13] Miklós preferred that his surname not be used, and in interviews with entrepreneurs between 1989 and 1991, this was generally the case. After 1991, however, my three "modern" entrepreneurs *insisted* that I use their full names, despite the concerns I voiced (for example, that they might be held liable, after the fact, for infractions of pre-1989 regulations that were so jumbled and contradictory that compliance was often impossible.

[14] He planned to raise his prices with inflation and the new individual income tax of 1989. Like others, he was confused about what he would owe; unlike many, he was candid about the net effect of the new income tax. Asked if people like him were putting aside money for taxes, he replied, chuckling, that even if he were to be charged 200,000 forints (then about $3,300, an unthinkably large sum in the still-socialist economy) in a lump sum, he would come out

Instead, he continued to operate according to his two sacrosant rules. One, "do not pay taxes." Two, "work *exclusively* for trustworthy customers referred by friends or long-standing clients."[15] The second rule minimized his concerns about possible anonymous denunciation from jealous individuals who might inform the authorities that he worked without registration and paid no taxes. The first rule, tax evasion, was, in his view, part of an *ethical code* that he had crafted out of a mixture of conviction, necessity, and his own interpretation of the anomalies of the official system. He did not, for example, pilfer materials from the state firm, and he refused to take advantage of his private customers. Indeed, he charged them a *lower* fee than that of his state firm, even though, as he noted with pride, the quality and timeliness of his work was far superior. The reasoning behind his pricing system was both normative and prudential: because he paid no taxes, he felt obliged to offer an *implicit discount*; and since overpricing might lead angry customers to inform on him, the discount was also the safer route. Of course, given the general shortage of service-providers, he knew that most people would not even consider denunciation, and that he could have charged more – many informal entrepreneurs did. But he also knew that even a single exception that confirmed the norm could ruin him – a prospect he dreaded.

Miklós's practices and ethos, multiplied by several millions, helped simultaneously to prop up and transform the socialist economy. Not that Miklós saw *himself* as an agent of change. If anything, even at our second interview in 1989, he was quite pessimistic about the chances of building a successful economy on the "ruins" of the old. As he put it: "It's much easier to tear down a house, even if all you have is a hammer and a chisel, than to build one. For forty years they've been tearing down this economy; it's going to take much longer to build it up." And when asked deliberately leading questions about the transformative possibilities inherent in his own informal work and that of others like him in various professions and trades, he replied that they merely represented remedial supplements to an impossibly inefficient system – one that, he added, was even more corrupt than the informal second economy itself.

immeasurably far ahead, given all of the tax-free money he had earned since 1956. At the time, an excellent industrial wage for a skilled worker at a state firm might have reached 27,000 forints/month, about $450. The nominal monthly average wage for workers in the state sector was 8,817 forints, or about $147/month. See Györgyi Baló and Iván Lipovecz, eds., *Tények Könyve '90 [Fact-Book 1990]*, (Debrecen, Hungary: Alföldi Nyomda [Alföldi Press], 1989), 733.

15 As was the case with many of my interview subjects – and *all* the "traditional" entrepreneurs – I met Miklós through someone both he and I knew and trusted – in this case, my uncle's ex-wife, who had informally employed him for many years. At the time, this was the only possible way to obtain interviews, let alone conduct a frank discussion, with informal entrepreneurs. The method had its advantages: the link to a third person made it a relatively easy matter to check the accuracy of many of the interview subject's specific claims, such as charges relative to others offering similar services, quality of work, and sometimes the entrepreneur's work-history, social origin, and educational background.

This dim view of the broader socio-economic import of informal second-economy production converges with that of analysts who focused on the privatization of state firms to the exclusion of other sectors of socialist economies. To be sure, judged by Schumpeterian standards of entrepreneurship, the informal entrepreneur represents a "weak case," not unlike the thousands of licensed artisans and retailers working legally and full time – the "traditional entrepreneurs" – featured in a statistical survey by Kuczi and Vajda.[16] Like these traditional entrepreneurs, Miklós did *not* seize the opportunity to expand in 1982. Like 51 percent of traditional artisans and retailers, he saw his enterprise simply as a way to supplement his state wage to make a better living. As with 62 percent of traditional artisans and retailers, habit was a strong motivation for the work he did. And as in their cases – and in sharp contrast to the post-1982 generation of entrepreneurs – capital shortage was typically *not* an obstacle to his work. Finally, like the traditional entrepreneurs, he had no more than a high school education and, like many of them, his father had specialized in the trade he himself pursued.[17]

But in another sense, the informal entrepreneur was also socialism's "strong case." He was not only ubiquitous – informal private work was far more prevalent than registered private business – but also more representative of state-socialist Hungary than the full-time artisans and small retailers who worked legally out of small shops. Because of him, shortages of goods and services were either eliminated or made less severe than they otherwise would have been. And since consumer and worker dissatisfaction was often channeled into productive (over)work, because of him the system functioned. Ultimately, it was partly because of millions like him – despite his own disclaimer – that the system was transformed.

If the 1982 reform did not radically alter the behavior of the traditional entrepreneur, it did give impetus to an incipient Schumpeterian elite. Most of these entrepreneurs were in their forties. Often they were highly educated, and just as often they came out of the state sector. In fact, only a small minority of managers of post-1982 private enterprises were carrying on a family tradition in business – approximately 6.7 percent of them, most of whose fathers had been employed as professionals or skilled workers (see Table 6.1). Some became wealthy only a few years after the reform; a few became home-grown millionaires before they even launched the large-scale expansion of their businesses that became possible in 1988.[18]

The high level of education of this entrepreneurial vanguard and its work experience in the state sector are also among the salient characteristics shared by the most successful entrepreneurs I interviewed. Those profiled in this chapter include a Ph.D. in mathematics who once worked at the Institute of

[16] Kuczi and Vajda, "The Social Composition of Small Entrepreneurs," 344.
[17] Ibid., 333–344.
[18] See the Law on Economic Association, *A Társasági Törvény: Az 1988.évi törvény a gazdasági társaságokról, magyarázatokkal, iratmintákkal*, Budapest: Lang, 1988.

TABLE 6.1 *Distribution of entrepreneurs by father's social group (percentages)*

	Self-employed (entrepreneurs)	Managers and intellectuals under age 60	Total wage and salary-earners in towns
Managers	12.9	4.7	2.5
Professionals	15.3	27.0	15.7
Skilled workers	29.3	22.0	23.8
Unskilled workers	15.7	15.8	23.5
Agricultural laborers	7.2	10.8	14.3
Farmers	5.2	9.1	12.6
Artisans and Retailers	10.9	6.7	7.8
Unknown	3.5	3.9	7.8

Note: "Self-employed" refers to both pre- and post-1982 entrepreneurs and artisans, and includes managers of private partnerships and cooperatives. "Managers and intellectuals under age 60" refers to managers of state-owned enterprises, and, more broadly, to the group usually called "professionals" in the U.S.
Source: Kuczi, T., and Vajda, A. 1990. "The Social Composition of Small Entrepreneurs," *Acta Oeconomica* 42, Akadémiai Kiado: Budapest, p. 332. Part of the authors' information came from a 1984 microsensus of the Hungarian Central Statistical Office.

Architecture; an industrial inventor with a background in applied research at a state institute; and an engineer, formerly employed by a state firm. The relatively advanced age – the late start – of the new entrepreneurs is a shared characteristic of my research pool, as it was of Kuczi and Vajda's larger one. In fact, we can think of this emerging elite as a cohort. One cohort member expanded on this point in 1989:

Our age group was left out of everything. We are the 40-something crowd. We could not be in major leadership positions because the older generation was still there. The 50, 60, 70 year-olds were so entrenched it was impossible to drive them out. The 45-year-olds should have been the next generation of political leaders, yet we are not. And now there will be a change: the 60-something crowd will leave, but we won't succeed them – the 30-year-old crowd will. We got left out of the decision-making process, and cannot oversee our own interests as responsibly as we would like.[19]

But their late start also reflected the fact that it took these entrepreneurs a decade or more to "acquire the capital, the goodwill, the connections, and the expertise

[19] Author's interview with Mihály Szabó, January 1989, Budapest. In subsequent rounds of interviews with the author, Szabó reaffirmed the views he expressed here and elsewhere in the book Budapest, fall 1991, summer 1994, and fall 1996. Szabó nicely summarizes the trend in directorships of state firms as well, which Kiser found in his 1980s interviews at state firms. See Kiser, *Communist Entrepreneurs: Unknown Innovators in the Global Economy*, 64–65.

on the specific market."[20] Of course, a few entrepreneurs inherited some of these key resources. Such was the case of Péter Futó, the son of a retailer of sweets. During what Futó called the "repressive years" – the 1950s and 1960s – his father slowly and cautiously built up a network of customers, and his sales provided the family with a stable living. The elder Futó's shop was a registered, legal one-man business, and as such was permitted to use the "occasional" help of family members. Young Futó, who sold candy on weekends as a traveling salesman for his father, remembers the shop as a vertically integrated, in-house operation.

In 1984, Futó Sr. died, leaving two shops (he had opened the second in 1982). This was a turning-point for his son. A change in his personal life – his father's death – came close on the heels of a change in public life: the 1982 reform of property rights. Although Futó held a Ph.D. in mathematics, he now chose to expand on his father's small business instead of taking a professorship at the Budapest Technical University. Like many others among the modern entrepreneurs, his original plans had not included business. After Futó finished university in 1969, he had no fixed idea about his career except that he wanted some "control" over his time. He worked for some years at the Institute of Architecture while making progress toward his doctorate, which he was awarded in 1979.[21]

As a professor, Futó would have earned a salary which, as he put it, " afforded neither financial nor intellectual independence."[22] In contrast, the businesses he "inherited" in 1984 (strictly speaking, socialist law only allowed him to inherit the businesses' "use value") were earning ten times what they had before the 1982 regulations allowed expansion and the hiring of non-family employees. Thus, in 1985, the mathematician who had never expected "to become his father" chose to increase his sense of autonomy and agency by building on his father's legacy. He founded *Fundy, Inc.* (combining *Futó* and *Candy* in the name), a confectionery firm that manufactures both hand- and machine-made sweets. The hand-made confections are of the kind that sold by high-end specialty stores in the United States, and are comparable to fine Swiss or Belgian chocolates. *Fundy's* machine-made products, though more standardized, are still comparable with many high-end imports widely available in the United States and Europe – from German "Gumi-bears" to French herbal candies and Swedish mints.

Familial endowment, however, was clearly not the most common platform for the launch of a Schumpeterian transformation. Technical experts, for example, began to leave the state sector with increasing frequency in the early 1980s,

---

[20] In 1984, the Central Statistical Office found that the average age of what Kuczi and Vajda termed "modern entrepreneurs" – the post 1982 group – was 40.3 years. Kuczi and Vajda, "The Social Composition of Small Entrepreneurs," 330.

[21] More precisely, he earned his "candidacy," or "kandidatus," which in the Soviet system then in effect in Hungary, actually ranked somewhat higher than the American Ph.D.

[22] His salary would have been about $140/month at the time.

taking their firms' knowledge with them. Consider Mihály Szábo. He produced high-quality, heavy glass that can be used for the large doors and windows of commercial buildings, as well as for smaller items such as mirrors or coffee-tables. It is extraordinarily strong, resistant to temperature changes, and takes permanent imprints with great precision. These might be delicate and complex designs etched in gold-leaf on furniture, or the bold logos of display-windows. Szábo's work includes the glass of the Hungarian National Opera House's candelabra and the massive, multiple windows of numerous Budapest department stores.

Szábo's professional biography is not unlike Futó's. In 1990, Szábo was in his forties, held a degree in mechanical engineering, and had worked for many years at one of Budapest's well-known industrial research institutes. He recalled his first few years there as good ones, but then budget cuts slowed down the institute's long range research program. Szábo and his team-members had less work and a surfeit of time on their hands.

We talked politics, which we enjoyed. But after a while we got on each others' nerves. We simply didn't have enough to do. I stayed on for a few years because I was building my house, and it was good for me that there was a phone at work, which I could use to organize the construction. But when the house was completed, I reached a kind of cross-roads.[23]

Szábo was in search of *meaningful* competition, by which he meant the chance to compete with himself and with peers. But at the state research institute, all he found was bitterness. He remembered the institute as "exploitative" of its research workers, and gave several examples. One example in particular bothered him. He recalled that he and his work-team had received a joint patent on a machine they developed, which, as he noted proudly, attained the standards of the American firm Corning. However, none of the team-members received any of the profits from the invention because they had used parts of discarded state-owned machines in its construction. And according to Hungarian accounting standards, the low value of the component parts reduced the book-value of the final product to near zero. "The institute, however, made several million forints in profit from our research," he concluded.

Not long after another incident of this type, Szábo announced to everyone's surprise that he would leave the institute and become a private entrepreneur. "One of the lawyers there," Szábo remembered, "advised me to do it within the framework of the research institute, and in exchange they would support me to a degree." Szábo rebuffed the offer on "financial, personal, and moral grounds." Or, as he summarized it: "I got to the point where I said, enough! I now want the patent for myself."

Szábo settled on the idea of producing heat-isolating glass largely because he had also worked to develop this product in the research institute, and as a result, he had connections with various large factories in Europe. He was

---

[23] Author's interview with Mihály Szabó, January 1989, Budapest.

also aware of an opening on the domestic market: in Hungary, only two state factories were able to make good quality *thermopan*; and the numerous small entrepreneurs engaged in the production of this type of glass were unable to achieve the level of quality he knew was within his grasp. Finally, Szábo knew that in order to attain such quality improvements, he would either have to invest in expensive Western machinery, or build it himself. He took the latter route, and in a few years received his patent.

He might have begun his business even earlier, but for a bureaucratic regulation. Szábo needed a trade-school certificate, proving that he had completed the eighth grade and two years' apprenticeship in industry.

I didn't have this! I had much *higher* degrees, but not this. However, in 1982 it became a citizen's right to enter into business. At first the authorities didn't want to give it to me, because I had no trade-school certificate. But later they realized that as a court-appointed expert, I had reached the highest level of expertise. So while it was true that I didn't actually know how to *cut* the glass – for that, I needed employees – I was nevertheless qualified. Eventually they approved my application.[24]

Bureaucratic barriers to entry into private business activity were as commonplace as the reasons for exiting the state sector. Consider the case of Pétér Gerő, who in 1982 founded *Colorplan*. The firm began as a manufacturer of electrostatic powder-coating systems – a sophisticated industrial-painting technology and one of the most advanced forms of industrial surface finishing. Electrostatic coating systems can be partially or fully automated, and are used to cover the surface of products as diverse as automobiles, metal furniture, modern lamps, and minute, intricate plastic toys – all with near-perfect homogeneity of color, evenness of distribution, and adhesiveness. The system produced by *Colorplan* was also environmentally friendly since it worked on a closed cycle, and it was highly efficient, since it avoided loss of materials.

Like the glass manufacturer we met earlier, Gerő felt that in state firms, people could not "implement their own ideas or realize themselves." In 1981, for instance, Gerő and his colleagues had submitted a proposal to the director of their state enterprise, arguing for a joint venture with *Wagner*, a German firm highly regarded in the field of industrial painting (in the United States, smaller *Wagner* products can be found in any hardware or home-improvement store). But after Gerő and his colleagues had obtained the proper authorizations and signatures, and even secured bank-loans, the director "got cold feet." Although the deal was off, Gerő and colleagues were loathe to give up their plan.

We had all the signatures except the director's. Had we had his signature, we would have been *the very first such firm* . . .we actually could have had a joint venture on January 1st! [1982][25]

---

[24] Ibid.
[25] Author's interview with Pétér Gerő, December 1988, Budapest.

Before 1982, only state ministries could establish firms. Gerő, however, was familiar with the new regulations allowing firms to found their own branches and joint ventures, and private individuals to establish several new types of firms. After the failure of the joint-venture idea, he founded an enterprise work partnership (GMK) with two colleagues.

For about six months, we planned our GMK on the side . . . Finally, in April 1983, we all left the state firm and started to work for ourselves full-time. Under the auspices of a [state-owned] foreign trade firm, we signed a contract retroactive to January 1, 1983 with *Wagner* – the German firm we had proposed as partner for a joint-venture with our state enterprise. Now we three would be their Hungarian representative and technical advisers. Of course, we brought the connection from our former workplace. Then in May we hired two workmen, and we operated this way for a year before expanding.

Once again, knowledge, skill, and potentially profitable connections left a state firm, thus contributing to an emerging brain-drain pattern. Like the confectioner and the glass maker, Gerő was highly educated. He had accumulated his technical expertise working in state firms as an engineer in painting technology, manufacturing industrial spray-painting machines. Unlike the others, however, he resembled many directors of modern Hungarian private firms in that he changed workplaces within the state-sector numerous times before exiting to full-time private enterprise.[26]

Gerő's family background, too, is more representative of the directors of modern private firms. Gerő's father began his career, if we follow the criteria used by the Kuczi and Vajda survey, as a "skilled worker" (Table 6.1). Later, however, Gerő senior earned two university degrees and became an engineer. He thus doubly fit the pattern identified in the survey mentioned: 58 percent of the fathers of 1982 private managers fell into the categories "managers, intellectuals in subordinate posts, and skilled workers."

By the 1980s, the social origins of state firm managers and private entrepreneurs were similar, with the notable exception that an even larger proportion of managers of private companies had fathers who themselves were "intellectuals, or holders of a university degree, or [state-firm] managers."[27] Gerő senior had also been a history professor and an army officer, and by the time his son started his firm, the father had become the director of a large state company. In 1990, at the age of sixty one, the father was working as a lathe-turner for his son at *Colorplan*, and also raised fruits and vegetables – "a serious peasant," his son declared, somewhat like the "urban peasants" we

---

[26] 24 percent of the Kuczi-Vajda sample changed place of employment three times, 19 percent four times, and 29 percent five or more times. Kuczi and Vajda, "The Social Composition of Small Entrepreneurs," 337.

[27] Ibid., 332.

encountered in Chapter 2. Gerő Sr. remade himself time and again: a plastic man in a rigid system.[28]

It should come as no surprise, then, that Gerő's response, when he was asked about the conventional wisdom that the system had killed the initiative and creativity of many of its employees, was reminiscent of Miklós Haraszti's famous description of skilled lathe-turners forced to make machine parts from disjointed pieces of blueprints without ever seeing the whole or knowing what machine they were intended for.[29]

The system may have battered the initiative and creativity of some people, but the system could not really kill the spirit. [At *Colorplan*] we have, for example, an engineer who is perfectly happy as an engineer – he doesn't want to direct things. But he's happier at our place because at the state firm his superiors were forever telling him how to do things: he was a simple drudge, the executor of their wishes.

At our place, all activities are result-oriented, and if within this framework someone is able to realize himself, he can do it freely and independently; only the framework is given. If he's talented, he solves problems; if not, sooner or later it will become apparent that he's incompetent. Then he can return to the state sector, where they will tell him exactly what to do.[30]

Clearly, there were some state firms and cooperatives that allowed workers space for creative initiative, especially as the relative autonomy of skilled workers in state firms increased after 1982 through VGMKs and various forms of auxiliary production (see Table 6.2). But state firms had always served as socialism's welfare net, and by the late 1980s, many had become workers' ghettos. Meanwhile, the new entrepreneurs embarked on a journey that would test their mettle and radically alter the developmental path of the Hungarian state-socialist system.

Founding and Consolidating the Private Firm

Hungarian entrepreneurs who founded businesses in or shortly after 1982 faced little or no competition, other than from state firms. This advantage naturally lasted longer in some areas of manufacturing than in the retail and service sector. Gerő was aware that *Colorplan*, too, had benefited.

We found a niche. In the mid-1980s, we alone in Hungary could offer, for forints, this Western technology. Of course, today [summer 1989] we have competition. We've been forced to concentrate on those areas in which we are better. But this terrain will get more and more crowded as the opportunities increase, and others start to find their place in it.[31]

---

[28] Ibid., 333. Gerő's grandfather was also an entrepreneur, a biographical *datum* that places Gerő among those two-fifths of entrepreneurs whose grandfathers were self-employed at some time in their lives.

[29] Miklós Haraszti, *A Worker in a Worker's State* (New York: Universe Books 1978).

[30] Author's interview with Péter Gerő, June 1989, Budapest.

[31] Ibid.

TABLE 6.2 *Small private enterprises* * – Hungary, 1982–1990*

Year	Industrial and cooperative specialist groups	VGMKs	GMKs
1982	——	——	——
1983	——	——	——
1984	2,327	17,765	7,346
1985	2,613	20,265	9,312
1986	2,758	21,527	10,920
1987	2,331	19,169	11,164
1988			11,399
1989			14,572
1990			19,896

*Selected enterprise forms; does not include private craftsmen, "small cooperatives," or Civil Law Partnerships (PJTs)
Sources: 1984–1987: Éva Kerpel and David G. Young, *Hungary to 1993: Risks and Rewards of Reform* (EIU Special Report No. 1153, London, November 1988); 1988–1990: *Hungarian Statistical Yearbook.*

When Gerő started his business, his only competitor had been a single state firm. By 1989, however, he faced competition from other private producers – firms that, like *Colorplan*, imported similar West German technology, or worked under license to German or other firms. This competition, as Gerő put it, was only "market-like" – not truly *of the market.*

A market-*like* relationship exists among us competitors. The reason is simple. The production of basic materials is monopolized by the state, so we have no open access to them. This means that our success or failure is not only determined by how well we operate, or how we find and deal with buyers, or even by the quality of our products. At least on a day-to-day basis, what matters most is how we obtain our raw materials.[32]

The new entrepreneurs also faced a wide range of legal obstacles, from limitations on the number of employees allowed to punitive tax laws. Initially, the entrepreneurs circumvented these obstacles; eventually, they helped bring them down. This was a slow, step-by-step process. Let's take the case of *Colorplan* first. Gerő and his partners limited their salaries, purchased a plot of land, and invested in machinery. In this way, they built the first part of a modern factory in three years, at the end of which they hired two more people.

However, the firm's activities soon outgrew the GMK organizational form.[33] For this reason, and in order to escape the disadvantageous tax laws then

[32] Ibid.
[33] For example, "commerce" (*kereskedelem*) and manufacturing were traditionally divided under socialist economic organization, and GMKs were not allowed to engage directly in retail trade until 1988. This was consistent with Marxist political economy, which separates economic

applicable to GMKs, the partners set out to found a "small cooperative" in 1987, retaining the GMK only as a legal entity to protect the partners' original investment. Founding the small cooperative was not easy, either. The law required the associates to present a business plan for the first year of operation, and stipulated a minimum founding capital of $20,000.[34] Gerő and his associates cobbled together $9,000, then presented their plan to the authorities.

We reported that the founding capital was $9,000 and that we were only aiming for a $400,000 turnover. They told us that this was impossible; that for such a turnover the founding capital had to be *at least* $600,000. We strongly questioned this judgement, and argued that *we* were the entrepreneurs, and that if we were mistaken it was *our* neck on the line. No matter, the authorities refused to accept the plan.

In the end, we stayed with the smaller founding capital, since that's all we had; and reduced our projected turnover, on paper, to $120,000. This plan was approved. We started the business with all papers in order. At long last, no one could interfere with us anymore. And yes, our turnover *was*, in fact, about $400,000.[35]

The authorities apparently wanted to ensure that private firms would not fail in their first year of operation.[36] The partners, however, tried to explain that theirs was not a mass-production operation requiring significant working capital. Their operation, though a manufacturing firm, was based primarily on intellectual work aimed at solving technological problems of customization. And so the associated material expenses were relatively small. Moreover, the founding partners already knew with some precision which markets were available to the firm, and as a result, returns from sales would be relatively rapid.

When asked whether the authorities might be trying to "plan the market," Gerő insisted that such a formulation conferred undue credit on the Hungarian administrative system. This was a simple matter of bureaucratic enervation.

Those who sit in that bureaucratic permit-granting office take out their old instruction books from the 1970s [for founding *state* cooperatives] and they read and say: 'Ah, that's the way it was. This must also apply to the founding of a small *private* cooperative.'

No wonder these bureaucrats hold onto their desks for dear life . . . while reasonable [entrepreneurs] think to themselves: 'once I've gotten my permit, I'll do things my way.'[37]

---

activity into "productive" and "non-productive," and holds that commerce belongs to the latter category.

[34] Or about 1 million forints at the time. An *individual* member's contribution to this amount only needed to be $2,000, or 100,000 forints at the time.

[35] Author's interview with Péter Gerő August 1989, Budapest.

[36] After 1988, it became illegal for the authorities to question the technical aspects of a firm's creation, its potential profitability, or its socio-economic or political "desirability"; the administrative authorities and courts could only ensure that newly registered firms met the legal requirements of the Law on Economic Association. *A Társasági Törvény: Az 1988. évi törvény a gazdasági társaságokról* (Budapest: Lang, 1988), 9.

[37] Interview with Gerő, 1989.

Whatever the difficulties of founding the firm and establishing new organizational forms, in his efforts to circumvent bureaucratic rigidity, Gerő was representative of a larger group of entrepreneurs. The Kuczi-Vajda survey showed that fluidity of organizational form was common among managers of modern private enterprises, who, because of their superior education, were better equipped to "see through" the morass of rapidly shifting, confusing, and often conflicting regulation, and were quicker to identify the organizational form or mixture of forms best suited to their changing needs.[38]

This nimbleness was key, precisely because while change was the order of the day, it was still imperative not to offend state-firm managers, especially while simultaneously (if often surreptitiously) absorbing their best human capital. For example, as Gerő's small cooperative rapidly expanded its activities, it had to take on more members. A former colleague from Gerő's state firm had gone to another state enterprise, where he headed his own independent section that manufactured rust-proof steel equipment. However, Gerő's former colleague now wanted to join *Colorplan* with his entire work-team from the state firm. Gerő had originally planned to establish a stable sub-contracting relationship with an outside firm to build stainless steel components, but when this opportunity presented itself, he decided to take on the work-group from the state firm.

> He was an old colleague . . . and we saw that his section group [of twenty] at the state firm was profitable, even though the firm as a whole was not. So we decided to have them come over. These were people who couldn't realize themselves at the state firms where they worked; they didn't let them work, and they were looking for someone who was interested in their skills. *We* were interested. We let them do their work independently, and develop themselves.[39]

Within five years, *Colorplan* expanded into four main areas of work, each organized as a separate profit center: the original painting technology; the manufacture of a variety of stainless-steel structures; the manufacture of a double-diaphragm pump of the firm's own conception and design; and a fire-detecting and extinguishing system. By 1990, the firm employed sixty people; its sales were in the neighborhood of $360,000 annually; the rate of growth in sales was remarkable;[40] and the firm had even purchased computer numerically

---

[38] Kuczi and Vajda, "The Social Composition of Small Entrepreneurs," 335.

[39] Author's interview with Pétér Gerő, July 1991, Budapest.

[40] $360,000 was about 220 million forints in 1990. Between 1987 (the year *Colorplan* essentially transformed itself from a GMK to a small cooperative) and 1990, Gerő estimated that its sales increased from 26 million forints to 140 million forints (an increase of 438 percent). However, as 1987 was only a half-year of operation for the small coop (prior to that time the firm was still functioning as a GMK), the next two years are more representative. In 1988, the cooperative earned about 201 million forints, an increase of 43.6 percent over the previous year. Its 1990 sales were about 220 million forints, an increase of 9.5 percent. (Adjusted for inflation, the 1989 increase in sales was about 15 percent, whereas the 1990 figure actually represents a decline of approximately 15 percent.)

controlled (CNC) equipment, which increased the flexibility and speed of specialized design work.

Two market-related factors contributed to the firm's success. On the one hand, the significant differential between Western and Hungarian wages lowered the price of *Colorplan*'s products.[41] On the other hand, the firm was able to pay its employees high wages relative to other Hungarian workers. But years of accumulated experience and dense networks of professional contacts were also crucial. These resources allowed *Colorplan* to develop new parts and equipment to improve the *Wagner* systems, and to redesign the machines to fit Hungarian firms' production processes.

> This was possible because we had been working with these machines for a long time, and we had developed our own "know-how" by solving problems which arose in the course of manufacturing and using the machines. For this reason we were ahead of our Hungarian competition.[42]

These adaptive and flexible productive strategies were in the beginning "completely unconscious," but Gerő then became aware of the international trend toward "flexible automation." Once armed with this knowledge – he had attended a conference on the subject organized in Budapest by Baden-Württemburg's Chamber of Commerce – he self-consciously borrowed from strategies deployed by the German and Swedish auto industries, and from the Japanese experience of imitative development.[43]

If the firms' creativity was on the rise, old disadvantages continued to impose a host of strategic requisites on entrepreneurs, from skillful deployment of contacts in the state sector to discrete exploitation of bureaucratic flaws. One major disadvantage was the old official mind-set, which only added to the bureaucratic confusion created by the innovative features of the property rights reform. In the early 1980s, for example, the authorities had trouble squaring the state directives to which they were accustomed with the fact that a private business might need to purchase vehicles and real estate *qua* businesses, not as individuals.

> Q: So you could be the owner of a firm but the firm couldn't own a truck?
> A: Precisely. And once we solved this problem, we faced the challenge of buying [rather than leasing] real estate. I went all the way to the Ministers of the Interior and Finance, and we were the first for whom they allowed the purchase of workplace real estate as a GMK. But they said, 'O.K., buy it, but *in the name of the joint representative of the GMK.*' We wanted to know why, since it wouldn't be his, but would belong to the firm, to the GMK. It was, of course, implicit in the 1982 regulation that the GMK could buy whatever it needed, but they didn't know how to handle it in terms of taxes. You just

---

[41] In 1990, the average industrial wage in Hungary was less than a quarter of the West German; wages overall were lower still.

[42] Author's interview with Pétér Gerő, July 1991, Budapest.

[43] Ibid. On "flexible specialization," see Charles Sabel, *Work and Politics* (Cambridge: Cambridge University Press, 1982); also Piore and Sabel, *The Second Industrial Divide*.

can't imagine the mess . . . Business purchases simply didn't fit into the existing mental or regulatory framework.[44]

In this and in other matters that would be typical business operations in the West, Gerő and his associates filed written requests and applications – which were frequently refused. But even after receiving half a dozen rejections, Gerő would still "climb in through the window after they had kicked him out the door." In other words, he and his associates petitioned time and again, until persistence paid off. In this way, Gerő's firm and many others helped to push forward particular institutional innovations. For instance, *Colorplan* appears to have been the first GMK to serve as the technical representative of a foreign firm. Pioneering, however, had to be carried out in a roundabout manner. As Gerő recalled, in 1983 the Ministry of Foreign Trade simply "could not grasp" *Colorplan*'s proposal. The Ministry was unable to tell *Colorplan* whether or not it could contract as the representatives of a foreign firm through a Hungarian state foreign trade firm, because there had "never been such a thing."[45]

So I had to explain it in person to the chief lawyer. He claimed to understand. But then, behind our backs they told the director of the foreign trade firm to be very cautious in handling our contract. [Caution] meant that we were unable to get the usual *proviso*, meaning a percentage after sales. So we had to do it *sub rosa*. Everyone knew it was a proviso, but it had to be called "engineering services." We had to charge "engineer days" instead of sales.

We did this for a year and a half, simply because the Foreign Trade Firm was afraid of what we were doing and the Ministry was unable to tell them what to do and how to do it. They didn't know how to handle this new arrangement. Then, after a year and a half we decided not to count "engineer days" anymore. We declared that this was going to be a *proviso*, period.[46]

The Director of the Foreign Trade Firm finally approved this unfamiliar practice, but only after finding and attaching to it an old label – an existing category – that could in no way upset the *status quo*. The Director thus protected himself from any possible political fallout, since he could not be fingered as the first to permit what might turn out to be a "deviance" from the socialist line. If anyone bore a political risk, it was the private entrepreneur.

   Other entrepreneurs took notice of Gerő's "model" – his approach to economic and bureaucratic challenges – and "copied it." By being in the vanguard, ironically, Gerő helped spawn his own competition. "Now we had to fight to be the best again. But we accepted it as part of the reality of the market." His activism *vis-à-vis* the bureaucracy clearly broadened the scope of possibility for

---

[44] Ibid.
[45] As in other state-socialist countries, private firms were not allowed to engage in foreign operations on their own until 1989. Such operations had to be carried out through state foreign trade firms and sanctioned by the Ministry of Foreign Trade.
[46] After the fact, *Colorplan* calculated days of services rendered to match actual sales, and charged that amount to their foreign trade intermediary (the state foreign trade firm). Authors' interview, Pétér Gerő, July 1991, Budapest.

others: six months after his bureaucratic coup, regulations appeared formally allowing "what *Colorplan* had done."

The more this demonstration effect spread, the more it helped intensify competitive pressures. By 1990, *Colorplan* had lost market share to expanded domestic and international competition. In a very real sense, and even aside from its export business, *Colorplan* was already competing on the world market even within Hungary, since rival West European, Japanese, and American products were being sold and/or manufactured by Hungarian firms. But as Gerő noted, because competition required the company to keep adapting machines and developing new ones, competition also served to keep the *Colorplan* team focused and productive.

Maintaining focused productivity also required a change in labor-management relations. At *Colorplan*, the line between worker and entrepreneur was blurred. Gerő emphasized this as a central difference from the state firms that once had employed *Colorplan*'s staff. "Here," he said, "the private owner controls only the *result* of the work, not the *details* of the work process, so the worker can achieve better results."

Colorplan also provided services for its employees that supplemented the national welfare net.[47] The firm extended loans to employees purchasing or renovating an apartment or house. From 1987 on, employees wishing to vacation at Hungary's Lake Balaton were entitled to two weeks with their families – rent-free, at half-board – in a large house rented by the firm. In addition, *Colorplan* compensated for the slowness of national sickness and disability disbursements, due in this case to the fact that private firms were not, like state firms, disbursement points. Specifically, *Colorplan* employees had to wait as much as three to four months to receive such payments from the state insurance system. So *Colorplan*'s management advanced employees the money due them from the government for sickness or disability benefits. Other efforts to build a team spirit included keeping social relations among management and workers relaxed and casual,[48] with Gerő himself acting as a kind of *primus inter pares*. (Management and employees, for example, regularly played soccer together on a field rented by the firm.)

These efforts at boosting employee morale and firming up their loyalty were worthwhile because they helped maintain focused productivity, something that was essential at a time when much of the managers' entrepreneurial attention and energy was spent not on supervising their businesses but on struggles with bureaucratic authorities. Repeatedly, entrepreneurs voiced deep resentment at the time and money dedicated to such "non-productive" activities.[49] Indeed,

---

[47] *Fundy* provided many similar services to its employees.

[48] This, at any rate, is what I was able to observe during interviews with Gerő and his associates, on multiple visits to the firm between late 1988 and August 1991.

[49] Asked, for example, whether he, like so many others, had found that payoffs to officials were part of the cost of doing business in socialist Hungary, Gerő replied that to a certain extent they were necessary, as well as related to a process of counter-selection in the bureaucracy." Honorable bureaucrats work for a while without corruption, perhaps out of sheer enthusiasm. A few stay,

successful entrepreneurs typically demonstrated a stubborn commitment to a long-term strategy, an equally abiding willingness to keep abreast of changing regulations, and last, but not least, the ability to convince state officials to implement both the letter and the spirit of the laws recently enacted.

The bundled aspect of these essential qualities was particularly evident when it came to business expansion. In 1989, our glass maker, Szábo, was uncertain as to how he might expand his business, primarily because of residual confusion about the rights accruing to him as an inventor. Even though his process had recently received first prize at a conference on innovation, Szábo could not collect the subventions he believed were his legal due. In effect, the patent office was unable to determine the *value of the patent* in the product, so that Szábo continued to pay tax at the 60 percent rate.[50] He argued his case:

The law says that if someone gets a patent for their own invention, works in their own business, and "uses" the patent, then they are allowed a tax break. However, by "use" they mean *use up* – that is, sell it. But if I myself employ it in my business, that's "use" too, it seems to me! This is where the disagreement comes in. They claim that I must *sell* this machine . . . But I would have to sell it to my competitors, and the total demand right now is probably for about three machines. With that, I would put myself out of business, since the competition could then match my quality. So for me the profit would come from *using* the machine and any spinoffs for ten, twenty years.

To circumvent what he perceived as "senseless" regulation, Szábo and another entrepreneur came up with a solution: he would establish a legal entity in the form of a corporation (KFT, the Hungarian acronym for a limited liability corporation, which became possible with the 1988 Law on Economic Association). The corporation would then "buy" the license for the machine from Szábo, and even help him evade taxes by "paying" him an artificially low sum, so that he could post a loss.

In the course of normal business, Szábo also spent quite a bit on bribes.[51] But what troubled him even more were the five hours a day he had to take from his productive work and devote to figuring out where and how to obtain inputs, solving various bureaucratic problems, and deciphering contradictory regulations. Purchasing a plot of land on which to build a new workshop – outside his home – proved challenging.

and remain honorable. But most get tired of all the meaningless struggle, and either leave for better pay, or just because they can't take it anymore. Fewer and fewer people get into the bureaucracy who know what the goal is, or who know how to achieve it if they have a sense of purpose." Author's interview with Péter Gerő, December 1988, Budapest. Gerő reaffirmed the views he expressed here and elsewhere in the book in subsequent rounds of interviews with the author. Budapest, summer and fall 1991, 1994 summer.

50 According to this law, the inventor who received a patent should have paid 30 percent instead of the standard 60 percent tax. But no one in the patent office had been able to determine what percentage of the price of *thermopan* was glass and glue vs *intellectual* value. Author's interview with Mihály Szabó, February 1989, Budapest.

51 Ibid. He estimated an additional 12 percent of the cost of his various materials (glass, steel, aluminum, and so on) in the 1980s.

This country needs entrepreneurs to build and expand. But I can't do it because I already own a house, and I'm not allowed another piece of real estate.

In late 1988, Szábo was reasonably certain that he would find the right "channels" out of this quandary, but he was also certain that considerable time and connections would be needed to get municipal council officials even to hear him out.

Q: In this case, do you also need to pay people?
A: Not necessarily. It's more a matter of knowing someone, perhaps because I made something for his house, or did him a favor of some sort. Then he speaks to so-and-so on my behalf. The logic is simple. If I get you bricks, you get me glass, and another one gets my kid into university . . .
Q: But what about the uncertainty? Can you get used to it?
A: No. It's impossible. It takes tremendous energy.
Q: And how do you know whom to trust?
A: Only through friends and connections.
Q: But even then you can go wrong and get into a jam, can't you, if what's involved is illegal, or even just not common practice?
A: Yes, but there are ways to be careful. You speak *only to one person at a time.* There must never be witnesses. *You never do business with three.*[52]

Because Szábo the tactician also had a broader perspective on the system, he knew that there was no other way to deal with the "insanity" of it all.

On the one hand, any petty official has great power. The lady who works as the gatekeeper at the Csepel Iron works, a huge state firm that employs thousands, wouldn't let the five cars of a Yugoslav delegation of journalists enter the other day, unless they all got into two cars – five were too many! They had to obey her.

On the other hand, many people with great power can do less than you think . . . I recall some years ago that the Director of a BM hospital [Belügy Miniszterium: one of the special hospitals for the Ministry of the Interior] wanted to replace some 5,000 bottles badly smeared with vaseline. But he lacked the power to make the decision. So he turned to me, since I was certified to testify as a court expert. I was to attest that these filthy bottles could no longer be cleaned properly and had to be discarded. For my services, he paid the state institute where I then worked 10,000 forints [then about $166], of which I got not a cent. The institute did, though – for a half-day of my work and my opinion that various acids and solvents could not fully clean the bottles! I wrote *four pages* to explain why they really did have to be thrown out.

Meanwhile, here in my own garage it is possible to invent new and useful things, perhaps even beautiful ones.[53]

Pointing to a gold-etched glass table in his living-room, which was indeed beautiful, Szábo mentioned that similar pieces had been exhibited in Budapest's National Gallery. As his work became better-known, the price of Szábo's glass

[52] Author's interview with Mihály Szábo, December 1988, Budapest.
[53] Ibid.

soared.[54] And yet he remained hesitant about expansion. Asked about the local stereotype of Hungarian entrepreneurs as largely incapable of long-term thinking and being interested only in fast money, Szábo acknowledged that the economic and regulatory climate quite often elicited short-sighted and greedy behavior. But he felt that the stereotype also grew out of public misperceptions created by the wheeling-and-dealing necessary to run a private business in a socialist system.

Connections are everything. An Austrian colleague was here a few years back and asked me how I got a hold of glass. In those days, Hungarians were not permitted to import raw materials. I explained that I knew people who made it possible for me to bring in the glass in a quasi-official manner. He then wanted to know where I got the Western glue. I explained that I was the informal middleman between the Hungarians and the English on a particular state firm deal, and I got my payment in glue samples. Finally, he told me that he didn't understand how it was possible to make *thermopan* without a steady and reliable source of glass, glue, or aluminum. And I told him: that's the *poetry* of it.[55]

In some ways, the story of these entrepreneurs is indeed a tale of poetic justice. The case of Futó the confectioner illustrates the point. When Futó started his business in 1986, he was required to take the confectioners' trade examination in order to be allowed to hire six trainee-employees. But he was unwilling to spend the time and energy to prepare for the exam. As result, his score was only middling. So he had to start with only three employees, who made all the candy by hand. By 1988, however, hiring regulations had eased. Futó now had fifteen employees, a completely automated plant (though some sweets were still hand-made), and was producing a greater variety and a higher quality product than his main competitor, the state candy factory in Budapest. Moreover, *Fundy* confections – then still manufactured in a small factory that appeared, from the street, to be a completely unimpressive private house – were sold in England, France, Austria, then-West Germany, Canada, and the United States. In the domestic market, *Fundy* had about 2,500 regular retail buyers, and profits were remarkable for the time.[56]

Success hinged partly on a particular sales strategy. In Hungary, *Fundy* sold automated manufactures. Taking advantage of the relatively low cost

---

[54] From about $33/square meter in 1983 to $250/square meter in 1989; at the time, about 2,000 forints/square meter and 15,000 forint/square meter, respectively.

[55] Author's interview with Mihály Szábo, December 1988, Budapest.

[56] In late 1988, Futó's official profits were recorded at approximately $120,000. But Futó admitted that this was a gross understatement of the truth. He felt that it was "unfair" that state firms were subsidized, and wanted to protect his business, which he worried could be taken from him at any time. By 1990, however, he had built a new factory outside Budapest on land owned by a state cooperative with which he had formed a joint venture, and his (certainly still understated) profits were in the neighborhood of $700,000/year (then 50 million forints/year). Author's interview with Pétér Futó, July 1991, Budapest. In subsequent rounds of interviews with the author, Futó reaffirmed the views he expressed here and elsewhere in the book. Budapest, summer 1994 and fall 1996.

of Hungarian labor, the firm exported old-fashioned, hand-made candies and chocolates to the West, where *Fundy Inc.*'s competitive edge was price-for-quality. But success also required reinventing labor-management relations. This was a delicate task. On the one hand, Futó provided a series of benefits that followed the traditional familial model, including on-site medical attention for employees and their families. On the other hand, he had to deal with the fact that the theft of materials – so prevalent in state firms – was becoming a problem for *Fundy* as well.

About 20 percent of our employees steal in spite of the highest standards of production . . . For example, when one of them was building a weekend-house, he decided to make sure the neighborhood was given candy, the better to secure his neighbors' help in the construction.

In 1990, Futó had no particular system for hiring new employees. Letters of reference were not used, and he advertised only for managers.

The way it works is, the worker appears and asks for a job. We send him around to the others, let them get to know each other a bit. If a number of them say not to take him on, we think about it. Of course, this system probably helps the friends of the present workers. On the other hand, if a worker we really trust says something, we listen. If there are no serious objections, we sit down and talk for a few minutes, and we ask him to come for two weeks trial.[57]

Futó was hopeful about instituting a better system of hiring and monitoring of employees. Networks would be of help in this task as well: he was preparing to hire a factory manager in his new plant at Gyál, just south of Budapest – an excellent manager with whom he had worked for a number of years, and who was scheduled to move there from the Budapest plant in 1991, when the two plants merged. In the meantime, Futó put his trust in the workers he already employed, and let them shape the hiring process. This method, obviously, enlarged the role of informal networks in the new economy.

Skillful deployment of informal relations was also key in other, more shady areas. Exporting, for example, entailed knowing whom to target for bribery in the Ministry of Foreign Trade.[58] Success in exports, in turn, created an opportunity for further business expansion, which required maintaining a delicate balance between competition and cooperation with state candy factories. One moment Futó "seduced" the best workers away from his state competitors and from the Budapest Confectionery Research Institute; the next he donated

---

57 Author's interview with Péter Futó, September 1990, Budapest.
58 Futó's export business started as a protective umbrella: foreign currency as a hedge against inflation. This was, however, double "protection": he also reported officially that three-quarters of his sales were from exports, and only one-quarter domestic, whereas the proportions were, in reality, exactly reversed. In this way, he shielded himself from what he saw as prohibitive and punitive tax rates (between 50 percent and 60 percent in 1988–89, with no tax credits for investment). He did not, however, evade taxes on employees; nor did he think the national health care tax or the pension contribution unfair.

money to help develop the first Hungarian prototype adapted from the one Italian packaging machine his main state competitor could afford. In this way, Futó secured the state-sector connections and goodwill that made him the only private businessman allowed to order one of the first ten such machines manufactured in Hungary.

The balancing act extended into every aspect of the business. Employees of the state's Budapest Confectionery Research Institute, for example, conducted product research for Futó as informal second-economy work.[59] Futó even found individuals in one of the state chocolate factories who could build specialized machines for him; they worked as part of a VGMK (the intra-firm work partnerships operating within state firms after 1982). And eventually, true to the pattern we have seen, he hired this group away from their state-factory.

The rapid growth underway inside Futó's factory soon had to be masked, lest his rising income catch the eye of the tax authorities or the economic police. This meant, among other things, hiding the fact that he was stealing workers from the very state factories upon whose cooperation he depended. So he devised "halfway" jobs for these individuals, who were officially listed as having joined GMKs formed by Futó's friends (GMKs were neither family nor individual enterprises; all their members bore liability to the full extent of their personal assets). Sometimes, "Potemkin GMKs" were created just for the purpose of concealing the true volume of production at *Fundy*. Meanwhile, and until 1991, Futó continued to operate out of a small house-factory, exploiting the appearance of retarded development to serve his goal of high rates of growth and accumulation.[60]

Working the system entailed both mutual corruption and mutual assistance between emerging private firms and the state. From the individual's perspective, the proximate objective was to keep up with the continually changing regulations and, as Futó put it, to "play the game optimally." He would not discuss hard figures, but claimed that at one time he was able to retain about 98 percent of his profits, although with the new tougher tax regulations of 1989, he would "only keep about 90 percent." By then, Futó had been anonymously "denounced" five times: to the economic police, to the Commercial Overseer, and to the National Trade Union.[61]

Tax evasion was considered by many entrepreneurs as "fair" – as a way of leveling the playing field *vis-à-vis* subsidized state firms. Most did successfully evade taxes to one degree or another, but Futó was exceptionally adept because his formal training in mathematics allowed him to construct on paper a convincing fictive, or shadow, factory. Unlike many small entrepreneurs, he did not

---

[59] Research, for instance, on the composition, viscosity, and packaging of various types of candy.

[60] In 1988, four trucks supplied Futó's network of 2,500 buyers, most of them private and state-owned shops. His deliverymen were private contractors who worked on a commission basis.

[61] The tax office, APEH (Adó és Pénzügyi Elszámolasi Hivatal), conducted a four-month examination, but his books came up clean. Futó reported that the tax authorities miscounted by a factor of ten and tried to force him to sign the document containing this calculation, but he refused.

have to keep two sets of books, or a "secret" warehouse.[62] His method was much more sophisticated. Every month, he prepared matrices of materials and energy expenditures, which in turn allowed him on any given day to have in the factory only as much material as needed for *one day's* production. Inventory not in the factory was on trucks being delivered to customers by sub-contractor deliverymen. This home-grown version of "just-in-time" inventory helped to protect Futó from prosecution, though not from the sort of repeated inquiry and "harassment" that our informal entrepreneur, Miklós, feared if he were to "go formal."

Futó also cultivated good relationships with the authorities. He got to know the director of the District Council's industry division; he became a directing member of the government's National Association of Small Manufacturers (KIOSZ) XIVth district and Budapest organizations, and within KIOSZ was president of the confectionery manufacturers group. He also enjoyed good relations with the Peoples' Front, or "Népfront."[63] "I've got to have the goodwill of the gangsters," Futó declared. "Later, they'll be corruptible."

Futó would have preferred not to have to "corrupt" anyone – not only because of ethical objections and higher costs and risks, but also because he was far more interested in solving the technical and financial puzzles of his business. Therefore, he tenaciously pursued another strategy: he repeatedly visited the office of a KIOSZ official whose acquaintance he had made, to learn as much as possible about regulations affecting private business. He was so successful that by 1988, KIOSZ considered him a valuable source of information on the fine points of the law, and KIOSZ's economic director often consulted Futó as a kind of behind-the-scenes technical adviser.[64]

KIOSZ turned out to be useful to Futó in more ways than one. In 1990, he hired László Gellei, the former director of the Budapest KIOSZ office, as commercial director for *Fundy*. And Gellei, in turn, recruited the former head of a provincial KIOSZ office to work for *him* at *Fundy*. Now Futó had

---

[62] Until 1989, many shopkeepers and manufacturers I interviewed told hair-raising stories of searches and seizures. One with whom I spoke had his tile-making operation shut down by the economic police with a store full of customers, and in 1983 he had been held for a full month without being officially charged. In 1989, he still preferred to remain anonymous. Péter X [tile-factory], interview with author, Budapest, January 1989.

[63] The titular functions of the People's Front (originally an anti-fascist coalition) remained acceptable to the HSWP because of the former's historical tradition of broad coalition (which had included the Communist Party). Although the People's Front never exercised real power, it served a formal, legitimating function for the HSWP. By the late 1980s, reform socialists were trying to reactivate the organization to advance their causes, and included non-Party members, much as Imre Nagy did in 1953.

[64] Indirect evidence of his influence with this particular state representative organization for small manufacturers was that it was Futó who managed to arrange an interview for me with the extremely reluctant Director of KIOSZ's Budapest office, László Gellei (over a year before Gellei went to work for Futó). In late 1988, Gellei was loath to permit an official interview with a Western researcher who wanted to discuss the second economy, and had refused when I contacted him on my own (see Chapter 7).

not one but two bureaucratically savvy people on his staff – an important coup for at least two reasons. First, both former KIOSZ functionaries were extremely well-connected inside the party-state apparatus, Second, Futó now had nothing to fear from one of the transmission-belt organizations originally meant to liquidate all private businesses (and which, even in 1988–89, tried, in various ways, at least to control them and to extract a variety of fees from them).

In any other period of the history of Hungarian socialism, this double-metamorphosis would have been unthinkable. In the brief span of five years, a trained mathematician became a small manufacturer, and then the head of a large and successful joint venture, and a Party member and high-level state official went from Director of the Budapest office of a state transmission-belt representative organization to Commercial Director of a private firm.

Yet despite clear indications of the new entrepreneurs' success, entrepreneurship had yet to be acknowledged in 1988 as a prestigious activity. No matter how much Futó emphasized the sophistication of his firm – its managerial "precision" and high production quality – he remained on the defensive. But by the autumn of 1991, Futó was less guarded, and consented to be profiled in my research using his own name and that of his firm.[65] He noted that changes such as the 1989 Association Law had enabled him to expand on his GMK and to start "playing in the major-leagues." He established a joint venture with a foreign investor in the newly available form of a limited liability corporation (KFT).[66] He began to manufacture and distribute candies for a large German company. Futó also started to think about updating his own products.

---

[65] Although Gerő was willing from the start to use his real name, he was an exception. Like Futó, Szábo agreed to do so only after 1991. And in the fall of 1991, most private entrepreneurs with whom I conducted follow-up interviews still requested anonymity. But Futó's only stipulation was that his foreign partner not be specified, and indeed, insisted that I use his real name. In any case, it would not have been possible to conceal his identity by then, since *Fundy* had become such a large and visible company.

[66] Futó became aware of a program administered by the Ministry of Finance that allowed a five-year tax-holiday for producers of foodstuffs, as long as a significant proportion of production was exportable. The founding capital required was about $340,000, and the requisite foreign participation was between 30 percent and 50 percent. Through a combination of luck and sheer persistence, Futó was able to take partial advantage of this program. The zero-tax was not automatically granted to foodstuff exporters: petitions were reviewed by the Ministry of Finance. Futó founded his joint-venture on October 1, 1989, but by the time he had finished the paperwork, the regulation was about to change. (Still in effect during 1989, it was revoked at the end of the year; thereafter, the lowest tax was about 11 percent.) In repeated petitions to the Ministry, Futó argued that he had founded the joint-venture on the basis of this regulation, and included an appeal to national honor: his commitment to a foreign partner should be the *country's* commitment: both would lose credibility with a foreign investor if it were not honored. He was finally granted a four-year tax holiday. Futó's point about his battles with the Ministry was that even in 1989–90, only a very persistent and well-connected individual would have been able to wrangle this concession from the Ministry, which in his view was at that time still far more concerned with raising tax-revenues than promoting foreign investment.

To do all this, however, he realized that he needed not the 100 square meters of space he had, but at least 1,000. Looking around for new sites, he discovered that one of the country's largest and best-known state cooperatives – the "Freedom Cooperative" (Szabadság MGTSZ) in Gyál – wanted to lease about 1,000 square meters of space. When he approached the director of the cooperative about an arrangement, Futó found that what the coop members really wanted was to form a corporation with his firm.

In the late 1980s and early 1990s, it was not unusual for private entrepreneurs to be approached by state firms and state-controlled cooperatives in search of successful vehicles to pull them into the emerging economic system. Nor did this apply only, or even mostly, to failing state firms: the Freedom Cooperative, for instance, was one of the most successful, with a highly diversified portfolio of which a considerable proportion was industrial production.[67] But whereas sophisticated private entrepreneurs were often willing to use decentralized parts of state firms or cooperatives in some limited capacity (for example, as job-shops), many were also wary of closer ties with state-controlled institutions. Futó decided upon the following solution:

I created an ESOP [Employee Stock Option Program], and through this the state coop (TSZ) as a legal entity participates in the firm to the tune of 6.6 percent. *Fundy's* employees have 10 percent, I have 33.3 percent, and 50 percent is with our foreign partner. The TSZ contributed the land and the existing building; we built a super-modern factory. I have my eight or ten key employees in the firm, including my wife, who left her research institute; each one of them has about a 1 percent financial participation of their own. Now, the TSZ continues to *lease* the land to us, but it's a perpetual lease. This is a strange situation: the TSZ can never take away its land from us, but it didn't have to sell it, either.

We pay rent in the following way: if our profit is large then we pay only a small rent; if the profit is small, we pay a set rent. In effect, we won't pay any rent next year, because it went well for us this year. This was my innovation: the TSZ director was angling for a fixed amount; I was betting on doing well and playing for the long term. We really pay only if the firm does badly.[68]

Of course, in the late 1980s, the TSZ "owned" its 12,000 square meters of land and its 1,000 square-meter building in a narrow sense: it enjoyed rights of use and limited alteration, but, before the 1988 Law on Economic Association, not rights of transfer or disposal. So the TSZ actually sold the legal right to the *use-value* of this real-estate, which it was able to do because Hungarian state firms and state-controlled cooperatives had long been permitted to operate auxiliary businesses (*mellékszólgáltatás*).

Futó and his team modernized the TSZ's building, and built a new factory of their own as well, and by 1991 had constructed a third building. In short order,

---

[67] Recall from Chapter 2 that from 1968 on, State Agricultural Cooperatives (MGTSZ, or, simply, TSZ) were allowed to engage in industrial production on the side.

[68] Author's interview with Pétér Futó, September 1990, Budapest.

Fundy had considerably more property on the land it leased from the TSZ than the latter had originally. Futó observed:

We hold that place with an iron fist. But the TSZ Director sees this clearly, and supports anything we can do to ensure that the state will not be able to take it from us later. He's in a great situation. He invested his money in a firm that will likely bring an 80–100 percent return on his investment. You don't find too many opportunities like this in Hungary, and the firm is growing. I have a well-developed circle of buyers, and we continue to expand this circle aggressively.[69]

The business savvy of this particular state coop (TSZ) director, while considerable, was not singular. Studies suggest that Futó was not wide of the mark when he asserted that a new "director class" was being formed as a result out of the networks emerging among enterprising directors of state firms and cooperatives on the one hand, and private entrepreneurs on the other.[70]

At times, the entire system seemed to be changing under the innovative pressures of entrepreneurs. As Futó expanded his business by hiring more salespeople, buying more trucks, and by selling to state stores, he also decided to take the product directly to the state groceries – leaving out commercial middlemen – and, if possible, settling the bill directly with the small retailers instead of with the central accounting organization that oversaw each state-owned retailer. In this way, Futó completely by-passed the state distribution system, which had by now been considerably decentralized, but still retained features of years of centralization.[71] Futó likened it to

a chain of retail stores in a semi-subordinate position to a kind of central office that has its own warehouses. In other words, the little stores have a 'boss' or 'owner,' of sorts. This boss or owner is either a state firm or a [state controlled] cooperative, which buys the supplies and pays for them.

It's hard to know what the little store can order, how much of that it actually gets, what [deliverymen] steal . . . Evidently, if the store-owner gives a nice gift to the deliveryman, he might favor that store, but on the other hand, maybe another store gives him more . . . so both the producer and the retailer are in a dependent situation.[72]

Fortunately, by 1990, the small groceries had enough independence to buy their products directly from producers, though not all pursued this possibility.[73] The

[69] Ibid.

[70] On the intertwining of the *nomenklatura* and the new entrepreneurs, see Elemér Hankiss, "A 'Nagy Koalicio' Avagy a Hatalom Konvertálása [The 'Grand Coalition' or the Conversion of Power], *Valoság*, no.1, 1989.

[71] In 1990, there were approximately eleven large commercial firms dealing in foodstuffs, each of which covered roughly two counties. Each large commercial firm had fifty eight depots where they took food for distribution. Such a firm typically distributed some 6,000–8,000 items to about 16,000 grocery stores, approximately 300 of which "belonged" to one such center. The central commercial firm supplied these stores about once a week.

[72] Author's interview with Pétér Futó, September 1990, Budapest.

[73] Ibid. Not surprisingly, Futó found that selling to the small groceries was preferable, since his salespeople were able to show his product directly to the store manager, who was better

planned economy was on its way out, and business planning was in. Futó never let the future out of his sights.

In Hungary, the confectionery market shrinks yearly by about 10 percent, as the real-wage level falls. Yet we entered this shrinking market with dynamic growth. The large state firms and cooperatives are falling apart, and we are in fact contributing to their downfall. And when they crumble, we'll try to buy them up cheaply. That's our plan. It may not work out. Maybe the state firms will get it together.

When asked what he thought about the chances of his state competitors, Futó replied that he was privy to information indicating that there was little hope for them. "You see," he whispered conspiratorially, "I have industrial spies."

Q: You are speaking figuratively, I take it.
A: Not at all. I mean paid spies in state firms. We have built an information system. In every large state firm [in my field], I have embedded people who inform me about everything: [laughing] horrid spies!
Q: You mean industrial spying.
A: Precisely. I know their product-development plans. How? The people who are in charge of various aspects of the candy industry – exports, procurement of foreign inputs to the production processes of state firms, and the direction of domestic sales of sweets – these people work for us, too, part-time.
Q: Don't they know this in the state factories?
A: No, they don't know.
Q: How much do you have to pay such people to do this?
A: Actually, it's a much more complicated and *infinitely* more dignified process. I invite them, for instance, to be on our board of directors, for which they receive an honorarium. Later, they come over and chat with us. And in the course of these chats, they 'accidentally' tell me stories. We question them; we try to learn from these fellows, and so they do come over to us as spies of sorts.
Q: Are you careful about what you, in turn, reveal?
A: Not really, I play with an open hand. The only difference is that they used to think that such a small firm was of little interest; today they're already afraid. And because of this 'spy network,' we know that there are weekly work-stoppages in the state factories. Meanwhile, we already do a tenth of the sales of the largest state candy factory. Not so long ago we sold only about 1 percent of that. So now they start to take notice and to be a bit afraid. The largest state factory's director called up to ask if it was true that we were working with fully automated assembly lines. I invited him over, he came, and he's already asked us to help them sell their products. In fact they want to merge with us, but I have no such intention. For the moment, our plan is to wait until the smaller state firms go broke and buy them up, and when we're big enough, then we'll see what happens next.[74]

acquainted with the local conditions and requirements. He frequently offered samples so that the managers could try out his product and gauge how it would sell. He was also comparatively satisfied with the payment schedules – a satisfaction I almost never encountered among other Hungarian entrepreneurs dealing with large state firms or central distribution systems. As Futó put it: "It's almost cash-and-carry, though of course not quite . . . but there's carry for sure, and the cash comes in about thirty days net, some slower."

74 Author's interview with Pétér Futó, September 1990, Budapest.

Thus, this entrepreneur turned the tables on the system that had once spied on him. Poetic justice indeed. Nevertheless, as we are about to see, the creative hyper-alertness that consumers had once exhibited in informal markets was still required of private managers on the production side.

Power and the Sense of Smell

By 1990, Futó faced a dilemma. He wanted an outside infusion of funds, but he did not wish to bring other partners into the firm. Moreover, he was still finding it quite difficult to obtain loans. One problem was that his business was already far too large to be considered a small firm, and thus did not qualify for loans offered by several new banks lending to such firms. At the same time, he could not hope to compete for credit with the mammoth state firms.[75] Eventually, Futó found a way to compete for subsidized loans through "connections."

Q: You need such connections even inside the banks?
A: Yes. First, we must find the person or persons who will support our project – win over a few internal lobbyists who will advance our cause. Everyone who has seen our proposal so far has said that if it depended upon them, ours would be the firm that would definitely get the loan, because it exports, honors its contracts, and is highly profitable. They are very sympathetic from every point of view, but when it comes right down to whether or not we'll get the loan, it seems that others have paid more, or found the right way to do it . . . Marx taught that finance capital rules, and here, in a crude sense, it does, although this has nothing in common with real finance capital.[76]

Futó voiced a complaint commonly heard among private entrepreneurs in the late 1980s and early 1990s: the banking-system, though advanced in comparison to its counterparts in the rest of Eastern Europe, was not yet sufficiently profit-motivated, and the new loan "competitions" were not sufficiently "objective." Part of the reason was the severe liquidity shortage in the banking system. But there was also a tendency to allocate funds through a multiplicity of very small loans, ranging, on average, from $4,300 to $7,100.[77] The idea – according to Futó and several other entrepreneurs with whom I spoke – was to put on a "better show" – for the banks to be able to claim that large numbers of people were able to secure loans.

Fast-growing enterprises, however, needed larger loans. To secure them, entrepreneurs had to rely on connections and pay-offs. Asked how he approached bankers to establish those connections, Futó replied:

---

[75] In the autumn of 1990, the commercial interest rate was still approximately 36–38 percent (at the time, official inflation was estimated at approximately 30 percent); but Futó was competing for funds at more favorable rates (between 18 percent and 25 percent). However, most of these more favorable loans were intended for start-up and very small businesses. A limited number of subsidized loans were available to entrepreneurs for the pursuit of various goals – for example, investment, increasing exports, or expansion of employment.
[76] Author's interview with Pétér Futó, September 1990, Budapest.
[77] Approximately 300,000–500,000 forints at the time.

I *smell* it. I figure out which person is the right one, and I ask him for help in writing the proposal, to have a look at it. When he comes over [for a visit to the firm], I tell him I'll give him X amount if it's successful. Period.

Q: No chance he would blow the whistle?
A: He won't. But if he does, I will deny it. There are no receipts to prove anything. Everyone tries to earn money in his *area of power*. And because the biggest source of money is money, the person who determines whether or not you'll get a loan, and at what rate of interest, has tremendous power.[78]

Futó's "area of power" was entrepreneurship, and that meant drawing on other people's power. In this, he excelled. He helped to change the balance of power between state and private firms, which in turn helped increase private firms' leverage with the banking sector. Other entrepreneurs had a similar impact. Let's revisit Szabó, the glass-maker. Recall that he had been a court-appointed expert in matters of construction involving glass, a role that not only allowed him to become familiar with the entire industry but also endowed him with a rich network of contacts. It was as a court expert, for example, that he built good relations with state firms. Asked how he did this, he replied that he always heard all sides.

They accepted me because I looked not for fault, but for solutions. So when I got to the judge, I could say this party to the dispute is 30 percent at fault, this one 70 percent. I would also stress that the nature of the "fault" was technical, not moral. Moreover, we would decide on the distribution of fault amongst ourselves, prior to the trial. So even those who ended up paying more accepted me, because they still did better than in a totally adversarial system. In this way, I developed good connections with all the glass factories.[79]

Szabó also learned the distinction between "good" and "bad" connections. The latter were unreliable and based exclusively on need. The former went beyond need and even sympathy to a sense of obligation and duty, so that even if one was only a *maszek* (the sometimes pejorative term for private businessmen[80]), one was still repaid in kind for past assistance rendered.

After I went private, some of these weren't such good connections anymore, because I didn't get court-appointed jobs, and so I was not needed. Even when I unselfishly helped solve technical problems or trained technically weak people, what I got later in return was a refusal to sell me glass! If I asked why, they would not give me a reason.

It got to the point that regardless of all the people I knew in these circles – from the manager to the chief engineer – I was just a "maszek." So the warehouseman became my best connection. He was literally in possession of the glass. I just had to get to know him.[81]

[78] Author's interview with Pétér Futó, September 1990, Budapest.
[79] Author's interview with Mihály Szabó, December 1988, Budapest.
[80] In Hungarian, *maszek* is a contraction of *magán* (private) and *szektor* (sector) – literally, private sector.
[81] Author's interview with Mihály Szabó, December 1988.

Though Szabó's position in the market was enviable – he alone produced at such high-quality levels – he was dissatisfied with the national system of quality-control and measurement, and believed that the corruption of government examiners put him at a competitive disadvantage.[82]

For a system of standards to work, the government has to pay its examiners sufficiently so that they aren't biased and corrupt. This is how it's done in the West. But here, it's different. Examiners try to cover as many firms as possible in order to make as much money as possible . . . If the companies you examine pay you, and that's how you make your living, then it's completely incorrect. You will say everybody's product is good, according to how much you're paid.

Q: Who gets this money?
A: The examiner, but I refuse to pay for this. A TSZ (state agricultural coop) will pay for the inspection. It has the money. And in return it gets the seal of approval for low-quality *thermopan*.

Szabó nevertheless continued to compete with state factories, but it was a competition limited by many other factors as well. His state competitors, for example, obtained inputs to the production process at subsidized prices.

Take the Orosháza Glass Factory. In terms of capacity, we can't even compare, they're so large. But they say we're competing. Well, I'm all for price competition. But what can I do? They get the glue for a third the price. And as a state factory, they have access to government reserves of foreign exchange necessary for importing materials from the west. I can only do this if I use my own foreign exchange.[83]

Nor did Szabó feel that he could take full advantage of the fact that he produced higher-quality glass and undercut his competition, say, by offering longer guarantees.

I would be willing to guarantee my products for twenty years, but I can't because Orosháza accepts only five years responsibility, and I get the glass from them. I am dependent upon them. If they know that I raised it to twenty years, they'll stop supplying me, and I'm finished.[84]

Partly because Szabó was caught in a system of complicated dependencies, in early 1989 he was at once skeptical and hopeful about change.

Among the top officials in the Party, the battle has begun. Who will win? The Party still doesn't take dramatic steps. It fears for its position. And as long as they are in power, it's not possible to have a real competitive economy. Consider competitive bidding for construction. Let's say there are five bidders. Suddenly the Party brings in a sixth. Next, the command comes from on high that this sixth bidder, for no apparent reason, should

[82] Hungarian firms were just beginning, in 1990–91, to think about ISO certification.
[83] Author's interview with Mihály Szabó, October 1990, Budapest.
[84] Ibid.

get the contract. Why? Because that contractor will later build something for free for some well-placed official.

At the same time, the Party hasn't much space to go backwards. It has to go forward. Now they're even talking about multi-party elections in the future. They say "let's preserve the one-party system for now, since we don't want to add to the chaos, but in the following elections, we'll see." They're always one step behind the demands of society. If they took these steps in advance, they might even get elected.[85]

Asked about the political power of the private sector, and why none of the emerging parties in 1989 seemed eager to embrace private producers of the official second economy, Szabó referred to the pre-war attitude against commerce. His former colleagues at the research institute, for example, could not fathom how he could "work with joy" out of his garage and "develop an innovation" by drawing on his own resources. To them, he was now a mere glazier and a *maszek*, a term that had first entered the common parlance in the 1950s, and in official discourse signified "opposition" and "degradation."

At official levels, the prejudice against the *maszek* still ran deep. The post-1982 generation of private entrepreneurs was often regarded – at best – as traditional and conservative, as "small" manufacturers or "craftsmen." Szabó attributed this partly to ignorance.

[Officials] don't know that 70 percent of patents in Hungary originate not from the large research institutes or firms, but from private individuals. So [officials] can barely bring themselves to tolerate the second economy.[86]

A strategy of obfuscation, partly enabled by the complexity of the law itself, helped entrepreneurs overcome prejudice. Szabó explained:

[After the enactment of the 1988 Company Law], if I form a KFT (limited liability corporation), then I become a firm, even if I'm its only employee. Now, with the KFTs there will be no official distinction between state and non-state firms. If I go to buy glue, or to a bank, they will not so easily be able to distinguish anymore between who is "private" and who is "state."[87]

And indeed, from 1989 on, KFTs could be formed both by state and private firms, separately or jointly, with or without foreign participation.[88] As a result, without access to the company's books, it was in fact impossible to know which KFT was private and which was part of a state-owned company. This had not been true, for instance, of the GMKs (the economic work-partnerships) or PJTs (civil law partnerships) founded in 1982 and after: formally, at least, "state" was state and "private" was private.[89] Private entrepreneurs who registered their

---

[85] Author's interview with Mihály Szabó, January 1989, Budapest.

[86] Ibid.

[87] Ibid.

[88] Before, GMKs had operated analogously, but with unlimited liability.

[89] In fact, the reality was more complicated. Many state-controlled cooperatives had transformed themselves into small cooperatives for tax purposes. Author's interview with Gyula Tellér, October 1990, Budapest. See also Chapter 7.

businesses in these and other institutional forms were still known collectively as *maszek*. Although, in reality, many GMKs and PJTs had complex connections with state firms and cooperatives (in the case of the VGMK functioning *within* state firms, as we have seen), they were legally not permitted to consolidate with state firms to form new companies with them until 1989.

This was an encouraging development. But almost as heartening to the entrepreneurs interviewed for this study was the fact that the younger generaton coming up in the mid-1980s started inverting the long-standing pejorative nomenclature. To them, *maszek* signified something "remarkable," even "excellent." The mixed atmospherics – old resentment mingling with emerging admiration – contributed to the entrepreneurs' tendency to live day-to-day between anxiety and hopeful divination. Gerő, for one, never felt secure, not even as his *Colorplan* expanded. He was always concerned that

> these interesting little GMKs and small coops could disappear with a signature . . . we could be nationalized anytime . . . Of course, if this were to happen, then obviously nothing would matter any more.[90]

And yet if others used uncertainty to justify conspicuous consumption and short-term business strategies, Gerő did the opposite: he planned for the long term. The anxiety that plagued him at night would give way in the morning to a deep, even prophetic sense of conviction. The "second economy," he was sure, would one day become "the first." In fact, he could envision a dynamic whereby, as competition increased, the well-known "inverted pyramid" – whose base consisted of large firms – would be righted, and "the base of the first economy [would] be the small and medium-sized firms," as in most market economies. He planned for that day.[91]

Careful, long-term planning even in the face of uncertainty was emblematic of the emerging "modern" Hungarian entrepreneur. Gerő's own assessment of "traditional" entrepreneurs in Hungary endorsed the Kuczi-Vajda survey, which found a fairly clear division in behavior and outlook between post-1982 entrepreneurs and traditional artisans.[92]

> In contrast to the new entrepreneur, the old craftsman-entrepreneur [*a nagyon régi vállalkozószellemű maszek*] thrives because of the completely unkempt system of taxation. Around him all is topsy-turvy, and he fishes in these agitated waters. This is not necessarily pejorative. These are old but very alert tough guys who are alive to the possibilities . . . They typically formed GMKs when the opportunity to do so arose, because this allowed them to engage in free enterprise – or, as some would have it – free robbery.[93]

[90] Author's interview with Pétér Gerő, December 1988, Budapest.
[91] Ibid.
[92] Kuczi and Vajda, "The Social Composition of Small Entrepreneurs," 342–344. Although the authors do emphasize the rather clear division between the two groups, they also mention that some traditional artisans "opened new workshops in 1982," which coincides with Gerő's observation concerning the second "sub-type" of traditional artisan.
[93] Author's interview with Pétér Gerő, July 1991, Budapest.

Connections Between Private and State Firms

By 1990, *Colorplan* regularly subcontracted orders it could not handle to half a dozen firms, without discriminating between private and state firms. After all, virtually all of *Colorplan*'s employees came from the state sector. *Colorplan*'s frustrating experience with the branch of one large state firm, however, illustrates some of the difficulties private firms faced in the effort to establish cooperative relations with such firms. The firm in question was a decentralized, nominally independent stock company of the former conglomerate *Medicor*, a huge vertically organized state firm that had broken up into ten stock companies. This particular stock company (RT) manufactured, among other things, industrial and military gas-masks.

Colorplan had purchased stock in the new *Medicor*, and Gerő and his associates had good personal relations with the director and the chief engineer of its gas-mask producing RT, where the machines were practically at a standstill.[94] Knowing the firm's capacity, Gerő arranged a meeting with a private Hungarian manufacturer who had just returned from an exploratory trip to Canada, where he wanted to export lamps. The entrepreneur did not have sufficient machine capacity, however, to do the job alone.

The private manufacturer wanted 300,000 lamp bodies. *Colorplan*'s primary interest in the deal was that it would have painted the lamps. The private manufacturer asked both the *Medicor* RT and *Colorplan* for estimates. Gerő and his associates waited for the factory's estimate, on which he would base his own. When the team had heard nothing after three days, they contacted the chief engineer, who equivocated about the reasons for the lack of response. Gerő offered to talk over whatever problems the chief engineer and director foresaw.

We went to lunch, and he told me that the retooling and resetting of his machines, which were set up for mass production, would take four days and would be very expensive. We asked him: 'why worry about those big machines; you've got so many molding presses, why not set up three next to one another and that'll do it.' 'Well,' he said, 'that isn't worth it, because on the big ones you can do 100,000 pieces in two days.' I asked: 'wait a minute, didn't you just say that now you're only producing 200,000–300,000 pieces per year and that you've only got that many orders for your own product? So what percentage of the time are the machines working?'

Summa summarum, the machines work one month out of the year! And in *this* context, these people were breaking their heads over why they couldn't take this order, instead of kissing the hand of the person who brings them the business so that their machines would at least be used at some minimal level of efficiency. That's a state firm for you.[95]

---

94 This stock company had once produced close to 1 million gas masks/year, and in 1988 was producing only about 200,000. Gerő's explanation for this included a decline in industrial pollution, smaller military orders, and the fact that Hungarian industry was not working at full capacity, so that demand for industrial products in general had dropped.

95 Author's interview with Péter Gerő, September 1990, Budapest.

But of course, there was more to the story, and Gerő finally got to the bottom of it. Almost 80 percent of the RT's stock, it turned out, was owned by the holding company of the original *Medicor*, which appropriated the majority of the profit and dividend, if any.[96] As a result, all of the *Medicor* RTs wanted the holding company to go under so that they could be truly independent. Simply put, the stock companies were doing their best *not* to take new work orders. As a result, nothing came of the deal in the end.

Colorplan, meanwhile, managed to compete successfully against the Hungarian state firm engaged in the manufacture of electrostatic painting technology. As previously mentioned, the firm had purchased stock in *Medicor*, and eventually put the former conglomerate's gas-mask-producing RT to work as *Colorplan*'s job-shop for painting orders. The director of the *Medicor* RT saw the writing on the wall, and told Gerő:

You fellows are partners in everything; you're good, enthusiastic kids. . . .but I'm afraid that soon we'll be whistling in the dark, and everything will be yours. Two years from now you'll be sitting here in my place, and everything will be yours.[97]

Gerő replied cheerfully that the RT director should "just go ahead and be afraid." And indeed, as we have seen, *Colorplan*'s sales grew dramatically. The cooperative also grew in size, and by 1990 had twenty six members and thirty employees. The value of the firm's assets also increased considerably. The cooperative's initial investment of founding capital had been 430,000 forints. In 1989, the American accounting firm Ernst and Young valued the machinery, materials, and employees' know-how of just one of *Colorplan*'s operations – the one in southern Budapest, where the firm rented space from *Medicor* – at 13 million forints. In addition, since the headquarters building, vehicles, machinery, and equipment at the central office were not counted in this figure, it is reasonable to assume that the firm's value measured by American accounting conventions was far in excess of 18 million forints by 1989.[98]

Colorplan also achieved significant success in exports thanks to the consistent high quality of its products, the timeliness of delivery, and continuity of contact

---

[96] As best Gerő and I were able to determine, the central office took about 80 percent of the profits and left 20 percent to be divided among the ten stock companies.

[97] Author's interview with Péter Gerő, September 1990, Budapest.

[98] At the time, the Hungarian system of valuation actually represented *investment* value rather than *estimated* value at auction. For example, machines were counted only at the rate at which they were amortized. If firm X spent the entire 10 million forints it earned in its first year of operation on a 10 million forint machine, then its value would still be counted only as the amount of its founding capital, and its book value would grow only by the yearly amortization of the debt on this machine. The amortized portion would then be viewed as part of the permanent value of the firm. This system was still in force in 1990; several entrepreneurs mentioned that it was not sustainable, and it was, in fact, soon revised. My thanks to Ákos Róna-Tas for alerting me to the 1991 *Számviteli Törvény* (Accounting Law) that brought Hungarian conventions into line with those of the United States and Western Europe.

with customers.[99] Lack of access to credit – not only capital for expansion, but even working capital – remained the firm's real handicap. Even payment of a transitory expense like the VAT,[100] for example, could present difficulties for Hungarian private firms, since the tax had to be paid at the moment of invoice-presentation, before receipt of payment for sale.

The result can be a significant cash-flow problem. In a normal market economy, banks will finance this with a temporary credit. But here, it's hardly possible to get such credits. The banks don't have any money; you can't get a working-capital loan. You can crash, because you haven't yet received the value of the goods commensurate with the value you've added, yet you have to pay the VAT up front.[101]

Increasing taxes also worried Gerő, but he emphasized that even if taxes were raised further and nothing changed with regard to the availability of credit, he believed that *Colorplan* would succeed, because all his partners and employees had worked at state firms, and

they've had enough. Here, we're essentially our own bosses, we enjoy our work, it's going pretty well, and we take some pride in the fact that we work pretty efficiently. If revenues fall, we'll pull it along somehow, because we'd rather do this than go back to a large state firm, which is awful. Then we'll just accept that it's a bad year, a bad couple of years, and *we'll just have to get through it rather than give up.*[102]

Not giving up meant dealing with a credit shortage. To this end, Gerő took the firm public in 1992, transforming it once again, this time into a stock company (RT), by combining the existing GMK and the small cooperative (reborn as *Unicolor*), and distributing a portion of the shares to cooperative members. By going public, Gerő hoped to circumvent the serious financing problems facing most Hungarian private firms.

Conclusion

Long before 1982, many state-sector workers became informal small producers or *de facto* business owners (see Table 6.3). They taught foreign languages, repaired cars, worked as electricians, seamstresses, and tailors, or painted houses. Dentists worked during the day at state clinics and hospitals and saw private patients at night and or on weekends. Sometimes even attorneys made analogous arrangements. Virtually none had official access to capital. Yet in their informal sphere of action, the cleaning-woman and the shoe repairman,

---

[99] Gerő estimated 1989 income from exports at 200,000 Deutschmarks (about 2.5 percent. of total sales) and 1990 export income at 1 million Deutschmarks (about 20 percent. of total sales).

[100] Transitory, that is, except for the tax on the additional value added by the producer (see Chapter 7 of the present book for a more detailed discussion of the VAT as part of a broader reform of the tax system).

[101] Author's interview with Pétér Gerő, August 1994, Budapest.

[102] Author's interview with Pétér Gerő, June 1994, Budapest.

TABLE 6.3 *Enterprise forms – Hungary, 1988–2000*

	1988	1989	1990	1991	1992	1993	1994	1995	
								Registered	Active*
Unlimited partnerships	11	203	418	463	1,187	2,492	3,348	3,951	2,935
GMKs (economic work groups)	21,262	15,976	20,600	19,999	17,595	15,323	13,416	—	—
Limited (deposit) Partnerships (PJTs, "small cooperatives")	71	1,162	5,789	22,977	41,218	67,301	89,045	107,106	80,950
Other corporations without legal status	8,313	6,802	7,288	8,697	10,597	12,920	16,335	19,913	1,077
Sole proprietors	290,877	320,619	393,450	510,459	606,207	688,843	778,036	791,496	417,487
Organization of ceasing legal form	—	—	—	—	—	—	13,618	13,846	8,297

TABLE 6.3 (*cont'd.*)

	1996		1997		1998		1999		2000	
	Registered	Active*	Registered	Active*	Registered	Active*	Registered	Active*	Registered	Active*
Unlimited partnerships	4,394	3,558	4,509	3,565	5,006	4,063	5,217	4,386	40,045	33,910
GMKs (working teams)	—	—	—	—	—	—	—	—	—	—
Limited (deposit) Partnerships (PJTs, "small cooperatives")	127,725	107,782	140,043	118,419	161,857	140,449	170,762	150,637	188,136	167,434
Other corporations without legal status	22,712	4,536	24,269	5,680	26,182	24,130	26,998	24,762	—	—
Sole proprietors	745,247	460,163	659,690	465,049	648,701	458,355	660,139	467,513	682,925	487,699
Organization of ceasing legal form	12,595	7,676	11,091	6,365	10,646	6,194	8,858	5,077	—	—

* Active as of December 31

Source: Hungarian Central Statistical Office, *Statistical Yearbook of Hungary* (1991, 1994, 1995, 1998, 1999); 2000 data from CSO website (http://www.ksh.hu).

the computer programmer and the moonlighting architect, all set the price of their own labor. And like the plumber we met at the beginning of this chapter, many served the same network of customers for decades.

No truly reliable information is available about the precise number of informal entrepreneurs who made the transition after 1982 to "modern," full-time entrepreneurs.[103] Sketchy statistical and other indirect evidence strongly suggest that many did, well before 1989 (see Table 6.3, as well as Chapter 7 for indirect evidence – for example, such entrepreneurs' membership in their new interest-representation organization, VOSZ). But like the registered artisans and retailers working in the small, pre-1982 private sector, many others remained conservative and traditional in their outlook and business strategies.

The modern entrepreneurs were different. Frustrated in their relatively low-paying and unimaginative state sector jobs, they turned first informally and then formally to entrepreneurial activity for self-realization and profit.[104] They took risks that far exceeded those normally faced by their capitalist counterparts elsewhere. Socialist entrepreneurs, for example, bore *unlimited* individual liability regardless of the partnership form they chose for their ventures, since limited partnerships were instituted only in 1989. In addition, they frequently confronted both the overt and tacit opposition of a bureaucrats dealing with new regulations they did not understand or, in some cases, support. These entrepreneurs even carried on with little or no access to credit. And manufacturers like those profiled here had to overcome great difficulties in procuring raw materials and other inputs for their production processes.

Far more, even, than in capitalist economies, personal connections were crucial to every aspect of entrepreneurship, and often decisive. Connections helped shape the entrepreneur's decision-making process: from the initial decision to exit the state sector, to the hiring of employees and decisions on mergers and aquisitions; from efforts to raise capital to choice of markets, both domestic and foreign. Connections were also used aggressively by entrepreneurs engaged in legal-bureaucratic activism – pushing for the implementation of both the letter and the spirit of the 1982 regulations, as well as the rationalization of regulatory details. In so doing, these activists broadened the scope of action for other entrepreneurs, and blurred the line between entrepreneurship and politics.

---

[103] Given the informal nature of such activities, statistics are incomplete and sometimes misleading. Many entrepreneurs continued their informal work well into the 1990s; some may still. Even retrospective studies are of little use in this regard, since we can safely infer that many who formalized their businesses in the 1980s now prefer anonymity, perhaps fearing a retroactive tax assessment on undeclared earnings or property.

[104] David Stark found just such frustrations among workers in VGMKs. He cited complaints that information was released only piecemeal; as a result, the work often had to be redone or was of poor quality, because it had been so segmented as to make it almost impossible for workers, whether manual laborers or engineers, to foresee and prevent problems. See also Haraszti, *A Worker in a Worker's State.*

Entrepreneurs also altered the nature of labor-management relations. Those profiled here and many others whom I interviewed – did not abrogate social responsibility, but tended to be paternalistic even as they emphasized individual enterprise and problem-solving. They changed the relationship between state-organized mass-production and small, private firms. They certainly competed with state firms. But they also cooperated with branches or divisions of state-owned firms and in some cases, even with their own state-sector competitors, through subcontracting or permanent job-shop arrangements. Finally, entrepreneurs crafted a business ethos that not only justified the manipulation of connections and knowledge – the better to circumvent and evade the state regulatory system – but also imposed on the entrepreneurs themselves standards of fairness, compliance, and quality.

When all is said and done, these modern socialist entrepreneurs approximated the Schumpeterian ideal at the micro-level, even as they struggled in a decidedly non-Schumpeterian context. They replaced old technologies with sophisticated, even novel, alternatives. They stretched a rigid legal-bureaucratic environment to its very limits, then pioneered solutions that transcended those limits. And they profoundly changed the way Hungarians thought about private business.

This Schumpeterian transformation could never have taken place without the 1982 reform. And those laws, in turn, would not have been possible without the bargained revolt that citizens waged from below for decades as both workers and as consumers, or the political-discursive strategies deployed at the top by state reformers in 1982. But as the 1980s came to a dramatic close, it was the post-1982 entrepreneurs who linked past and future in Hungary. They stood out as the "powerhouses" of that country's post-socialist private sector, fueling a spurt in productive cooperative ventures and technical learning.[105] And they were crucial to the "head start" that post-socialist Hungary enjoyed over virtually all other transforming state-socialist countries. Because of them, Hungary's longer history of a well-institutionalized and relatively diversified private sector allowed for the evolution of a more sophisticated system of labor-management relations, deeper learning of productive processes, and higher productivity and profitability.[106] Above all, Hungary's head start was the result of its institutionalization of private property-rights, as well as the legal apparatus to enforce those rights and to uphold contracts between parties to economic transactions. As we have seen here, virtually all of these pieces were in place by the end of 1988.

The individuals featured here who helped blaze this transformative trail remain energetic and highly successful businessmen, even if in one case, the 1990s brought unexpected problems and challenges. In 1995, Gerő's *Color-plan* went bankrupt after the German firm *Wagner* first urged him to expand

[105] Leila Webster, "The Emergence of Private Sector Manufacturing in Hungary" (World Bank Technical Paper 229, Washington DC: 1993).

[106] Blachard, et al., *Reform in Eastern Europe* (Cambridge, MA: MIT Press, 1991), 11.

by taking on debt (which he had up to then avoided), and then later reneged on their agreement, deciding it no longer needed a partner, and would sell its products directly on all the Hungarian market. In retrospect, this is hardly surprising, since Hungarian regulations did not discriminate between foreign and domestic firms, and in fact favored direct foreign investment in myriad ways. But with typical determination, Gerő soon started a new business along the same lines. His new venture in electrostatic painting was even more successful and more self-reliant, since it no longer needed to licence technology. Meanwhile, Szábo the glass maker, who was somewhat more risk-averse than either Gerő or Futó, continued his business on a more intensive and larger scale than before, but without major plans for expansion. Finally, Futó the confectioner continues to be extremely successful. By the mid-1990s, *Fundy* was among the largest candy and sweets manufacturers in the country, and by 2002, was considered a "major food multinational."[107]

By the end of the 1980s, these three entrepreneurs, like many others, had also learned the importance of aggregating and channeling their economic interests. In different ways, all three had joined others in attempts to influence the policy-making process, and to shape laws pertaining to the private sector. From 1987 on, the National Association of Entrepreneurs (VOSZ), of which Gerő was a founding member, exerted pressure on the government to level the playing field between state and private firms in matters of regulation and taxation. The founders, to be sure, had specific inequities in mind, most notably the unequal access to material and financial inputs in a system of predominantly monopoly producers characterized by shortage. But they also wanted the power that comes from organized activism. As Gerő put it,

VOSZ was founded as a forum, so that when a lot of people start to yell, they should yell out of a single bullhorn to shake those it reaches. If everyone yells separately, no one is heard.[108]

Shaking the system into action, of course, was not the same as demolishing it. In the summer of 1988, most entrepreneurs expected additional, incremental reforms, and they anticipated new rounds of bureaucratic struggles. Futó, for one, remained a member of KIOSZ, the government's National Association of Small Industrialists. Although he approved of VOSZ, Futó never joined, continuing instead to learn as much as he could through KIOSZ. This was partly because VOSZ was founded only in 1987, and partly because of the firm's history: Futó's father had begun as a traditional small manufacturer, and had been required by law to be a member of KIOSZ, which exercised strict oversight and control of such firms.

---

[107] *Fundy, Inc.* remained competitive through the 1990s even as Hungary's market opened up to imports. In 1999, the multinational candy manufacturer Van Melle aquired *Fundy*; in 2002, Candy Plus (formerly owned by Nestlé) acquired *Fundy's* trademark and factory in Gyál; and in 2002, *Fundy*, which was by then listed in the "Directory of Major Food Multinationals & Global Food Operators," bought out its foreign investors.

[108] Author's interview with Pétér Gerő, June 1995, Budapest.

However, there was also another reason. Futó was planning to join GYOSZ – the National Association of (private, large) factory-owners, which in 1990 had just been reestablished after having been shut down in the late 1940s. In the autumn of 1990, GYOSZ identified only about thirty private firms it judged large enough in terms of their sales to qualify as members, but Futó was convinced that his firm had a good chance of growing to three or four times its 1990 size in a year, at which point it would be "as large as some of the large state firms." His 1990 sales exceeded $2 million.[109] Futó was counting on the assistance of an old acquaintance who was one of GYOSZ's directors, and president of a well-known private software firm, to help *Fundy* gain admission.

Even as these entrepreneurs organized into formal interest groups, they could not see the extent to which they already had helped further change the outlook of the officials at the apex of that system – the men who once had controlled their fate. Yet already in 1988, a member of the Party's Central Committee and the President of the Hungarian Chamber of Commerce asserted in an official publication that

for Hungary, an orientation to the world market, an open external economic policy is of vital importance. It is this recognition that requires a promotion of the attraction of foreign capital. In Hungary so far nearly 140 joint ventures have been established.[110]

Not long afterward, in October of 1988, the Act on Economic Associations[111] – variously known as the Enterprise Law or Company Law – was approved in Parliament, and became effective in January of 1989. In the works since 1987, the law grew directly out of the 1982 reform, and although the Company Law was vastly more coherent and comprehensive, it was in many respects an extension of the earlier regulations. As the next chapter demonstrates in detail, the 1988 law was instituted in an effort to solve the regulatory and bureaucratic contradictions unleashed by the 1982 reform, and in response to the constant petitioning and arguments from the new entrepreneurs' lobbies. The Company Law, was, as its drafter put it, a 'bonus" because in addition to raising the cap to 500 employees per private firm, it allowed

not only small businesses, but also large business with real capital. People could now purchase shares without restrictions, and *individuals* – not only state firms – could establish joint-stock companies. This was the supplement the Company Law added to the Partnership Law that had already been developed between 1979 and 1981. That, you see, paved the road. Already in 1982 a GMK could have thirty employees. Think about it. Private individuals with thirty employees. This wasn't possible in other countries even in 1990. And don't forget: few could afford it, but if a Hungarian entrepreneur wanted 500 employees, it wasn't that hard to do it even before the 1988 law. To get around the

---

[109] Approximately 150 million forints at the time.

[110] Mihály Beck, "Joint Ventures in the Light of the Reform Process in Hungary," *Hungarian Business Herald*, 3, 1988, 5.

[111] A gazdasági társaságokról szóló 1988. évi VI. törvény (Act VI of 1988 on Economic Associations).

restriction, all he had to do was to establish several small cooperatives, maybe add a few PJTs and GMKs, each with the maximum number of employees . . . [112]

Thus, in 1980s Hungary, we find the early efflorescence of private entrepreneurship, the beginnings of organized activism to support it, and much of the legal-institutional infrastructure needed to undergird the more fully developed post-transition capitalist system. As we will see in the next chapter, the results – including an increasingly responsive party-state apparatus – were a far cry from the days when organizations like KIOSZ existed to exert strict control, and ultimately to liquidate, the very interests they formally represented.

---

[112] Author's interview with Tamás Sárközy, legal scholar and author of the 1989 Association Law, of which the 1988 Company Law regulating enterprise association was part, June 1994, Budapest.

7

Action and Reaction

Institutional Consequences of Private-Sector Expansion

> It is an important precondition of any organization to have greater coherence between its parts than between any of these parts and the environment of the organization.
>
> László Garai[1]

The Hungarian entrepreneurs who burst onto the scene in 1982 partially remolded socialism's institutional logic to fit their business agendas. But they were by no means the only source of disruptive pressure bearing on the system's internal coherence. Within the structures of the state apparatus, too, conflicting interests and passions arose. In non-profit institutions such as hospitals, universities, and legal-services cooperatives, high-ranking administrators were outraged by the new laws, which motivated their professional staffs – surgeons and nurses, professors and researchers, lawyers and legal secretaries – to pursue independent careers. In the sectoral bureaus, ministers feared the loss of monopolistic power in their particular "spheres" of the economy. And in state firms, directors resented the new legal "freedoms" enjoyed by their private competitors.

Indeed, the reform itself (and the widespread reaction to it) so thoroughly compromised the institutional logic of the economy that the Ministry of Finance actually had to take on the role of "protector" of private enterprise, constantly trying to prevent resentful state-firm directors and hostile bureaucrats from "turning" on the new entrepreneurs. The Ministry's protective role – entailing complex politico-administrative lobbying – partially reflected the fact that it was the reform's institutional sponsor. But it also reflected recognition of the fact, by then taking hold at the highest levels of authority, that the macro-economy had become vitally dependent for growth on the private and semi-private sectors, which between 1982 and 1985 quintupled in size.

---

[1] László Garai, "The Bureaucratic State Governed by an Illegal Movement: Soviet-Type Societies and Bolshevik-Type Parties," *Political Psychology* 12, no. 1 (March 1991).

Thus the complications introduced by the new private sector transcended state-firm resentment, bureaucratic hostility, and the partial role-inversion of a number of oversight organizations of the socialist state. Complications also arose because private enterprise radically altered the web of power relations running through the system. Despite initial resentment, state firms soon learned that they could benefit from openly cooperative relations with private entrepreneurs, often by incorporating quasi-private work in the form of the VGMKs. And as state firms exploited the advantageous conditions created by private enterprise, central planners' control over state firms diminished even further. Central planners, in turn, got caught in a double-bind: because of private businesses they were losing leverage over state-firms; but as the planners themselves knew only too well, absent the expanding private businesses, the economy – and particularly private consumption – would suffer significantly.

In an effort to escape this dilemma, central planners successfully pressed for a taxation policy that shifted the lion's share of the fiscal burden to the private sector. The strategy backfired precisely because it worked. That is to say, the policy was predictably punitive of the private sector. But now punishment of the private sector also meant punishment of the economy as a whole. To avoid economic catastrophe, key decision-makers managed to substitute this prejudicial tax policy with a value-added-tax in 1988. The VAT's distributive consequences were momentous, among other things, because the tax made no distinction between private and state firms, or between large and small, and this in turn meant the end of the long-standing practice of redistributive taxation that had enabled unprofitable companies to survive at the expense of profitable ones.

By 1988, the "rules of engagement" for both the private and state sectors had changed to the point that a Department Head at the Ministry of Finance could cut straight to the underlying problem. "The 1982 law," the official explained, "carried within it the political duality of which it was born."[2] As a result of this duality, even official interest-representation organizations were undergoing an identity crisis. Although originally intended to act as the "liquidators" of the private enterprise interests they "represented," these organizations by the 1970s had actually come to function as "transmission belts" that conveyed the center's "suggestions" to the organizations' memberships. But with the 1982 reform, citizen entrepreneurs were no longer obligated to belong to these interest-representation entities. And so the organizations suddenly faced an existential challenge: reinvent themselves in order to attract members, or become obsolete and wither away.

László Gellei, the KIOSZ director we met in Chapter 6, spontaneously borrowed from Western theories of political economy in an effort to explain the root of the problem. Echoing Albert Hirschman, he noted that under mandatory membership, the organizations' members enjoyed neither "voice" nor "exit." But his next observation was reminiscent of Mancur Olson. Gellei also pointed

---

[2] Author's interview with Anna Székács, Ministry of Finance, Budapest, December 1988.

out that making membership optional would cause a free-rider problem, since no one would want to pay membership dues. And then, how would the organizations finance their activities?

Separate Spheres of Work

The clearest institutional-organizational disruption and attendant challenge to authority structures occurred in non-profit organizations, known in state-socialist systems as state budgetary organizations. Over the years, many non-profit organizations had come to tolerate internal procedures and financial arrangements that allowed their workers to expand their fixed incomes. This was a kind of second economy inside schools, hospitals, and other not-for-profit organizations.[3] Health-care professionals, for example, routinely received separate "private" payments for nominally free medical procedures, usually remitted directly by patients to the provider. Similar arrangements existed in the field of law between clients and attorneys who worked for the state lawyers' cooperatives. Finally, there were some open and official, semi-private financial arrangements that linked not private consumers and official state providers, but branches of the socialist economy.

Representative of the latter was "KK work" (*külön keret munka*: literally, "work in a separate sphere"), an arrangement that allowed university faculty and research staff to do work on a separate account, in addition to their regular, salaried work. The development of KK work was not unlike the more general history of the bargained revolt described in Chapter 6. In the 1960s, universities regularly received research orders from industry and from research institutes. University staff, however, were not motivated to undertake extra work as long as their official work orders were elaborated in terms of course-hours held. Indeed, even when it came to course work, many faculty members spent little time or energy because it meant nothing in terms of "wages," which were essentially fixed at low levels.[4] Hence the emergence of KK work in the early 1970s. The arrangement was simple. Universities received orders for projects and assigned them to a particular team of professors and/or researchers. This team then undertook the research in exchange for extra income. A portion of the payment for their work went to the universities' welfare institutions,[5] and another portion to the central university budget.[6] Beyond this officially

---

[3] A careful reader might note that most state firms and cooperatives were not, strictly speaking, "for profit" institutions, either (although, as noted earlier, the profit motive was considerably stronger by this time in Hungary than elsewhere in the state-socialist world). The difference here is that State Budgetary Institutions were funded directly and, in theory, exclusively from the state budget, and offered social services, not products *per se*.

[4] Author's interview with Székács, December 1988.

[5] Like state firms, budgetary institutions provided their own vacation spots with housing, a "mensa" for subsidized meals, and so on. Thus university budgets covered many areas besides education *per se*.

[6] Author's interview with Székács, December 1988.

sanctioned distribution, a department head or two always had to be paid off as well.

But the financial and political consequences of this simple arrangement were complex. The pay-off requirement made those who actually completed the work resentful. This dissatisfaction, in turn, only made it more tempting in 1982 for professors and researchers to leave their official posts and form independent consulting companies. Such an exodus, however, represented a mortal threat to the universities, because the KK arrangement had become so entrenched that a financial symbiosis had developed between KK revenues and the universities' official budgets (determined as part of the national annual plan). This was almost as if agricultural workers were suddenly to walk away from their state cooperatives, taking their private plots with them, if such a thing were physically possible. (Recall from Chapter 2 the intense and profitable symbiosis that developed between the state farms and cooperatives, on the one hand, and the household plots, on the other.) Moreover, department heads and administrators were also personally affected, although many professors and researchers would have been willing to take research orders as sub-contracting units in the name of the university (in a manner analogous to VGMKs or specialized groups in state firms), they were unwilling to continue making payoffs to the higher-ups who did nothing.

An internal struggle soon ensued between administrators, on the one hand, and faculty and staff, on the other. In an atmosphere rife with accumulated indignation and growing jealousy, the Finance Ministry had to step in as mediator.

We had to go everywhere, starting with the Academic Political Committee (*Tudomány politikai bizottság*) and ending who knows where. We had to explain that it was impossible to leave [universities] out of the new entrepreneurial options because otherwise professors would simply quit, and then they'd do other intellectual work, like research and consulting, independently.[7]

Ministry officials had to fight the same battle in one or another university every year until 1989.[8] Finally, professors and researchers were allowed to form consulting companies both within the university system and independently, without having to resign from their teaching posts. To gauge the implications of the Ministry's success, consider this: the Karl Marx University of Economics,[9] no less, came to harbor the well-known and quite profitable consulting company, ECONOMIX. Here was a turn of events that would have perplexed Marx himself.

---

[7] Ibid.
[8] Ibid.
[9] Later renamed the Budapest University of Economics, and again in 2004 renamed Corvinus University.

Ambivalent Relations in a Bureaucratically Controlled Economy

The logic of socialist regulation was plainly ill-suited for the integration of private and quasi-private activities.

For instance, one regulation held that local councils could only grant business permits for operations *within* their own jurisdictions. This meant that the fifth-district council could issue a permit to the fifth-district taxi-driver allowing him to operate his taxi *only* in the fifth district [of Budapest].[10]

For a city cab to be confined to a single district was, of course, a death warrant. But the Minister of Transport had to worry about death warrants of his own. His monopoly over "his" sphere of the economy was now imperiled. And so were his constituents – the state taxi firms now threatened by the private taxi services that had rapidly proliferated within weeks of the 1982 reform.

State taxi firms were not happy. They wrote petitions, went up and down the Party lines of authority protesting; they couldn't stand the competition. They lost customers, and could no longer support their large office-buildings. Every time the government raised the price of gasoline, these firms used to come regularly and say: 'well, now are you going to let us raise the taxi fare?' By contrast, the private firms undercut the state taxi rate considerably, the chauffeur was courteous [as compared to the state company]; so the state taxi firm couldn't go to the authorities any more saying it wanted permission to raise prices.[11]

Once again, it fell to the Ministry of Finance to overcome institutional and bureaucratic resistance through endless lobbying, until the Minister of Transport reluctantly released a circular allowing private cabs to operate across districts.

Tedious and burdensome as these repeated regulatory changes were for Ministry officials, they were nothing compared with the more widespread and complex problems arising from the reactions of state-firm managers and the regulatory bureaucracy. Some state-firm managers – particularly high-level directors – begrudged the fact that private firms were not subject to the direct, centralized redistributive taxation of profits, and in general were bound by fewer restrictions.[12] Their resentment came to the fore in the two years following the implementation of the 1982 regulations. Anna Székács, the department head in the Ministry of Finance who oversaw most aspects of the reform's implementation, commented on this problem in late 1988.

[10] Author's interview with Székács, December 1988.
[11] Ibid.
[12] Author's interview with Judit Fekete, ELTE Legal Faculty, Budapest, October 1988. On the other hand, private firms enjoyed none of the privileges of state firms and none of the subsidies either. As we saw in the last chapter, they were at a serious disadvantage in materials procurement, access to credit, and imports, and had none of the help state firms could expect from the state trading companies in export development. For an overview of the structural position of socialist private sectors, see János Kornai, *The Socialist System: The Political Economy of Communism* (Princeton: Princeton University Press, 1992), especially 83–90.

From the beginning, we knew that two things were unsustainable. First, the tax system would have to change. It was impossible to take away 80–90 percent of the pure profit from state firms, and to be *much more lenient* with the private firms. It was a contradiction, and the state firms would not stand for it. Either they demanded the same rights as the private firms – this, obviously, could not happen – or after a while, the state firms turned on the small [private and semi-private] ones. This could be expected not only with respect to the VGMK's [intra-firm work-partnerships], but in general.

Second: if the internal logic of the state regulatory system required a mode of thinking very different from that required by the small [private] firms, then the entire bureaucratic class would turn against the small entrepreneur, since it only caused them more work, and so they would do anything to make the life of the entrepreneur harder.[13]

Many state-firm managers did begrudge the "advantages" of private firms, and bureaucrats were often uninterested in helping private entrepreneurs achieve their goals; or worse, actually tried to obstruct them. Often, as have already seen, connections and bribes could ameliorate the latter problem, at least for those private entrepreneurs with sufficient resources. But the issue of differential taxation was a sticky one, and certainly not only because some state-firm managers resented the inconsistency of wage and tax regulation.[14] A government spokesman quoted in *Népszabadság*, the Party daily, claimed that "the populace [was also] irritated by the high incomes of . . . private enterprises and that taxes [would be] one method of keeping down disproportionately high earnings."[15]

It is, of course, impossible to assess the role that popular sentiment played in various governmental decisions to increase the tax burden of the new partnerships: whether it precipitated action or was simply used to "ratify" decisions taken for other reasons. What Party and Ministry of Finance documents do show very clearly is that officials faced a new dilemma. Resentment of the relatively low taxes and high incomes of private and quasi-private partnerships might be widespread, and raising the new partnerships' taxes might be expedient in the short term, since it would provide new inflows to the national budget. But increased taxation (or the administrative restrictions suggested by some) could backfire at the level of the macro-economy. After all, by 1984, the number of private and quasi-private businesses had grown so dramatically that the Ministry of Finance recognized that

---

[13] Author's interview with Anna Székács, Budapest, February 1989. Székács subsequently reaffirmed her earlier interpretation of events and perception of the political and economic landscape discussed here and elsewhere in the book in interviews with the author, Budapest, summer 1994 and fall 1996.

[14] The Hungarian tax system was gradually revised between 1968 and 1988; these revisions and attempts at rationalization were part and parcel of broader reform packages aimed at increasing the efficiency of state-firm performance. See Györgyi Varga, "The Reform of Taxation in Hungary," Chapter 3, in Roger Clarke, ed., *Hungary: The Second Decade of Economic Reform* (London: Longman Group UK Ltd., 1989).

[15] Economist Intelligence Unit, *EIU Country Report: Hungary*, no. 3 (London: Economist Ltd. Publications, 1986), 10.

there was no going back. Our growth now came unambiguously from these small enterprises. There were years when, if not for these enterprises, instead of 1 percent growth, we would have had negative growth. And we put this in writing. Every year between 1982 and 1988, there were governmental meetings on the issue of the private businesses. The political bodies requested data and analysis concerning what the private businesses did during that year. We gave an account of their number, activities, political effects; and we *always* indicated that without them, we would have no growth whatsoever.[16]

In fact, according to an internal document of the Ministry of Finance, from 1982 to the first quarter of 1985, the private and quasi-private sector – which, as previously mentioned, had quintupled in size in this period, accounted for *all* economic growth; viewed against the record of a longer period that included two years preceding private-sector expansion (1980–1985), the sector's contribution accounted for *half* of all economic growth.[17]

And yet, even though the output of the new partnerships provided a temporary "breathing space" for the ailing Hungarian economy, opponents of the reform frequently claimed that the partnerships were responsible for a considerable outflow of potential state revenue. In accounting terms, this was probably an accurate representation of state firms' and state-controlled cooperatives' financial relations with their internal sub-contracting partnerships (the VGMKs and the specialized groups, respectively). Because firms paid sub-contractors from their expense funds (instead of from wage funds), they managed to circumvent centrally determined wage ceilings, and managers regularly paid the members of internal sub-contracting partnerships more than during regular working hours.

But if the number of legal internal sub-contracting units grew rapidly after 1982, the underlying reasons for their existence were not new. To some degree, as we have seen, VGMKs and specialized groups in industrial and service cooperatives represented an *ex post facto* formalization of earlier informal overtime and sub-contracting schemes between managers and groups of key workers.[18] Prior to 1982, firm directors and especially shop-floor managers had learned to appreciate the flexibility that private and quasi-private sub-contracting arrangements could provide. Many managers – even some who may have been unhappy about the promotion of the private sector as a whole – had encouraged the development of a variety of official semi-private work-arrangements that increased their degrees of freedom precisely by undermining the central bureaucratic

---

[16] Author's interview with Székács, February 1989.
[17] "A kisvállalkozások helye, szerepe és távlatai," Feljegyzés egy GPB előterjesztéséhez ["The place, role and outlook of small enterprises"]. Notes to a (Political-Economic Committee) report, Budapest: Ministry of Finance Internal Document, signed by László Lengyel, 1986, 2, 6.
[18] We saw in Chapter 2 that specialized groups had been permitted in agricultural cooperatives since 1968; both members and non-members (often pensioners) could contract with the cooperative to raise, for example, bees, rabbits, and so on, and the cooperative would market their production. The right to form specialized groups was extended to industrial and service cooperatives in 1982.

system of financial control over state enterprises. The post-1982 proliferation of VGMKs and specialized groups showed that state-firm managers were gaining a new appreciation of the advantages of semi-private partnership arrangements that now could be pursued openly. Through such subcontracting arrangements, for example, managers were better able to encourage key workers' cooperation by raising their pay, and better-paid subcontractors could be counted on to fulfill work-orders to specification and on time. Alternatively, through independent initiatives, subcontracting groups both earned extra income for their members and raised the profits of host institutions to which they paid an operating fee: if the host-institution marketed the subcontractor's production, the former also shared directly in the profits. Unlike earlier informal subcontracting arrangements, management and VGMK or specialized-group members now signed contracts that protected both.

Like middle-level managers, top firm management was motivated to earn the centrally awarded bonuses and promotions that resulted from productivity increases. In addition, state firms received tax-breaks and extra resources if they increased productivity. By supporting VGMKs, state firms could produce more efficiently without additional capital investment.[19] Moreover, internal subcontracting arrangements had a deeper, institutional significance for top management: they forestalled decentralization of state firms – and therefore managers' loss of power. Thus, whatever their resentments of the wider private sector, many state-firm managers increased their freedom of maneuver through internal subcontracting.[20]

The increase in managers' degrees of freedom, as previously mentioned, came at the expense of the central authorities' financial control over state firms. But if the loss of control was undoubtedly a serious concern for many planners and officials (for example, in the State Office of Wage and Labor), these concerns resonated with the Central Committee for another, more immediate reason: the country's growing international debt. Hungary's hard-currency debt rose dramatically between 1984 and 1985 (from US$ 12.2 billion to 15.1 billion), and the increased proportion of short-term debt was an even more immediate worry.[21] Officials thus had to be concerned about international money markets' perceptions of the country's creditworthiness, and all the more so since Hungary had joined the World Bank in 1982 and the country's political leadership was unwilling to reschedule its debt or default, as Poland did (in effect if not quite officially). If potential revenue was escaping via private and quasi-private partnerships, more stringent taxation might – some hoped – nourish a

---

[19] Recall also from Chapter 2 managers' attitudes toward centrally allocated investment goods – what Kornai called their "investment hunger." János Kornai, *The Socialist System: The Political Economy of Communism* (Princeton: Princeton University Press, 1992), chapter 9.

[20] David Stark, "Bending the Bars of the Iron Cage: Bureaucratization and Informalization in Capitalism and Socialism," *Sociological Forum* 4, no. 4 (1989).

[21] From $2.4 billion to $2.7 billion in the same year. Economist Intelligence Unit, *EIU Country Profile, Hungary 1986–87* (London: Economist Ltd. Publications, 1988), 40.

state budget perpetually in deficit partly because of heavy interest and capital payments on the hard-currency debt.[22]

Reform-minded officials at the Ministry of Finance did their best to show that the growth of private sector *output* exceeded its income growth, and that the majority of the outflow of potential state revenue relative to output growth actually occurred in the *state* sector (for example, through the long-standing problems of work-shirking and theft of materials, but above all, as the result of government subsidization of price-insensitive state firms).[23] Nevertheless, the State Office of Wage and Labor pushed hard for additional taxes, and soon the command came from the Central Committee (via the Ministry of Planning): levy additional taxes on the private sector, because the "escaping revenues" are unacceptably high.[24]

As a result, the tax-burden of the private sector was substantially increased, and by 1985,

the situation for many private enterprises became exceedingly tight. Gross output value rose by 30% but taxes and social security contributions increased by 64%, while total average enterprise income grew by only 13.2%. . . . Furthermore government tax auditors receive[d] bonuses for finding bookkeeping mistakes at private enterprises. No corresponding system of perks exist[ed] for those checking the books at state companies.[25]

In addition, company taxes (the fees paid in exchange for the right to conduct business) for private enterprises in 1986 were increased dramatically for the second time since 1982.

The Ministry of Finance strongly opposed heavy taxation of the private sector on the grounds that far from enjoying any true advantage over state firms, private firms suffered from every conceivable form of discrimination (for example, impaired access to credit, materials, equipment, machinery, real-estate and land, bureaucratic and social hostility, and so on). But increased taxation of the new partnerships was congenial to many *apparatchiks* in the State Office of Wage and Labor and in the Ministry of Planning "who were capable of thinking only in terms of the 'people's economy measures' of what is 'owed'

---

[22] In socialist systems, the relationship between the national budget and the balance of payments is direct, since virtually all credits from foreign banks are incurred by the government. In accounting terms, this changed after the institution of the two-tier banking system in 1987; in practice, little changed, since these "commercial" banks behaved essentially like branches of the central bank and lent mostly to state firms and state-controlled cooperatives.

[23] For instance, in 1986, the total of subsidies and benefits allocated to state firms "equaled the total profit of [state] enterprises and [state-controlled] cooperatives." See Varga, "The Reform of Taxation in Hungary," 31. For a comprehensive discussion of the systemic roots of this phenomenon, centralized redistribution of profits, see János Kornai and Ágnes Matits, *A vállalatok nyereségének bürokratikus újraelosztása* ["The Bureaucratic Redistribution of Firm Profits"] (Budapest: Közgazdasági és Jogi Könyvkiadó, 1987).

[24] Author's interview with Székács, February 1989.

[25] Economist Intelligence Unit, *EIU Country Report, Hungary*, no. 3 (London: Economist Ltd. Publications, 1986), 10.

to the Center."[26] Nor, it seems, was an increased *general* level of taxation of partnerships sufficient to satisfy those most concerned about the loss of control over the hidden wage expenditures of state enterprises.

> The Ministry of Finance tried, to no avail, to stem the tide. Minister Hetényi even threatened resignation. But they still forced the so-called "separate tax" on us.[27]

Originally levied at the rate of 10 percent, the separate tax was raised to 15 percent in June of 1986 and again to 20 percent in 1987.[28] Though it also applied to private work partnerships (GMKs), and to civil law partnerships (PJTs), the "separate tax" was first and foremost a targeted effort to recapture a portion of moneys that state firms and state-controlled cooperatives paid to *internal* subcontractors (VGMKs).

The separate tax was to have been implemented in January of 1985, but it was only introduced in the middle of the year, because Minister of Finance Hetényi continued to fight against it.[29] The separate tax, after all, discriminated not only between state and private enterprise, but between "new" and "old" private sector firms. State firm transactions with the pre-1982 traditional small "mom and pop" private businesses were less common, but in any case, were *not* subject to the tax. However, if state firms did business with the new partnership forms, the separate tax obtained.[30] Only one new partnership form was not subject to the separate tax. Given the ideological framework of the 1982 regulations that brought these organizational forms into being, it is not surprising that this was the single officially classified "socialist form": the small cooperative.[31]

Thus, despite clear discrimination, the separate tax was implemented over the strong official objections of the Ministry of Finance. Three years later, Finance Ministry Official Székács recalled that she was so "ashamed and embarrassed" about this tax that she would have preferred not to give her regular bi-monthly presentations to would-be entrepreneurs, lawyers, and others throughout the country who were interested in becoming involved in private enterprise. Clearly, she was not the only high-level official representing the interests of the private sector who was angered. In a show of passive resistance, *the Ministry of Finance*

---

[26] Székács knew the individual in the State Office of Wage and Labor responsible for the development of the "separate tax," who was "simply acting on orders from 'on high,'" and had since moved to Canada to enjoy a "more peaceful life." Author's interview with Székács, February 1989.

[27] Ibid.

[28] Economist Intelligence Unit, *EIU Country Report: Hungary*, no. 1 (London: Economist Ltd. Publications, 1987), 11.

[29] Author's interview with Székács, February 1989.

[30] Pénzügyminisztérium 2345/1988 Jogi Főosztály, "Előterjesztés: A Gazdaságpolitikai Bizottság részére a kisüzemi gazdálkodás helyzetéről" ["Report for the Political Economic Committee (of the HSWP) on the situation of the small-firm economy"]. Internal document 2345/1988, Budapest: Ministry of Finance Legal Department, 1988, 5.

[31] Actually, there was one more "socialist" form, the so-called "Small Firm"; however, this was essentially a small state firm. See Teréz Laky, "Small Enterprises in Hungary: Myth and Reality," *Acta Oeconomica*, 32, no. 1–2 (1984): 39–63.

refused to release any instructions or explanations concerning the new tax regulation:

The directive [for instructions] came from the Council of Ministers [Minister Tanács], which the Council issued in spite of the opposing vote of the Minister of Finance, who then refused to release a single order of implementation.[32]

Activists in the Ministry of Finance were right to think that the separate tax would prove detrimental to the interests of the new private sector (and, they argued, to those of the economy overall). Even though it was the state firms that were technically responsible for paying the separate tax, they often managed to shift a significant portion of it onto their private partners.[33] As a result, many private partnerships became unprofitable as they were forced to lower their prices enough to cover the state firms' increased expenditures.[34] The immediate effect of the separate tax was to restrict the fastest growing sub-sector of the larger private sector, the quasi-private VGMKs, since the preponderance of their business was conducted exclusively with state firms in which they operated.

This was clearly a punitive tax against the new private sector, which some thought was "earning too much at the expense of the state sector and the national economy."[35] And indeed, from the tax authorities' perspective, the most striking consequence of the separate tax was that it supplied upward of 10 billion forints annually to the national budget in 1986 and 1987.[36]

Thus far, it would seem that the private sector was losing out, and that the predominantly socialist principles of economic organization it had upset were beginning to reassert themselves. However, subsequent events suggest a different conclusion. It is true that because of its significant contribution to the budget, the Ministry of Finance did not succeed in reversing the separate tax ruling until 1988. Nevertheless, when the Ministry did finally convince the Political-Economic Committee of the HSWP to rescind the separate tax, its success was part of a process far more significant than the reversal of a particular tax. As of January 1, 1988, a comprehensive new tax law, including a modern

---

[32] Author's interview with Székács, December 1988.

[33] Pénzügyminisztérium 2345/1988 Jogi Főosztály, "Előterjesztés: A Gazdaságpolitikai Bizottság részére a kisüzemi gazdálkodás helyzetéről" ["Report for the Political Economic Committee (of the HSWP) on the situation of the small-firm economy"]. Internal document 2345/1988, Budapest: Ministry of Finance Legal Department, 1988, 7.

[34] This was by no means always the case. Sometimes, state firms were dependent enough on a private supplier or sub-contractor that they absorbed the extra cost themselves. Or, in the event that a private firm supplied a state firm with a good or a service in seriously short supply, it even happened that it might earn such a high profit that it could afford to lower its price significantly.

[35] János Palotás, then-Director of VOSZ, the National Association of Entrepreneurs, Budapest, characterized the views of "orthodox thinkers" in the party-state apparatus. Author's interview with János Palotás, Budapest, January 1989.

[36] Author's interview with Székács, February 1989.

VAT would be applied to *all* private and state firms.[37] The VAT would replace the earlier "preferential direct tax system . . . characterized by different rates for almost every company, with a unified indirect tax system that [was] indifferent as to whether a firm [was] private or state, large or small . . . and [would shift] the tax burden from production to trade."[38]

The new tax system was prepared in the framework of a concept that had been under discussion at high levels since at least 1983: "sector neutrality."[39] Ministry of Finance officials had seized on the term as a reference to the need for a level playing field for private and state firms, and within this, the need for "tax neutrality." However, the Tax Reform Act of 1987 was developed over many years in response to systemic economic pressures far more profound than the ones brought to bear by the "separate tax" on private partnerships. Indeed, the economic distortions caused by the separate tax were only the "last straw" for a seriously troubled economy, and by 1986, the need for a complete overhaul of the tax system was evident. Hence the intense debate over tax reform that began in 1986.[40]

In its 1988 position paper written for the Political-Economic Sub-Committee of the HSWP's Central Committee, the Finance Ministry stated:

The separate tax paid by [state firms] has caused the greatest tension for small [private] enterprises . . . The separate tax offends the principles of tax neutrality and competitive neutrality [between the sectors]; we cannot put off rescinding it past 1989.[41]

Although the VAT was not applied in an entirely consistent manner (the system still allowed for several rates, which permitted the government to protect firms making a loss[42]), its implementation was a big step forward in the liberalization of the economy – specifically in the effort to end the long-standing redistributive taxation of state firms whereby unprofitable companies survived directly at the expense of profitable ones.[43]

---

[37] A comprehensive income tax was also being prepared at this time, and took effect on January 1, 1989. Incomes were taxed at a progressive rate (from 15 percent to 37.5 percent up to 250,000 forints/year; income from bonds was also taxed. The VAT keys were 0 percent, 15 percent, and 25 percent; for more detailed information, see Varga, "The Reform of Taxation in Hungary."

[38] Economist Intelligence Unit, *EIU Country Report, Hungary*, no. 2 (London: Economist Ltd. Publications, 1987), 10.

[39] See for instance, PM, "Előterjesztés a Miniszteri Értekezlet részére," Közgazdasági és költségvetési Főosztály ["Ministry of Finance Report to the Council of Ministers, Economic and Budgetary Department"], Budapest: Ministry of Finance, November 1983, 22.

[40] On the intensity of the debate, see Varga, "The Reform of Taxation in Hungary," 29.

[41] Pénzügyminisztérium 2345/1988 Jogi Főosztály, "Előterjesztés: A Gazdaságpolitikai Bizottság részére a kisüzemi gazdálkodás helyzetéről" ["Report for the Political Economic Committee (of the HSWP) on the situation of the small-firm economy"]. Internal document 2345/1988, Budapest: Ministry of Finance Legal Department, 1988, 5–7.

[42] Economist Intelligence Unit, *EIU Country Report, Hungary*, no. 2 (London: Economist Ltd. Publications, 1987), 10.

[43] Kornai, *The Socialist System*, especially chapter 13.

A Communist Party Introduces the VAT

The new enterprise tax system implied a serious potential loss of control for the Hungarian Socialist Workers' Party (HSWP) and redirection of the economy.[44] So why did the Party allow its implementation? Official documents indicate that a variety of experts managed to persuade key members of the ruling elite that the "contradictions and inefficiencies inherent in the . . . underdeveloped system of taxes and subsidies" had to be changed.[45] The Ministry of Finance and its associated research group (Penzügykutató RT), in particular, believed that the incoherent system of subsidies and taxes could not be corrected without a comprehensive tax reform; further, that

the obsolete tax system . . . played a role in conserving the economic structure; and that the resentment created by the ever-increasing differentiation of incomes, for instance, could only be overcome by means of a system of personal income tax that resulted in a more equitable distribution of public burdens.[46]

Still, neither sound technical advice nor the strong convictions of high-level officials in the Ministry of Finance tell the whole story. To be sure, a reformed tax system (compared with that of the classical socialist model) had been evolving in Hungary since 1968. A complicated turnover tax had been implemented with the New Economic Mechanism (NEM) of that year, and although it was a far cry from a modern VAT,[47] here, too, reform legacies made subsequent steps easier.

Another part of the answer to the question of why the HSWP allowed implementation of the VAT is to be found in private-sector expansion. According to one estimate, by the mid-1980s, approximately 2.6 million of Hungary's 4.8 million employees had some form of income originating in legal private or quasi-private work. This figure includes marginal incomes such as those sometimes earned from household plots and auxiliary farming, but it also includes significant incomes. Approximately 1 million of these 2.6 million employees were involved in formal, registered private or quasi-private business, whether of the traditional variety, which expanded after 1982 to employ approximately 400,000, or in private and quasi-private post-1982 partnerships, which by the mid-1980s employed approximately 600,000 individuals.[48] Thus it was

---

[44] The earlier tax system allowed for wide discretion of various branches of the apparatus (for example, the tax office and the State Office of Wage and Labor). Its overall structure was ultimately dependent upon rulings of the Ministry of Finance, rather than on the constitution, for instance. See Varga, "The Reform of Taxation in Hungary," 29.

[45] Economist Intelligence Unit, *EIU Country Report, Hungary,* no. 3, (London: Economist Ltd. Publications, 1986), 11.

[46] Varga, 29.

[47] The turnover tax of 1968 was "highly differentiated . . . the number of tax rates was around 2,000 – with some items zero-rated and some enjoying subsidies." Varga, 32. A modern VAT (value-added tax) usually has three or four clear, uniformly applied rates.

[48] Varga, "The Reform of Taxation in Hungary," 32.

increasingly impossible to regulate incomes directly at workplaces, and "an *ex post* correction," in the form of a personal income tax, became necessary.[49]

Yet if the central authorities wanted revenue from the private sector, they would have to allow it to grow, and this it could not do past a certain point if it were to be forever hampered by outright discrimination. One example of such discrimination was the way many private ventures had to purchase inputs. In principle, they were free to buy from the wholesalers that supplied state firms; in practice, as we saw in the cases of two entrepreneurs in Chapter 6, private businesses had to buy "secondhand" from state firms in the same line of production, or from retail outlets, because the wholesalers were uninterested in selling small quantities, and were not administratively forced to do so. Thus private firms generally paid retail prices for inputs, unless through bribes and special bargains they were able to arrange better deals.[50] This was one reason why private producers also tended to charge more, thus narrowing their market to those with relatively higher incomes. But with the introduction of the VAT, this effective price discrimination against private industry came to an end. By forcing state firms to behave in greater accord with the discipline of market principles, the VAT increased their incentive to supply *all* potential buyers.[51]

The "sector-neutrality" of the VAT was good news for private manufacturers capable of competing with state firms, but was potentially quite disruptive of the comfortable position of inefficient loss-makers in the state sector. The "separate tax" was, of course, entirely incompatible with the VAT framework. In any case, the spontaneous reaction of private and quasi-private firms affected by the separate tax (and by other unfavorable financial regulations) showed that arbitrary treatment of one sector would simply force it to redirect its activity. By 1988, a striking reorganization had occurred in the "completer

---

[49] Ibid.

[50] Traditional pre-1982 small private manufacturers were still obliged to purchase some of their inputs through KIOSZ, whereas retailers were free to try to purchase them on the domestic market. The situation for all private firms (pre- and post-1982) was very difficult with respect to imports, in part because foreign trade enterprises had little incentive to cultivate the business of small private firms. Until the 1989 order of the Trade Ministry that allowed natural persons to import in the same way as legal persons (corporations), and required foreign trade companies to handle their orders, many private entrepreneurs imported through friends in foreign countries or through personal purchases of goods abroad.

[51] VAT is essentially an indirect tax on final consumption that is "collected fractionally along the production-distribution chain," and as such does not penalize producing firms (which would still, of course, pay taxes on profits, just as in the West). Though firms pay the VAT with each purchase of an input, they are entitled to claim refunds on any intermediate good used in the production process. In principle, all firms would have to pay the VAT according to a clear guideline that differentiated only on the basis of activity, not ownership form (for example, different pre-determined rates for exports, services, and final manufactured products). The VAT simply cannot comfortably coexist with *direct* methods of price control, because it requires producer and consumer prices to move in tandem. Moreover, though by itself it never guarantees wholesale reform of any particular economic mechanism, it is in harmony with the tax systems of many market economies, and tends to increase integration into the world market. See Varga, "The Reform of Taxation in Hungary," 36–37.

and helper economy" – as State and party documents still sometimes called it. With this reorganization, the long-term viability of the separate tax was called into question, since many of the partnership forms affected by the tax simply transformed themselves into small cooperatives in order to avoid it. Whereas in 1985 there were 713 small cooperatives, by mid-1987 they numbered 2,200. Partly as the result of this wholesale switch, by 1987 small cooperatives provided 41 percent of the production value of industrial cooperatives as a whole (that is, traditional state-controlled and small "private" cooperatives together), a contribution of more than US$ 1 billion.[52] The small industrial cooperatives employed approximately 90,000 people, and, as the Ministry of Finance put it: "unambiguously [came to] represent a significant economic force."[53] A Ministry of Finance position paper explained to the Political-Economic Sub-Committee of the HSWP's Central Committee that the rapid growth of the small cooperatives was attributable first and foremost to the separate tax, which rendered the other organizational forms less attractive, and secondly to other regulations that were not "organizationally neutral."[54]

The private sector's reaction to the separate tax was just one case in which firms used their new opportunities to transform themselves to evade restrictions of various kinds. Starting in 1982, some *state* cooperatives also began reorganizing themselves into multiple small (private) cooperatives to escape state regulation. As late as 1988, the Ministry of Finance, in a report to the Central Committee's Political Economic Sub-Committee, raised the question of whether it would be necessary to restrict this development.[55] However, it concluded almost in the same breath that such restriction would "arouse opposition and the feeling that [our] regulations are unreliable, not only among the small cooperatives, but in a wider sphere."[56]

By 1988, Finance Minister Miklós Villányi, who briefly succeeded Hetényi in 1987, could state with confidence:

The organizational structure of the economy needs state, cooperative, and private institutions equally. The basic requirement for their undisturbed functioning is that . . . the [possibility for] mutual influence and transition between them be insured. This . . . will be solved by the 1989 Act on Economic Association, now under preparation.[57]

But even before 1989, the central authorities undertook further significant liberalization of the private sector. In late 1987, for example, the Political-Economic

---

[52] At the time, about 55 billion forints at official exchange rates.

[53] Figures and quote are from the Ministry of Finance's position-paper: Pénzügyminisztérium 2345/1988 Jogi Főosztály, "Előterjesztés: A Gazdaságpolitikai Bizottság részére a kisüzemi gazdálkodás helyzetéről" ["Report for the Political Economic Committee (of the HSWP) on the situation of the small-firm economy"]. Internal document 2345/1988, Budapest: Ministry of Finance Legal Department, 8.

[54] Ibid.

[55] Ibid., 9.

[56] Ibid., 10.

[57] Ibid., 13.

Sub-Committee, following the advice of the Ministry of Finance, raised most of the numerical limits on employees in the various private sector organizational forms. The Sub-Committee took this decision with a view to avoiding the "tensions" caused by different rules that obtained for the traditional pre-1982 private sector and the post-1982 partnerships. Much of the information about these tensions, and the direct bureaucratic impetus for this liberalization, came from the interest-representation organizations that oversaw the traditional private sector (e.g., KIOSZ, the National Association of Small Manufacturers, and KISOSZ, the National Association of Small Retailers). Their membership consisted primarily of traditional (pre-1982) private manufacturers and retailers, who had long objected through official channels to unfair treatment: why, for instance, could *they* not employ as many workers as the new partnerships?

In a 1987 proposal to the Ministers of Finance, Justice, Industry, and Domestic Commerce, The Central Committee's Political-Economic Sub-Committee noted that:

> The state and interest-representation organizations concerned . . . have reached the conclusion that it is not expedient to make separate decisions concerning the number of employees permitted [for] the [traditional] private sector and the [new] private entrepreneurs. In the interest of avoiding contradictions and tensions, it is necessary to handle the entire private sphere in a unified manner.[58]

The same official document also pointed out the achievements of the private sector: it satisfied consumer demand, providing high-quality parts, fittings, and equipment; it supplied shortage goods, and produced for export. By playing its assigned role as the "background economy," it gave rise to a "many-sided cooperation" with large (state) industry. Therefore, the position paper concluded, "it is important to the interests of the people's economy that the activities of the private enterprises be expanded."[59]

So by 1987, many high-level officials were aware that the growing private and quasi-private sector had wrought significant changes in the socialist regulatory system. From the foregoing examples, we can see that it had become problematic to treat the "old" and "new" private sectors – or, for that matter, the private and state sectors – differently. Step by step, discrimination would either have to be clearly justified, or ended, in the official regulatory framework, because the economy had come irrevocably to depend on private and quasi-private activities. What party-state documents never stated directly, but couched gently in terms of latent "tensions," was that the *political* cost of discrimination against the private sector had increased in direct proportion to the percentage of the population that depended on private or quasi-private activity for all or part of its income. At the same time, the quasi-private household plots

---

[58] "*Előterjesztés az a MSZMP KB Gazdaságpolitikai Bizottságának a magánvállalkozásokban foglalkoztatottak létszámának növelésére,*" ["Proposal to the HSWP's Central Committee's Political-Economic Committee (concerning) increasing the number of employees in the private sector"]. Internal document, Budapest: HSWP Central Committee, September 1987, 4.

[59] Ibid., 5.

and private farms were producing a significant share of agricultural output on which the population depended (see Tables 3.1 and 3.2 for sample years).

In fact, the roles of the state apparatus and private sector had been partially reversed. Prior to 1982, the latter had been in a dependent and subservient position *vis-à-vis* the authorities; until 1989, it often remained so in practice. However, the Party Central Committee became increasingly aware of the need to "woo" private entrepreneurs, even as it tried to "reassure" those who needed reassuring – mainly hard-liners within the apparatus and some traditional state firm managers. This is evident in the Political-Economic Sub-Committee's support of the Finance Ministry decision to eschew direct and "outdated" methods of regulating the size of the private sector. On the one hand, the position paper spoke to those who were nervous about private-sector expansion, informing them that "in any case, the number of small entrepreneurs who employ really large numbers of workers is insignificant [sic], and is typical only of those who are involved in export." On the other hand – and in almost the same breath – it went on to state that the modernization of the regulatory system (and abandoning all attempts at direct control over firm-size) would "strengthen the trust of private enterprise; it would express [the fact] that their activities are needed in the long term."[60]

Interest-Representation Organizations

Early communist doctrine held that "pluralistic institutions of interest mediation" were nothing more than "instruments of bourgeois dictatorship, whose existence was undesirable even in the transitional period."[61] Accordingly, by 1948, the Hungarian socialist system had abolished a network of "several thousand associations and representative organizations," including all guilds and local chambers of commerce, and substituted a system consisting of a few large organizations that functioned as "quasi-ministries."[62] We have already encountered two of these: KIOSZ and KISOSZ. These institutions, established by the Communist Party in 1946, tried to "appear above party [politics], but were in fact under Communist direction,"[63] and functioned as "organizations

---

[60] Ibid., 6
[61] Péter Tölgyessy, "Economic Interest Representation in Hungary," unpublished manuscript (1988), 114.
[62] Béla Pokol, "Changes in the System of Political Representation in Hungary," in Rudolf Andorka and László Bertalan, eds., *Economy and Society in Hungary*, published by the Department of Sociology of the Karl Marx University of Economic Sciences (Budapest: Alfaprint, 1986), 272. Pokol also notes that whereas it is normal for the "more developed societies of the West" to have "several thousand" representative organizations, Hungary in 1980 still had only 225; if we discount a number of professional organizations, associations of foreign students, and the like, "no more than 5 associations remain . . . when talking about the political institutionalization of interests." Ibid., 277.
[63] Géza Kovács, "A Magánkisipar útja a magyar szocialista gazdaságfejlődés különböző szakaszaiban" ["The path of small private industry in the various phases of Hungarian socialist economic development"]. Unpublished paper, Budapest: Research Institute of Labor Affairs, 1988, 16.

of political agitation."[64] In fact, as already mentioned, their original role was that of "liquidator" of the private sector: in the 1950s, KIOSZ and KISOSZ worked hand in hand with the economic police to rid the economy of most private enterprise, although this was not clearly stated as a goal in the beginning.[65] Instead,

[KIOSZ's] first director, who ran on the Communist ticket in 1947, explained the [newly disadvantaged] socio-economic status of small businesspeople [by citing] 'the counter-revolutionary forces [at work] in the Ministry of Industrial Affairs.'[66]

Those small (usually one person) private businesses that were allowed to survive were kept under strict economic and political control. A Hungarian scholar cites, by way of example, an incident in 1958 – already a less repressive period, five years after Stalin's death – when a Hungarian newspaper wrote about an unnamed small private manufacturer who was "overcharging." KIOSZ's internal newspaper found out the individual's name and made a public example of him.[67]

After 1948, KIOSZ and KISOSZ did take on nominal functions of interest-representation, and after 1956, the Party recognized KIOSZ as the only official interest representation organization for private manufacturers. In 1958, membership for all private manufacturers became mandatory; KISOSZ, which had analogous authority over private retailers, was renamed the National Association of Small Retailers. The authorities granted licenses for private business only to members in good standing.

An official interest-representation organization similarly "represented" every other productive sector of the Hungarian economy to the Party and the Parliament. For example, when in the early 1950s most private industry was forced into some 1,500 state producers' cooperatives, OKISZ, the National Association of Small Industrial Cooperatives, became their interest representation organization; similarly, state-controlled agricultural cooperatives had TOT, the National Organization of Agricultural Cooperatives. Household plots, in contrast, had no real interest-representation, since they were considered to be organically integrated into the agricultural cooperatives.[68] The one remaining chamber of commerce was not a transmission-belt organization in the same sense as KIOSZ, KISOSZ, or OKISZ, but it did serve as a kind of

---

[64] Péter Tölgyessy, (1988) "Gazdasági érdekképviseletek Magyarországon" ["Economic Interest Representation in Hungary]," unpublished manuscript (1988), 202, note 19.

[65] Author's interview with Peter Szirmai, Budapest Technical University, Budapest, November 1988. See also Pokol, "Changes in the System of Political Representation," 273.

[66] Kovács, "A Magánkisipar útja a magyar szocialista gazdaságfejlődés különböző szakaszaiban," 16.

[67] Ibid., 47, note 75.

[68] They could, if they wished, attach themselves to the People's Front "friends of gardens" circles. Péter Tölgyessy, "Gazdasági érdekképviseletek Magyarországon ["Economic interest representation in Hungary"], unpublished manuscript (1988), 78, 242, note 118.

"self-government" for the eighty to hundred largest state firms, and focused primarily on developing export possibilities. However, all economic units, including non-profit institutions and cooperatives, could join; and in the 1980s, the Chamber of Commerce took some 3,500 new private partnerships under its wing for a time in its "small entrepreneurs' section," but was not able to advance their interests significantly; indeed, it had no real reason to do so.[69]

In the parlance of Hungarian socialism, interest-representation organizations such as KIOSZ, KISOSZ, OKISZ, or SZOT (the National Council of Trade Unions) were known officially as "social organizations," a term with a very broad meaning. The Party did not conceive of SZOT, for instance, simply as an organization of workers, nor was OKISZ merely an organization for small industrial cooperatives. Instead, these were mass organizations that transmitted the concerns, wishes, and commands of the Center to their memberships; hence the term "transmission-belts."[70]

The interest-representation organizations' role as transmission-belts included the effective power to determine which traditional, pre-1982 firms could function and which could not. KIOSZ, for instance, was able to decide which small manufacturers would obtain access to materials and on what terms, and until 1987, it determined its members' annual taxes by fiat. OKISZ's mandate included, for example, oversight of the industrial cooperatives' cost-calculations and wage-determination.[71]

Although all-powerful with regard to the traditional small private sector that survived nationalization, the official interest-representation organizations were not especially powerful at the high level of national politics. KIOSZ, for instance, was in regular contact only with "the lowest level of the central party-state apparatus," and, despite a great deal of internal bureaucratic activity and a constant round of national meetings, the institution lacked "even organized information about the true situation of small [private] manufacturing" in the country.[72] (On the other hand, for the sake of perspective, it is worth pointing out that interest-representation organizations had fairly well-defined functions and fully equipped permanent headquarters. By comparison, most members of Parliament had neither offices nor official telephones.)

Over time, these transmission belts took on more of the role of facilitators for small traditional enterprises, though by many accounts, they remained considerably more assiduous about "transmitting" the wishes of the Center to their memberships than vice versa. Nevertheless, with the 1968 NEM, KIOSZ, KISOSZ, and other interest-representation organizations lost some of their rights of control. This change amounted mostly to a procedural one:

---

[69] Ibid., 66–69, 78–79, and 232, note 94.

[70] Ibid., 116.

[71] Ibid., 205.

[72] Péter Tölgyessy, "A kisiparosság érdekstruktúrája és szervezete" ["The interest-structure and organizations of the small manufacturers"], unpublished manuscript, Budapest, 1984, quoted in Kovács, (1988), 47. On the other hand, the director of OKISZ in 1988 was also a member of the Politburo. Author's interview with Szirmai, November 1988, Budapest.

interest-representation organizations now issued non-binding "suggestions" instead of orders to their memberships (suggestions that became binding once accepted, according to the standard principle of democratic centralism). These organizations also maintained direct ties to state oversight institutions and to the Party. For instance, the Ministry of Industry exercised oversight control of KIOSZ, whose director was appointed jointly by the Ministry and the Party, and only in 1976 was "the old cadre of the apparatus who had been trained on the centralized system of tasks and commands" replaced.[73] Even after this modest liberalization of the late 1970s, the interest-representation organizations rarely openly asserted the real political-economic interests of private businesspeople; much less did they actually do public battle on their behalf where those interests came into conflict with those of the party-state apparatus.[74]

It was only the creation of new private and quasi-private enterprise forms in 1982 that really undercut the system of interest-representation that had obtained for the traditional private sector. Since the new partnership forms were instituted on the basis of *citizens' rights to engage in them*, their membership in the official interest-representation organizations was *not* mandatory; although it remained so for the traditional, pre-1982 private sector. Thus the 1982 reform presented both an immediate challenge and a long-term threat to these organizations. The challenge was whether they could attract a new, enlarged, and *voluntary* membership from among the private partnerships. The threat was that if they could not, they would become obsolete. Indeed, one close observer – a Hungarian professor of Marxism-Leninism who was also a "post-1982" entrepreneur – saw in the 1982 reform the "death" of KIOSZ and KISOSZ.[75]

In the early 1980s, KIOSZ tried to modernize itself in response to this challenge: it developed local and regional information and training centers with a view to helping small private businesses develop new products and services; in some places, it also offered legal services. However, both KIOSZ and KISOSZ "remained rigidly centralized," and still tended to rid themselves of "radical officials, who . . . demanded reform but transgressed expectations of internal behavior."[76]

Neither organization was up to the challenge presented by 1982, and very few of the new partnerships joined KIOSZ or KISOSZ. For instance, of some 11,000 GMKs registered in 1987, only about 500 joined KIOSZ. The story at OKISZ was somewhat different, at least on the surface, mostly because so many state-controlled industrial cooperatives transformed themselves into small (private) cooperatives. By 1988, close to 80 percent of OKISZ's membership consisted of small cooperatives; by 1986, five directors of small cooperatives were

---

[73] See also Pokol, "Changes in the System of Political Representation," 273.
[74] Tölgyessy, 51.
[75] Author's interview with Szirmai, November 1988.
[76] Tölgyessy, 243.

represented in OKISZ's national directorate; and at the beginning of 1988, the small cooperatives formed a commission of their own within OKISZ.[77]

Why did so few "new" entrepreneurs join the interest representation organizations, despite attempts at modernization and liberalization and despite the fact that KIOSZ, for instance, even created a separate department to try to accommodate GMKs? Simply put, the fact that these organizations remained closely tied to the state was enough to discourage many from joining, nor did new entrepreneurs easily forget the well-known historical role of these organizations in the near-extinction of Hungarian private enterprise. The memory of unsavory tactics also remained strong. KIOSZ, for instance, determined small private manufacturers' taxes, as mentioned earlier, and its methods reveal a good deal about the kind of organization it was. Before it lost its tax functions, KIOSZ forced small private manufacturers to join "tax communities" of, say, a hundred others working in the same branch of industry. Of these, a smaller number, perhaps five, would be "elected" (always with prior KIOSZ approval) as delegates. Their job would be to examine the income of the others and determine the proportion each would pay of the total tax the group owed – an amount that had been centrally pre-determined, and an approximation of which KIOSZ officials had informally communicated to the delegates. In this zero-sum process, the small manufacturers frequently turned on each other in violent meetings, since the manufacturer who understated his ability to pay forced others to bear a greater burden. KIOSZ officials often cleverly pre-selected delegates for their vulnerability to blackmail – ambitious manufacturers who had committed infractions of various regulations or even broken serious laws (for example, trafficking in stolen goods, or bringing in foreign goods without paying customs). In this way, KIOSZ increased the likelihood that it could keep them well in line and that they, in turn, could be trusted to discourage any serious show of group independence or solidarity against the institution.[78]

KIOSZ and the other interest representation organizations had changed, but not enough to attract a significant new membership on a voluntary basis. As late as 1988, even a relatively highly placed KIOSZ official stated that the organizations' biggest problem was that the "transmission" function, on the one hand, and the function of lobbying the center in favor of its memberships' needs and opinions, on the other, were "not of equal weight":

[T]he root of our current problems ... [is] that people in the highest positions at KIOSZ are people with political backgrounds rather than economic expertise, and they take the first function much more seriously than the second.[79]

---

[77] Ibid., 241–2.

[78] Author's interview with István Gábor, Budapest University of Economics, Budapest, October 1991. Gábor also pointed out that some types of solidarity did exist in the tax circles: the group might decide that someone with a larger family could afford to pay less, etc. Nevertheless, he emphasized the efficacy of KIOSZ's "salami tactics" as a method of political control.

[79] Author's interview with György Vass, KIOSZ Department Head, Budapest, September 1988.

Indeed, the individual who was president of KIOSZ in 1988 came to the organization from the Budapest district committee of the Communist Party.

If, however, the interest-representation organizations had not changed enough to attract the new entrepreneurs, they had changed sufficiently to resist the imposition of control from above. The election of KIOSZ's director in 1986, for instance, was entirely unlike others before it. For the first time in its history, many delegates to KIOSZ's national assembly of deputies had voted against this particular nominee; similarly, in one county, the membership had flatly refused (again, for the first time) to elect the official nominee for regional director.[80] Yet they had not managed to come up with a candidate of their own, either, even after a year:

It is easier to vote *against* than to organize independently, especially given the level of mistrust in KIOSZ. Because of this, the membership hardly cares who is president. It's a vicious circle.[81]

Nevertheless, a significant portion of the membership was pressuring KIOSZ to nominate a private manufacturer for president at the next national elections. To be sure, even reform-minded KIOSZ functionaries were torn about this, for obvious reasons. A small private entrepreneur could never be a member of the Central Committee, like the (then) head of OKISZ, for instance. The power of such an individual would have to come exclusively from a grass-roots lobbying effort – hardly the way that KIOSZ officials or members were accustomed to operating. Nor was there a consensus even among the membership that a small manufacturer as president could, in practice, serve their interests. Even with this question unresolved, however, KIOSZ did become somewhat more activist in the late 1980s, and successfully confronted the government for the first time on a major issue in 1988 by protesting a large increase in social security taxes that would have raised the cost of labor so much that it would have put many entrepreneurs out of business.[82]

Moreover, if purposeful change was slow, unintended change was not. Despite both fundamental continuities *and* concerted attempts to reform, private-sector expansion disrupted the business of the interest representation organizations in fundamentally *disorderly* ways. In a late 1988 interview, the head of Budapest's KIOSZ office at first declined to discuss internal political problems in his organization, preferring to discuss those of KIOSZ's companion organization, KISOSZ. There, the president, who had been nominated by the Minister of Domestic Commerce and had been elected in the usual way, was having trouble gaining cooperation on policy issues, and asked for a vote of confidence by secret ballot.

---

[80] Ibid. Vass refers to events in Csongrád County in 1988.
[81] Ibid.
[82] Ibid.

In five minutes, he lost his job! He's been looking for a new one for four months. This is the bureaucracy's nightmare.[83]

Later, having apparently exhausted his store of information about KISOSZ's problems, the director of KIOSZ's Budapest office mused aloud about his own organization. His opinions – expressed in a manner one would not have expected of a high-ranking functionary of the organization, especially one who had only reluctantly agreed to be interviewed at all – were themselves evidence of institutional disruption. KIOSZ, he said, was not an interest representation organization at all, but "parasitic" on the private sector it purported to assist.

It is clear that this rather bleak assessment of KIOSZ was based not only on the fact that the organization could not seem to attract new entrepreneurs as members, but also on the growing dissatisfactions of KIOSZ's captive membership – the traditional small manufacturers. For one thing, as mentioned earlier, the latter were allowed far fewer employees. And whereas small cooperatives, PJTs, and GMKs filed taxes on their own, the central tax authorities still determined the taxes of traditional small private manufacturers – even though KIOSZ itself had been divested of this function.

Small [traditional] manufacturers were not treated as adults; they had to file forms with all sorts of information on their activities and then the tax authorities assessed how much tax the manufacturer owed them . . . It could happen that of three people filing the same incomes, one had to pay 20,000 [forints], the other 50,000, and the third nothing.[84]

As we would expect, one result of the relatively disadvantaged circumstances of traditional businesspeople after 1982 was that many gave up their licenses and formed GMKs or other partnerships. KIOSZ officials were unhappy about this because, as one said, "people got out from under its control."[85] Thus the organization tried to attract GMKs as members, but with little success: those who *did* join were often former traditional small manufacturers who reorganized their activities to fit the guidelines for GMKs in order to take advantage of the freedom this property form afforded, but because of their earlier histories they were accustomed to having ties to KIOSZ. However, the relationship between KIOSZ and member-GMKs was an uneasy one:

These GMKs weren't dependent upon KIOSZ because their membership was voluntary, and they tried to bargain with the organization. KIOSZ was not at all used to this.[86]

A few prescient KIOSZ officials wanted the organization to become much more open to the needs of GMKs, foreseeing that the days of mandatory membership

---

[83] Author's interview with László Gellei, Director of KIOSZ's Central Budapest Office, Budapest, December 1988. (Recall Gellei from the preceding chapter when a year or so after my interview with him, he went to work for a private manufacturer.)

[84] Author's interview with Péter Gábriel, KIOSZ, Budapest, September 1991.

[85] Ibid.

[86] Ibid.

were numbered, even for the "traditional" small entrepreneurs. Unfortunately, this proposal met with indifference at the highest levels.[87] Although by the mid-1980s, manufacturers and "non-political" technicians often exercised power at lower levels of the organization, KIOSZ's top leadership remained out of touch with its "base," and significant structural changes came only after 1989.

Even OKISZ, which by 1988 seemed to have changed the composition of its membership rather dramatically, went through a serious upheaval that was representative of the broader tensions between the two kinds of cooperatives: the state-controlled cooperatives, on the one hand, and the small private cooperatives, on the other. In the early 1980s, OKISZ tried to block the formation of the small cooperatives, which nevertheless proliferated, as we have seen. But OKISZ had not been set up to direct these small cooperatives, and lacked the expertise even to advise them. Reflecting on developments in the cooperative sector from the vantage point of 1990, one of Hungary's preeminent experts on cooperatives (and member of Parliament at the time) summarized the dynamic that ensued:

The small coops snuck out from under OKISZ's authority, and OKISZ was left to direct its own traditional coops as before. A conflict ensued between the new and the old coops . . . OKISZ wasn't prepared to deal with the transformation of enterprise forms, and there was tremendous envy of the small private cooperatives, for example, on the part of traditional coop directors, who earned less money. Of course, people in general earned more in the small coops. And the directors of the state coops started to demand that they earn as much as those of the small coops. Thus began a struggle within the OKISZ apparatus . . . Then *bureaucrats* in OKISZ started to complain that if the coop *directors* were going to get paid more, then *they* should also be paid more as department heads! The new [small cooperatives] were free to criticize OKISZ, since it no longer controlled them. Soon, all concerned started to disparage OKISZ, which hadn't been the fashion, since after all, it was part of the government, an oversight agency. But coop directors complained that it was good for nothing, and so it went. It was a big upheaval . . . The whole cooperative system was falling apart.[88]

As if their internal problems were not enough, all the official interest-representation organizations soon faced outside competition. In 1987, a group of post-1982 entrepreneurs formed VOSZ. Its leaders had also run the afore-mentioned Chamber of Commerce's Department of Small Entrepreneurs, VOSZ's predecessor organization. VOSZ, in fact, was the first completely autonomous official political interest-representation organization of any kind since the inception of the socialist system in Hungary. After two years of negoti-ations with the government, the Politburo permitted VOSZ to begin its formal activities in February of 1988.[89] Its leadership and staff were composed of

---

[87] Ibid.

[88] Author's interview with Gyula Tellér, Budapest, September 1990.

[89] Author's interview with Szirmai, 1988. The organization began in Budapest with 849 voting members. See Éva Kerpel and David Young, *Hungary to 1993*, EIU London: Special Report no. 1153, November 1988.

active private entrepreneurs, and it was widely perceived as the first genuine political forum for the new business partnerships, which had not really "fit in" anywhere else.

Our MP and expert on cooperatives also had personal experience in private business, and summarized a central difference between the state's interest-representation organizations and VOSZ:

KIOSZ is made up of paid state workers. [In the early years], nobody at VOSZ [was] paid; they volunteered. At VOSZ, they all had their own jobs, but on the side, they did their politics. I'm about to leave KIOSZ and go over to VOSZ. If Palotás [the managing director] extracts some concession from the government for VOSZ, then the private firm he works for benefits. His motivation is clear![90]

KIOSZ had actually begun to cooperate with VOSZ in a number of ways by 1989. According to one KIOSZ department head, both organizations realized that their memberships were partially overlapping.

KIOSZ represents small, undifferentiated firms where one and the same person is manufacturer, bookkeeper, administrator, etc.; VOSZ represents much more differentiated and sophisticated firms. But where the interests of the entire private sector are concerned, we join forces [and] coordinate our plans because otherwise the government is the winner in a situation of 'divide et impera.'[91]

However, this cooperation had not been automatic. It required direct pressure from VOSZ, which in 1987 could not even get replies to the official letters it sent to the state transmission organizations.[92] Starting in 1987, VOSZ's well-educated, articulate, and assertive co-directors lobbied both the Ministry of Finance and Parliament on tax issues and vociferously protested regulations it deemed unreasonable. In these efforts, the organization always tried to enlist KIOSZ and other state interest-representation organizations, with varying degrees of success.[93] VOSZ also took clear and feisty positions on issues affecting the private sector, and published them in *Heti Világgazdaság*, or HVG ("*Weekly World Economy*," Hungary's *Economist*) and other national publications. Political activists trying to form new political parties in late 1988 and 1989 could not have failed to learn from VOSZ's tactics, which were unlike anything the party-state apparatus had been required to contend with until then. Opinion polls showed that VOSZ's co-director, János Palotás, quickly had become one of Hungary's most popular politicians. In a 1992 poll, he still ranked among the top three.

Finally, on January 1, 1989, under the authority of the Act on Economic Association, KIOSZ, KISOSZ, and OKISZ, like the official trade union SZOT and other associations, lost their privileged positions. None could impose

---

[90] Author's interview with Tellér, September 1990.
[91] Author's interview with Gábriel, September 1991.
[92] "Tizenkét Hónap Tükrében: Dokumentumok, levelek, állásfoglalások," ["A twelve-month retrospective: Documents, letters, editorials"] (1988), VOSZ/Népszava kiadvány: Budapest.
[93] Author's interview with János Palotás, Budapest, January 1989.

mandatory membership any longer, of course; some quickly underwent name changes and substantial organizational transformation.[94]

In 1988, academic and scientific workers formed the first autonomous labor union (TDDSZ), and the next two years saw an explosion of interest representation organizations and associations of all kinds. Then in 1991, GYOSZ, the National Association of Hungarian Industrialists, was reestablished. GYOSZ had been the most influential organization representing large private industry in Hungary until the Communist Party dissolved it in 1948.[95] We have already seen that some so-called "small private partnerships" considered themselves too large to join VOSZ (although VOSZ itself was open to all sizes and types of private business), and opted instead to join GYOSZ (for example, Futó the manufacturer from Chapter 6).

Conclusion

Although the proliferation of formal *political* interest-representation organizations began a few years prior to 1989 in Hungary, this process, like that the formation of political parties, was clearly still in its early stages, especially when compared with Poland.[96] The internal dissolution of state interest-representation organizations overseeing the private sector, however, was complete; their successor organizations would have to operate on a fundamentally different basis and face increasing competition from new, autonomous organizations.

We have seen in this chapter that the Hungarian party-state's efforts to incorporate an expanded private sector into the state-socialist system caused regulatory and institutional upheaval – despite considerable cooperation and even a degree of symbiosis between the state and private sectors. Some cases of disruption were resolved when a state budgetary institution (for example, universities) grudgingly incorporated the new private property rights of its employees. Other types of disruption were more complex and considerably harder to contain. Some required that the party-state apparatus elaborate and institutionalize new systems of regulation (for example, consistent financial regulation of firms). The authorities were altogether incapable of resolving other problems, which in the end could be addressed effectively only through the creation of new or completely restructured institutions (as in the case of interest-representation organizations). In addition, the new system of indirect personal taxation that went into effect at the beginning of 1989 also altered the relationship between the citizenry and the party-state. When the latter decided that the former would henceforth "bear the common expenses of society" through indirect, progressive taxation,

---

[94] KIOSZ, for instance, became IPOSZ, the National Association of Manufacturers.

[95] See George Deák, "The Economy and Polity in Early 20th Century Hungary: The Role of the National Association of Industrialists." Unpublished dissertation, Columbia University (1980).

[96] See, for example, Elemér Hankiss, *East European Alternatives* (Cambridge: Cambridge University Press, 1990) on the formation of informal associations in the 1980s.

it opened itself to explicit popular demands for increased civil oversight and control.[97]

These examples are indicative of a wide variety of political and economic repercussions of incorporating a growing private sector into the Hungarian state-socialist system. By explicitly legitimizing the autonomy of the private sector, the party-state opened itself to new pressures for similarly increased autonomy from state firms and state-controlled cooperatives.[98] Soon it lost all ability to control the private sector through directives transmitted downward via the interest-representation organizations. If in the late 1980s, the socialist system remained in many ways an inhospitable environment for the unfettered development of the private sector, private-sector expansion nevertheless dramatically raised the economic and political costs of purposeful discrimination by state authorities. There were some, of course, within the party-state apparatus who tried unsuccessfully until the end to restrict private enterprise through arbitrary regulation.[99]

When they formed VOSZ, and with multi-party elections still nearly three years away, private entrepreneurs became the first officially recognized, explicitly political autonomous actors since the inception of state socialism in Hungary.[100] There can be no doubt that free elections represented the culmination of many years of less obvious forms of political transformation. However, democracy requires more than multiple parties, which never by itself guarantees democratic government. Equally important are autonomous social groups with constitutionally guaranteed rights to organize politically. To be sure, VOSZ operated without explicit constitutional guarantees until 1989, but by then, the Party would not have been able to mount an effective constitutional challenge to its activities even if it had wished to do so. Because it had taken the prior step of establishing citizens' rights to form private *economic* associations, the Party

[97] Of course, the citizenry had always borne "the common expenses of society," but it had previously not been asked to do so explicitly, since the state simply withheld "tax" in the form of artificially low wages. See Varga, "The Reform of Taxation in Hungary," Appendix, 44. Because the new personal income tax system went into effect only in 1989, this particular regulatory disruption was, of course, overshadowed by many others that went far beyond demands to know how the party-state was spending tax revenues.

[98] That the actual behavior of many private firms was not – and could not realistically be – "autonomous" of the state sector is important for our story, and has been noted several times. But the point to be made here is that in principle, the Party had vigorously and publicly *sanctioned* private firms' autonomous economic action.

[99] In fact, restriction of private-sector growth was due not so much to active discriminatory regulation as to an understandable lack of confidence on the part of many potential entrepreneurs. This changed dramatically in 1990 with the fall of the HSWP and subsequent constitutional changes guaranteeing private property. Other factors limiting private-sector growth included economic recession and, as we saw in Chapter 6, continued logistical difficulties deriving from a preponderance of the state sector in the economy (one consequence of which was limited access to bank credit).

[100] In 1987 – its first year – VOSZ was officially entitled to negotiate with the government only through the Chamber of Commerce. However, its representatives sat on parliamentary committees on reform and, as already noted, its high-profile activities were in every respect autonomous.

was also bound by the constitution and socialist doctrine to permit citizens to express themselves politically through an interest-representation organization. Indeed, every year between 1982 and 1988, the Central Committee's Economic Sub-Committee noted disapprovingly that this need still remained essentially unmet.[101]

In effect, the HSWP had combined some of the tenets of liberal democracy (citizens' rights to private economic activity, guarantee of property-rights) with the socialist principle of "interest representation" for all officially sanctioned groups (hence VOSZ's unquestioned right to create an interest-representation association). In its efforts to solve "economic" problems pragmatically, the HSWP forced itself to remake not only its economic regulatory systems, but its system of *political* representation for economic actors as well.

---

[101] See, for instance, Ministry of Finance, "Előterjesztés a Miniszteri Értekezlet részére," 1983, op cit; "Jelentés (tervezet) a GPB-nak a kisüzemi termelést, a kisegitő tevékenységet végzo vállalkozások müködési tapasztalatairól," 1984 majus (announcement [planned] to the Political Economic Subcommittee of the Central Committee on the experiences of the enterprises undertaking small-scale production and helper activities); PM, "A kiegészitő és kisegitő gazdaságok működésének 1985 évi tapasztalatai" (Ministry of Finance, internal document, "1985 experiences with the completer and helper economy"; 1986 (untitled internal Ministry of Finance document reporting on the 1986 situation of the *completer* and *helper* economy); and Pénzügyminisztérium 2345/1988 Jogi Főosztály, Előterjesztés: A Gazdaságpolitikai Bizottság részére a kisüzemi gazdálkodás helyzetéröl. pp. 5 and 7. (Ministry of Finance, 2345/1988 Legal Department, Report for the Political Economic Committee (of the HSWP) on the situation of the small-firm economy.

Conclusion

Despotism, Discovery, and Surprise

No puzzle draws greater attention from social scientists than radical change in entrenched political and economic systems. The fascination is understandable. Issues of power, justice, and the conception of progress itself are implicated in large-scale, complex shifts such as the industrialization of agrarian societies and the development of capitalism. This is also the case with one of the great surprises of our time – the systemic transformation of state-socialist planned economies.

In the early 1980s, few foresaw that by decade's end the very ideology and institutions of state socialism would be exposed as brittle shells. Fewer still foresaw that a mere twenty years later, most of the nations of eastern Europe – trapped since the end of World War II within a bloc meant to isolate them from the West – would be entering a union of thoroughly western Europeans. This book has addressed the surprise itself, but has concentrated on the long transformation that preceded the collapse of the Berlin Wall, and the legacies that to this day shape the new capitalist democracies of two very different transformational leaders: Poland and Hungary. In so doing, the book sheds light on the political economy of state socialism and post-socialism and on existing theories of marketization and democratization. The book is also relevant to our current understanding of vast structural change and, more particularly, to long-standing debates on the relationship between agency and structure – a relationship best analyzed by focusing on what I have called points of permeable contact between state and society.

This last claim is crucial because, whether explicitly rendered or merely implied, scholars' views on agency and structure have strongly shaped social-scientific inquiries into the origins and development of different types of state-society relations and, more broadly, the logic and contradictions of complex political economies. State socialism is no exception. Friedrich Hayek once called state-socialist planning a "fatal conceit." He was right, of course. The ultra-rationalist presumption that an economy can be designed and ordered from above is bound to lead to nightmarish dysfunctions. But the conceit was in the end fatal for other reasons as well, reasons unforeseen both by state-socialist planners and by Hayek himself.

Economic agents, according to Hayek, generate solutions to economic problems through competition, which he conceived as a "discovery procedure" that gradually unveils the secrets of efficiency. Cooperation – one possible alternative to competition – Hayek dismissed as problematic on at least three counts. First, it requires collective agreement on both means and ends. Second, cooperation, while possible in small groups, is unrealistic on a large-scale systemic basis. Third, even if such cooperation were feasible, it still could not provide the kind of prescience required for systemic adjustment in a complex and, by extension, unpredictable economy.[1]

Putting an end to unpredictability was in fact a major objective of state-socialist systems. The plan itself represented the state's hubristic attempt at prescience, which would eliminate resource waste and, by extension, establish socialism's claim to superiority over market capitalism. But, as Hayek argued, the performance of the planned economy turned out to be dismal. And yet, in a variation on Hayek's vision, individuals living under state socialism soon found themselves involved in a discovery procedure based on complicity, trust, and mutual masking. Through these means, citizens *qua* agents created pockets of autonomy and wove them into networks that allowed them in massive numbers to circumvent economic strictures and avoid political reprisal. In Hungary, these alternative networks of production and services even penetrated the state sector, and eventually established informal cooperative relations with management. Thus, citizens radically altered the structural base – the micro-foundations – of state socialism.

To ignore this alternative discovery procedure is to assume an excessively atomistic view of communist society. Moreover, to believe that a state-socialist system could survive the ramifications of this alternative procedure unscathed is to accept a static view of state-society relations. And yet, macro-level analyses time and again fall into these traps. In 1990, for example, Mancur Olson wrote something that scholars and observers alike not too long before had believed perfectly applicable to state-socialist systems in particular and to despotic systems more broadly.

When there are no free elections and governments are able and willing to use force, political outcomes do not mainly depend on the hearts and minds of the people . . . Very often governments can be massively unpopular yet continue in power . . . Even though the aggregate benefits to the group or population of overthrowing the regime are many times the total costs, each typical individual finds that his costs of working to

---

[1] Friedrich Hayek, *The Fatal Conceit: The Errors of Socialism*, W. W. Bartley, ed. (Chicago: University of Chicago Press, 1991), 6–22. See also James Scott, *Seeing Like a State: How Growth Schemes to Improve the Human Condition Have Failed* (New Haven: Yale University Press, 1998).

overthrow an undemocratic regime are normally much greater than the benefits he would receive.[2]

This collective action problem, while very much in evidence in communist systems, turned out not to be wholly insurmountable – even on the political front. The opposition strategies deployed at great risk by Poles vividly make the point that although rational actors feared the state, their fear was not paralyzing. Citizens' informal economic activities in Hungarian and Polish societys' political-organizational innovations, to be sure, never posed the kind of direct threat that the ballot poses to discredited incumbents in a democratic regime, or the equally direct threat that a massive armed rebellion poses to a despised dictator. But each did significantly remake the system, all without a single democratic ballot cast or a single bullet fired – at least by opposition actors after 1956.

Indeed, in several cases, communist regimes themselves also contributed to the system's transformation. In Hungary, reform waves launched from above interacted with second-economy activities springing from below. Over time, this interaction created an *institutional residue* that served as a transformative resource for reformers and citizens alike. Though operating at different structural levels, reformers and citizens gradually turned, even if sometimes unwittingly, into cooperative agents. The upshot of all this was nothing less than a reformist revolution that radically altered the system's internal power relations, functional boundaries, and the very logic of identity-formation.

In the most specific terms possible, the 1982 legalization of much of the second economy granted property-rights to private entrepreneurs. This landmark legislation went into effect a full seven years before the fall of the Berlin Wall. In the time that passed between these two events, the Hungarian party-state adopted many more radical reforms that shifted *the possibility frontier of private economic activity* outward, even as most domestic players failed to recognize their long-term political ramifications. These included the gradual emergence of an entrepreneurial capitalist class – a profoundly significant development that eluded sophisticated *foreign* analysts even twenty years later.[3]

---

[2] Mancur Olson, "The Logic of Collective Action in Soviet-type Societies," *Journal of Soviet Nationalities*, 1 (Summer 1990): 9, 10–11. Cited in Jerry F. Hough, *Democratization and Revolution in the USSR, 1985–1991* (Washington DC: Brookings Institution Press, 1997), 7.

[3] David Stark, for instance, insisted even in the second half of the 1990s that the Hungarian economy was not based primarily on private ownership. Rather, he argued, an entirely new structure of "recombinant" property had emerged. This structure, far from clarifying property rights, blurred them, obscuring the line between state and private ownership. David Stark, "Recombinant Property in East European Capitalism," *American Journal of Sociology* 101 (4): 1996, 993–1027. Eric Hanley, Lawrence King, and István Tóth János showed that this argument was empirically unfounded in "The State, International Agencies, and Property Transformation in Postcommunist Hungary," *America Journal of Sociology* 108 (1) July 2002, 129–167, Nevertheless, many scholars' understanding of the Hungarian economy – and by extension their views of post-socialist development – have been shaped by Stark's thesis. Neil Fligstein, for example, claims

This odd combination of radical structural change and intersubjective myopia stemmed from the dynamics that made significant change possible in the first place. At the micro-level, individual Hungarians attained their self-seeking goals through accommodation and cooperation with the state, presumably the faithful guardian of socialist orthodoxy. At the macro-level, the state freed itself from the practical constraints of orthodoxy. It accomplished this through discursive adaptations that gutted state-socialist dogma but often left its exterior untouched. To the extent that a public sphere existed in Hungary, anyone who stood in it or looked from outside saw little more than this immutable facade.

In Poland, the state was unable to escape the constraints of dogma. Similarly, workers fixated on what they perceived to be the unjust irrationality of dogmatic policymaking. Economic management, therefore, was *the* point of contention between state and society. In fact, struggles over economic management shifted outward the possibility frontier of *political* collective action. But even as this shift occurred, the motivating preoccupations of state and society remained unresolved: the state continued to fight for unchallenged economic control, while workers in particular and Solidarity more broadly operated on the premise that the regime retained its stranglehold on the political-economic system. As in Hungary, Poles were simultaneously transforming the system and – at least before 1980 – perpetuating the illusion that it remained the same.

Because Hungarians and Poles discovered various networking solutions to the collective action problem in *practice* without cognitively grasping the full extent of the changes they were effecting, the events of 1989 perplexed governments, citizens, and analysts alike. Elster, Offe, and Preuss, however, argue otherwise.

[Since] the people of state socialist societies had *not* 'made' the breakdown of the old regime but just experienced it with the same degree of surprise and amazement as outside observers, they had remained 'the same' while the institutional shell of their society was crumbling.[4] [emphasis added]

In fact, however, Hungarians, Poles, and many other East Europeans contributed mightily to the system's breakdown, even though the breakdown was for them a nearly unimaginable possibility precisely because the system's

---

that in Hungary, "[t]he policy domains of the state that will deal directly with . . . ownership, financing and employment are still being built. Market reformers will have a difficult time producing these institutions without an indigenous entrepreneurial and capitalist class that proposes how to do so." Neil Fligstein, *The Architecture of Markets: An Economic Sociology of Twenty-First-Century Capitalist Societies* (Princeton: Princeton University Press, 2001), 89. Yet, as we have seen, many key institutions were already in place by the time of the transition, notably the Company Law of 1988 and the Association Law of 1989. Other institutional reforms followed in rapid succession during the first half of the 1990s, including bank privatization, a variety of privatization programs for the transformation of state-owned firms overseen by the State Property Agency, the reestablishment of the Budapest Stock Exchange, and the Tripartite Commission, through which management, labor, and the government negotiated state policy.

[4] Jon Elster, Claus Offe, and Ulrich K. Preuss, *Institutional Design in Post-Communist Societies* (New York: Cambridge University Press, 1998), 26.

institutional shell remained intact until the end. Even permissive signals from the Soviet hegemon were not enough to shatter this illusory integrity.[5] Hungarians and Poles may have remained the same to the extent that they did not see how much they had changed their world, but change it they did.

The Isnstitutional Residue and the Dual Transition

In the mid-1980s, economists and other observers still hoped that "Kádárization" would take hold in Poland. One regional specialist opined:

> As in Hungary after 1956 – where . . . substantial domestic reforms were introduced – the Polish upheaval in 1980–81 may bring about a similar delayed effect, and some time before the end of this decade domestic relaxation in the country will take place. . . . The prospect of Kádárization in Poland, despite all the existing obstacles, may still be possible.[6]

This same expert even argued against U.S. economic sanctions and proposed instead that aid ought to be made contingent upon reform "along the Hungarian pattern."[7] By 1984, however, it was clear that convergence through imitation was improbable at best. By then, Poland's state-society relations had been locked for decades in a tightening antagonistic hold. And by then, too, Hungary had been engaged in a prolonged process of spontaneous "privatization" from below that was typically ratified and ultimately publicly encouraged from above.[8]

Consider how these divergent legacies influenced privatization of state-owned enterprises. Hungary's long history of economic reform and precocious institutionalization of private enterprise largely spared the Hungarian state the spectacle unleashed in the 1990s by economic liberalization in the Soviet Union, where officials bent on extracting fungible assets "actively pulled apart" state institutions.[9] The Hungarian state did not share in this fate, first,

---

[5] Even in the midst of democratic elections, prominent opposition leaders in both countries expressed pessimism regarding election outcomes, and later, their shock at winning. See, for instance, Adam Michnik, "Independence Reborn and the Demons of the Velvet Revolution," in Sorin Antohi and Vladimir Tismaneanu, eds., *Between Past and Future: The Revolutions of 1989 and Their Aftermath* (New York: Central European University Press, 2000), 85.

[6] Adam Bromke, "Four Stages or Five or More? Eastern Europe in the 1980s," *Coexistence* 21 (1984): 137–165, 152, 163.

[7] Ibid.

[8] Here I refer to privatization not literally of state-assets – although *de facto* privatization of state assets did occur on a large scale in the 1980s, and private use of state equipment had always been a feature of the system – but of work-time, methods, and income streams. See, for instance, the detailed description and categorization of such "privatization" by István Kemény, "The Unregistered Economy in Hungary," *Soviet Studies* 34, no. 3 (July 1982): 349–366. I am referring also, of course, to the reform process detailed in Chapters 5 and 6 of the present book: the legalization of the second economy and the establishment of half a dozen private and quasi-private organizational forms newly available to Hungarians after January 1, 1982.

[9] Steven L. Solnick, *Stealing the State: Control and Collapse in the Soviet Union* (Cambridge: Harvard University Press, 1998), 7. To be sure, spontaneous privatization did occur in Hungary,

because the state sector had already become considerably more decentralized and flexible, and state-firm managers' ideas about their futures – and hence their perceived material interests – were far more diverse as a result of many years of protracted quasi-privatization.[10] Second, by the late 1980s some highly successful private entrepreneurs – including several who appeared in Chapter 6, but also others who operated on a far larger scale[11] – had already begun to compete with the *nomenklatura* for such assets. Finally, and perhaps most importantly, the legal infrastructure already in place to support both Hungary's indigenous private sector and its state firms attracted far more foreign investment than elsewhere in Eastern Europe. Indeed, between 1990 and 1997, Hungary absorbed approximately 50 percent of all foreign capital invested in Central Europe.[12]

The foreign currency proffered by such investors was a powerful incentive for political elites to conduct a significant portion of privatization deals on the basis of relatively open competition. In fact, private entrepreneurs played a role in making this process among the most transparent in Eastern Europe – though it was certainly not without its problems.[13]

If convergence with the Hungarian pragmatic politics of reform was improbable in 1984, it was virtually impossible for Poland by 1988–89. For one thing, in 1989, labor was far better organized and politically endowed at the state-firm level in Poland than in Hungary, even though, ironically, the

especially between 1989 and 1991. But the government gained control of the privatization process relatively quickly, imposing a variety of plans through the State Property Agency, most of which were overseen by Western auditors. Such programs, too, were open to side-payments, but not to the amassing of astronomical fortunes by large numbers of the *nomenklatura*. Author's interviews with George Holló, Senior Advisor, State Property Agency, Budapest, December 1992, and Cambridge, MA, March 1993.

[10] In this case, I refer first to the long process of official decentralization of state firms, traced in Chapter 2, and of which specific examples are also found in Chapter 6; and second, to *de facto* if not always *de jure* privatization of state-sector firms or their subsidiaries. As we also saw in Chapters 2, 6, and 7, both kinds of privatization were linked to the extension of the second economy's unofficial and, after 1982, official role in the state sector. See also Charles F. Sabel and David Stark, "Planning, Politics, and Shop-Floor Power: Hidden Forms of Bargaining in Soviet-Imposed State-Socialist Societies," *Politics and Society* 11, no. 4 (December 1982): 439–475; and David Stark, "The Micropolitics of the Firm and the Macropolitics of Reform: New Forms of Workplace Bargaining in Hungarian Enterprises," in Peter Evans, Dietrich Rueschemeyer, and Evelyn Huber Stephens, ed., *States Versus Markets in the World System* (Beverly Hills: Sage, 1985).

[11] One of these was Műszertechnika RT, a PJT (civil law partnership) established by two engineers in 1981, which had a 25 percent share of the Hungarian personal computer market and was exporting to Germany, Switzerland, and the United States and bought the remaining assets of its state counterpart. Many others are now internationally known in their respective fields: Grafisoft, Cygron Kft. and Recognita come to mind.

[12] Bartołmiej Kaminski, "Hungary's Integration into EU Markets: Production and Trade Restructuring," unpublished paper (College Park and Washington, DC: University of Maryland and World Bank), 2.

[13] On the role of private entrepreneurs in privatization, see Ákos Róna-Tas, *The Great Surprise of the Small Transformation: The Demise of Communism and the Rise of the Private Sector in Hungary* (Ann Arbor: University of Michigan Press, 1997)

state sector remained much closer to the classical bureaucratic state-socialist blueprint than its Hungarian counterpart. During much of the 1980s, workers' self-management may have been officially out of favor in Poland, but it was precisely in that decade that workers' councils attained a high profile both *de facto* and *de jure*. This hard-won presence was not to be let go easily during the transition. As one scholar writing in 1992 put it:

Employee councils continue to function, and will probably still function for a long time during the transition period, but their activism and importance must dwindle systemically. Self-management activists perceive such dangers and try to defend not the institution itself but the principle of the participation of the staffs in management. Shares in the hands of employees are to be the form of the adaptation of that principle to the conditions prevailing in the economy which is being privatized.[14]

Workers' councils in Poland did, in fact, exercise *de facto* veto power over privatization decisions, especially in the early post-transition years. They maintained a degree of influence in many enterprises, and used it to establish numerous ESOPs,[15] as well as to veto some privatization arrangements. This was obviously not the case in Hungary, where organized labor remained weak.

This book has shown that post-communist structural configurations differed from one country to the other because, whereas the potential for systemic transformation stemmed everywhere from the citizenries' alteration of state socialism's micro-foundations, the state's policy response to initiatives from below ultimately determined specific outcomes. But the book has also made another argument: the success of state-policy responses hinged in large part on major actors' capacity to enhance their ideological degrees of freedom. In this sense, the book underscored the crucial importance of the *conceptual frames, discourses, and informal political processes* that actors use to select their core conflicts and organize their modes of conflict resolution. This argument applies to the post-communist period as well. The structural inheritance of the *ancien régime* has undoubtedly shaped countries' post-communist development. But so have its more intangible legacies: the frames, discourses, and processes that continue to structure the political agenda, order debate and shape identities even in radically altered contexts of political, legal, and economic incentives, and even where elite circulation has been significant.

This claim implies, among other things, the need to re-examine contemporary understandings of legacies in transformative politics and, more specifically, their role in dual transitions and consolidations. For some analysts, the past and its legacies do matter to the political-economic development of post-authoritarian societies in general and post-communist systems in particular. For others, the past and its legacies have been overruled by new institutional arrangements and

---

[14] Barbara Gaçiarz, "Employee Self-Management in the 1980s," in Jerzy Hausner and Tadeusz Klementewicz, eds., *The Protracted Death Agony of Real-Socialism* (Warsaw: Institute of Political Studies, Polish Academy of Sciences, 1992), 121; Slay 1995; Jarosch 1994.

[15] Employee Stock Option Programs, which typically allow workers to purchase all or most of the firm's shares.

attendant sets of incentives. Both views, however, often converge on one key point: marketization and democratization, when simultaneously occurring, are likely to interfere with one another. The debate has important implications not only for the study of state socialist transformations, but also for our understanding of political-economic change more broadly.

From a comparative-historical perspective, Claus Offe outlined the contradiction he found at the core of dual transitions in post-communist Europe. With an eye on the centuries-long experience of capitalist development in the West, Offe starts from the premise that a market economy can only be created if democratic rights are held in check while the initial capital accumulation required by markets takes place. In post-communist Europe, however, this sequence was largely reversed, since it was newly democratic regimes that were called upon to marketize their economies. Thus marketization can only succeed on the basis of "strong democratic legitimation." But Offe argues that this legitimation may not be forthcoming if citizen majorities, acculturated under communism, hold neither democracy nor a market economy to be desirable.[16]

From an ahistorical starting point, collective action theorists arrive at a similarly disheartening conclusion. On this theory, pressure groups in particular and the electorate more broadly are rent-seekers who "lobby, bribe, strike, and vote" to persuade politicians to distribute resources their way. To avoid punishment by dissatisfied rent-seekers – as when voters take revenge by ejecting unreliable incumbents – politicians pursue a targeted distribution strategy. They allocate resources to concentrated, highly organized interest groups and to party activists who can mobilize "external constituencies whose rewards may be delayed and whose support is not ensured." Furthermore, animated by the imperative of political survival, politicians forestall liberal reform and "perpetuate state intervention" in order to draw on the resources they need to buy rent-seekers' support.[17] In this context, new democracies can implement market reform only if three conditions are met. First, a good portion of the net benefits of reform accrue to powerful coalitions – the winners – capable of supporting reform politicians. Second, politicians are either shielded from losers bent on punishment, or losers simply have no punitive capacity. And third, politicians can make side-payments to losers.[18]

The Russian debacle of the 1990s and the Balkans' implosion appear at first glance to confirm Offe's pessimism. Similarly, collective-action theory seemed vindicated when communist parties returned to power in Hungary (1993) and in Poland (1994) – the two countries that, at the time, seemed to be advancing the fastest in post-socialist economic restructuring. But *contra* Offe's legacy-based

---

[16] Claus Offe, *Varieties of Transition: The East European and East German Experience* (Cambridge, MA: MIT Press, 1997), 41.

[17] Beverly Crawford, "Post-Communist Political Economy," in Beverly Crawford, ed., *Markets, State and Democracy: The Political Economy of Communist Transformation* (Boulder, CO: Westview Press, 1995), 4.

[18] Ibid., 5.

perspective, David Bartlett has argued that democratization need not release anti-market forces. He found that, if anything, democratization in Hungary actually diminished popular aversion to market reform.[19] Moreover, in contradistinction to the collective-action problem presumably posed by net losers, others have suggested that it is not the net losers but the "earliest and biggest" winners who engage in selective obstructionism of economic reform, suspending the process in a state of "partial-reform equilibrium" that allows them as privileged insiders selfishly to exploit their asset-stripping opportunities, arbitrage capabilities, and monopolistic positions.[20]

The inconclusiveness of debates about the precise connection between dual transformations and the political economy of post-communist reform has helped render the focus on reform suspect. Some have even argued that focusing on the political economy of reform not only reduces politics to allocative jockeying and arbitration, but also obscures prior, more fundamental struggles over sovereignty.[21] And indeed, to the extent that collective action accounts ignore the latter, they can be justly indicted on charges of reductionism. But focusing on reform politics is not *per se* reductionist. The fact that Poland "caught up" to Hungary in private-sector development and growth in the 1990s, for instance, does nothing to lessen the significance of the foregoing comparative analysis, which employed the analytic lens of the states' relationship with the private sphere under socialism to focus more sharply on fundamental struggles.

Reform struggles and their outcomes, in fact, help account for important differences in the countries' economies that persisted throughout most of the crucial decade of the 1990s, as reflected in key *per capita* indicators. For the period 1990–2002, Hungary vastly outperformed Poland in cumulative *per capita* FDI, and came in second in the region only to the Czech Republic (see Table C.1). As for average *per capita* GDP, even as late as 1997–2000 it was significantly higher in Hungary (US $4,641) than in Poland (US $3,992).[22] More importantly, the politics of reform is not just about who gets what, or how. Reform politics is also about contestations over programmatic visions and authority – contestations that implicate actors internal to the state, as well as the state in relation to society.

One major question that arises at the dawn of the twenty-first century, then, is whether understanding communist legacies and post-communist collective-action problems provides us with any theoretical or analytical purchase on the social-scientific study of dual transformations, and more profoundly, on the relationship between agency and structure in politics. This book argues that

---

[19] David Bartlett, *The Political Economy of Dual Transformations: Market Reform and Democratization in Hungary* (Ann Arbor: The University of Michigan Press, 1997), 2–3.

[20] Joel Hellman, "Winners Take All: The Politics of Partial Reform in Post-Communist Transitions," *World Politics*, 50, no 2 (January, 1988): 204

[21] David Woodruff, *Money Unmade: Barter and the Fate of Russian Capitalism* (Ithaca: Cornell University Press, 1999).

[22] Averages calculated from the Economist Country Briefings, Hungary and Poland economic data (Economist Intelligence Unit, May 4, 2001), available at http://www.economist.com/countries.

TABLE C.I *FDI in Central and Eastern Europe, 1990–2002 (U.S. $)*

	Cumulative FDI	Per capita cumulative FDI
Croatia	6,956	1,568
Czech Republic	35,186	3,413
Estonia	2,535	1,864
Hungary	22,534	2,253
Latvia	3,040	1,336
Lithuania	3,540	1,024
Poland	38,552	997
Slovak Republic	9,636	1,784
Slovenia	3,437	1,722
CEE and Baltic states	118,461	1,774

Source: Transition Report Update 2003 (London: European Bank for Reconstruction and Development, 2003).

there is much to be gained from an approach that takes into account *both* the power of legacies and the post-transition dynamics of collective action. But it also argues that we can do this only if we first grapple with the *formation* of those legacies and the *nature* of collective action under the *ancien régime*. As Ken Jowitt cautions, to dismiss the legacies of communism would be to repeat the grave "intellectual mistake" made by the Leninists who, after 1948, rejected their own Eastern European heritages as mere remnants of an old and irrelevant era.[23]

There is also the danger that we buy into the "vacuum" fallacy – the idea that in the struggle between state and society, the one so thoroughly destroyed the other that no usable parts were left behind.[24] The evidence presented in this book shows there was no vacuum in the cases at hand because extensive informal institution-building took place under communism. In Poland, as in Hungary, some "alternative" institution-building arose from within the state sector, but far more arose from "below" than from "above," emerging from shop-floors and among students and intellectuals. Unlike in Hungary, however, much of it was in direct and explicit opposition to the institutions of state

---

[23] Ken Jowitt, "The Leninist Legacy," in Valdimir Tismaneanu, ed., *The Revolutions of 1989* (New York: Routledge, 1999), 215.

[24] It is from this perspective, for instance, that one scholar goes so far as to claim that "controlled liberalization" was impossible in post-communist systems because state socialism's attack on civil society precluded pact-making between elites and society; and as a result, no "organized body existed that was capable, so to speak, of disciplining its troops." John Hall, "After the Vacuum: Post-Communism in the Light of Tocqueville," in Crawford, ed., *Markets, State and Democracy*, 83, 85. But this book has shown that a kind of informal "pact-making" was pervasive. No "organized body" was necessary; and in fact, in such a rigid system, might actually have disadvantaged social actors.

socialism, and enjoyed the backing and support at crucial junctures of the Catholic Church – by any standard the most independent and powerful church in the Eastern bloc. In Hungary, meanwhile, informal institutions and networks emerged, sometimes at the very heart of the state apparatus. Members of an influential pro-market network, as we saw in Chapter 5, could be found in the Ministry of Finance, research institutes, and elsewhere. Just as importantly, the settlement of conflicts between them and hard-liners typically took the shape of economic reforms, some of which were partially revocable, most of which were not.

The *institutionalization* of property-rights implemented by the Hungarian regime in 1982 is at the center of this book's analysis of Hungary in part because – though hardly noticed by analysts at the time – it was as momentous as it was irreversible.[25] Property-rights, once given by law and publicly trumpeted, are difficult, if not impossible, to reverse without a new round of violent nationalization. Thus, institutional change may – and if it is profound enough, almost certainly will – establish a new equilibrium that proves as difficult to change as the set of institutions preceding it. Institutions, as Peter Gourevitch argues, "obviously affect the struggle for power: for a specified production profile, different institutional arrangements promote different outcomes." But, he continues, "culture also matters: actors rarely understand a situation solely of itself . . . [and] variables cannot be lifted out of social context and fired off as explanatory cannon. *How* institutions matter depends on *who* is trying to use them."[26] In the more specific language of this study, the relationship between agency and structure reflects the fact that institutions change partly in response to the conceptual frames of those who use them to achieve their ends. The political-discursive struggles preceding the 1982 reform in Hungary illustrate this clearly, and cast in sharp relief the strikingly different conceptual frames of Polish state and opposition actors of 1980–81 – an additional reason for this particular choice of focus.

Another finding of this book is also related to our understanding of agency and structure: the possibility of institutional change is partly contingent on the political discourse that pre-commits the actors who repeatedly use it in an effort to legitimize their ideas and their goals. Such a discourse can either limit or open up degrees of flexibility in policymaking. In Poland, for example, the Socialists' fear of, and uneven discourse concerning the private sphere sharply limited their ability to promote either its institutional diversification or links with the state sector. And despite the fact that, because of agriculture, Poland had the largest private sector in the state-socialist world, not even the most

[25] Naturally, this is not to suggest that by itself the 1982 reform would have been sufficient to bring about full system-change. Although pivotal, we saw in Chapter 2 that several important reforms preceded it, and in Chapter 7 that it was followed by numerous other radical reforms (for example, bank decentralization, the Company Law and the Law on Associations).

[26] Peter Alexis Gourevitch, "Breaking with Orthodoxy: The Politics of Econonomic Policy Responses to the Depression of the 1930s," *International Organization* 38, no. 1 (Winter 1984): 95–129. [emphasis added]

reform-minded among pre-transition Polish leaders enjoyed the degrees of freedom in policymaking needed for a Hungarian-style embrace of private entrepreneurship, much less for constructing the legal infrastructure that a sophisticated private sector requires in order to advance. We saw, of course, that the Polish government's narrowing degrees of freedom in economic policymaking more generally was first and foremost the result of its profoundly adversarial relationship with workers, farmers, and intellectuals. This prevailing relationship between state and society, in turn, made it even more difficult for the Polish government to negotiate the economic obstacle course of the 1980s that all relatively open trading economies within the state-socialist world faced to one degree or another.

Paying careful attention to the legacies of state socialism is also warranted because these legacies structure post-communist collective-action dynamics, which we must firmly grasp if we are to avoid the dangers of a purely elitist approach to politics. To be sure, elites play a key role everywhere.[27] State-socialist elites were no different, and neither are the elites of the post-communist era. But millions of individuals – workers and farmers, producers and consumers – spontaneously reshaped a number of state-socialist economies, and millions, too, used the past to navigate the transition and beyond. As Elster, Offe, and Preuss have observed about the uncertain moment of transition:

[A]s individual actors made their transition from the old to the new, all of them retained and kept hold of their skills, their positions and the material resources attached to them, their formal and informal ties to other agents, their memories of their own and other peoples' past actions, their habits and frames, feelings of guilt and pride, loyalties and hostilities, fears and hopes – *all of which can now be employed in the struggle for social power and the defense against that power.*[28] [emphasis added]

Although this broad-strokes depiction of the transition environment may not capture the loss of position and resources that some (especially top) elites experienced in Hungary, Poland and in several other countries, it does indicate the importance of a synthetic understanding of communist legacies and new collective-action dynamics. More specific findings regarding dual transitions point in a similar direction. Kullberg and Zimmerman, for example, have shown that citizens' support for democratic institutions is not solely based on macro-economic performance. It also matters crucially whether or not citizens are in "possession of economic rights and genuine economic opportunity." It depends, in other words, on the economic opportunity structure.[29]

---

[27] See John Higley and Jan Pakulsi et al., eds., *Post-Communist Elites and Democracy in Eastern Europe* (London: Macmillan Press, 1998).

[28] Elster, Offe, and Preuss, *Institutional Design in Post-Communist Societies* (New York: Cambridge 1998) 26.

[29] Judith S. Kullberg and William Zimmerman, "Liberal Elites, Socialist Masses and Problems of Russian Democracies," *World Politics*, 51, no. 3 (April 1999): 327.

The economic-opportunity structure is partly shaped by government policy. For example, the liberalizing measures of Rakowski's December 1988 reforms notwithstanding, Polish citizens wishing to start a legitimate private firm *de novo* did not enjoy nearly the range of institutional choices, legal support, or potential financial assistance as their counterparts in Hungary.[30] As late as 1991, and despite impressive growth, the legal private sector in Poland still had to "jump through hoops."[31] But the economic-opportunity structure is also shaped by relevant legacies. Two stand out: one is the informal institutions that began to show themselves more clearly after formal institutions crumbled. These informal institutions included the socio-economic and political practices and the conflict-resolution modes that each country developed during the state-socialist period. The other legacy is the structural-economic effects of those institutions, such as the degree of institutionalization of property rights, the suppleness of markets, the sophistication of private enterprise, and regnant notions of public obligation in the face of unemployment and income inequality. These are some of the factors that account for the varying degrees of distress of state-socialist economies at the time of regime collapse. Thus, Romania was not Poland, and Poland was not Hungary.

Nor were their transitions uniform. In Hungary's positive-sum transformation to a market economy, it was sometimes hard to distinguish between winners and losers.[32] In Poland, on the other hand, a large "reserve army" of marginal peasants enjoyed "private farmer" status under state socialism, but were prevented from developing their human or material capital, and consequently years later stood to lose dramatically with the country's accession to the European Union (EU).

Of course, both Poland and Hungary now have thriving private sectors. The lion's share of GDP is privately produced, and along with numerous countries in Central Europe, both have consolidated their democratic capitalist systems. But these "macro facts" obscure an important connection between markets as institutions and their social underpinnings, on the one hand, and the distinctive characteristics of the new democracies, on the other. First, the middle class in these countries is not yet the middle class of Western Europe or the United States. Difficult as it is to define any middle class, given its breadth and diversity in industrialized democracies, the West European and American middle classes

---

[30] Financial support, as we saw in Chapter 6, was difficult for Hungarian entrepreneurs to obtain as well, since banks had little incentive to lend to private entrepreneurs. Nevertheless, it was possible and perfectly legal for private entrepreneurs to obtain bank financing, and the Ministry of Finance even sponsored several funding competitions for new entrepreneurs.

[31] Janine R. Wedel, ed., *The Unplanned Society: Poland During and After Communism* (New York: Columbia University Press, 1992), 126.

[32] Aside, that is, from those who typically lose in other reforming economies, whether state socialist or capitalist: the elderly and others on fixed incomes, and those who were dependent on state transfers.

have strong, positive identities that are largely lacking in Eastern Europe. As the sociologist Ákos Róna-Tas explains:

Before Communist rule, a large part of the Romanian middle class was of foreign ethnic origin – Germans, Jews, or Hungarians. Bulgaria had no strong middle stratum. In Poland, just as in Hungary, the middle stratum was recruited from the large lesser nobility, as well as from ethnic Germans and Jews. The non-ethnic members of the middle class in all countries were often employed by the state in some bureaucratic function. Czechoslovakia had the strongest middle class, although an important part of it was of German origin. All over Eastern Europe these middle classes suffered enormously during and after World War II. The massacre of the Jews, the Polish resistance, and the postwar expulsion of ethnic Germans decimated the ranks of these middle layers. The newly formed Communist states declared war on the bourgeoisie . . . Today in East-Central Europe the principal rival of middle class identity is ethnic nationalism. Ethnic nationalism serves the same unifying function as the concept of the middle class, as it can bring various groups under the umbrella of a shared identity.[33]

It will take time before an ethos of "middle-class liberalism" is strong enough in either Hungary or Poland that it cannot be shaken by competing ideologies. Hungary, however, may have some advantages in this respect. Partly as the result of the private sector's deeper roots there, and particularly because of its better-developed legal infrastructure – itself in part an artifact of private sector development, as we have seen – the country received much higher levels of FDI than Poland through the 1990s,[34] and as previously mentioned, higher still on a *per capita* cumulative basis for the period 1990–2002 (Table C.1).

Some portion of the performance differentials in FDI and, as we saw earlier, in *per capita* income, are likely attributable to Hungary's earlier and deeper commitment to an indigenous and institutionally diverse private sector.[35] It is reasonable to infer this for at least two reasons. First, a segment of the population had a longer period of time in which to grow their businesses; to leave state sector employment for higher wages in the private sector; or even more commonly, to take part-time jobs in the private sector to supplement their primary incomes. The second reason involves the feedback mechanisms at work between foreign investment and the private sector. The presence of a wider background economy of small and medium-sized private firms able to serve as sub-contractors and suppliers to large multinationals establishing themselves in Hungary played a role in attracting such a relatively large share of FDI in Eastern Europe (about half of all foreign capital invested in Central Europe

---

[33] Ákos Róna-Tas, "Post-Communist Transition and the Absent Middle Class in East-Central Europe," in Victoria Bonnell, ed., *Identities in Transition* (Berkeley: University of California Press, 1996), 42–43.

[34] FDI inflows have since increased in Poland.

[35] Of course, any reliable measurement of the income effects of the two countries' different paces and degrees of private sector development under state socialism is beyond the scope of this study; nor is it central to the arguments made here.

between 1990 and 1997).[36] This role was secondary only to the country's well-developed legal infrastructure, as previously mentioned. The result was that in mid-1998, Hungary had attracted $18 billion, and – it bears repeating – on a *per capita* basis, Hungary attracted the highest levels of FDI of all transition economies, *including China*.[37] The "second generation" foreign-owned firms, in turn, appear on average to export more and to be more profitable than domestic Hungarian firms, and played a key role in Hungary's export-led recovery, which began in 1994 with the first increase in real GDP since 1989.[38]

Chapter 4 showed that private economic activity *per se* prior to regime change was equally important in Poland as in Hungary; indeed, counting private agriculture, we saw that Poland had by far the largest private sector of all state-socialist countries (See Table C.2 and Table C.2a). We also saw, however, that the government's treatment of the Polish private sector – while at times during the 1980s more liberal than in most Eastern bloc countries besides Hungary – was generally hostile, and mirrored the conflicts that defined Polish state-society relations.

It should be obvious from the foregoing analysis that Poland's position relative to Hungary's on FDI or any other vector of transition and economic transformation does not result from any dearth of talent or vision on the part of its post-transition policymakers, who included some remarkably able and well-known figures. (If post-transition policy mistakes were determinative, Hungarian policymakers blundered enough that, arguably, the country's relative roles might be reversed.) This book, then, should not be read as a scorecard, unless perhaps in the narrow sense, for instance, of Poland's relative "failure" to develop a deeper, institutionally richer, and better integrated private sphere before 1990, or of Hungary's relative "failure," prior to the regime transition, to develop a civil society as robust and broad as Poland's. The point here is that different political-economic outcomes are at least as much consequences of each country's institutional legacies and state-society relations as of recent institutional and policy choices.

From this perspective, then, any assessment of a country's degree of success in, say, privatization of state enterprises, involves much more than numbers of firms privatized. Among others factors to be considered are the depth of corruption involved (spontaneous privatization, or *nomenklatura* privatization, occurred everywhere in Eastern Europe, but to different degrees and for varying lengths of time); revenues generated from privatization and the use to which states put them; and last, but certainly not least, the type and quality of corporate governance that results from different privatization schemes. In both

---

[36] Bartołomiej Kamiński, "Hungary's integration into EU Markets: Production and Trade Restructuring" (College Park and Washington DC: University of Maryland and World Bank, 2002), 2.

[37] Paul Marer, "Economic Transformation, 1990–1998," in Aurel Braun and Zoltan Barany, *Dilemmas of Transition: The Hungarian Experience* (New York: Rowman & Littlefield, 1999), 188; and on other factors that help to account for Hungary's popularity as a destination for FDI, see 189.

[38] Kamiński, 9; Marer, 189.

TABLE C.2 *Organizational breakdown of economic entities: Corporations with legal entity – Hungary, 1988–2004*

	1988	1989	1990	1991	1992	1993	1994	1995 Registered	1995 Active*	1996 Registered	1996 Active	1997 Registered	1997 Active*	1998 Registered	1998 Active*
State-owned enterprises**	2,378	2,400	2,363	2,233	1,733	1,130	821	761	425	683	335	655	262	619	141
Companies with legal entity	919	5,191	19,401	42,695	59,363	75,654	91,229	106,245	88,455	125,940	107,589	147,388	127,961	162,588	138,014
Cooperatives	7,414	7,546	7,641	7,766	8,229	7,694	8,252	8,321	4,879	8,362	4,858	8,330	4,989	8,230	5,668
Agricultural	1,333	1,333	1,348	1,421	1,388	–	2,038	2,105	1,952	2,119	1,919	2,131	1,902	2,125	1,808

TABLE C.2 (cont'd.)

	1999		2000		2001		2002		2003		2004***	
	Registered	Active*	Registered	Active	Registered	Active*	Registered	Active*	Registered	Active*	Registered	Active*
State-owned enterprises	506	93	411	54	341	49	298	26	270	27	256	17
Companies with legal entity	165,307	140,791	171,495	148,495	177,424	154,153	186,744	162,232	197,667	175,749	210,367	180,751
Cooperatives	8,191	5,892	7,516	5,922	7,074	5,715	6,768	5,392	6,790	5,546	6,590	5,242
Agricultural	2,252	1,932										

* Active as of December 31.

** After 1997, categorized as "Economic organization bound to reform."

*** Third quarter.

Source: Hungarian Central Statistical Office, Statistical Yearbook of Hungary (1991, 1994, 1995, 1998, 1999); 2000–2004 data from CSO website (http://www.ksh.hu).

TABLE C.2a *Organizational breakdown of economic entities: Corporations with legal entity – Poland, 1990–2004*

	1990	1991	1992	1993	1994	1995	1996	1997	1998	1999	2000	2001	2002	2003*	2004**
State-owned enterprises	8,453	8,228	7,245	5,924	4,955	4,357	3,847	3,369	2,906	2,599	2,268	2,054	1,951	1,736	1,306
Municipal enterprises	32	741	542	647	564	481	444	265	–	–	–	–	–	–	–
Commercial law companies	36,267	53,771	69,907	83,283	95,017	104,922	115,739	126,465	136,497	146,859	159,660	177,085	196,681	208,753	220,162
Other companies	978	703	894	945	994	1,031	1,237	1,385	1,507	1,561	–	–	–	–	–
Cooperatives	18,575	18,949	19,372	19,746	19,816	19,822	19,868	19,775	19,638	19,328	19,011	18,812	18,682	18,548	18435

* 12 October 2003.

** 12 October 2004 from : Central Statistical Office, *Statistical Yearbook of the Republic of Poland* Table 39, National Economy Entities, end of quarter.

Source: Central Statistical Office, *Statistical Yearbook of the Republic of Poland* (1994–2000).

Poland and Hungary, as elsewhere, the results in these and other aspects of privatization were clearly influenced by prevailing macro-economic circumstances, but even more crucially, by the formal and informal institutions and practices left in place by each country's history of reform under state socialism. This is in part because, as the prominent Polish economist Włodzimierz Brus explains, under the old system,

> . . . state assets . . . were seldom . . . properly assigned to a well-defined public entity with clearly delineated property rights, but instead could be shifted between and by various layers of the organizational structure of economic management supervised by corresponding ranks of the communist party hierarchy.[39]

While this was true everywhere in the state-socialist world, by the late 1980s the lines of authority and the distribution of effective property rights were considerably more confused and contested in Poland than in Hungary – partly because of the residual power of workers' councils there, and partly because of union strength and proliferation. (In the 1990s, sometimes as many as three unions were represented in Polish state firms; consequently, privatization was often "a scene of bitter contest.")[40] In contrast, recall from Chapters 2 and 7 the "dominant role of enterprise management" in Hungary, which emerged from the long history and relative strength of "pro-managerial economic reform."[41]

In Poland after 1990, many state enterprises filed requests for "commercialization" rather than privatization, in an effort to "solve the dilemma over the running of the enterprise." Commercialization was frequently a code word for decentralization and self-management, and self-management bodies and union councils often tied the hands of management. The three together were sometimes called the "three corners of the Bermuda triangle."[42] It is not surprising, then, that privatization of state enterprises moved relatively slowly in Poland. In 1997, about a third of Poland's 16 million workforce still worked in the state sector (see Tables C.2 and C.2a for an organizational breakdown of firms in Hungary and Poland, and Table 3.2 for sectoral employment in the latter).[43]

---

[39] Włodzimierz Brus, in Yilmaz Akyüz, Detlef Kotte, András Köves, and László Számuely, eds., *Privatization in the Transition Process: Recent Experiences in Eastern Europe* (Geneva: United Nations 1994), 47.

[40] Béla Greskovits, "Hunger Strikers, the Unions, the Government and the Parties: A Case Study of Hungarian Tranformation – Conflict, the Social Pact and Democratic Development" (manuscript, Budapest: Central European University, 1994), 10, and Grzegorz Ekiert and Jan Kubik, "Collective Protest and Democratic Consolidation in Poland, 1989–93" (Princeton: Princeton University Center of International Studies, Pew Papers on Central European Reform and Regionalism, No. 3), 22.

[41] George Blazyca, review of Jerzy Hausner, Bob Jessop, and Klaus Nielsen, eds., *Stategic Choice and Path-Dependency in Post-Socialism* (Cheltenham: Edward Elgar 1995), in *Europe-Asia Studies* 48, no 6 (1996): 1239.

[42] Ciechoncinska, 223.

[43] See *Poland: International Economic Report* 1997/98 (Warsaw: World Economy Research Institute, 1998), 94. For a more general comparative assessment of privatization and other instituitonal reforms, see Paul Marer. "Economic Transformation, 1990–1998" in Aurel Braun and

Models of Democracy

As we have seen, Hungary and Poland developed markedly different patterns of core conflict-resolution during the communist period. These patterns seemed, however, to reverse as the system's formal structures began to collapse. After decades of both overt and covert confrontation between broad sectors of Polish society and the authorities, the 1989 roundtable negotiations appeared to herald the end of confrontational politics. Similarly, in Hungary, the opposition seemed to abandon its initial preference for compromise with the leadership, opting instead for fully competitive elections – a move rejected by the better organized and much stronger Polish opposition.[44]

But as any student of democratic development in *Western* Europe knows, transition-based theorizing about consolidation that ignores pre-transition history can be a dangerous pitfall. Equally so in both Poland and Hungary, where as the transition progressed, long-standing patterns of confrontation reemerged. Once the Polish negotiations achieved their immediate goal of re-legalizing Solidarity and making concessions to other groups, participating actors saw no reason to extend the compromise moment beyond the procedures necessary to ensure the implementation of the roundtable itself.[45] Similarly, Hungarian politics quickly returned to a pattern of pragmatic compromise more closely resembling that of the 1963–1988 period.

In the early 1990s, different models of consolidated democracies began to emerge. Elsewhere I have described Poland's model as basically *confrontational-pluralist*, and its Hungarian counterpart as a *compromise-corporatist* model.[46] These classifications are more finely grained than the commonly available categories of newly consolidated democracies, which typically distinguish only between presumably homogenous clusters of stable, essentially consolidated democracies (for example, the Czech Republic, Hungary, Poland, Slovakia, Slovenia, and the Baltics),[47] and highly problematic camps (Albania, Bulgaria, Romania, Russia, and most of the former Yugoslavia). The cases of Poland and Hungary show that there is much more to be said about the way new democracies actually work. Actors, if they are to approach emerging economic and political opportunity-structures rationally, must craft effective blends of inherited resources and novel solutions to collective-action problems. In so doing,

Zoltán Bárány, *Dilemmas of Transition: The Hungarian Experience* (New York: Rowman & Littlefield 1999), pp. 157–201.

[44] László Bruszt and David Stark, "Remaking the Political Field in Hungary: From the Politics of Confrontation to the Politics of Competition," in Ivo Banac, ed., *Eastern Europe in Revolution* (Ithaca: Cornell University Press 1992), 21–23.

[45] On the calculations of Solidarity leaders see Jan Gross, "Poland: From Civil Society to Political Nation," in Ivo Banac, ed., *Eastern Europe in Revolution* (Ithaca: Cornell University Press, 1992).

[46] Anna Seleny, "Old Political Rationalities and New Democracies: Compromise and Confrontation in Hungary and Poland," *World Politics* 51 (July 1999).

[47] Rupnik sees a tripartite classification, with the Balkans and Russia in separate categories. Jacques Rupnik, "The Postcommunist Divide," *Journal of Democracy*, 10, no.1 (January 1999): 57–62.

they cannot help but bring to bear upon themselves and each other the formal and informal resources accumulated under the *ancien régime*, including the concepts and discourses that frame their suspicions and aspirations – all of which, as Elster, Offe, and Preuss assert, *can be employed in the struggle for social power and the defense against that power.*[48]

Actors' combination of legacy-based resources and political innovation in the face of collective-action problems translates into distinctive institutional-political democratic alloys. For much of the period since 1990, Poland's *confrontational-pluralist* model of consolidation was characterized by high levels of political mobilization, contentious party competition around several overlapping, deep ethical-ideological cleavages, relatively low levels of elite consensus, and a moralistic political discourse. The Hungarian *compromise-corporatist* model of consolidation was, for much of the same period, characterized by low levels of political mobilization, relatively high levels of elite consensus and bargaining, and a generally "economistic" or pragmatic political discourse.[49]

Protest actions, especially by unions, and the direct confrontation of the state by societal actors, became the hallmark of democratic Polish politics in the early to mid-1990s.[50] (At the start of the new millennium, the degree of unionization was still significantly higher in Poland than in Hungary.)[51] Hungary, on the other hand, was relatively free of such activity until the end of the decade, when the governing coalition of center-right and right-wing parties headed by FIDESZ explicitly espoused a more confrontational ideology and pushed for a more clearly demarcated two-party "British" system.[52] Yet fifteen years after the transition, following a major shakeup within the Socialist Party that amounted to an internal "coup," Hungarian politics remains among the most stable in the region.[53]

---

[48] Elster, Offe, and Preuss, *Institutional Design in Post-Communist Societies*, 26.

[49] During the May 1998 election campaign, as in the previous two election cycles since 1989, other strains of moralistic politics more similar to the Polish could be heard in Hungary. As discussed later, this trend has become somewhat more pronounced since then. Similarly, one finds myriad examples of political compromise in everyday Polish politics, as well as a few more dramatic ones: the original political compromise of the 1989 Roundtable Agreements, Adam Michnik's rapprochement with General Jaruzelski, and so on. Thus my characterization is intended only as shorthand for describing overall trends in the political development of the two countries.

[50] Grzegorz Ekiert and Jan Kubik, *Rebellious Civil Society: Popular Protest and Democratic Consolidation in Poland, 1989–93* (Ann Arbor: University of Michigan Press, 1999).

[51] In 2000, 61 percent of employees were in unions in Poland, compared with 40 percent in Hungary. See *Transition Report 2000* (London: European Bank for Reconstruction and Development), 99.

[52] Yet on an index of measuring polarization in Hungary between 1994 and 1998 and in Poland between 1993 and 1998, Hungary scored 11.4 compared with Poland's 31.8. See Timothy Frye, "The Perils of Polarization: Economic Performance in the Post-Communist World," *World Politics* 54 (April 2002), 335.

[53] Lehman Brothers/Eurasia Group ranks the country as the most stable in the region, for instance. See Lehman Brothers/Eurasia Group Stability Index, *Stability Summary and Outlook* (New York: January 2003).

Despite some evidence of greater convergence in recent years, other features of Polish and Hungarian democracy in the 1990s support characterizing them as *conflictual-pluralist* and *compromise-corporatist* models of consolidation: among them, the role of the courts, the informal rules of legislative-judicial interaction, and the two countries' constitution-making processes more broadly. Indeed, some of Poland's most intractable core conflicts are enshrined in the body of the Polish Constitution, and the deeply embedded *Us vs. Them* cleavage evident in final debates on the constitution can also be seen in the ongoing debates over "decommunization," a concept almost never invoked in Hungarian politics until the late 1990s, and then seemingly rejected by voters in 2002. Attitudes toward lustration and former communists were also clearly mirrored in these different models of political interaction.[54]

Another good illustration of the countries' contrasting democratic models is the nature of party competition and coalition-building. Hungarian political elites have tended to split the difference and find compromise solutions. In Poland, on the other hand, core political conflicts have been considerably clearer and deeper, making stable alliances between ideological and historical opponents impossible even in the 2001 parliamentary elections.

Markedly different conceptual frames, political discourses, and governing styles also predominated through much of the 1990s. Polish political elites often showed themselves to be consummate activists – "maximalists" ready to wage political battles and to emphasize the "zero sum" nature of conflicts, drenching political action in meaning and symbol, creating a "moralistic" political discourse, often with strong religious overtones. Moreover, post-transition Polish politics were highly personalized, and in the mid-1990s, survey respondents tended to favor "a strong leader, while Hungarians tended to believe in strong *government*."[55] In 2001, surveys showed that 33 percent of Poles – the highest percentage in the region – *including* Russia and Romania – favored an authoritarian leader, compared with only 17 percent of Hungarians (see Table C.3).[56]

Since the Roundtable Agreements of 1989 and through most of the 1990s, party politics in Poland was indicative of a "broader process of re-polarization" between neo-liberalism and state welfarism, on the one hand, and between "confessional and secular visions of political order," on the other.[57] As Krzysztof Jasiewicz showed, however, it is the latter cleavage that explained the frequent changes of government in Poland during the 1990s. Between 1992

54 For more detail, see Seleny, "Old Political Rationalities in New Democracies."

55 Mira Marody, "Three Stages of Party System Emergence in Poland." Manuscript (Warsaw: Institute for Social Studies, University of Warsaw, 1994), 2–4; and author's interview, Warsaw, November 1994.

56 New Europe Barometer 2001, http://www.cspp.strath.ac.uk/.

57 Krzysztof Jasiewicz explains that this cleavage overlaps with others, for example, nationalist vs. pro-Western orientations, in *The Woodrow Wilson Center East European Studies Newsletter*, March–April 1997.

TABLE C.3 *Percentage favoring an authoritarian leader*

Poland	33
Czech Republic	13
Romania	32
Hungary	17
Russia	31

Source: New Europe Barometer (2001).

and 1997, in fact, polarization on the religious/secular dimension intensified more rapidly than on the neo-liberal/state-welfare dimension.[58] In Hungary, these cleavages were far less salient in national politics during the same period, and have not been core political conflicts – even though the acrimony of the 2002 elections suggests that such cleavages can at least temporarily be reactivated even in a country where they had weakened long before the elections of 1990.

The lower intensity of political cleavage in Hungary can also be inferred from the stability of governments. In May 1998, Hungarians elected their third post-1989 democratic government without incident, the previous two having served out their terms without serious parliamentary upsets. During the same period, Poland had seven governments. After the Polish Roundtable Agreements and the first, partially contested elections, party fragmentation became endemic to party formation as Solidarity split apart. Hungary, by contrast, saw little fragmentation of its main parties in the 1990s. Moreover, sociological research shows that the cleavage structure of Hungarian politics was indistinct in this period, and the citizenry "consensus oriented."[59] Finally, as previously mentioned, there is the alliance-structure of politics in the two countries, which in Hungary allowed former communist-era enemies to rule in coalition, and largely foreclosed this option in Poland.[60]

To say that in the 1990s, Hungarian elites developed a tradition of consensus politics, however, is not to say that they are invulnerable either to the exigencies or the temptations that come with changing circumstances. Allies, for instance, may find that under conditions of strong party discipline, entrenched consensual procedure does not provide sufficient space for debate and open dissent even *within* government. Rivals, for their part, may be tempted to exploit the rules of the game to selfish advantage, and if the potential payoff seems worthwhile, they may actually seek to alter the rules. A tradition of consensus-building,

---

[58] Markowski, 22.

[59] György Markus, 19.

[60] In 1994, following a victory that granted it more than enough seats to govern alone, the Hungarian Socialist Party (the successor party to the Hungarian Socialist Workers Party) formed a coalition with the Alliance of Free Democrats.

however, *does* entail a particular structure of costs and benefits for political actors. In 2002, for instance, the FIDESZ coalition certainly alienated many with its distinctly confrontational style and increasingly nationalistic tone; in the event, it lost the election to the Socialists, albeit narrowly.

The key point here is simply that in Hungary, as in Poland, the cost-benefit structure is shaped by the very real consequences that flow from dominant conceptual and discursive frames, which bear the mark of each country's distinctive struggles under state socialism. Formal modeling of the relationship between attitudes toward economic reforms and voting behavior in Poland demonstrates, for instance, that "understandings of the past exert as much of an effect on attitudes toward reforms as do personal economic assessments," and more specifically, that "prior understandings of the transition history, manifested as blame attributions, serve as a heuristic frame for sifting through complicated political and economic situations."[61]

Transitions in which clearly defined, distinct protagonists emerge are likely to crystallize and focus public debate in a way that creates a cleavage and perpetuates it in the future. Subsequent reconciliations and accommodations, such as those in Chile or Poland (the 'thick line' demarcating past and present) do not necessarily eliminate distinctions between the opposition and the old regime; they may only recast the form of public discourse. If the truce seems hollow or inauthentic on some level, then it will not resonate with the citizenry and may intensify the cleavage. . . . [On the other hand], the existence of moderate forces or splinter groups in the old elite may blur the distinctions of past and present and make conflicts less pronounced. This seems to be the case in Hungary.[62]

The power of conceptual frames and their explanatory and legitimating discourses, in other words, is not spent in the process of transformation. Like Hungary, Poland today is radically different from its former self. But it is also the case that Poland's post-transitional politics have suffered from a deficit of moderation, as noted by intellectuals and political actors alike.[63] And in both nations, distinctive legacies continue to shape their political economies, even after turning West and binding their futures to the European Union.

---

[61] Denise Powers and James Cox, "Echoes from the Past: The Relationship Between Satisfaction with Economic Reforms and Voting Behavior in Poland," *American Political Science Review* 91, no. 3 (September 1997): 629. The data on which the study is based concerns only political transitions, leading the authors to underestimate the processes that brought them about in the first place. Nevertheless, they clearly grasp the power of political discourse and historical legacies.

[62] Ibid.

[63] No less a light than Adam Michnik had long advocated greater temperance, and Prime Minister Aleksander Kwasniewski promised in 2002 to work toward that goal. Because of the party's large majority in government, Kwasniewski appeared to be the main brake on the old-style communists still remaining in Poland's reformed Socialist Party, the SLD (Alliance of the Democratic Left). See Maciej Lukasiewicz, "The Polish President's Mission," *Washington Post*, July 16, 2002.

From Bloc to Union: Legacies and State Capacity

The 1992 Maastricht Treaty created the EU as an internal market with aspirations to monetary and eventual political unity.[64] More fundamentally, however, the Union represented from the start a concerted effort at deep integration by a group of nations steeped in the lessons of two world conflagrations and the long hostility of the Cold War.[65] The Union, in brief, is an expression of faith in the harmonizing powers of shared interests. So, too, is the EU's enlargement project, which expressly aimed to widen integration, and by extension, peace and prosperity. Even in its most prosaic articulation – that is, enlargement conceived simply as a bid for control over the traffic of illegal migrants and organized criminals, and as an attempt to promote trade, investment, and tourism – the project has been laden with great expectations.[66]

This is particularly applicable to the Union's new entrants from the former Soviet bloc. Isolated from the West since the end of World War II, eight Central and Eastern European countries became EU members in May of 2004. Their accession (together with that of Cypress and Malta) expanded the Union's population from 380 million to 454 million, signaled a renewal of these countries' commitment to democracy and market principles, and served as capstone to a process that began even before 1989 and the establishment of the Union itself. This process gathered momentum early on, as overtures by the CMEA countries toward the European Community met with a positive response from the European Council in 1988.[67] By 1990, the European Council had decided, within the framework of the Group of 24, to aid the Central and Eastern European countries, stating that

the [European] community has a duty to consolidate and develop the general process of reform being undertaken in these countries notably by playing its part in the stabilization of their financial situation.[68]

Once again, Poland and Hungary led the way.[69] They were the first to receive balance-of-payments assistance from the European Council, the first to sign

---

[64] Or more precisely, the members of the European Community signed the Maastricht Treaty (the Treaty on European Union) on February 7, 1992, but it did not enter into force until the following November.

[65] O. Neill Nugent, *The Government and Politics of the European Union*, 5th ed. (New York: Palgrave Macmillan, 2003), 499.

[66] Jan Zielonka, "Europe Moves Eastward: Challenges of EU Enlargement," *Journal of Democracy* 15, no. 1 (January 2004): 22–35.

[67] Declaration of European Council on the International Role of the European Community. Rhodes, December 2–3, 1988 SN 4446/88 as Annex to European Council Conclusions of the Presidency. Rhodes, 2–3 December 1988. SN 4443/1/88.

[68] European Council. "Conclusions of the Presidency." Rome, October 27–28, 1990. SN 304/90 Rev 2.

[69] The G-7 summit of July 1989 asked the European Community, as it was called at the time, to coordinate aid to Hungary and Poland. Subsequently, the aid was extended to all Eastern European countries.

Association and Europe Agreements with the European Community,[70] and in 1994, the first to submit their applications for membership.[71] Other Central and Eastern European countries quickly followed, and by the time of the European Summit in Luxembourg (December 1997), the path toward accession had been opened: negotiations with six of eleven candidate countries were set to start in March 1998.[72]

In December 1999, the European Summit proclaimed: "The candidate states are participating in the accession process on an equal footing."[73] Like most EU public statements, this enunciation was exceedingly diplomatic. All applicant countries, to be sure, were required without exception to accept the treaty provisions (as amended since the Treaty of Rome), and to integrate and implement the *acquis communautaire* – the whole body of EU law, which includes all directives, regulations, and decisions. And certainly, a common set of criteria was used for the evaluation of all countries applying for membership. But the *process* was far from uniform, since each applicant negotiated its own terms of admission, and the EU, in turn, analyzed each country separately.[74] Moreover, individual negotiations produced specific arrangements, and on several occasions, transition periods and delays in implementation were included in negotiation packages to help smooth accession.

At the most obvious level, the unevenness of the enlargement process reflected the predictable clash of national and interest group pressures.[75] At a more fundamental level, however, it reflected different legacies that will likely continue to shape the countries' experiences as members of the Union. Fulfillment of

---

[70] "Europe Agreement establishing an association between the European Communities and their Member States, of the one part, and the Republic of Hungary, of the other part." *Official Journal* L 347, 31/12/1993, 0002–0266; "Europe Agreement establishing an association between the European Communities and their Member States, of the one part, and the Republic of Poland, of the other part." *Official Journal* L 348, 31/12/1993, 0002–0180. Further amendments were added to the Europe Agreement, until finally it was replaced by later agreements between each of the two countries and the European Union.

[71] Their application followed the 1993 Copenhagen European Council, which set the foundation for enlargement by stating in its conclusions that "the associated countries in Central and Eastern Europe that so desire shall become members of the European Union" as long as they fulfill specific economic, political, and general membership conditions. These conditions were set out in the "Conclusions of the Danish Presidency," and have become known as the Copenhagen criteria. *Conclusions of the Presidency*, Copenhagen, June 21–22, 1993. SN 180/93 (paragraph 7/A iii).

[72] Presidency Conclusions. Luxembourg, December 12–13, 1997, paragraph 2. The first six were the Czech Republic, Estonia, Hungary, Poland, Slovenia, and Cyprus, though the latter was on a different track as a result of its unique political situation. The remaining five applicants – Bulgaria, Latvia, Lithuania, Malta, Romania, and Slovakia – did not make the first cut but were given assurances that depending on their performance, they could join the first group and become candidate countries. Ibid., paragraphs 27–28.

[73] Presidency Conclusions, Helsinki, December 10–11, 1999, paragraph 4.

[74] This provision was made clear from the early stages of the accession process and is in line with the 1997 Luxembourg Presidency Conclusions, 1997, paragraph 13.

[75] For an excellent analysis, see Jan Zielonka, "Europe Moves Eastward: Challenges of EU Enlargement," *Journal of Democracy* 15, no. 1 (January 2004): 23.

the *acquis communautaire* illustrates the point. Like all the applicants, both Hungary and Poland had to adjust their legal, administrative, and economic structures to meet EU demands. For example, both countries were expected to implement austerity measures and tight budgets in compliance with convergence criteria. Formally, both met these criteria. But the rate of privatization, the extent of public finance reform, and the pace of industrial restructuring slowed significantly in Poland during the year before its entry. Hungary, on the other hand, despite some specific shortcomings, was encouraged to follow through with the "credible" reforms underway to reverse deteriorating economic trends.[76]

Indeed, Hungary was perceived as a successful candidate country, whereas the Polish situation was more ambiguous.[77] The difference in the 2003 Country Report's judgment of the two candidates was significant, with Hungary scoring higher in almost all the requisites for accession. Although Poland's administrative institutions, for example, were largely prepared to implement the *acquis,* the report emphasized the need to reinforce areas critical to Poland's proper functioning within the Union,[78] calling, among other things, for swift and effective enactment of legislation regarding public procurement.[79] And although both Poland and Hungary were found wanting in some of the institutional mechanisms necessary to absorb the structural funds and Common Agricultural Policy (CAP) subsidies,[80] Poland lagged behind considerably in a number of specific aspects of agriculture for which the Union has developed an extensive body of legislation.[81] The Commission's report also expressed concern about Poland's ability to implement social and employment policy.[82]

Public-sector corruption remained one of the most significant challenges for both countries. But again, there were differences (see Table C.4). In Poland, measures to curb corruption proved largely inefficient, and in fact corruption

---

[76] The general performance of the economy in each of the two countries is presented in section B1, *Economic Developments*, in each of the two 2003 Comprehensive Monitoring reports.

[77] "Poland and the EU: A nervous new arrival on the European Union's Block," *The Economist*. August 28, 2003. For a report detailing Hungary's positive track record towards EU accession, see World Bank, *Hungary: On the Road to the European Union* (World Bank Country Study 19923, November 1999).

[78] *Comprehensive Monitoring Report* on Poland, 2003, 14.

[79] *Comprehensive Monitoring Report* on Poland, 2003, 21.

[80] For example, both in transposing the legislation and in the implementation of the measures themselves. *Comprehensive Monitoring Report* on Poland, 2003, 33, 47–8. *Comprehensive Monitoring Report* on Hungary, 2003, 30, 41–3.

[81] European Commission, *Comprehensive Monitoring Report* on Poland, 31–2.

[82] The country still lacked the necessary administrative and institutional capacity to monitor compliance – for instance, in the areas of workplace health and safety – and had yet to transpose some of the more recent additions to the labor *acquis* such as workers' information and consultation, among others. *Comprehensive Monitoring Report* on Poland, 39–41. Hungary, on the other hand, had largely transposed the employment *acquis*, though concern about discrimination against the Roma community remained. European Commission, *Comprehensive Monitoring Report* on Hungary, 36.

TABLE C.4 *Corruption perceptions index, 2004*

Rank (10 = highest)	Country	2004 CPI score
1	Finland	9.7
24	Japan	6.96
42	**Hungary**	4.8
42	Italy	4.8
51	Czech Republic	4.2
54	Bulgaria	4.1
67	**Poland**	3.5
67	Peru	3.5
71	China	3.4
71	Syria	3.4

Source: 2004 Transparency International Corruption Perceptions Index, available at *ti@transparency.org*.

was perceived as increasing.[83] On the other hand, independent rankings placed Hungary among the least corrupt of the post-communist countries, and the Open Society Institute found that Hungary has "one of the highest numbers of convictions for corruption among the post-Communist countries."[84]

Yet despite the greater severity of Poland's problems, it was Poland that took a hard-line position in the accession negotiations with Brussels.[85] Moreover, the Polish political elite more commonly resorted to an adversarial discourse in matters pertaining to accession.[86] This was a somewhat risky approach, especially because until late 2002, it was unclear which countries would be included in the first round of Eastern enlargement.[87] Indeed, at the eleventh hour, there were fears that the European Parliament, whose approval was needed for enlargement to take place, might vote down some of the countries'

[83] *Comprehensive Monitoring Report* on Poland, 16. The most recent reports on Polish and Hungarian corruption are from the Council of Europe Group of States against Corruption(GRECO). See *Evaluation Report on Hungary* (Council of Europe, GRECO Secretariat: Strasbourg 28 March 2002) and *Evaluation Report on Poland* (Council of Europe, GRECO Secretariat: Strasbourg 14 May 2003), available at: http://www.greco.coe.int/.

[84] Though the EU's Comprehensive Monitoring Report saw significant improvement for Hungary since the 2001 new anti-corruption legislation, it did caution the country on the need for tighter controls in public administration. See also Transparency International Corruption Perceptions Index at www.transparency.org.

[85] To be sure, seen from a domestic political perspective, the Polish government had little choice. Since a fifth of the population in 2005 is employed in agriculture, for instance, the degree and terms of the agricultural subsidy to be offered by the EU were crucial.

[86] Christopher Bobinski, "Polish Illusions and Reality," in Anatol Lieven and Dmitri Trenin, eds., *Ambivalent Neighbors: The EU, NATO, and the Price of Membership* (Washington DC: Carnegie Endowment for International Peace, 2003), 237–238.

[87] To be sure, it might be argued that even if Poland's problems had been far more serious, enlargement simply could not have proceeded without the most populous and most symbolically important of the eight candidate countries.

negotiation packages.[88] In the event, the packages were approved[89] and put to a public vote in the accession countries, each of which held successful referenda on joining the Union. Subsequently the Accession Treaty was also put to a vote in the national parliaments of the existing member states, all of which gave the green light.[90]

However, in the run-up to accession, there were concerns about support for the project among the candidate countries' electorates. In the EU referendum in Hungary, held on April 12, 2003, 45.6 percent of the citizens went to the polls, and of these, 83.8 percent voted in favor of accession. Many analysts were concerned about the low turnout. Two main explanations have been advanced. The positive interpretation hinges on the classical free-rider problem. That is: given expectations of overwhelming support for accession, many people decided not to vote. More pessimistic analysts, however, argue that the low turnout was at best a demonstration of apathy. In the Polish accession referendum, turnout was higher but approval was somewhat lower. On June 7 and 8, 2003, 58.9 percent of the electorate went to the polls, and 77.5 percent of voters said "yes" to accession.[91]

Regardless of how we interpret these data, the demonstration of enthusiasm for accession was not as high as many had anticipated in either country. Furthermore, in both countries, support appeared to weaken as their publics recognized that additional sacrifices would be required.[92] This is hardly surprising.

---

[88] "European Parliament Votes in favor of EU Enlargement," *EurActiv.com*, 10 April 2003.

[89] European Parliament resolution on the conclusions of the negotiations on enlargement in Copenhagen (2003/2014(INI)). P5˙TA(2003)0168. The vote at the European Parliament was held separately for each country. For the separate resolutions on each Member State, see *Official Journal*, L 236, 23 September 2003. For an overview of the voting, see "Key EU enlargement vote passed," *BBC News Online*. 9 April, 2003. http://news.bbc.co.uk/1/hi/world/europe/2931865.stm and "European Parliament Votes in Favor of EU Enlargement" *EurActiv.com*, 10 April 2003. For the details of the vote, see the *Daily Notebook of the European Parliament* for April 9, 2003.

[90] Although the first Irish referendum failed to approve the Nice Treaty, which was drafted in order to reform the EU institutional structure in preparation for enlargement. For results from national parliaments of the existing fifteen member states, see: http://europa.eu.int/comm/enlargement/negotiations/accession_process.htm.

[91] The Polish government decided to hold the referendum over two days, fearing that the turnout on one day would not reach the threshold of 50 percent of the electorate. The ten new entrants signed the Accession Treaty in an extraordinary European Summit in Athens on 16 April 2003, and in May 2004, the European Union became a Union of twenty five member states. Despite concerns about Bulgaria and Romania's ability to fulfill the accession criteria, the EU is likely to become a Union of twenty seven or more. *Treaty between the Kingdom of Belgium . . . and the Slovak Republic, concerning the accession of the Czech Republic . . . and the Slovak Republic to the European Union. AA2003/TR/X 3*. For the accession documents, European Parliament resolutions, and the treaty between the governments of the twenty five countries, see the *Official Journal*, L 236, 23 September 2003. See also "Croatia toasts EU green light," *BBC News Online*. 21 April 2004: http://news.bbc.co.uk/2/hi/europe/3646113.stm.

[92] Pre-referenda polls for both for Poland and Hungary are available at http://europa.eu.int/comm/public_opinion/enlargement_en.htm. For an analysis of the public support towards the EU with data up to 2002, see Slomczynski, Kazimierz and Glodie. "Dynamics of support

Europe's new common life does not spring fully formed from the sheer will and power of its member states, as underscored by the 2005 "No" vote in France and the Netherlands. But the capacity of states and, more specifically, the resources and competencies necessary to conciliate domestic exigencies and those of the Union, will be of paramount importance as integration proceeds. Integration, after all, is in good part about accommodation. In the initial phases, the prospect of accession serves as a powerful incentive for potential entrants to compromise, and even to comply voluntarily with the terms they are offered. Once accession takes place, however, accommodation becomes a stiffer challenge.

Old Europe, New Europe

The capacity to accommodate is particularly important in areas where the state-socialist legacies of the Union's new members may clash with the old members' vision of the Union's future. At the Lisbon and Gotenborg summits in 2000 and 2001, the EU declared its intention to become "the most competitive and dynamic knowledge-based economy in the world capable of sustainable economic growth with more and better jobs and greater social cohesion."[93]

The Union's commitment to the principle of convergence in economic and social indicators between the wealthier West and the poorer East[94] is part and parcel of this grand vision. But compelling as this vision may be, there is no denying the conflicts and constraints inherent in the enlargement project. Key among these is the CAP, which consumes approximately half the Union's budget. Integrating the East European countries without any policy change toward them or reform of the CAP would have increased the Union's spending on agriculture by more than a third. As a result, Eastern Europe was offered considerably less favorable terms for entry than Spain, Portugal, or Greece. And even so, the Union's budget is bound to be strained by significant transfers to the East.[95]

The EU's budgetary limits are only part of the story, however; the other key part has to do with the new members' state-socialist legacies. Recall the differences in agricultural development among East European countries under communism. At one end stood countries such as Romania, where even in the 1980s, as Katherine Verdery notes, slaughtering and eating your own cow was

for European integration in post-communist Poland," *European Journal of Political Research* 42 (2003): 503–539. More recent opinion polls on the EU in Central and Eastern Europe are available at http://europa.eu.int/comm/public_opinion/cceb_en.htm.

[93] European Council "Lisbon Extraordinary European Council" Presidency Conclusions, 23 and 24 March 2000.

[94] Nugent, 503–504; Paul Brenton, "The Economic Impact of Enlargement on the European Economy: Problems and Perspectives," CEPS Working Document no. 188, October 2002. http://www.ceps.be.

[95] Via the structural funds and the extension of the CAP's benefits to the farmers of the new member states. Silvia Weyerbrock, "East-West European Integration: A General Equilibrium Analysis of Alternative Agricultural Policies," *Review of International Economics*, 9, no.3 (2001): 462–481.

a "political act" – a defiance of state directives aimed at reserving beef for export.[96] At the other end stood Hungary, which gradually but significantly reorganized agriculture after 1956. Recall from Chapter 2 the state's support of the highly profitable symbiosis between state cooperative farms and the individual private "household plots" of their members.

Uniquely in Hungary, as Lerman, Csáki, and Feder note in a recent study of agriculture in transition countries, both household plots and small private farmers eventually "received official recognition and were often treated as a formal production sector in large cooperatives, with all that this implied for allocation of resources and product marketing."[97] Recall also the efflorescence of "auxiliary production" on the agricultural cooperatives following the 1967 Hungarian Law on Agricultural Cooperatives, which permitted "industrial sub-divisions, with little explicit regulation."[98] Together with the New Economic Mechanism Reform of the following year (which among other things empha-sized profitability, permitted state firms to trade more freely, and individuals to change jobs more easily), this law significantly diversified the cooperatives' pro-duction, since it encompassed almost any kind of light manufacturing, from the production of down comforters to industrial construction, as well as all manner of specialty food processing.[99] By the 1970s, Hungary exported over one-third of its agricultural output, and by the mid-1980s, its *per capita* production value was the highest among the CMEA countries. In Europe as a whole, it was second only to Denmark's.[100]

Between the extremes of Romania and Hungary stood Poland. There (as in Yugoslavia), agriculture remained mostly in private hands after World War II, yet central controls continued to rein in farmers as in other Eastern bloc coun-tries. In addition, Poland's post-war land reform had fragmented the farm structure, and legal restrictions on the transfer of property-rights "froze" the land-use pattern and blocked the adjustment of farm sizes.[101] Consequently, Poland became a net food importer, and after briefly evening out its agri-cultural trade imbalance in 1990–91, returned to that status in 1992 (for Poland, comparisons with Hungary, and more recent years, see Table C.5).

[96] Katherine Verdery, *What Was Socialism and What Comes Next?* (Princeton: Princeton Univer-sity Press, 1996), 27–28.

[97] Zvi Lerman, Csaba Csáki, and Gershon Feder, *Agriculture in Transition: Land Policies and Evolving Farm Structures in Post-Soviet Countries* (Lanham, MD: Lexington Books, 2004), 25, 74.

[98] Kálmán Rupp, *Entrepreneurs in Red: Structure and Organizational Innovation in the Centrally Planned Economy* (Albany: State University of New York Press, 1983), 2.

[99] See Ákos Róna-Tas, *The Great Surprise of the Small Transformation: The Demise of Commu-nism and the Rise of the Private Sector in Hungary* (Ann Arbor: University of Michigan Press, 1997).

[100] Hungary exported one-third of its "net total output . . . the highest among CMEA countries." Donáth, ibid., 4–5. See also Timothy N. Ash, "Agricultural Reform in Central and Eastern Europe: Marketisation, Privatisation, Developing a New Role for the State," in *Communist Economies and Economic Transformation* 4, no. 4 (1992).

[101] Lerman, Csáki, and Feder, *Agriculture in Transition*, 49.

TABLE C.5 *Agriculture: Hungary and Poland, 1990–2001*

	1990	1991	1992	1993	1994	1995	1996	1997	1998	1999	2000	2001ᵖ
1. Share of agriculture in GDP/Hungary	14.5	8.9	7.5	6.8	7.1	7.1	6.9	6	4.9	4.2	3.6	4.5
2. Share of agriculture in GDP/Poland	10.5	4.6	4.9	5.3	5	4.9	6	4.8	4.2	4	4	n.a.
3. Share of agriculture in total employment/Hungary*	17.9	n.a.	11.4	9.3	8.9	8.1	8.5	8.1	7.7	7.2	6.5	6.2
4. Share of agriculture in total employment/Poland**	26.9	26.9	25	24.8	23.8	26.5	27.3	27.3	25.6	28.1	28.2	27.6
5. Share of agriculture and food exports in total exports/Hungary	n.a.	n.a.	24.7	22.3	21.6	22.4	20.9	15	12	9.1	8	7.5
6. Share of agriculture and food exports in total exports/Poland	14	16.6	15	11.6	11.7	10.5	11.4	12.2	10.5	9.1	7.9	8.4
7. Share of agriculture and food imports in total imports/Hungary	n.a.	n.a.	6.4	6.6	7.9	6.5	6.1	5.4	4.7	3.6	3.2	2.9
8. Share of agriculture and food imports in total imports/Poland	8.2	13.6	12.6	12.1	11.6	10.9	10.8	9	8	7.1	6.5	6.1
9. Agricultural and food trade balance/Hungary	1,586	1,962	1,968	1,151	1,214	1,894	1,713	1,685	1,525	1,270	1,153	1,410
10. Agricultural and food trade balance/Poland	642	503	–105	–672	–532	–792	–1461	–705	–743	–707	–533	–376
11. Agricultural productivity***/Hungary (1988–90/1998–2000)	5,133										5,016	
12. Agricultural productivity***/Poland (1988–90/1998–2000)	1,632										1,874	

p: preliminary; n.a.: not available

*Includes agriculture, forestry, hunting, and fishing.

**Includes agriculture, forestry, and hunting.

***Agricultural value added per agricultural worker, 1995 dollars.

Source: lines 1–10, OECD, Agricultural policies in transition economies: Trends in policies and support (London: European Bank for Reconstruction and Development, 2003), 88–91, 120; lines 11 and 12, World Development Report 2003, *Sustainable development in a dynamic world: transforming institutions, growth, and quality of life* (New York: Oxford University Press, 2003), 238, 239.

TABLE C.5a *Agriculture and national income in Hungary and Poland in the 1980s*

Country	Rural population (%)	Employed in agriculture (%)	Agriculture in GDP* (%)	Arable land in agricultural output** (%)
Hungary	40.8	17	17	77.5
Poland	40.3	28.8	12.1	76.7

*Average 1980–1989.
**Average 1987–1989.
Source: Adapted from Lerman, Csaki, and Feder, Table A2.1, p.55 (Annex to Chapter 2).

Indeed, during the state-socialist period, food shortages and rationing were a common occurrence in Poland, and the country ranked near the bottom of the Soviet bloc countries in the availability of food.[102]

Careful scrutiny of the Polish and Hungarian experiences shows that Hungary's relative success during transition was largely attributable to the economic reforms that the country introduced as early as 1953, and especially after 1956. This is not a stretch, given the beneficial ramifications of reform, detailed earlier in Chapter 2. Here one need only glance at the higher levels of efficiency that Hungarian agriculture had attained by the 1980s relative to that of Poland (see Table C.5 for sample years and Table C.5a for the 1980s average). Even after the transition from state socialism, Poland retained relatively high transaction costs in an officially unfettered land market, including negative social policy incentives.[103] The implications for Poland as a member of the EU are serious. Even though the agrarian sector's contribution to GDP has decreased dramatically, one-third of Poland's population still lives in the countryside, and more than a quarter remain employed in the country's "dwarf agriculture."[104] The average size of a Polish farm is about 7 hectares (approximately 17 acres), less than half the EU average of 16 hectares.[105]

The state-socialist legacy is also evident in quality produced. Poland's farmers and food-processing industry often do not reach the quality level of imports, which Poles can now afford and easily obtain. Uncompetitive farms will not survive long inside the Union; this means that many farmers will join the sizable ranks of the unemployed in Polish cities, where unemployment is already higher than in most European countries (nearly 20 percent in 2004).[106]

---

[102] Zygmut Nagorski, "Lifting of Sanctions Challenges Poland," *New York Times*, February 1987.

[103] For example, people owning more than 2 hectares of land stood to lose their unemployment benefits from non-agricultural jobs. Lerman, Csáki, and Feder, *Agriculture in Transition*, 80.

[104] Michael Bernhard's apt characterization for Poland's ubiquitous small farms. Personal communication, June 2002.

[105] Lerman, Csáki, and Feder, *Agriculture in Transition*, 90, table 3.13, and 91.

[106] *Economist Country Briefings*, Poland economic data (Economist Intelligence Unit, May 4 2001), available at http://www.ecnomist.com/countries.

The prospects of these impoverished sectors are likely to remain dim. Reforming agriculture has proved extremely difficult.[107] And as mentioned earlier, the Union's political and economic constraints precluded massive transfers of resources to the poorer Eastern regions. The EU-15, in fact, were initially reluctant to agree to any increase in the EU budget that would benefit the new members.[108] In January 2002, the Union announced that the existing agricultural subsidies could not be extended to the new member states. Having done so would have led to a dramatic increase in the financial burdens of existing member states, since beneficiaries of these subsidies – most notably, French farmers – were unwilling to tolerate any reduction in their allocations.

Criticism of the Union and its commitment to the enlargement process by the accession countries – Poland in particular – did little to change the realities of EU power relations.[109] The agreement that was finally reached in October 2002 and endorsed soon thereafter held that the new member states would receive only one-fourth of the subsidies allocated to Western farmers. Moreover, the decision to reduce existing EU-15 farmers' subsidies was postponed until 2013.[110] (Postponement of the CAP reform discussion was the result of the same Franco-German agreement that stipulated a ceiling on national contributions to the EU budget in order to spare Germany, the Union's largest contributor, the burden of increased expenditures.)

This is not to say that the stronger EU members have escaped vigorous challenges from the entrants. The 2003 Constitutional debate, ostensibly waged over the number of Commissioners and the allocation of votes in the European Council, was fundamentally a power struggle between the larger states that wanted to control the direction of the EU, and the smaller states that wanted an equal say in the process. Three points are worth noting here, however. The first is perhaps so obvious as to be easily forgotten: conflictual negotiations among union-builders can be costly in terms of prestige, good will, and political capital more generally, even for those who hold the upper hand. The immediate outcome of this particular struggle, for example, was the collapse of the inter-governmental conference, as well as stalled negotiations among the members of the expanded European Council in Brussels.[111] (The reasons for the "No" votes in France and the Netherlands were complex, but earlier acrimonious debates surely did nothing for the constitution's cause.)

---

[107] Timothy N. Ash, "Agricultural Reform in Central and Eastern Europe: Marketisation, Privatisation, Developing a New Role for the State," *Communist Economies and Economic Transformation* 4 (4) 1992, 524.

[108] "Big Players Want to Reduce Cost of EU Enlargement," *EurActiv.com* February 11, 2002.

[109] "Candidates Outraged by EU Aid," *BBC News Online*, 30 January 2002. http://news.bbc.co.uk/1/hi/world/europe/1789765.stm and "Poland's farming woes," *BBC News Online*, 30 January 2002. http://news.bbc.co.uk/1/hi/world/europe/1791480.stm.

[110] European Council, Presidency Conclusions, Copenhagen, 12–13 December 2002. At this summit, Heads of State endorsed an agreement that had already been reached in October 2002.

[111] European Council. Presidency Conclusions. Brussels, 12–13 December 2003, paragraph 2. See the revised Presidency Conclusions that also include the Declaration of the President.

The second point is less obvious but equally important: countries that find themselves in a subordinate position may nevertheless pursue a risky, even aggressive negotiation strategy *vis-à-vis* stronger members. Most of the applicant countries, for example, grasped the need for compromise on the matter of the Council votes, but Poland, with the active support of Spain, tried to block the process of adoption of the European constitution unless its position in the Council was strongly reaffirmed.[112]

The third point follows from the previous two: because conflict can be costly to the negotiating parties, and because even a weak party may risk conflict in the pursuit of particular benefits, countries with the upper hand have a compelling incentive to preempt rather than confront or face down challenges. On December 16, 2003, Germany, Austria, France, the Netherlands, and Sweden signed a letter affirming their position that the EU budget should not exceed 1 percent of the Union's gross national product from 2007 onward.[113] The letter, which coincided with the start of negotiations on the 2007–2013 financial perspective of the EU, came just days after Spain and Poland created a deadlock in the negotiations on the Union's constitution. In its first budget proposal, the European Commission sought an increase of 1.44 percent of the Union's GNP, but the letter, threatening to impose a ceiling on the Union's budget drove home the point to Poland that it would be required to conform to the Community method of negotiation.[114]

The net contributors' reaction sent a clear warning to Poland and a reminder to Spain: power relations matter, even within the EU. (Although Spain acted in

---

[112] "Member States' Divisions Loom Over IGC Start on 4 October," *EurActiv.com*, 1 October 2003. With the proposed revisions, their number of votes will be reduced while a standard of "double majority" of population size and member states would mean that their relative power would be reduced. Poland and Spain, which are comparable in population size, were allocated the same number of votes in the European Council in the Nice Treaty. The Polish-Spanish coalition was particularly fierce as the debate over the war on Iraq continued, since both countries were allied with the United States rather than with the Germany and France. Hungary, Poland, Spain, the UK, Italy, Portugal, Denmark, and the Czech Republic signed a letter of declaration supporting the US position on Iraq. "European leaders rally behind U.S.," *BBC News Online* 30 January 2003. http://news.bbc.co.uk/1/hi/world/europe/2708023.stm. Moreover, in September 2003, Poland led an international force of about 9,000 troops, including over 2,000 Polish personnel, which was responsible for bringing stability to south-central Iraq. The previous month, Hungarian soldiers had also been sent to Iraq to participate in the peacekeeping activities that would come under Polish leadership. Jacques Chirac, who belittled the role of the ten not-yet-member states in foreign policy, heightened the tensions during the debate on the Future of Europe. "Chirac blasts EU candidates," *BBC News Online*. 18 February 2003. http://news.bbc.co.uk/1/hi/world/europe/2774139.stm, and John Vinocur, "News analysis: A big unhappy family: How friendly can Europe be with US?" *International Herald Tribune*. February 19, 2003. Nevertheless, since December 2003, and especially after the Madrid terrorist attack on March 11, 2004, the Polish-Spanish coalition became more tolerant of the proposed changes to the voting rules. "A Constitutional Revival: Despite its re-emergence, the draft constitution has remarkably few friends," *The Economist*. April 1, 2004.

[113] George Parker, "EU budget plan sets up clash with big states," *Financial Times Europe*, 19 January 2004, 1–2.

[114] "How to blow a trillion euros: The start of two years of argument over the European Union budget," *The Economist*, 22 January, 2004.

concert with Poland, some observers have suggested that if Spain had been the only party to the negotiations, an agreement would have been reached. Poland, largely unfamiliar with the European Council's horse-trading process, was not really prepared to negotiate.)[115]

Poland's approach should not have come as a surprise. Not only is Poland the country most affected by the Union's decisions on agriculture, it is also a country of some 38 million people and, as such, feels entitled to have a proportionate influence. More importantly still, as we have seen, Poland's model of democracy and patterns of collective action have been as confrontational-pluralist as Hungary's have been compromising-corporatist, and in both cases, the underlying cost-benefit structures in which actors operate shape the strategies and responses of political and interest groups. Just a few months before joining the EU, Polish farmers took to the streets *en masse* to protest the reduction in the subsidies they had expected.[116] In Hungary, meanwhile, not only were protests much less dramatic, but more importantly, the Hungarian government refused to endorse the protesters' concerns, and remained committed to ensuring that all Copenhagen criteria had been met.[117] The Hungarian elites, in short, took a technocratic approach, whereas their Polish counterparts chose a principled and confrontational alternative by channeling domestic public concerns into a struggle over the European Constitution.

The structural and political exigencies of the enlargement project thus reanimate and test the different legacies of state socialism in the new members. So too do the uncertainties inherent in the project. From the existing member states' perspective, the question that naturally arises is whether a common European identity can be forged, and if so, whether it will be sufficiently strong and supple to accommodate the newcomers. Some argue that no common identity exists even among the older fifteen member states; others fear that whatever identity does exist will be weakened with the addition of the ten new countries.[118]

At a minimum, member countries will continue to face classic issues of national power and prerogative *vis-à-vis* other states, and they will continue to face the challenges of distributing sacrifices and rewards among their citizenries at home. They may even come to face serious friction over the very definition of the political-cultural values and practices on which any viable association ultimately hinges. Hints of this last scenario were already discernable in Poland's

---

[115] "Those Pesky Poles: In which old members offer new ones some lessons in negotiation," *The Economist*, 27 November 2003.

[116] For a review of CEE reform in the agriculture sector in the 1989–99 decade, see Alexandra Trzeciak-Duval, "A Decade of Transition in Central Eastern European Agriculture" *European Review of Agricultural Economics* 26 (3) (1999): 283–304. Also see World Bank. *Structural Changes in the Farming Sectors in Central and Eastern Europe*, Lessons for EU Accession – Second World Bank/FAO Workshop, June 27–29, 2000. World Bank Technical Paper no. 465. WTP 465 April 2000.

[117] "Hungarian farmers step up protest," *BBC News Online*, February 23, 2004.

[118] Nugent, 502. Questions also have emerged about Europe's future eastern borders. See Jan Zielonka, "How New Enlarged Borders Will Reshape the European Union," *Journal of Common Market Studies* 39, no. 3 (September 2001): 507–36.

2004 elections for representatives to the European Parliament (EP). The Center-Right Civic Platform (PO) and Law and Justice (PiS) parties won the majority of votes (24 percent and 13 percent, respectively), but the Catholic and adamantly anti-EU League of Polish Families (LPR) received 16 percent of the vote, doubling its showing in the 2001 domestic parliamentary elections. Moreover, the Self-Defense Party (Samoobrona), a left-wing, anti-EU farmers' movement, won 11 percent, while the ruling Social Democrats (SLD) came in at fifth place with only 9 percent of the vote.

Assessing the depth and significance of this rightward trend is no simple matter, since fewer than 21 percent of the Polish electorate voted in the elections, the second lowest turnout (after Slovakia) among the new member states of Eastern Europe.[119] In addition, though more pronounced, in Poland as in Hungary and several other states among the new entrants, the EP votes were as much protest against the governing coalition as expressions of abiding support for opposition parties. However, in Poland, these parties performed well in the October 2002 local elections, and domestic polling results tend to support the EP election results, with two important exceptions. First, the far-right League of Polish families, which "would like to see the European Union disintegrate" and which "denounces the EU as a vehicle for German domination,"[120] did twice as well as polls would have suggested. Second, the Self-Defense Party did less well than it is likely to do in domestic elections. It has consistently polled around 20 percent of the vote, and since most of its supporters – among them many farmers and unemployed people – have little interest in European affairs, it is likely that they were under-represented in the EP elections.[121] In any case, these populist, anti-EU parties will likely have significant representation in the Sejm (lower house of the Polish Parliament), where their "uncivil" behavior has been marked enough to cause concern about the "strength of Poland's democratic political culture."[122]

Poland's democracy, as of 2005, remains remarkably pluralist and confrontational;[123] and governmental instability remains a problem as well.[124] However,

[119] RFE/RL, Thursday 17 June 2004.
[120] Maciej Giertych, on of the party's candidates who was elected to the European Parliament, quoted in *the Economist*, June 19, 2004, 51.
[121] RFE/RL, Thursday 17 June 2004.
[122] Preston Keat, "Poland," Freedom House 2003, 456.
[123] In the three years leading up to parliamentary elections in 2001, the Social Democrats (SLD) opposed virtually all legislation proposed by the Solidarity Electoral Action (AWS) government. Thus when the SLD-UP government assumed power in 2001, it did so under the weight of high expectations for change and improvement. These expectations were dashed. Polish politics in the early years of the new century came to be dominated by major corruption scandals, a growing public perception of cronyism, and a stalled reform and restructuring in a context of economic conditions little improved since 2001, when unemployment was about the same as in early 2005 (nearly 20 percent). In the two years following the 2001 elections, Poland had three finance ministers and therefore little policy continuity.
[124] Prime Minister Lezsek Miller resigned under pressure from the SLD on May 2, 2004, the day after Poland joined the EU. In the autumn of 2003, the government's approval ratings had been at an all-time low of about 16 percent; nor have they improved much since Marek Belka took

as this book has also emphasized, actors can combine legacy-based resources and political innovation to create startling possibilities. In this respect, there are a few hopeful signs in Poland. The centrist Freedom Union (UW), which joined Solidarity-dominated coalitions in the 1990s, won 7 percent of the vote in EP elections after most analysts had concluded that it was no longer a viable party, raising expectations for a centrist revival in the 2005 electoral campaign.[125] In early 2005, in fact, a variety of political groups publicly endorsed a centrist agenda; they were joined by prominent figures like Tadeusz Mazowiecki (prime minister in 1989–90) and Jerzy Hausner, who had recently resigned from the SLD. Interestingly enough, the UW's political council harkened back to the opposition's discursive "clarity" under the *ancien régime* by advocating a "courageous and stable formation at the political center that will focus on a clear democratic, European program,"[126] while President Aleksander Kwasniewski (SLD) spoke publicly about the need for political stability in general and in particular for a "bloc of pro-European and economically liberal groupings, which exclude radicalism with respect to vetting and the communist past."[127]

Hungary's political divisions over European integration are far less pronounced than in Poland, as we saw earlier. Moreover, as Hungary approaches its fifth electoral cycle since the 1989 transition, a majority of its electorate is divided along lines that any Western European voter would recognize, approximating Social Democratic and Christian Democratic camps. Overall, Hungary is consistently rated one of the most successful transition cases, and the most

---

office. To make matters worse, street protests became common, aroused in part by proposed liberalization of the labor code and by the so-called Hausner Plan's cutbacks in social spending. The plan called for cuts in government spending over a four-year period to reduce Poland's budget deficit – approximately 5.3 percent of GDP in 2004 – to comply with the Eurozone's limit, set at 3 percent of GDP.

[125] Meanwhile, the Ordynacka Association – composed mainly of former students who in the 1970s and 1980s belonged to the Communist Union of Polish Students (ZSP, later renamed the Socialist Union of Polish Students, or SZSP) – was established in 2001, and seemed ready to enter the fray on the Left, either as an adjunct to, or challenger of, the SLD. However, it was unclear whether Ordynacka could pass the 5 percent vote threshhold for entry to parliament, or that it could present Polish voters with a true alternative to the SLD, since many of its highest-profile members also belonged to, or have strong ties with, the SLD itself.

[126] By 2004, Aleksander Smolar, a member of that political council, had come to believe that the only "destabilizing factor" in Poland was politics, not economics. He also had concluded that a new centrist party was both necessary and possible, given the Polish electorate's disaffection and low confidence in the current parties. Only about 30 percent of Poles said they intended to vote in the parliamentary elections. The UW called for parliamentary elections in June (rather than the planned autumn 2005 elections), and held talks with the Centrum Party. The UW's leadership even talked to Prime Minister Marek Belka, and some speculate that President Aleksander Kwasniewski might leave the SLD before the end of his term, joining the new party that would likely include other members of the SLD as well as of the Civic Platform. See Lehman Brothers/Eurasia Group Stability Index, *Stability Summary and Outlook* (New York: January 2003), p. 79.

[127] Witold Zygulski, "Finding the Center," *The Warsaw Times*, February 16, 2005.

politically stable country in Eastern Europe.[128] In December 2004, Hungary became the second member state (after Lithuania) to ratify the treaty on the EU Constitution by a simple parliamentary vote, 304 to 9.[129] And even though the question of informants and of lustration began to attract the attention of the media, the power of the past to sustain deep political antagonisms remains much weaker than in Poland. This is in line with Hungarians' more positive assessment of the socialist period. We know from large *n* surveys of the region that at the start of the new millennium, the percentage of Hungarians who have a positive attitude toward the ancien régime is by far the highest in the region (75 percent), compared with only 33 percent of Poles and an East European mean of 61 percent.[130]

Of course, it bears repeating that Hungary's model of democratic consolidation, with its pro-consensus cost-benefit structure and fundamental stability, does not insulate the country from all the problems facing the other new democracies in the region.[131] Nor does it spare the country from the challenges

---

[128] See, for example, Lehman Brothers Eurasia Group Stability Index, *Stability Summary and Outlook* (New York: Lehman Eurasia Group LLC January 2003).

[129] The requisite two-thirds majority was easily reached despite eight abstentions and the absence of sixty-four MPs. In addition to Hungary, as of July 2005, Austria, Belgium, Cyprus, Germany, Greece, Italy, Latvia, Lithuania, Malta, Slovakia, Slovenia, and Spain had ratified the treaty. But on May 29, 2005, 55 percent of the French electorate rejected it, as did almost 62 percent of Dutch voters on June 2, 2005. As Article IV-447 of the Constitution itself makes clear, rejection by even a single country would have been enough to sink it; and in any case, the outcome in several other countries that have yet to hold referenda – Britain, Denmark, and even Poland, for instance – was always in doubt. Some analysts and policymakers hold out hope that France and the Netherlands may vote again after elections that will be held in both countries in 2007. At a June meeting in Brussels, EU leaders extended the November 2006 deadline for ratifying the charter, apparently indefinitely.

[130] 2001 New Europe Barometer.

[131] For instance, despite relatively favorable Transparency International Corruption Perceptions ratings, corruption (especially in public procurement) remains a problem. Hungary's ongoing "media wars" are also potentially damaging to public trust. Freedom House notes that "the 2002 OSCE election observation team found, for instance, that Hungarian state television 'consistently demonstrated a bias in favor of the government and FIDESZ'; nor has the socialist-dominated government that followed implemented significant improvements in the "impartiality of the state media." Dan Roberts, "Hungary" in *Nations in Transit* 2003 (New York: Freedom House), 298–299. At the end of the summer of 2004, the Hungarian Prime Minister, Péter Medgyessy – whom we met in his 1980s role at the Ministry of Finance in Chapter 5 – resigned following intense disagreements about government reshuffling with his Socialist Party's liberal coalition partner, the Alliance of Free Democrats (SZDSZ). Socialist Party president László Kovács proclaimed that the party was determined to "[maintain] the coalition and . . . a successful government," and the Socialists nominated Ferenc Gyurcsány, who was subsequently confirmed as prime minister. They also used the occasion to clean house by dismissing the few remaining vestiges of the far Left "old guard" from the party's pre-transition Communist era. (*The Economist*, June 19, 2004, 51.)

Like Lezsek Miller in Poland, Medgyessy had been dogged by his past, and was weakened in particular by his belated admission that he had worked as a counter-intelligence agent while at the Ministry of Finance in the 1980s. He claimed that he had been protecting secret plans for Hungary to join the World Bank in 1982, which the Soviets opposed. Although Hungary

inherent in the process of integration, which is bound to test the competencies and resources of all the members, particularly the new entrants. A 2003 survey of EU enlargement estimated that the GDP *per capita* of the entrants from East and Central Europe will take decades to catch up with the GDP per capita of the EU-15. But if the survey proves reasonably accurate, it is crucial to note that the decades will be not equally long for the entrants. It will take Romania 80 years, Bulgaria 63, Poland 59, and Lithuania 53 to catch up – in contrast to 39 years for the Czech Republic, 38 for Slovakia, 34 for Hungary, and 31 for Slovenia.[132]

Tentative but telling lines emerge from these estimates – lines that separate not only East and West, but also the countries of the former Soviet bloc. Among the latter, Hungary appears nearly as well-positioned for integration as Slovenia, long the trade beneficiary of a Mediterranean outlet before losing the port of Trieste to Fascist Italy. The survey estimates further suggest that Hungary is at least equally well-positioned for integration as the former Czechoslovakia – the most industrialized, economically advanced country in Eastern Europe during the inter-war period and, consequently, the closest developmentally to its Western neighbors at that time. Finally, the estimates suggest that the distance between Poland and Hungary, so often classed together by analysts, is actually quite significant. The challenges of integration, in other words, are themselves likely to vary in degrees of difficulty from one country to another. For as this book has demonstrated, contrasting histories of state-society relations under the *ancien régime* also left in place different structural legacies.

Yet no matter how difficult the road, the EU's most brilliant success, Ireland, offers the entrants a powerful incentive to carry on. In 1973, when Ireland began its integration process, its *per capita* income was 62 percent of the EU average; by 2001 it was 121 percent. Does Ireland hold up the mirror of the future to those who now seek to emulate it? Or does Greece? In 1981, when Greece joined the EU, its *per capita* income was 64 percent of the EU average.[133] In 2002, it was still no more than 70 percent.

The analytical framework at the core of this book points clearly to divergent outcomes for the newcomers – even for countries widely presumed to have followed analogous trajectories and attained similar levels of political-economic development. State socialism may be a thing of the past, but its past is part of the future.

---

did join the World Bank that year, it is not surprising that this claim was met with considerable skepticism by the opposition, and by many citizens. (On the other hand, two well-respected Hungarian scholars have opined in personal conversations that Medgyessy's claim was at least partly plausible). The main point here, however, is that despite facing challenges similar to its Polish counterpart, the Hungarian Socialist Party shows no sign of disintegrating.

[132] "When East Meets West," *The Economist*, November 23, 2003, in special section on survey of EU enlargement, 4.

[133] "Dancing an Irish jig," *Economist.com*, April 15, 2004.

Index